Contents

Part 1 How To

Create a Word Document   59

Format a Word Document   95

Build an Excel Worksheet   129

Format an Excel Worksheet   161

Create an Excel Chart   191

Create an Excel Database   211

Track Appointments, Meetings, and Other Events with Outlook — 333

Create an Outlook Contacts List — 347

Use Outlook to Keep Track of Things to Do — 359

Create and Maintain an Outlook Journal — 369

Print Office 97 Files — 377

Use Office 97 on the Web — 385

Share Office 97 Data   417

Part 2   Do It Yourself

Combine Excel Data and Charts with Your Word Documents   443

Find a Job with Microsoft Office   455

On the Job with Microsoft Office   481

Part 3 Quick Fixes

Part 4 Handy References

Introduction

Advertisers have spent a lot of money over the years telling us that technology makes life easier. Have you seen the new America Online commercials focusing on busy family members scrambling around in their kitchen and in their car, but still managing to stay in contact with work, school, and the world with the use of the latest technologies (such as car phones and online services)? Remember the simpler days when your life was readily improved with the purchase of a nifty technologically advanced gadget? What about the commercial with the woman who claps and a lamp turns off or on? Or how about the one where the man points to his garage door and then presses a button on his remote control to open the door. Life is supposed to be easy and simple when you've got a technologically advanced gadget, right?

The computer industry wants to convey the same message about computer technology. PC and software makers advertise that using a computer is as easy as driving a car—just turn on the ignition, put it in drive, and head on out on the information superhighway. Sure it sounds easy, but in reality it's not—the technological roadway has plenty of skid marks made by frustrated computer users to prove otherwise.

Computers and software have a long, long, LONG way to go to become truly simple to use. Sure, programs and computers have become somewhat easier to use since their arrival on the market in the 1980s, but they're still a far cry from being effortless or making life a breeze. And regardless of what the PC and software manufacturers tell you, using a computer is not like driving a car. You definitely need some help to get started.

In the eyes of the computer industry, help usually takes the form of a fat technical manual that comes with a computer program. Such manuals are written by someone who obviously knows the program really well. The manual includes all the features in an order that is logical to someone who knows the program, but what about the beginner? Most manuals don't explain the why of a feature. Why would I use this feature? What's the benefit? Give me an example! Also, most manuals include a lot of text with perhaps one figure (or picture). That figure may have many arrows and callouts that explain each and every option you can select. You are left to muddle through all the confusing text and hope you don't make a mistake.

Thankfully, you've picked up a book that can help you sort through all the confusion of learning new computer programs. Welcome to the *Big Basics Book of Microsoft Office 97*. While this book can't make the programs any more intuitive, it can help you learn the programs in the easiest way possible. Here are the top five reasons why this book is so easy to use:

1. This book explains the why of a feature and gives you examples of when that feature might come in handy. If you read something that sounds like it might make your work easier, you can read through the steps. If not, you can skip the section.

2. This book includes easy-to-follow *illustrated* steps called Guided Tours. The design of the book is similar to popular how-to books for home repair, cooking, and gardening. This book presents each step clearly; plus, you see what your screen should look like for each step. You don't have to wonder whether you got off track. You can follow along with the figures, step-by-step.

3. The How-To section consists of manageable topics so you can find what you need to know. For example, you don't have to read an entire chapter's worth of material just to find out how to insert page numbers in a document. You can quickly go to the topic on page numbers and follow the steps.

4. This book covers more than just the basic, simple features that can get you only so far in a program. It also covers useful features and concepts that will help you build your skills and get the most from your Microsoft Office 97 programs.

5. You'll find a project section packed with useful projects you can do yourself. The Do-It-Yourself section includes practical tips and steps for creating documents you'll use over and over.

6. This book anticipates common problems that may pop up and includes a handy problem-solving section called "Quick Fixes." If you encounter a problem, you can look it up and find an answer. You can also look up refer ence information, such as help in identifying toolbar buttons.

What Is Microsoft Office 97?

Microsoft Office 97 is a group of powerful programs designed to easily share information, utilize the Windows 95 operating system, and share information on the Internet, too. The Office 97 suite of programs includes Word, Excel, PowerPoint, and Outlook.

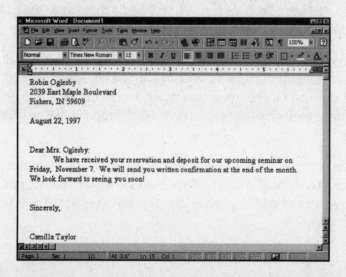

Word is a word-processing program that enables you to create all kinds of documents: letters, memos, reports, newsletters, and more.

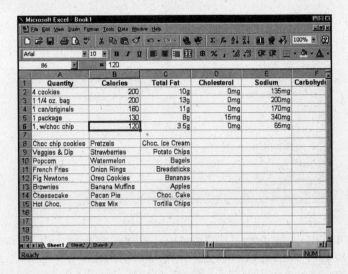

Excel is a spreadsheet program that enables you to track data. You can perform calculations on this data and even create charts from it. You can use this program to present numerical and other kinds of information; you can also use it to build databases.

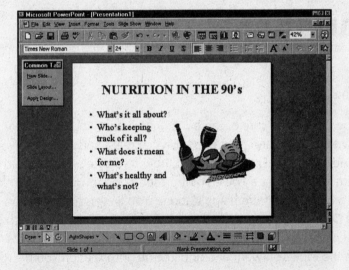

PowerPoint is a presentation graphics program that enables you to set up information in a graphic format for use in slide shows and other business presentations.

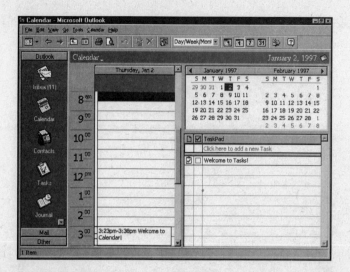

Outlook is an innovative new desktop information management program designed to help you organize your everyday activities, communicate with others through electronic mail, and more. You can use Outlook to compile To Do lists, jot down ideas in a daily journal, and keep a database of addresses and phone numbers. (Outlook replaces the old Schedule+ program found in previous versions of Microsoft Office.)

What This Book Contains

This book has four parts:

Part 1, "How To," is the core of the book. In this part, you find sections on Office 97 basics, how to manage and print files, how to create and format a Word document, how to create and format an Excel worksheet, how to create an Excel chart and Excel database, how to create and format a PowerPoint presentation, how to use Outlook, and how to share data among the different applications. You'll even find a section detailing how to use the various Office programs on the Internet and the World Wide Web. The sections clearly explain when a feature is useful and provide detailed, illustrated steps for each task. You can turn to the topic you want and find just the information you need.

Part 2, "Do It Yourself," provides real-world examples of how you can use the skills you learned in Part 1. All of the projects in this section involve using one or more of the Office 97 programs to create a finished product. By trying out the projects, you will learn how to harness the power of Microsoft Office 97 to quickly create polished documents.

Part 3, "Quick Fixes," provides answers or solutions to 101 common questions and problems that you may encounter. You can use this troubleshooting section to pinpoint and solve problems as they occur. Use the QuickFinder table at the beginning of this section to go directly to the answer you need.

Part 4, "Handy References," includes all the reference information you need in one easy-to-find spot. Here, you will find lists of keyboard shortcuts as well as a description of the toolbar buttons in each of the programs. Also included is a list of Excel functions along with an explanation of what each one does.

You can do many exciting, wonderful things with Microsoft Office 97; and with this book, you can take advantage of all that Microsoft Office 97 offers now.

A Word About Conventions

This book was specially designed to make it easy to use. In each task you'll find an explanation about the task and examples of how and why you use it. Immediately following is a Guided Tour, which shows you step-by-step how to perform the task. The following figure shows you how the Guided Tour works.

There are a few special conventions that make the book easier to use:

Text to be typed appears bold. For example, if you read, type **win** and press **Enter**, type the command "win" and press the Enter key on your keyboard. Keys you are supposed to press are bold, too, to make them easier to spot.

Key+Key combinations are used when you have to press two or more keys to enter a command. When you encounter one of these bolded combinations, hold down the first key while pressing the second key indicated.

Menu names and commands are also bold. When told to open a menu or select a command, move the mouse pointer over it, and press and release the left mouse button.

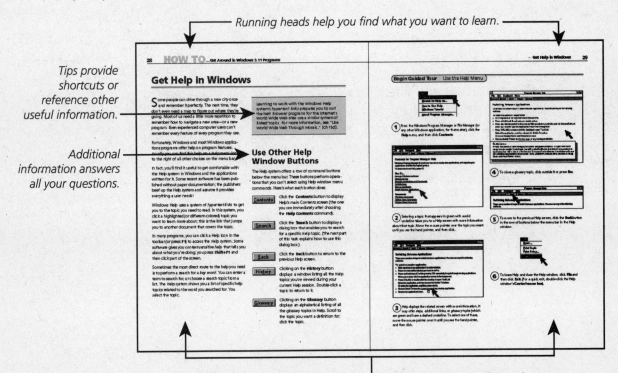

Running heads help you find what you want to learn.

Tips provide shortcuts or reference other useful information.

Additional information answers all your questions.

The Guided Tour shows you how to complete a computer task step-by-step.

Acknowledgments

When you read a book, it is easy to assume that the author(s) is the person responsible for creating what you hold in your hands. But that's not true; the book is really the result of the efforts of many individuals. Thanks go to Martha O'Sullivan, Melanie Palaisa, and Katie Purdum for all their brainstorming and administrating. Extra special thanks go to all in the Production Department for putting this book together.

Dedications

Sherry Kinkoph — To Robin and Alan Oglesby

Joe Kraynak — To Cecie

Jennifer Fulton — To Era Pool: Thank you for your kindness, your love, and most of all, your grandson—my husband.

PART 1

How To...

The first part of this book is a How To guide covering all the basic operations needed to use Microsoft Office 97 applications. Plus, you'll learn how to use the new elements of Windows 95, how to install the Office 97 programs, and how to manage the files you create. Each section is jam-packed full of information about using each of the Office 97 programs—you'll learn the details needed to put Word, Excel, PowerPoint, and Outlook to work for you. First, you'll learn how to use each Office 97 application individually and then how to make the Office 97 applications work together and on the Internet!

What You Will Find in This Part

HOW TO...

Use Basic Windows 95 Elements

Are you new to Windows 95? Microsoft has made quite a few changes to the Windows interface since Windows 3.1. Windows 95 looks a lot different, works a lot differently, and has many new features to learn about. Before you begin learning all about using Microsoft Office 97, you need to know a few things about Windows 95. One way to learn the detailed ins and outs of the Windows 95 operating system is to buy a book about the subject...but if you're just looking for instructions about the essentials of Windows 95, then this first section of the *Big Basics Book of Microsoft Office 97* is just for you.

In this section of the book, you learn how to start and stop Windows 95, familiarize yourself with some of the features, such as the taskbar and the Programs menu, and find out how to manipulate windows on your screen. These basic skills are fundamental for using the Office 97 programs. (If you're already an experienced Windows 95 user, you can skip ahead to the next section of the book and start using Microsoft Office 97.)

What You Will Find in This Section

Work with Windows 95

Microsoft Windows 95 can greatly enhance the way you run your computer system. Because it's so different from the old Windows (version 3.1), software companies are creating new software programs or versions to run on Windows 95 and "everybody" includes the Microsoft Office creators. Microsoft's first suite of Windows 95 included Office 95, a whole new set of Office applications created to run on the new Windows 95 interface. Today, Microsoft has released another upgrade for its popular Office suite called Office 97.

To help you understand the new Windows 95 system, you should first know a little about its history. Before Windows ever existed, people were using DOS—an operating system that tells your computer to act like a computer. DOS is command-driven, which means you have to type in cryptic words and abbreviations at a strange-looking prompt symbol to get the computer to do anything. Then, thankfully, Microsoft invented Windows, which is a graphical user interface program, GUI ("GOO-ey"), that ran on top of DOS.

Windows makes the computer easier to use and much nicer to look at. All you have to do is point and click your mouse button on icons (little pictures or graphics), select commands from pull-down menus (lists), and open dialog boxes (mini-windows) to make the computer perform various tasks—hence the name *graphical user interface*.

The Microsoft people decided they could improve Windows, making it even better and easier to use— eliminating its dependence on DOS. That improvement comes in the form of Windows 95. With Windows 95, you never have to deal with command-driven DOS again. Windows 95 is faster, more powerful, and gives you better performance when doing several computer things at the same time.

The Guided Tour below will show you some of Windows 95's many features, in no particular order.

Begin Guided Tour   Windows 95 Features

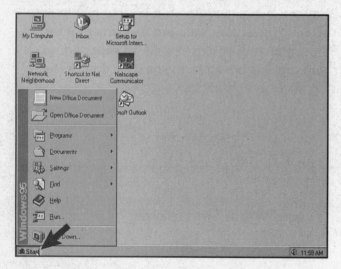

1 You can open any program or document by clicking the **Start** button, which is on a convenient taskbar, located by default, at the bottom of your Windows 95 screen.

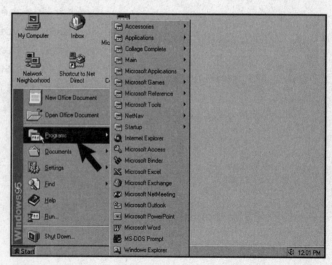

2 Instead of arranging programs and files into program group boxes and directories as in Windows 3.1, you now arrange them in folders in a **Programs** menu, accessed by clicking **Start** and then moving the mouse pointer to **Programs**.

> ## Guided Tour   Windows 95 Features

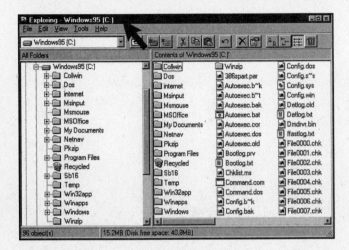

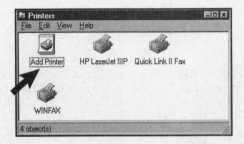

6 Print Manager's still around, too, using a new name. Access it through the **Start** menu by choosing **Settings** and **Printers**. It's easier to add new printers and change settings with the Add Printer Wizard feature.

3 Microsoft replaced Windows 3.1 File Manager with the **Windows Explorer**. You can use it to manage files, just like the old File Manager, but you access it from the **Programs** option on the **Start** menu.

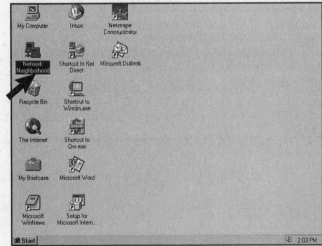

7 Networking is easier now with the Windows 95 **Network Neighborhood** icon. This is handy when you're hooked up to other computers in an office situation.

8 You can dump files you no longer want by tossing them, electronically, into the **Recycle Bin**, a temporary storage place for items you're cleaning off your system. The great thing about the Recycle Bin is you can get any files back that you accidentally deleted (if you haven't emptied the Recycle Bin yet).

4 You can view the contents of your computer's drives by opening the **My Computer** icon. You can also access the Windows 95 Control Panel and Printers folder using this icon.

5 The Control Panel is still around; you can find it by opening the **Start** menu and choosing **Settings**.

9 Windows 95 makes full use of Plug and Play hardware technology. With it, you can easily install new hardware devices, without all the headaches of hardware/software clashes. Microsoft also made it easier to install software.

(continues)

Guided Tour Windows 95 Features

(continued)

10 You can jump into cyberspace without much fuss using Microsoft's online service, aptly named **The Microsoft Network**. You'll also find built-in Internet support on Windows 95.

Start and Stop Windows 95

The new Windows 95 starts immediately whenever you turn on your computer system. Mind you, immediately isn't necessarily a fast thing on a computer. Most computers, when started, hum and whir for a few seconds, and strange text appears on the screen. After that, the Windows 95 opening screen appears; then you're presented with a logon box.

You can set up your logon box so that you have to use a password in order to use your computer. This feature is for people who want to safeguard their computers from others and keep computer data protected. If you have important files that you don't want other users viewing or changing, then it's a good idea to set up a password. If you're using a networked computer, you'll also have to use a password to access the network.

After you log on to the computer with the logon box, Windows 95 opens up. From your Windows 95 desktop, you can run other applications, use other Windows 95 features, and proceed with your own computer business. You'll always start from this opening screen, which you can think of as your Windows 95 lobby. When you're ready to turn off your computer, there's a new way to exit. You'll find a Shut Down option when you click the Start button on the taskbar. It opens a dialog box containing various exiting routes to apply. If you haven't saved your Windows work, Windows will ask you to do so before exiting. A little dialog box pops up with several choices about saving.

Change Your Windows 95 Password

One of the new features used in Windows 95 is a logon box. You can use the box to set up a password to log on with. You can use the password to keep other people from using your computer. Once you assign yourself a password, however, you'll have to remember it every time you open Windows 95.

Passwords are quite common in computer programs today. People use passwords to help keep important data safe. It's a good idea to change your password often, every few weeks or so, to keep your computer data secure. If you're using your computer at home, you may not have to be so diligent in computer security, unless you're trying to keep family members from deleting important files.

Use these steps to change your Windows 95 password:

1. To change your Windows 95 password, click the **Start** button; select **Settings** and **Control Panel**.

2. Double-click the **Passwords** icon in the Control Panel box.

3. This opens a dialog box that lets you change the password. Click the **Passwords** tab to bring its information to the front of the box; then click the **Change Windows Password** button.

4. In the Change Windows Password dialog box, type in your old password (if applicable), type in a new password, and then retype the new password again in the Confirm dialog box.

5. Click **OK** to exit the box. The next time you log on to Windows 95, you can use your new password.

Be sure to consult your Windows 95 manual for help with setting up your own logon box with a password. If you set up a password the first time you used Windows 95, you'll have to type it in exactly as you designated it each time you log on to your computer.

Begin Guided Tour   Start Windows 95

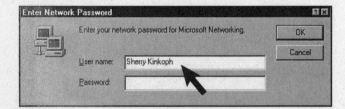

1 Turn on your computer. Windows 95 loads itself without any prompting. If you're using Windows 95 on a network, a logon box might appear. Type in your password (if applicable) and click **OK**. If you didn't set up a password and don't require a logon box, you can proceed directly to step 2.

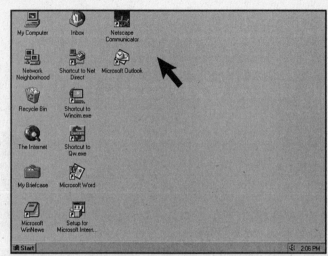

2 The Windows 95 desktop opens onto your screen.

Begin Guided Tour   Exit Windows 95

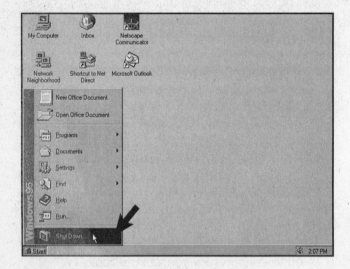

1 Open the **Start** menu and choose **Shut Down**.

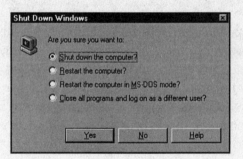

2 In the Shut Down Windows dialog box, choose an appropriate exit option (typically the first one), and then click **Yes**. Your computer prepares for shutdown and prompts you when it's safe to turn off the computer.

If you haven't saved your work, you'll be prompted to do so before turning off the computer.

Move Around in Windows 95

One of the primary tools for navigating Windows 95 and Windows-based programs is the mouse. You can use your mouse to point at items on-screen and move them around. You can also use your mouse buttons to select items and perform tasks.

Ever use a mouse before? Don't worry. It gets easier and easier each time you work with it. The mouse is a piece of hardware (as is your printer and keyboard). As you move the mouse around on your desktop, a little arrow appears on-screen and moves as well. That's your mouse pointer. It seems a little disorienting at first, but keep at it; using your mouse will become a natural part of your computer life.

Microsoft is now bundling a new mouse, called an IntelliMouse, with some copies of its Office 97 products. Perhaps you purchased such a bundle. The IntelliMouse makes use of a new wheel button in the middle of the mouse. The wheel lets you scroll up and down a document without having to point and click on the document window's scroll bar.

There are four basic mouse actions to learn about, and three actions that can only be performed with the IntelliMouse from within an Office 97 program. Here's a rundown of each mouse action:

- **Click**   To tap lightly on the mouse button quickly, usually the left button unless otherwise specified.

- **Double-click**   To lightly tap on the left mouse button twice in quick succession.

- **Right-click**   To tap lightly on the right mouse button quickly.

- **Drag**   To move the mouse while simultaneously holding down the left mouse button.

- **Scrolling**   To scroll quickly up or down a page in any Office 97 program, move the IntelliMouse wheel in an upward or downward direction. This

lets you scroll without having to click a scroll bar arrow or drag a scroll box.

- **Panning**   Hold down the IntelliMouse wheel button and move the mouse to scroll around an entire Office 97 document in any direction without using the scroll bars.

- **Zooming**   To zoom your view of a document to see text up close or far away, press the **Ctrl** key and hold down the IntelliMouse wheel button.

Although most people use a mouse to work with Windows 95, you can use the keyboard to navigate the many windows, too. You have to memorize keystrokes to perform certain tasks:

- **Selection letters**   Underlined letters found on menu commands.

- **Shortcut keys**   Keystroke combinations you use to perform tasks.

- **Arrow keys**   Use to move up, down, left, and right on your screen.

- **The Ctrl and Alt keys**   Use to open menus and carry out commands.

The Ctrl key and the Alt key are used in conjunction with other keys to activate commands. All of the menu bars and most of the menu commands have underlined letters in them, called selection letters. If you press the Alt key and one of these selection letters, it's the same as opening the menu or selecting the command with the mouse. For example, you can press Alt+F to open the File menu.

Also on the menu lists, you'll find keypress combinations, called shortcut keys, for activating commands. If available, these are located to the right of the menu commands. They will come in handy as you become more familiar with the programs. Because they're shortcuts, you can save time and effort in selecting commands.

Begin Guided Tour   Move Around with the Mouse

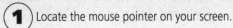

1 Locate the mouse pointer on your screen.

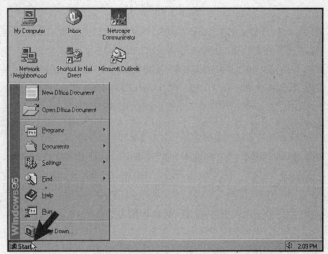

2 To move the mouse pointer, simply move your mouse. To select an item on-screen, move the pointer over the item and click the left mouse button. For example, if you move the pointer over the **Start** button on the taskbar and click, the Start menu opens. To open an icon on the desktop (a small picture representing a feature, command, or program), move your pointer over the icon and double-click.

Begin Guided Tour   Move Around with the Keyboard

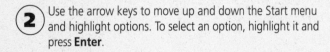

1 To move around on the Windows 95 desktop using the keyboard, use the arrow keys to move from icon to icon. When you've selected an icon, it appears highlighted. Press the Enter key to open the feature.

2 Use the arrow keys to move up and down the Start menu and highlight options. To select an option, highlight it and press **Enter**.

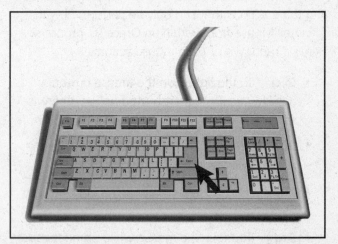

3 Press the **Tab** key to move back and forth from the desktop to the taskbar. Once you highlight the **Start** button, which appears to have a dotted outline of a box around the button's edge, you can press **Enter** to open the Start menu.

View the Windows 95 Desktop

Windows 95 focuses on a desktop look, which means that the most common elements appear on your screen much like your own office elements, such as the way you might arrange your stapler, phone, pens, and paper on your desk. Here are some common elements you'll find on your Windows 95 desktop:

- **My Computer**   This icon opens to reveal all of the drives you have on your computer. You can use this feature to open each drive's contents and find out what folders and files you have. For example, to find out what's on your floppy disk, you can put the disk in your floppy drive, open the My Computer window, and select the floppy disk drive. It will list what's on the disk in the drive. The My Computer icon also lets you access the Control Panel and Printers folders.

- **Network Neighborhood**   Use this icon when you're connected to a network of other computers. It displays the various elements found on your network and lets you use them.

- **Recycle Bin**   This is where you toss things you no longer want on your system, such as old files. When you're ready to remove items, empty the recycle bin and confirm the deletions.

- **The Microsoft Network**   This icon helps you get online with Microsoft's commercial online service. You'll need a modem to use this feature and a credit card to sign up and pay for the service.

- **Taskbar**   Use the taskbar to open and use one or more programs at the same time. For every program you open, a button for it appears on the taskbar. You can easily click the buttons to switch to other programs.

- **Start button**   To start any program, use this button. It displays a Start menu for launching programs, accessing the Control Panel, finding files, finding online help, and shutting down the computer.

Use Windows Accessories

There's more to Windows 95 than the items found on the desktop. Windows 95 comes with several applications, although you can certainly add others such as Office 97. The Accessories folder contains some fun Windows 95 features, such as a painting program and a calculator. You don't absolutely need to know about these accessories, but they may come in handy. I'll describe these for you, and then you can explore them at your leisure.

- **WordPad**   A simple word processing program that lets you work with text. It's not as sophisticated as Microsoft Word, but it can handle basic word processing tasks. (WordPad is the replacement for the old Windows 3.1 Write program.)

- **Paint**   A drawing and painting program for creating computer graphics. Paint has various tools for illustrating, making shapes, and using colors and patterns.

- **Calculator**   An on-screen calculator for handling simple operations such as addition, subtraction, division, and multiplication, as well as complex operations (like a scientific calculator).

- **Calendar**   Helps you keep track of your schedule (kind of like a streamlined version of Outlook, which comes with your Office 97 pack). You'll only have this accessory if you upgraded from Windows 3.1.

- **Cardfile**   A very simple database program that resembles a card catalog or Rolodex. Use it to keep track of information such as addresses, phone numbers, and so on. (You'll only have this accessory if you upgraded from Windows 3.1.)

- **HyperTerminal** Helps you use your modem to dial online services. HyperTerminal is a new Windows Terminal (a feature from Windows 3.1).

Be sure to check your Windows 95 manual for more information about using each of these accessories.

Begin Guided Tour   Tour the Windows 95 Desktop

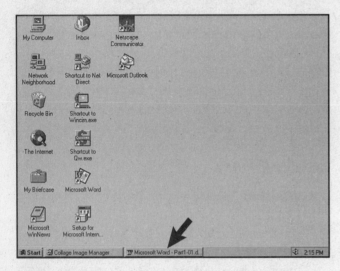

1 Windows 95 taskbar lets you switch back and forth between open programs. The program names appear as buttons on the taskbar.

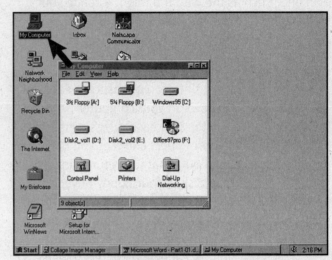

3 The rest of the Windows 95 desktop holds icons representing various features such as the Recycle Bin and My Computer. To open any feature on the desktop, double-click the icon.

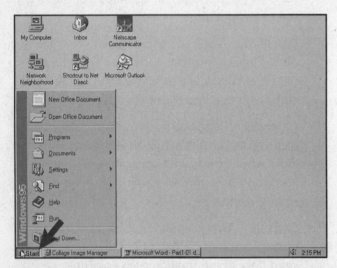

2 Also located on the taskbar is the **Start** button. When you click the **Start** button, a menu appears with various options you can select.

View Drives with My Computer

The My Computer icon presents you with another way to look at your drives and the files they contain. To open the My Computer feature, double-click its icon. It opens into a window revealing all of your drives. The My Computer window lets you see your drives' contents and find out how much space they each have. You can even check the contents of your floppy disk drives or CD-ROM drive. It also provides quick access to the Control Panel (for controlling Windows 95 settings), and the Printers folders (for handling printers).

To see how much space your hard drive is using, click the drive icon to select it, then look at the bottom of the My Computer window to see how much free space you have left. You'll also see what your drive's capacity is, listed in megabytes (or at times, giga-bytes).

To open a drive and see its contents, just double-click the drive's icon. To close the window at any time, click the Close button—the button with an X on it in the upper-right corner of the opened window. If you open a floppy drive or CD-ROM drive and it doesn't have a disk in it, you'll see an error message.

Begin Guided Tour   Open My Computer

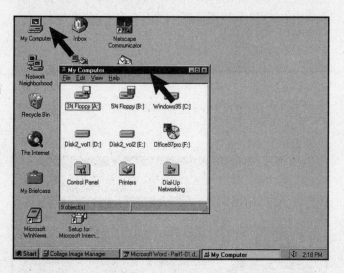

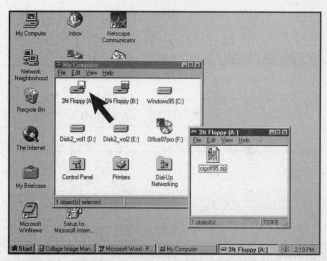

1 Double-click the **My Computer** icon to open a window revealing the contents of your computer. You see an icon for each drive on your computer, plus the Control Panel and Printers folders.

2 To see what's in a floppy or CD-ROM drive, double-click the drive icon. This opens a window revealing the contents of the drive.

You can open as many drive windows as you want. You can even move and copy files and folders from window to window. To close the My Computer window or drive windows you've opened, click the **Close** button in the upper-right corner. The button with the **X** on it is the **Close** button.

Use Windows Explorer to Manage Files

Windows 95 does not have a File Manager like Windows 3.1; it has been replaced with the Windows Explorer. You can do the same things with the Explorer that you did with File Manager, including moving and copying files to new locations, deleting files, printing files, and even launching programs. You can view your computer's file structure and folder hierarchy with Explorer. Windows Explorer looks very much like the old File Manager, with a few stylish touches added.

To find the Windows Explorer, you must first click the **Start** button to display the Start menu, then select **Programs** and **Windows Explorer**. When selected, it opens the Explorer window. Inside this window, you'll find menus, toolbar buttons, and a listing of your computer's file and folder hierarchy. To change the folders in view, click the drop-down list and choose a drive or folder you want to display. You can use the toolbar buttons to quickly view files, expand or

collapse the folder hierarchy, delete files, cut, copy, or paste, and more.

To open a folder and view its contents, double-click the folder icon or name. Use the scroll bars to move back and forth along the list of folders or files displayed.

There are lots of ways to do the same thing in Windows 95. For example, with Windows Explorer, you can view different drives using the Drives drop-down list, or by clicking the drive name in the left column list. The plus and minus signs in front of the folder and drive names can be used to expand or collapse the list too. A plus sign means there's more to see; a minus sign means the contents are already displayed. A quick click on the plus sign will expand the list. But you can also double-click the drive or folder name to do the same thing.

Begin Guided Tour   Open and View Windows Explorer

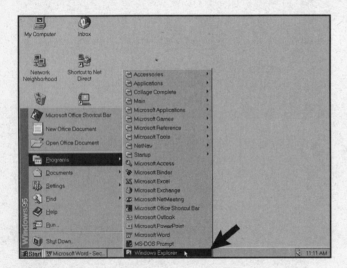

1 Open the **Start** menu and choose **Programs**. The Programs menu appears. Locate **Windows Explorer** at the end of the Programs menu list, and click it to select it.

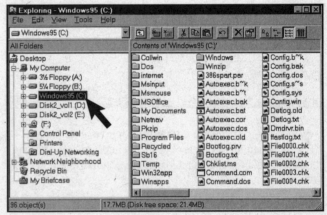

2 The Exploring - Windows 95 window appears, which looks very much like the Windows 3.1 File Manager. From here, you can use the menu bar and the toolbar to manage your computer's files and folders.

Guided Tour Open and View Windows Explorer

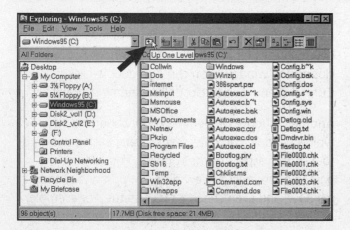

3 To find out what a toolbar button does, hover your mouse pointer over the button to see the ScreenTip name.

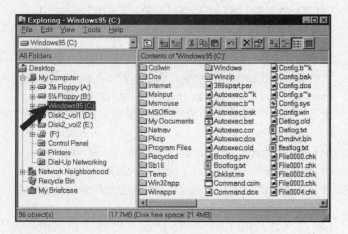

4 The left side of the Explorer window lists drives and program folders—the directory tree. The right side of the window lists individual files within a folder. To expand the directory tree, double-click the drive folder. For example, to view the C: drive, double-click the C: drive folder name.

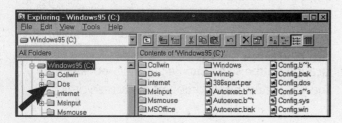

5 This expands the list and you see the folders contained within the drive. To view the contents of a folder, double-click the folder name.

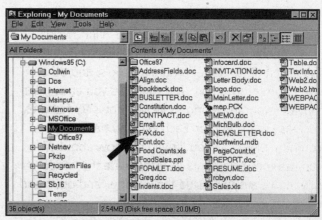

6 The right side of your screen will list the individual files found within a folder, as well as any subfolders.

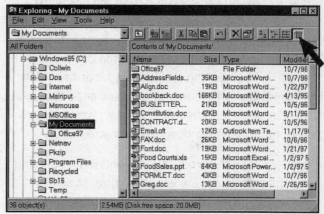

7 To see the file list in more detail, click the **Details** button, the very last button on the toolbar. The file list now shows detailed information about every file in the folder.

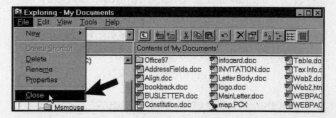

8 To close the Windows Explorer window, click the **Close (X)** button in the upper-right corner of the window. You can also open the **File** menu and select **Close**. Work with Window Elements

Work with Windows Elements

Microsoft appropriately named Windows 95 because of all the windows (also called boxes) that open up to reveal programs, tools, and other computer information. The windows you encounter may be program windows, or Windows 95 features, such as My Computer. Each window has some common elements you'll need to know about. You can use these elements to manipulate the window's size, move around inside the window, and open and close the window.

For example, each window has a border that you can use to resize the window. Move your mouse pointer over a border; when the pointer becomes a directional arrow, you can click-and-drag the border to make the window larger or smaller. You can drag any of the four sides of your window to change its size in that direction. You can drag any of the corners with the mouse to make the window bigger or smaller in two directions at the same time. You'll need to know how to resize windows when you start working with two or more open windows on your screen.

In the upper-right corner of your windows, you'll find three buttons. Those are your Minimize, Maximize, and Close buttons. You can click any of these buttons to control your window. The Minimize button, when selected, reduces your window into a button on the taskbar (which you can open again by clicking it). The Maximize button enlarges your window to take up the entire screen space. Once a window has been maximized, a Restore button appears. Click the Restore button to reduce the window to its original size. The Close (X) button does just as its name implies; it closes the window completely.

In the upper-left corner of most windows is a Control-menu icon. It sits to the left of the window title. If you click your mouse pointer on the Control-menu icon, it reveals a menu for controlling the window. You'll find commands listed for changing the window's size or closing the window. You can also double-click the Control-menu icon to close the window completely.

Another window element to know about is a bar. The typical window can have several bars, each pertaining to a certain aspect of the window. You can use the bars to open menus, view different portions of the window, and even check a task's status. For example, a window's title bar tells what program or feature it is, and the menu bar lists all of the menu groups you can choose from. A window's status bar might display information about the task you're performing. A window's scroll bar lets you quickly move backward and forward in a list of items.

Scroll bars are common throughout Windows 95 and Windows 95 programs (like Office 97). A scroll bar is used to view different portions of lists or on-screen documents. You'll find both vertical scroll bars (which are located on the far-right side of your window) and horizontal scroll bars (which are located at the bottom of your window). To scroll up, just click the up arrow at the top of a vertical scroll bar. To scroll down, click the down arrow. To scroll right on a horizontal scroll bar, click the right arrow. To scroll left, click the left arrow.

There are a few more ways to move around with the scroll bars. You can click anywhere inside a scroll bar to move your view. Or, you can use the scroll box, the tiny box inside the scroll bar. You can drag the scroll box to move up and down, or right and left. Simply click the box with your mouse pointer, hold down the left mouse button, and move the mouse to a new location on the scroll bar. Release the mouse button, and you view a new portion of the screen or list.

Work with Multiple Windows

The useful feature about Windows 95 is that you can open as many windows as you want. You can also move from window to window by clicking each one. (You can use the taskbar to do this, too.)

Multiple-opened windows make it easier than ever to move items from one window and place them in another. However, there's a downside to multiple windows. The more you open, the more cluttered your desktop becomes. Each time you open a window, it will sit on top of the previous window. This makes things a little messy sometimes. If you're opening all kinds of folder windows, for example, a stack of opened windows piles up fast. Not only that, but the more windows you have open, the slower your computer will run.

> The active window's title bar is always a solid color so you know which one you're currently using.

There are some options for tidying up these multiple windows. If you're working with multiple program windows, you can use the program's Windows menu commands (the Windows menu is on the program's main menu bar). If you're working with windows from My Computer or Network Neighborhood, you can tidy up multiple windows with the Options dialog box:

1. Open your window's **View** menu and select **Options**. This opens the Options dialog box with tabs for controlling windows.

2. Click the **Folders** tab to bring it to the front of the dialog box. There are two options for

viewing your windows. The first option opens a new window for every folder you view. The second option replaces the previous window with the new window's contents. In other words, when you select this option, only one window appears on-screen no matter how many you open—only the window's contents change.

3. Choose an option, and click **OK** to exit the box. You can open the Options dialog box at any time and change the selection for viewing your folder windows.

Another way to keep things tidy is with a Shortcut menu (a menu that appears when you right-click) on the taskbar. If you're working with multiple windows opened on your screen, you can arrange them neatly by tiling or cascading them on your desktop. To do so:

1. Move your mouse pointer down to the taskbar and right-click. This opens a Shortcut menu for arranging windows.

2. Select a command from the menu, such as **Cascade** (stacks the windows nicely) or one of the **Tile** commands (displays the windows side-by-side either horizontally or vertically), and the windows will appear neatly on-screen for you.

3. If you want to minimize all the windows opened on your desktop, select the **Minimize All Windows** command from the Shortcut menu. This will reduce all the opened windows to buttons on your taskbar.

> If you're looking for more detailed information about using Windows 95, pick up a copy of *Big Basics Book of Windows 95*.

Begin Guided Tour Use the Windows Elements

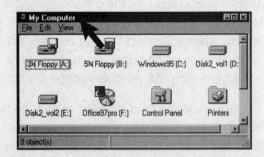

1 At the top portion of the window is a *title bar* that displays the program or file name. If you're not sure which program or window you're in, look at the title bar for a clue. You can move a window by pointing at the title bar, holding down the left mouse button, and dragging the mouse.

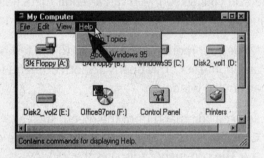

2 Located below the title bar, the *menu bar* displays a row of menu names. To open a menu, click the menu name, and a list of commands will appear. To select a command, click it.

3 You can find *scroll bars* along the right side or bottom of the window (or both), which you can use to view other parts of the window that aren't currently visible on-screen. Click the scroll bar arrows to move up and down, or right and left.

4 At the bottom of your window the *status bar* displays information about the file you're working on. In some programs, the status bar may even contain buttons you can activate.

5 Clicking the **Minimize** button reduces the window to a button on your taskbar. (Click the button on the taskbar to open the window again.)

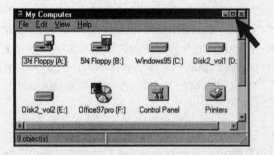

6 Clicking the **Maximize** button enlarges the window so that it takes up the entire screen.

Guided Tour Use the Windows Elements

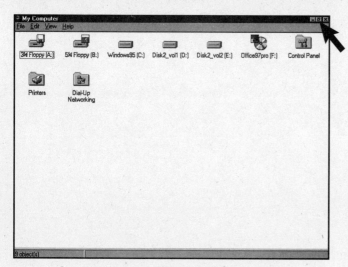

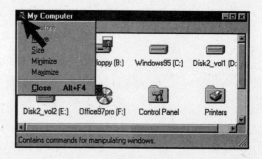

9 If you click your mouse pointer on the **Control-menu** icon, it reveals a menu for controlling the window. You'll find commands listed for changing the window's size or closing the window. You can also double-click the **Control-menu** icon to close the window completely.

7 When you maximize a window, a **Restore** button appears. You can click it to restore the window to its original size.

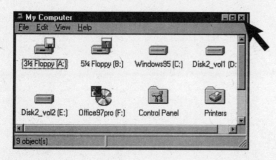

8 The **Close** button stands out because it has a big **X** in its box. Click it to close the window.

HOW TO...

Perform Basic Office Skills

I f you're already familiar with the new Windows 95 operating environment, then you're ready to dive in and start using Microsoft Office 97. If you're a new Windows user, you might want to back up and read the previous section for fundamental information about using the Windows 95 features.

If you're a seasoned veteran of the old Microsoft Office programs, you'll feel right at home using Office 97. All of your favorite features from the other programs are still around, plus there are plenty of new ones to try. The installation procedures are a little different, but simple and easy to handle. If you're a brand new user of the Office suite of applications, don't worry; this book will show you in detail how to use each program to its fullest, regardless of your comfort level.

In this section, you learn how to set up Microsoft Office 97, open and close applications, and understand the on-screen elements that will help you use the programs. With these skills, you can start using any of the Office 97 applications.

What You Will Find in This Section

Install Microsoft Office 97

Before you can take advantage of all the great things you can do with Microsoft Office 97, you first have to install the programs. If you are installing Microsoft Office 97 using floppy disks, you'll have a bunch of disks to juggle. Each disk, however, is labeled so you'll know which one to insert. If you purchased a CD-ROM version of Office 97, you'll just have the one CD. If you're installing Office 97 from a network, however, you'll need to ask your network administrator for assistance. Network installation works a little differently, depending on the type of network you have.

To make it as easy as possible to install Microsoft Office 97, the package includes a Setup program that will lead you through the installation process, asking you to make and confirm selections. You can choose to install the entire Office 97 package or just a single program. This same Setup program can help you uninstall Office 97 programs later.

The Setup program offers you several installation options, such as Typical or Custom. If you are installing the system on a desktop computer (not a laptop), the best choice is Typical. The Custom installation is for users who like to customize the setup of their Office 97 programs. If you're using a laptop computer, you may want to use the **Run from CD-ROM** option. This option lets you minimize the amount of space the programs occupy on your hard disk drive and run them from the CD-ROM instead. You can always go back later and make changes or customize how the programs are set up.

During installation, the Setup program will prompt you to select the drive and folder where you want to place the program files. You can select the default suggestions or change the folder, if necessary. You can also select which programs you want to install. After you make your choices, the Setup program will prompt you to insert the appropriate disks. Simply follow the on-screen instructions as necessary.

Begin Guided Tour   Install Microsoft Office 97

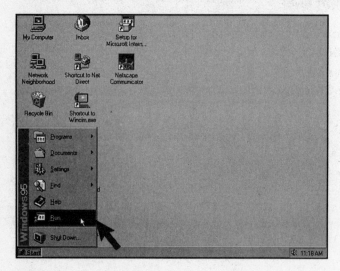

1 With Windows 95 running, click the **Start** button and select **Run** on the Start menu.

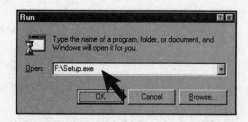

2 The Run dialog box opens onto your screen. In the **Open** text box, type in the drive letter you're installing from and the name of the setup program (**Setup.exe**). For example, if you're installing from your CD-ROM drive, you might type **D:/Setup.exe**. If you're installing from floppy disks, you might type **A:/Setup.exe**. Click **OK** or press **Enter** to continue installing.

If your computer is having trouble finding the setup program, you can select the **Browse** button to look for it.

Guided Tour Install Microsoft Office 97

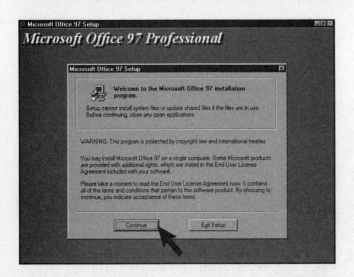

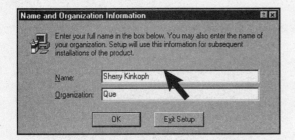

3 The Microsoft Office 97 Setup program opens onto your screen. The Setup program includes a series of boxes that lead you through the installation process. To start installing, click the **Continue** button or press **Enter**.

4 In the Name and Organization Information box, type in your name and company; then click **OK**. A confirmation box appears where you can recheck the information. If you need to edit your entry, click the **Change** button. If everything's correct, click **OK** again.

5 If you're installing from a CD-ROM, the next box that appears prompts you to enter the CD's 10-digit key code found on the CD liner notes or sleeve. Type the number and click **OK**.

6 In the next box, you'll confirm your product ID number. Be sure to write this number down and keep it in a safe place. You'll need this number if you ever contact Microsoft's technical support people. Click **OK** to continue installing.

(continues)

Guided Tour Install Microsoft Office 97

(continued)

7 The Setup program prompts you to install Office 97 in a folder named Microsoft Office. To install the program files to this folder, click **OK**. If you prefer to install Office 97 to another folder or drive, click the **Change Folder** button and designate another destination for the program files.

8 The next setup box lets you pick an installation option: **Typical**, **Custom**, or **Run from CD-ROM**. Click the option button to select the installation type you want. For most users, the **Typical** installation is the best option to choose; it installs the most common features the average computer user needs.

Depending on the installation option you selected in the previous step, more on-screen prompts may appear. Read the instructions and make the appropriate choices for you and your computer.

If you choose a Custom install, you can pick and choose which Office 97 program elements are installed. Use the **Change Option** button to access the options list and specify which elements you want.

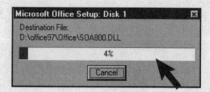

9 Finally, the installation process begins in earnest, copying program files onto your computer. A little installation-gauge box appears on-screen, indicating how much of the program is installed. If you're installing the program from floppy disks, just follow the on-screen prompts, inserting each disk as needed.

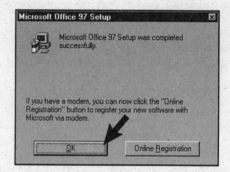

10 When you have installed everything, Setup displays a box telling you the procedure was successful. Click **OK** to exit the Setup program. (You can register your copy of Microsoft Office 97 electronically with your modem. Click the **Online Registration** button and follow the prompts.)

To install a single program, find the first disk, usually called the Setup disk, for the program. Then follow the Guided Tour for installing Microsoft Office 97.

Use the Office Shortcut Bar

One of the first things you'll notice after installing the Office 97 programs is the Office Shortcut bar. This toolbar appears on-screen, in the upper-right corner, as soon as you start Windows 95 (unless it's been turned off). The Office Shortcut bar is a unique feature that connects all of the Office 97 applications and literally acts as a manager, delegating work and bossing the other programs around. You can open documents with it, set up appointments, quickly access online help, and even launch the various applications with it. Basically, the Shortcut bar can save you time and effort as you work with the Office 97 programs. When you start Windows 95, the Office Shortcut bar feature starts up by default. You'll see the toolbar regardless of what program you're using (unless you choose to hide it or close it). For instance,

the toolbar doesn't appear only in Office 97 applications; you will also see it in any other programs you have running. By default, the toolbar is quite small and anchored in the upper-right corner of your screen; however, you can enlarge it and move it around on the screen.

Each of your Shortcut buttons provides you with a shortcut to starting a program or document. A click of a button may open a generalized dialog box that helps you choose a particular file or task, or it may take you directly into a program window, such as Outlook.

The following table explains each of the default toolbar buttons.

The Office Shortcut Bar

Icon	Name	Description
	New Office Document	Click this button when you're ready to start a new Office 97 document. It opens the New dialog box for choosing among Word, Excel, Access, and PowerPoint documents.
	Open Office Document	Opens a dialog box from which you can choose existing Office documents you've already created and saved.
	Internet Explorer	Opens the Internet Explorer Web browser program.
	Getting Results	Opens the Internet Explorer browser program to access the Getting Results Web page.
	Access	Opens the Access program (this button appears only if you've installed the Professional version of Office 97).
	PowerPoint	Opens the PowerPoint program.
	Excel	Opens the Excel program.
	Bookshelf Basics	Opens Microsoft's CD-ROM reference documentation.
	New Note	Opens Outlook's Note feature to record a note.
	New Message	Opens Outlook's e-mail feature for sending e-mail messages.
	New Journal Entry	Open's Outlook's Journal feature for recording a journal entry.

(continues)

The Office Shortcut Bar *Continued*

Icon	Name	Description
	Microsoft Outlook	Opens the Outlook program.
	New Appointment	Opens Outlook's Appointment feature for setting up a calendar appointment.
	New Task	Opens Outlook's Tasks feature that lets you add an item to your task list.
	New Contact	Opens Outlook's Contacts feature and lets you add a contact name to your list.

You can customize the buttons to represent each Office application you've installed or other common tasks you'll use frequently. With some modifications, this toolbar will let you open any of the Office 97 programs by simply clicking the respective icon. You can also add other buttons to this toolbar, even buttons for other non-Microsoft programs that you use frequently.

Customize the Shortcut Bar

If you click the Microsoft Office icon in the Shortcut bar (the puzzle icon at the very left of the bar), the Microsoft Office menu drops down. If your Shortcut bar is floating (not touching any of the four sides of the monitor screen), you can also right-click the title bar to see the menu. You can use the Microsoft Office menu to perform a variety of tasks, including opening the Customize dialog box or turning off the Shortcut bar (covered in a Guided Tour later in this task).

Here's what's on your menu:

Restore and **Minimize**   Commands for controlling your Shortcut bar. For example, when you choose the Minimize command, your Shortcut bar becomes an icon button on the Windows 95 taskbar.

Auto Hide   Instructs your computer to automatically conceal the Shortcut bar when you open a program.

Customize   Opens a dialog box for retooling (customizing) your Shortcut bar.

Add/Remove Office Programs   Opens the setup program (which you used to install the Office applications). You can use the setup program to add and delete Office 97 programs.

Contents and Index   Hooks you up with the online Help system.

About Microsoft Office   Displays some copyright information about the Office 97 product version and serial numbers.

Exit   Removes the Shortcut bar from your screen.

Add Program Buttons

Microsoft Office programs aren't the only applications you can add to the Shortcut bar. You can also add non-Microsoft programs that you use frequently. You can even add Windows 95 features, such as the Windows Explorer to the bar. To do any of these things, you first have to open the Customize dialog box.

Follow these steps to customize your own Shortcut bar:

1. Click the **Microsoft Office** icon to access the Office menu.

2. Select the **Customize** command.

3. In the Customize dialog box, click the **Buttons** tab to bring the button options to the front of the box.

4. Click the **Add File** button. The Add File dialog box appears.

5. In the Add File dialog box, select the program file you want to add to the Shortcut bar. Use the **Look in** drop-down list to locate the program, or use the **File name** text box to look it up directly.

6. Once you select the program file, click the **Add** button to close the dialog box and return to the Buttons tab.

7. Make sure the check box for the newly added program has a check mark in it, and then click **OK** to close the Customize dialog box.

You can use the Add Folder button in the Add File dialog box to add a folder to your Shortcut bar. For example, if you want speedy access to your My Documents folder, add it to the bar following the preceding steps (except click the **Add Folder** button instead of the **Add File** button). Then whenever you click its icon, the folder window opens on your screen.

Moving Your Shortcut Buttons Around

By default, your Office Shortcut bar buttons appear in a set order. However, you can customize the buttons to be in any order that you want. Why would you want to rearrange the buttons? Perhaps you're used to clicking the first icon on a toolbar. You may want to move the buttons you use the most to the left end of the bar where you click the most often. Or maybe you want similar icons or tasks grouped together. It's easy to move the buttons to other locations on the bar and place the buttons you use the most in the places you'll click most often.

Use these steps to change the order of your Shortcut bar buttons:

1. Click the **Microsoft Office** icon to access the Microsoft Office menu.

2. Select the **Customize** command.

3. In the Customize dialog box, click the **Buttons** tab to bring the button options to the front of the box.

4. Select the name of the button you want to move.

5. Click the up or down **Move** arrow to move the program to another place on the list. (Don't click the scroll bar arrows; that won't do the trick.)

6. When you're finished, click **OK**. The Shortcut bar reflects your icon changes.

If you want to delete buttons from the bar and from the list of buttons in the Customize dialog box, access the Buttons tab of the Customize dialog box, select the program, and click the **Delete** button.

Begin Guided Tour   Start and Close the Office Shortcut Bar

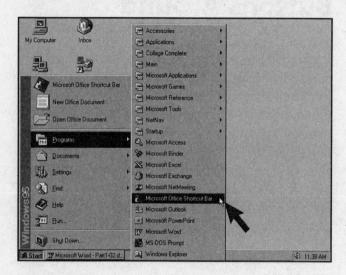

1 Click the **Start** button on your Windows 95 taskbar, then select **Programs** and **Microsoft Office Shortcut Bar** or open the **MSOFFICE** folder and click the **Microsoft Office Shortcut Bar** icon.

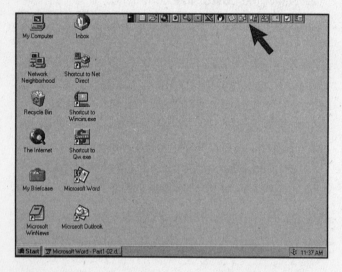

2 The Microsoft Office Shortcut bar opens and places the toolbar in the upper-right corner of your Windows 95 desktop.

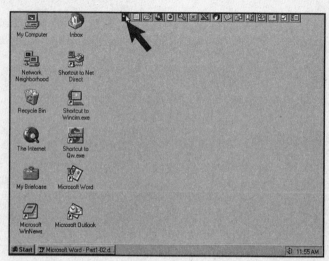

3 To close the Shortcut bar and remove it from your screen, click the **Microsoft Office** icon (the little puzzle icon at the very left of the bar).

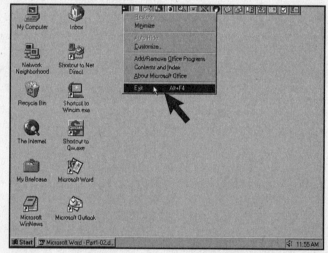

4 The Microsoft Office menu drops down. Click the **Exit** command to close down the Shortcut bar.

Begin Guided Tour Customize the Shortcut Bar

1 Click the **Microsoft Office** icon to access the Microsoft Office menu.

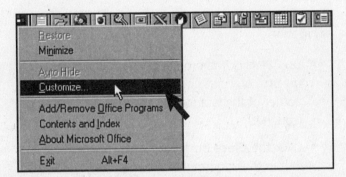

2 Select the **Customize** command from the menu.

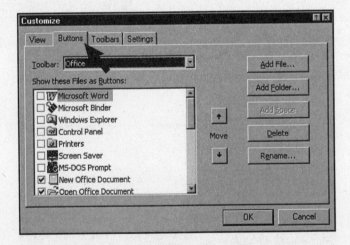

3 In the Customize dialog box, click the **Buttons** tab to bring the button options to the front of the dialog box.

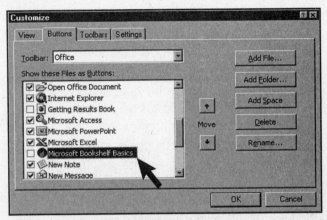

4 In the **Show these Files as Buttons** list, you can add or remove icons from the Shortcut bar by clicking the check box next to the icon. When the check box is activated, a check mark appears inside the box and the icon appears in the Shortcut bar. Use the **Move** arrow buttons to reposition the selected buttons on the bar. Use the scroll bars to move through the list of available icons to see all of the programs and features you can add to the Shortcut bar.

The Move arrows (the buttons to the right of the icon list that point up and down) are used to reposition icons on the Shortcut bar. Select the icon you want to move, then click the up arrow to move the button left on the bar, or click the down arrow to move the button to the right. A single click moves the icon one spot over in the arrangement.

5 When you finish redoing your buttons, click **OK**, and the Shortcut bar reflects your changes.

You can use the **Add Space** button in the dialog box to add spacers between your Shortcut bar buttons. Click the button list (in the Customize box) where you want space, and then click the **Add Space** button.

Start and Exit an Office 97 Application

Starting up an application is one of the easiest things you can do with your computer. To start an application, click the **Start** button, open the **Programs** menu, and click the application's icon. If the Office Shortcut bar appears on your screen, you can also start programs using the toolbar buttons. Aside from the startup methods just described, you can also launch your Office applications from the Windows Explorer or My Computer windows by double-clicking the application's executable file. With Windows 95, you can have several programs running at the same time. You can switch back and forth between them as needed using the taskbar.

When you finish working with a program, be sure to save all your work (see the task "Save a File"on page 48), and then exit the program. Why is it important to exit when you can have a lot of programs running? It's a good idea to exit the program to conserve memory and ensure your system runs as efficiently as

possible. You can think of exiting a program as clearing off your desk. When you clear off the desk, you have more working room. If you exit a program without saving your work, you will be prompted to save it.

There are many different ways to exit an Office application:

- Double-click the program window's **Control-menu** icon (that tiny icon in the upper-left corner of the window on the title bar with a tiny icon in it).

- Click the **Close** button (that tiny box with an X in it in the upper-right corner of the window).

- Pull down the program's **File** menu and select **Exit**.

- Press **Alt+F4** on your keyboard.

Begin Guided Tour   Start a Program

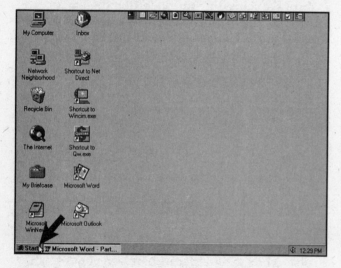

1 Click the **Start** button on the Windows 95 taskbar.

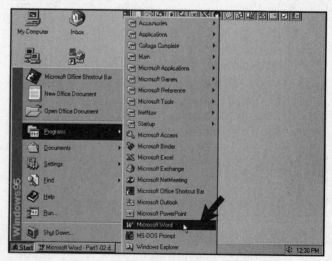

2 Select **Programs** from the Start menu; then in the Programs menu click the Office 97 program you want to open. The application opens onto your screen.

Begin Guided Tour   Exit a Program

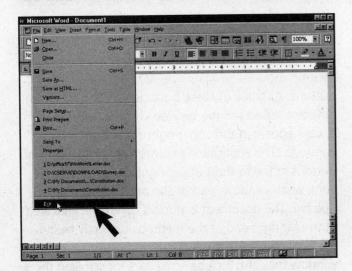

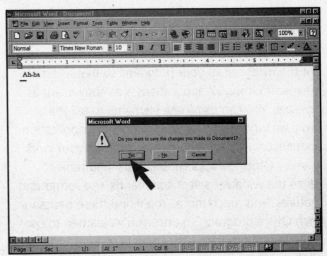

1 From any open program window, open the **File** menu and choose the **Exit** command. (You can also click the program's **Close** button.)

2 If you have saved the document, exit the program and return to the Windows 95 desktop. If you didn't save, you are prompted to save. Click the **Yes** button to save the document, the **No** button to exit without saving, or the **Cancel** button to cancel the exit.

When you finish working with the computer and want to turn it off, make sure you exit Windows 95 properly. You shouldn't turn off your computer with Windows 95 still running because Windows 95 takes care of some housekeeping (getting rid of temporary files and other things) when you exit. Use the exit steps you learned in "Start and Stop Windows 95" on page 7. Click the **Start** button, select **Shut Down**; then click **Yes** to turn off your computer.

Use Basic Office 97 Program Elements

The program creators have put several basic elements in the application window to help you get the most out of your programs so that using Microsoft Office 97 applications is as convenient as possible. You can use these elements to tell the program what to do, to control how the application appears on your screen, and to speed up your work. In every Office 97 application, you'll find tools to resize the window, select commands, use formatting features, and much more. You'll find these basics in each Office program, so once you've learned to use them in one program, you know how to use them for all the programs.

Keep in mind that when you are working in a document within an application, you may actually have two windows open: the application window and the document window (which appears inside the application window). Each window has its own set of controls: the standard window controls. The window controls include the Minimize, Maximize, and Close buttons. All three of these buttons are used to control different aspects of the windows. These buttons always appear in the upper-right corners of the windows. The application's controls are the first set of buttons in the farthest upper-right corner of the application window, part of the program window's title bar. The document window's controls are located at the far right end of the menu bar (directly below the application window's controls). The document window may also include scroll bars for scrolling the document.

Let's take a look at each of the common elements you'll see on your own Office program screens.

Begin Guided Tour Use Basic Office 97 Elements

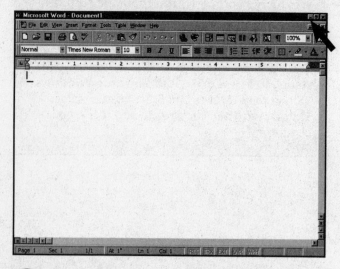

1 Click the **Minimize** button to turn the application window into an icon that appears on the taskbar.

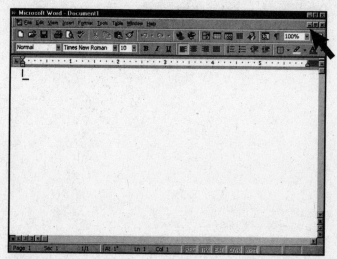

2 With some programs, such as Microsoft Word, you're working with a program window and a document window on-screen at the same time, so you will see two sets of window control buttons. If you click the document window's **Minimize** button, the document turns into an icon that appears at the bottom of the document window, but the application remains open.

Guided Tour   Use Basic Office 97 Elements

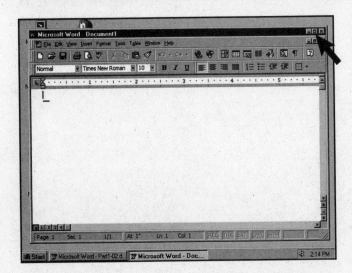

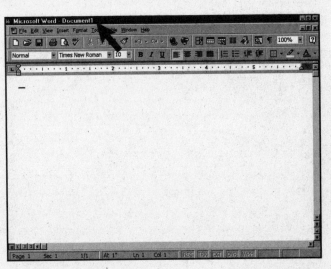

③ Click the **Maximize** button to expand the window to fill the entire screen. When you maximize a window, you see the **Restore** button, which you can then use to restore the window to its original size.

⑤ The application window's *title bar* shows you the name of the program and file you're currently working on.

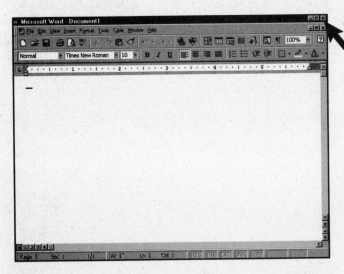

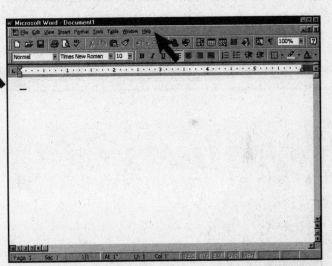

④ Click the **Close** button to exit the program at any time. In some programs, you're working with a program window and a document window, so you'll see two sets of window control buttons. If you click the document window's **Close** (X) button, you'll close the document you were working on, but the program stays open. If you click the program window's **Close** (X) button, you'll close the entire program, including any open documents.

⑥ The *menu bar* lists the menu names that contain commands for controlling tasks and features in your program.

(continues)

Guided Tour Use Basic Office 97 Elements *(continued)*

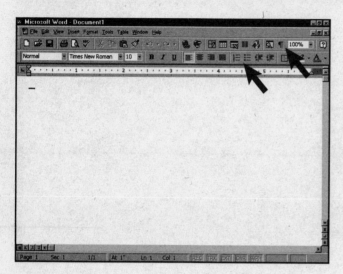

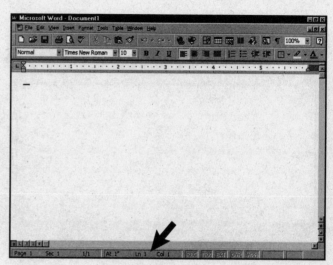

7 The *toolbars* include buttons for frequently used commands. These buttons can speed up your computer work. You can simply click the appropriate button to select a command.

9 The *status bar* contains information about the current document, such as what page you are on. For example, in Word, you can see what page you're working on, and the current location in the document. In PowerPoint, the status bar even contains buttons for activating commands.

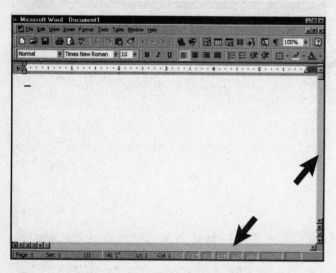

8 Use the *scroll bars* to view other portions of your file. You can scroll up and down, or right and left to view your document. Use the scroll arrows to move in specific directions. To scroll quickly, drag the scroll box in the appropriate direction.

Use Menu Commands

Menus are where most of your Office 97 commands hang out. Because menus contain all of the necessary tools for making the computer do things, opening a menu is kind of like opening your desk drawer to grab your stapler or a paper clip. When you're not using your desk tools, they stay in your drawer. It's the same with your computer tools: the menu is shut until you need the necessary command.

When you open a particular menu group, which you do by clicking the menu name, a list appears revealing related menu commands. (These menus are said to *drop down* because the menu list literally drops down from the menu bar.) To select a command from the menu list, click it with your mouse. After you choose a command, the menu disappears until you pull it down again. Here's what you'll encounter on your Office 97 menus:

Selection letters The underlined letters you see in the menu commands. You can press the selection letter in conjunction with the Alt key to choose a command with the keyboard (instead of clicking the screen with the mouse).

Shortcut keys Off to the right of some menu commands are keypress combinations that

activate commands. For example, the shortcut key for the Copy command is **Ctrl+C**. If you memorize them, you won't even have to open the menu; simply press the shortcut key to activate the command instead.

Ellipsis The three dots following a menu command. The ellipsis indicates that a dialog box will appear when you select that command. (See "Work with Dialog Boxes" on page 36.)

Arrow to the right of a menu command Indicates there is an additional menu to view (a submenu). The additional menu appears after you select the menu command.

Inactive commands Any faded-looking or grayish-colored commands on the menu. When a command appears gray, you can't use it for the moment.

Icons For those of you trying to learn toolbar buttons, you'll notice that the Office 97 menus also show toolbar icons, when applicable. This helps you learn which toolbar icon is associated with the command. Once you learn which icon to use, you can click it in the toolbar rather than display the menu.

Begin Guided Tour   Select Menu Commands

1 Click the name of the menu you want to open.

2 The menu drops down, and you see a list of commands. Click the command you want to execute. (Some menu commands open dialog boxes asking for additional information before executing the task.)

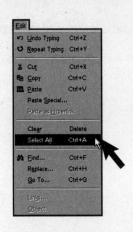

Work with Dialog Boxes

On many occasions when you select a command, the computer needs additional information from you before it can carry out the task. When it does, a dialog box pops up on your screen. A dialog box is like a mini-window within your program window for making additional decisions. It presents you with a bunch of options from which to choose, places in which to type text, and buttons for activating the options.

To make selections in a dialog box, click the various options with your mouse. In some cases, selecting

something might open yet another dialog box. When you finish with the dialog box, click the **OK** button (or whichever activating button resides in the box), or press the **Enter** key to put your changes into action. If you change your mind about the dialog box selections, click the **Cancel** button (or press **Esc**).

A dialog box contains quite a variety of components, as shown in the guided tour.

Begin Guided Tour   Use Dialog Boxes

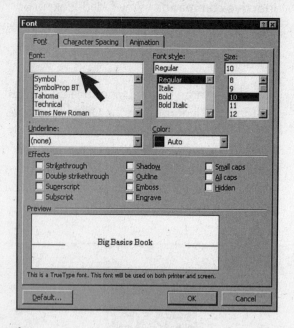

Text box   An area in which you type text such as a file name. When you click inside the text box, the mouse pointer becomes a cursor for typing.

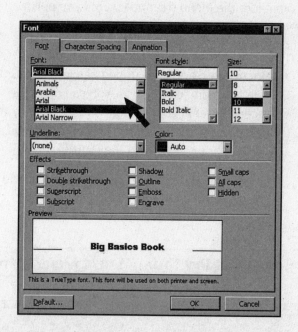

List boxes   Exactly what their name implies: lists in a box. To select an item in a list, click it to highlight it. If the list is a long one, scroll bars may appear. Use them to move backward and forward in the displayed list.

Guided Tour   Use Dialog Boxes

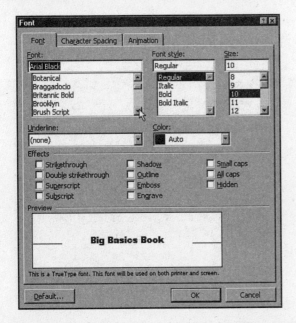

Scroll bars   Use to move back and forth through a list. Click the arrows to move up or down.

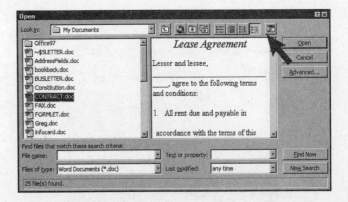

Toolbars   May appear in some of the dialog boxes you use. Toolbars have icon buttons that act as shortcuts for performing tasks. Click the icon to activate the task.

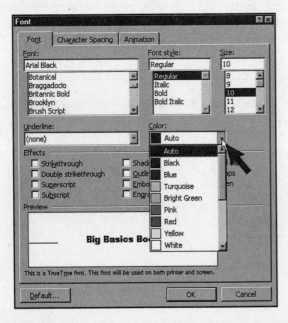

Drop-down lists   Have a downward-pointing arrow next to the first list item. When you click the arrow, a continuation of the list appears for you to view and choose from.

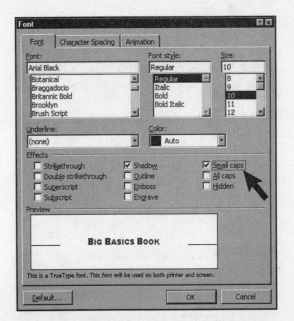

Check boxes   Tiny square boxes that turn a feature on or off. A check mark in a check box means the option is on; no check mark means it's off. You can turn on as many of these check boxes as you want. There's no limit.

(continues)

Guided Tour Use Dialog Boxes *(continued)*

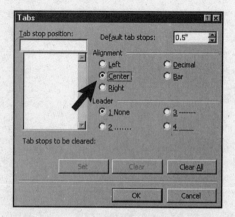

Option buttons Little round buttons that turn a feature on or off. A black dot in the option button means the feature is turned on. Option buttons usually represent a group of choices from which you can choose only one at a time.

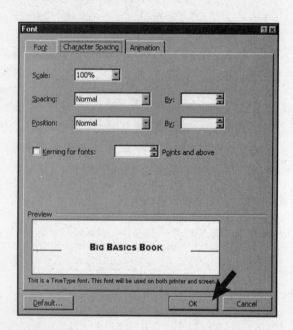

Command buttons Look like real buttons that you can click with the mouse to make things happen. Just about every dialog box has a command button that says **OK**. Click the **OK** button to have the computer carry out all of the dialog box selections you've made. Some command buttons even open additional dialog boxes.

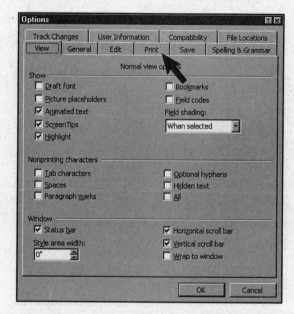

Tabs Appear in some dialog boxes. You'll know them when you see them because they look like they have little folders tabs at the top of them. Each tab has a name on it describing its options. In order to select options from one of the hidden tab pages, you must first click its tab name to move it to the front of the dialog box.

To quickly close a dialog box without implementing the options, click the **Close** button (if available) in the upper-right corner of the dialog box or press **Esc**. In some dialog boxes you can click a **Cancel** command to exit the dialog box.

Use Toolbars

Icons are little pictures or symbols. Buttons are small squares that you click with your mouse. Combine icons and buttons, and you have a *toolbar*. Toolbars are a part of every Microsoft Office program. So what's so hot about toolbars? Toolbars are collections of icon buttons that represent specific computer tasks, and they're the fastest way to select frequently used commands. Toolbar buttons represent commands you'll find among the program's menus. You'll quickly learn that selecting a toolbar button is a lot faster than opening a menu and looking for the command you want to use.

You'll find several toolbars available for every Office 97 application. For example, Word has 13 toolbars to choose from. When any of the Office 97 programs first start up, the default toolbar will appear. With some of the Office 97 programs, such as Word and Excel, there are two or more default toolbars.

As you work with the program, you can change toolbars to access the icon buttons that meet your current needs. To change toolbars, move your mouse pointer over the toolbar and right-click (click the right mouse button). This displays a shortcut menu listing all of the available toolbars, with a check mark next to each one that currently appears. To change toolbars,

click the one you want from the list, and the new toolbar appears. You can also change toolbars through the **View** menu, if available.

Microsoft has tried to come up with every possible toolbar combination you could want, but they've also made it easy for you to tailor the toolbars to fit your needs. You can edit the toolbars with the Customize button found in the Tools menu.

The ScreenTips Give You a Clue

The pictures on the toolbar buttons give you a visual clue as to what task the button performs. However, discerning what these pictures mean isn't always easy. If you're ever in doubt about what task the button performs, move your mouse pointer over it, and the button's name appears. This is a ScreenTip. This won't work if the ScreenTip feature is turned off. By default, it's on when you first use the Office 97 programs. If it is off, open the **View** menu, select **Toolbars**, click the **Customize** button, click the **Options** tab, then select the **Show ScreenTips on toolbars** check box. This turns the ScreenTips feature on again.

Begin Guided Tour   Select a Button from a Toolbar

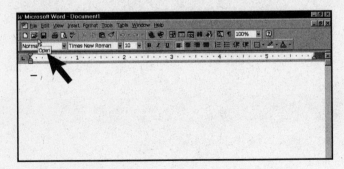

1 Move your mouse pointer over the toolbar button you want to activate. For example, click the **Open** button on the Standard toolbar to display the Open dialog box.

2 The Open dialog box appears on-screen. To exit the dialog box, click the **Cancel** button or the **Close** button in the upper-right corner of the box.

Begin Guided Tour   Change Toolbars

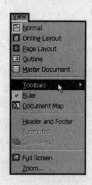

1 Open the **View** menu and select the **Toolbars** command.

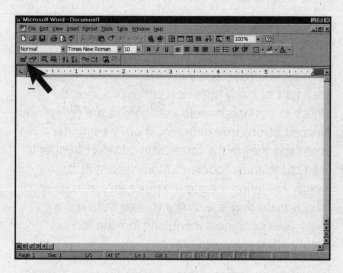

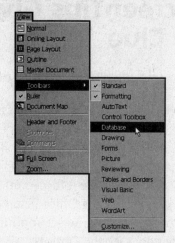

2 A list appears from which you can select toolbars to show. You can deselect those that are already selected, so that none are displayed, or you can display every toolbar.

3 If you selected a new toolbar from the list, the program now displays the toolbar on-screen, as shown in this figure. If you deselected a toolbar, it no longer appears on-screen.

Get Help in Office 97

When you can't remember how to do something in an application, you can use online help to refresh your memory. All Microsoft Office 97 applications include a Help menu and various ways to access the help features. For starters, you can ask the Office Assistant for help.

The Office Assistant is a new animated help feature that readily assists you with any questions or tasks you may have in any of the Office 97 programs. You can access the Office Assistant by opening the **Help** menu and selecting **Microsoft Help**, pressing **F1** on the keyboard, or you can click the **Office Assistant** button on the toolbar (the button with a question mark icon). Once you've accessed Office Assistant, you can type in a question, conduct a search, or view tips about the particular program you're using. You can even change options and customize the appearance of the animated feature. The Office Assistant may pop up on-screen from time to time to help you with common tasks.

If dealing with an animated help feature isn't your cup of tea, you can also find help the old-fashioned way, using a help dialog box. You can look up a topic in online help just like you do in a book: you can look up a topic in a table of contents or in the index. Unlike a book, though, you can also use the Help system to search for a particular topic.

> To get help on a particular on-screen element or command, open the **Help** menu and select **What's This**. Your mouse pointer changes to a question mark. Click the on-screen item or command for which you want help and a box appears detailing that item and how it's used.

If you're an avid Internet user, you can also access help via the World Wide Web. The Office 97 Help menus include a **Microsoft on the Web** command that lets you find help online, view the Microsoft Office Home Page, or check out an index of frequently asked questions.

Begin Guided Tour   Use Help

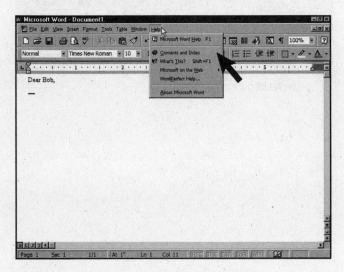

1 Open the **Help** menu and select the **Contents and Index** command from any Office 97 program.

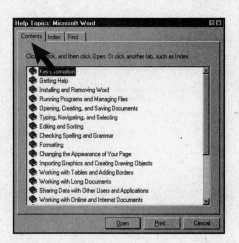

2 Click the **Contents** tab to view a list of topics.

(continues)

Guided Tour Use Help *(continued)*

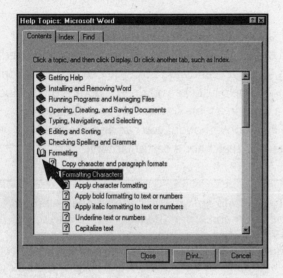

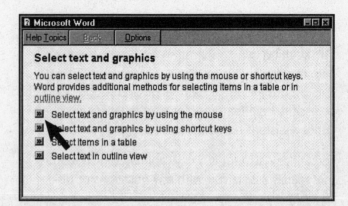

③ To choose a topic, double-click its name or icon. In many instances, this reveals a sublist of more topics. Keep double-clicking to find the exact topic you want to view information about. You'll see the following icons among the lists:

A closed book icon means there's a more-detailed list of topics to view.

An opened book icon means the topic is selected.

A question mark icon means there's detailed text to view about the topic.

⑤ Some topics you'll run across in the help text appear underlined and in a different color. You can jump to that topic by clicking it. Some topics appear underlined with a dotted line; click these hot spots to display a definition of the term.

⑥ Click the **Find** tab in the Help dialog box. The first time you click the Find tab, the Find Wizard opens on-screen. Click the **Next** button to continue.

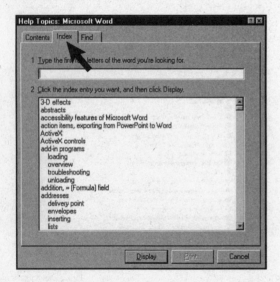

④ Click the **Index** tab in the Help Topics dialog box. The Index tab lets you look up topics from an exhaustive index list. Simply type in the word you're looking for and the index scrolls alphabetically to similar words. Double-click to display topics.

Guided Tour Use Help

7 The Find feature can help you look up a specific topic based on words you type in. In the first text box, type in the word or words you want to find help on, then select from the matching words or topics displayed in the second list. In the third area, click a specific topic to display an explanation about it.

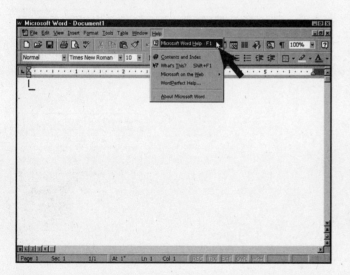

8 The newest addition to the Office help system is the Office Assistant. To open the Office Assistant, open the **Help** menu and select **Microsoft Help**, or click the **Office Assistant** button on the toolbar.

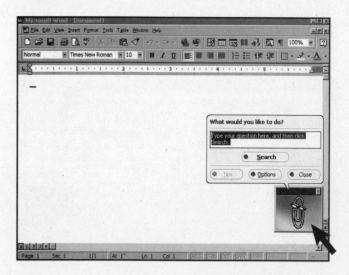

9 The Office Assistant appears on-screen as an animated character in a box with a dialog balloon. From the dialog balloon, you can type in a help question, access program tips, or customize the animated character. To close the feature at any time, click the **Close** option or click the **Close** button in the character's box.

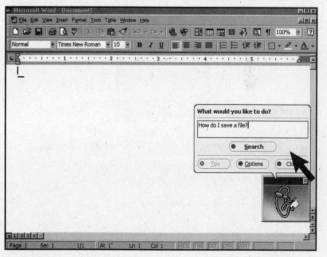

10 For example, you're having trouble saving a file. Type in a question like "How do I save a file?" and click the **Search** button. The Office Assistant will try to answer you.

(continues)

Guided Tour   Use Help   *(continued)*

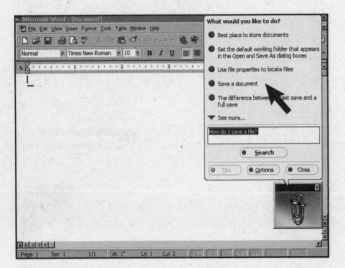

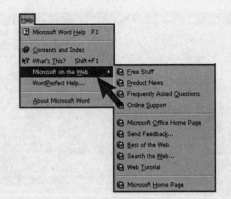

11 The Office Assistant displays a list of related topics. When you see something close to your request listed, click it to see detailed information about the subject matter.

12 To access the Microsoft Web site for help, open the **Help** menu and select **Microsoft on the Web**. This displays a list of online options you can pursue for more information. Select any option to start your Internet account and Web browser program.

Begin Guided Tour   Customize the Office Assistant

1 To open the Office Assistant, click the **Office Assistant** button on the toolbar, or open the **Help** menu and select **Microsoft Help**.

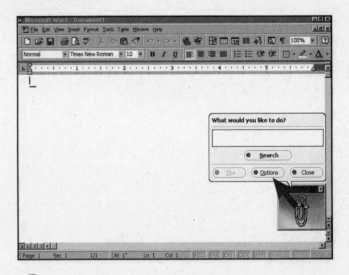

2 Click the Office Assistant's **Options** button.

Guided Tour   Customize the Office Assistant

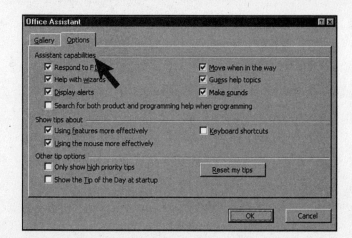

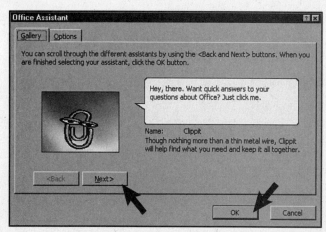

3 The Office Assistant dialog box appears. From here, you can turn options on or off pertaining to the Office Assistant feature. To change the animated character that appears each time you access Office Assistant, click the **Gallery** tab.

4 Click the Next button to scroll through a gallery of different animated characters. To select a particular character, simply click the **OK** button. This closes the dialog box.

HOW TO...

Manage Office 97 Files

One of the best things about using a suite of applications such as Microsoft Office 97 is that you can perform many common tasks the same way—for example, saving a file. Once you learn how to save a file in one application, you will know how to save a file in any of the applications. This section of the book covers common file management tasks.

If you've used Microsoft Office programs in the past with Windows 3.1, you'll notice Microsoft has radically changed the appearance of the dialog boxes associated with saving and opening files in Windows 95. The new Save As and Open dialog boxes used in Office 97 may confuse you a little. In Windows 95, you no longer store files in directories, but in folders. The hierarchy of a drive's contents appears the same way as before, but the way in which you display a drive works a little differently. But don't worry, this section will show you how to use each dialog box and its new features.

What You Will Find in This Section

Save a File

When you create a file (a letter, memo, budget, database), also called a *document*, your computer stores that information only temporarily in its memory. To make a permanent copy, you need to save the file to your hard disk or onto a floppy disk. It's important that you remember to save often. Why? Because if you don't and something happens to the power (such as an outage or an interruption in power just long enough to make the lights blink), all your hard work will be lost.

There are several different ways you can save files with the Office 97 programs:

- You can save a new file to a folder on your hard disk drive or save the file onto a floppy disk.

- You can save previously saved files, and even give them new names and put them in different folders.

- You can save files of different types to use with non-Microsoft Office programs.

The first time you save a file, you need to enter a file name. For the file name, you can type up to 255 characters, including spaces. In Windows 3.1, you could only use 8 characters in a file name, which was very limiting. Windows 95's new capacity for longer file names will go a long way in helping you clearly identify your documents.

However, you can't use any of the following characters when naming files:

\ ? : * " < > |

With some DOS and Windows 3.1 programs, the longer file names you create in Windows 95 may be truncated to 8 characters. When this happens, a tilde (~) is added to the name to indicate the name has been shortened.

Also, if you've worked with Windows 3.1, you might remember using three-letter file extensions in previous versions of Office. A file extension provides a unique way of identifying which program you created the file in and what type of file it was. File extensions are still around in Windows 95; however, they do not appear by default. Instead, you can identify files by icons next to the file name. For example, when you create a file in Word, a Word icon appears in front of the file name as it appears in a list of saved files. Knowing the Office-related icons will help you recognize files and file types in the lists you may come across, especially when you're looking at files in the Windows Explorer or My Computer windows.

You can still choose to view extensions, when needed. For example, if you want to view file extensions again while in the Windows Explorer, open the **View** menu and select **Options**. Click the **View** tab. Make sure you deselect the **Hide MS-DOS file extensions** check box. This will display the file names with their extensions.

By default, the following extensions are assigned by Office 97 applications:

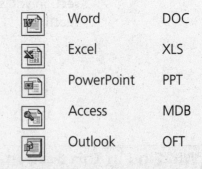

	Word	DOC
	Excel	XLS
	PowerPoint	PPT
	Access	MDB
	Outlook	OFT

When you save a file, the application will automatically save the document to the My Document folder. If you want to put the document in a different location or folder, you can use the **Save in** drop-down list in the Save As dialog box to change drives or folders.

It's a good idea to get in the habit of saving every five or 10 minutes so that your computer updates the disk version with the changes you make. After you've saved the first time, you simply select the **Save** command in the **File** menu to save again, or click the **Save** button on the toolbar. You won't be prompted for the name.

All of the applications, with the exception of Outlook, include a **Save** button in the toolbar. You can also use the keyboard shortcut **Ctrl+S** to save a file.

The Save As Dialog Box

The Save As dialog box has changed quite a bit from the previous Windows 3.1 versions of Office. There are new elements to learn about and new ways to save your data. In Windows 3.1, you saved files in directories, but in Windows 95, you save files in *folders*—which are just like the old Windows 3.1 directories. Folders can hold files and other folders (*subfolders*). Each of the Office programs appear as folders on your computer.

The toolbar buttons inside the Save As box let you view folders and files in various detail. Click a button to apply its function. Each button has a specific function, as shown in this table.

Button	Button Name	Function
	Up One Level	Moves your current drive's hierarchy list back one level.
	Look in Favorites	Opens the Favorites folder: a folder you can use to store your most popular document files in.
	Add to Favorites	Moves the selected file into the Favorites folder.
	List	Lists the folders and files by name.
	Details	Lists the files by details such as when the files were created, how much disk space they consume, their file type, and so on.
	Properties	Lists each file's individual details such as how many pages, name of the original author, what template the file's based on, and so on.
	Commands and Settings	Opens a submenu with additional file commands.

Begin Guided Tour   Save a File

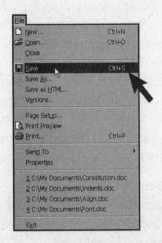

1 In your new, unsaved document, open the **File** menu and select the **Save** command. (You can also click the **Save** button on your application's toolbar.)

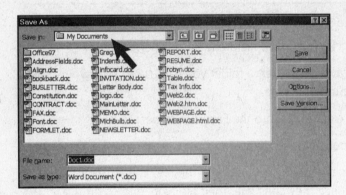

2 You see the Save As dialog box. Type a name for your document in the **File name** text box. You can type up to 255 characters.

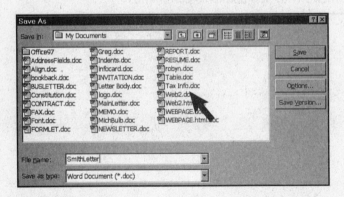

3 To save the document to another drive, click the **Save in** drop-down arrow.

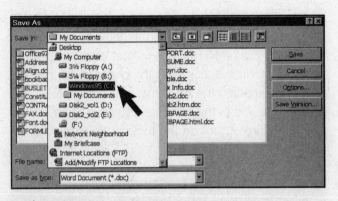

4 Click the drive you want from the list that appears. If you are saving to a floppy drive, be sure to insert the disk into the floppy drive.

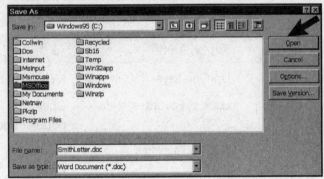

5 To save the document to another folder, click the folder name. Then click the **Open** button, or double-click the folder name to open it.

You may have to back up through the folder/ directory tree to get to the folder you want. You can do so by clicking the **Up One Level** toolbar button in the dialog box. For example, if you are in the MEMO subfolder of WINWORD and want to move to the PRO- POSAL folder (another subfolder you may have created in WINWORD), you have to back up to WINWORD and then change to PROPOSAL.

Guided Tour   Save a File

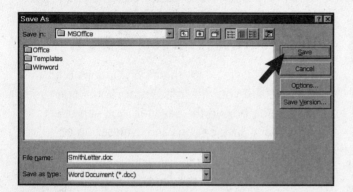

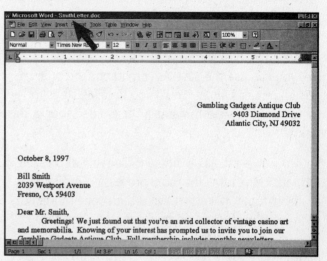

6 Once you give the file a name and decide which folder to save it in, click the **Save** command button.

7 The application saves the document. You see the new file name in the title bar of the application.

To save a previously saved file you're working on, simply click the **Save** button on your application's toolbar. If you want to rename the file or save it to a different location, open the **File** menu, select **Save As**, and then type in a new file name or location for the document.

Save an Existing File Under a New Name

If you don't like the name you originally used to save a file, or if you want to make a copy of the file, you can use the Save As command. The original version remains intact. You'll find detailed steps for using the Save As command in the Guided Tour in this task.

You can save a file as a different file type (also called *format*). Think of all the word processing programs available today. Microsoft Word is just one of many. Each word processing program creates a specific file type, even though the content focus (creating text pages) is the same. When it comes to word processing file types, you'll find choices such as Word for Windows, Word for DOS, WordPerfect, Word Pro, and Word for Macintosh, just to name a few. Unfortunately, not every program recognizes files from other programs. If you share documents with users who have different programs, you may want to save a document as another file type.

Use Automatic Save

In the Save As dialog box, there's an Options button you can press. If you click this button, you'll open yet another dialog box. In the Save tab, you can select from the many Save options and even set up a password to protect your file.

Pay careful attention to the **Save AutoRecover info every** option. You can set up your Office 97 application so it automatically saves the file you're working on every few minutes. Should a power failure or surge occur while you're in the middle of creating an important file, your computer will save the file contents automatically, without any instructions from you.

In the Save As dialog box, select the **Save AutoRecover info every** option, and set a minute increment from the Minutes box. Three minutes is a good choice. Click **OK** to return to the Save As box.

Begin Guided Tour   Save A File Under a New Name

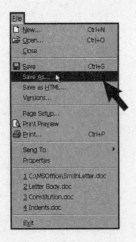

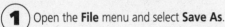

1 Open the **File** menu and select **Save As**.

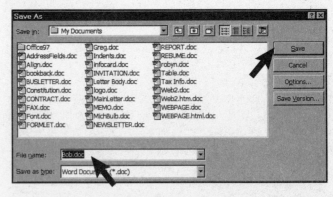

2 In the Save As dialog box, type in a new name in the **File name** text box. The existing name already appears highlighted in the box, but you can type right over it.

3 Click the **Save** button, and the existing file is saved under the new name.

Begin Guided Tour   Save a File Under a New Format

1 Open the **File** menu and choose **Save As**.

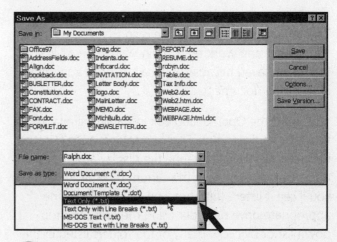

3 From the list that appears, select the appropriate file type.

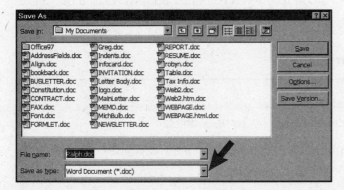

2 The Save As dialog box appears. To save the file in a different format, click the down arrow to the right of the **Save as type** text box.

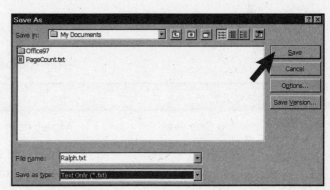

4 Click the **Save** button and the file is saved in a different file format.

If you're saving the file for the first time, you can also choose **File**, **Save** from the **File** menu, or click the **Save** button on the toolbar. If this is the first time you're saving the file, be sure to give it a name.

Open a File

The purpose of saving a file is so that you can open it and work on it again. You open a file you previously saved because you may want to edit, reuse, or print the document.

You'll find the Open dialog box looks very similar to the Save As dialog box. Files and folders appear in the list box, and you can change the display at any time. If the file you want is in the current drive or folder, you'll see it listed. If it's not, you can switch to the appropriate drive or folder using the **Look in** drop-down list or by clicking any of the folders listed in the list box.

You can also open documents in another file format. For example, in Word, you can open WordPerfect, Word Pro, and several other document types. To display other file types in the Open dialog box, use the **Files of type** drop-down list and select the file format you want.

Once you find the file you want to open and select it, you can click the **Open** button to display the file on your application screen.

The Open dialog box differs from the previous versions of Office you may have worked with. The dialog box displays files and folders in a new format. A new edition to the box is toolbar buttons. Click a button to apply its function as described in the table.

The Toolbar Buttons

Button	Button Name	Function
	Up One Level	Moves your drive's hierarchy list back one level.
	Search the Web	Opens your Internet Web browser program so you can open a Web document on-screen.
	Look in Favorites	Opens the Favorites folder: a folder you can use to store your most popular document files in.
	Create New Folder	Creates a new folder.
	List	Lists the folders and files by name.
	Details	Provides details such as when the files were created, how much disk space they consume, their file type, and so on.
	Properties	Lists each file's individual details such as how many pages, name of the original author, what template the file's based on, and so on.
	Preview	Lets you preview the contents of a selected file before opening. The Preview command isn't available for all Office programs.
	Commands and Settings	Opens a submenu with commands for viewing properties, sorting files, and mapping your network drive. You can also resize windows using the techniques you learned about in the first section of this book.

Using Multiple Files

Just like you can have several papers on your desk, you can have several files open on your "electronic" desktop—the computer screen. You may need to review information in one document to create a second document. You may need to copy information from one document to another. With Office 97, you can have as many documents open as your computer memory allows.

To work on more than one document, open the first document and then open the next document. The application displays the last document you opened on top. You can use the following features to move among the different open documents:

- To switch to a different document, open the **Window** menu. You see the names of the open documents displayed. Click the one you want.

- To arrange the documents so that you can see at least part of each of them on-screen at the same time, open the **Window** menu. For Word and PowerPoint, select the **Arrange All** command. For Excel, select the **Arrange** command, select how you want the windows arranged, and click **OK**.

- To return a document to a full-screen display, move to the document window you want to expand and click the **Maximize** button.

- If you have several files open at once, you can minimize the ones you aren't using. If you click the **Minimize** button, the file window reduces to a button on the Windows 95 taskbar. To open the window again, click its button on the taskbar.

Begin Guided Tour   Open a File

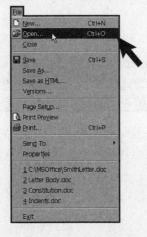

1 Open the **File** menu and select the **Open** command. (You can also click the **Open** button on the application's toolbar.)

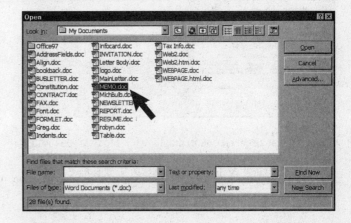

2 You see the Open dialog box. If you see the file you want to open, double-click the name and the document will open on-screen.

(continues)

Guided Tour   Open a File   *(continued)*

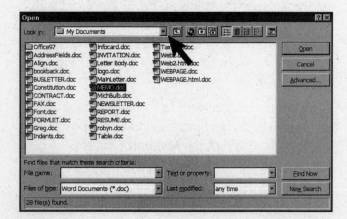

3 If you don't see the document you want listed, click the **Look in** drop-down list to locate the file. Click the down arrow button next to the Look in text box.

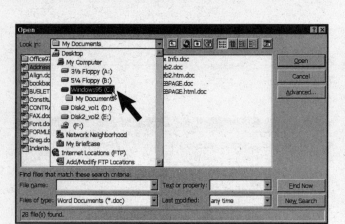

4 You can use the **Look in** drop-down list to help you locate the drive or folder containing the file you're looking for. Click a folder or drive from the list to view its files.

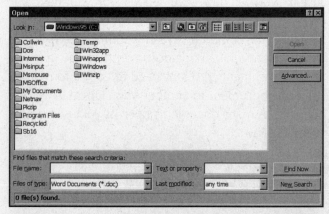

5 The list box displays a new list of folders or files. Remember, to view the contents of any folder, simply double-click the folder name.

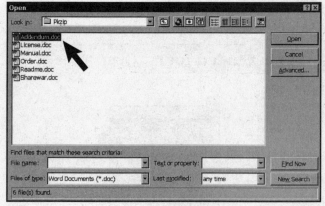

6 When the file you want to open appears in the list, double-click it. The document will open on-screen.

Close a File

You can have a lot of documents open at once, but doing so hogs your computer's memory (working space) and may slow down the performance of your computer. Instead, you should close a document when you finish working on it.

There are several different ways you can close a file. You can choose to close the entire application, which also closes the file, or you can choose to close only the opened document.

If you're closing the entire program, you can use any of these methods:

- Click the application's **Close (X)** button in the upper-right corner.
- Open the **File** menu and select **Exit**.
- Double-click the program's **Control-menu** icon located in the upper-left corner.

- Press **Alt+F4** on the keyboard.

If you're only closing the open file, you don't have to close the entire program. You can use one of these methods:

- Click the file window's **Close** button.
- Double-click the file's **Control-menu** icon. Again, depending on what program you're using, this icon may appear below the program's Control-menu icon. (Don't confuse the two buttons, or you'll end up closing the entire application.)
- Open the **File** menu, and select **Close**.

If you haven't saved your work before closing the file or application, the program will prompt you to do so before exiting.

Begin Guided Tour   Close a File Using the File Menu

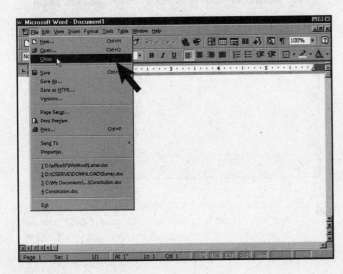

1 Open the **File** menu and select **Close**.

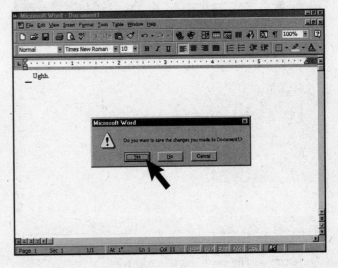

2 If you haven't saved your work, a box appears prompting you to do so. Click **No** to exit without saving. Click **Yes** to save your file first. Click **Cancel** to return to the document.

Create a New File

When you start Word and Excel, both display a new document for you to start working in. In Word, you can start typing away. In Excel, you can start entering the figures and data for the worksheet. If you want to create another new document, you can do so using the New button in the toolbar—a button found on most of the Office programs.

Another way to start a new file is to open the **File** menu and select **New**. In the dialog box that appears, you'll see tabs that list sample documents and templates you can use to help you build your file. A *template* is simply a pre-made design and structure for a file. Some of the samples you see are, in fact, wizards—special templates that walk you step by step through the process of building a file design and structure.

PowerPoint works differently. When you start Power-Point, you see the startup dialog box. Here, you can select to create a new presentation from scratch, use a wizard or template, or open an existing presentation.

> Are you creating a new file based on a template? Whenever you open a template that contains macros, Office 97 displays a warning. If you think that your system may have been infected by a macro virus (if you share files with other people), you can click **Disable Macros** to prevent the macros from running. However, if you disable the macros, the template won't do everything it is designed to do. To load the macros again, click **Enable Macros**.

Begin Guided Tour   Create a New File Using the File Menu

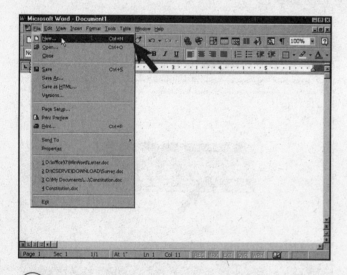

1 Open the **File** menu and select the **New** command.

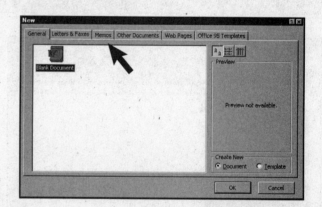

2 The New dialog box appears on-screen. Click the various tabs to see sample documents you can use to base your file on. (You can even choose from wizards that will lead you through the steps for building a document.)

3 Select the template you want to use (if you haven't already). Use the Preview area to see what the document sample looks like (if applicable). Click the **OK** button. You see a new document on-screen.

HOW TO...

Create a Word Document

The most popular type of computer program is a word processing program, and Microsoft Word is the most popular word processing program around today. You can use this program to create any type of document you want, from simple memos to multi-page reports, from flyers to newsletters. To open Word 97, click the **Start** menu; select **Programs** and **Microsoft Word**.

The basics of creating a document are simple; you just type the text you want in your document. Word includes many features that not only make typing the text easier but that also help you with the finer points of document creation, such as proofreading and revising your document. In this section, you learn about these features.

What You Will Find in This Section

Type in Text

In the simplest terms, a word processing program such as Word is similar to a typewriter; you type on the keyboard just like you type on a typewriter. However, a word processing program offers many advantages over manual typing.

For one thing, the words appear on-screen as you type. A flashing vertical line, called the *insertion point*, indicates the place where new text will appear. As you type, the insertion point moves to the right. If you make a mistake, you can easily correct it by using the keyboard's Backspace or Delete keys. You can press **Backspace** to delete characters to the left of the insertion point, or press **Delete** to delete characters to the right of the insertion point.

With a typewriter, you have to be careful not to type past the end of the line margin. When the carriage reaches the end of the line, you must press the carriage return key to go to the next line. With Word, you don't—and shouldn't—press the return key (called the *Enter* key on the keyboard) at the end of each line. Just keep typing. The program will automatically wrap words to the next document line. This is called *word wrapping*. Because of this feature, you can easily add or delete text without fear of messing up the words on a line. Word will move the existing text over to make room for new text or fill in the gap left when you delete text. You should press **Enter** *only* when you want to end one paragraph and start another or when you want to insert a blank line in your document.

Aside from the insertion point, there's also a horizontal line on your Word screen, called the *end of document line*. The end of document line marks the end of your document, the point where you typed your last line of text. Both the insertion point and the end of document line start out at the same place on your screen, until you start typing in text. The end of document line will always be under the last line of text in your document, but the insertion point can be anywhere you place it.

Just like Word adjusts line breaks, the program also automatically inserts page breaks, as necessary. If you add or delete text to one of the pages, Word automatically adjusts the page breaks.

Also, because the words aren't committed to paper, you can easily make changes—move text around, copy text, and make formatting changes. This section of the book covers making editing changes to existing text; see the next section for help on all the available formatting features.

By default, Word is set up to start you out in Normal view mode. Word lets you view your documents in several different modes. Normal view lets you see a simplified version of your document. This mode also uses the least amount of computer memory, which makes it faster to scroll and view pages. Page Layout view shows you how your document will actually appear on paper. Outline view lets you see how your document looks in an outline format. Online Layout view, new to Office 97, lets you see your document using two window panes. Normal view is the easiest view mode in which to see your documents on-screen. To switch to the different views, click one of the four view buttons located at the bottom-left corner of the window.

There are a few more view modes you can use, and you'll find them on the View menu: Master Document, Document Map, and Full Screen modes. Master Document mode lets you organize and manage a large document by breaking it into smaller sections. Document Map mode looks a lot like Online Layout mode, displaying a two-pane window; the left pane gives you an overall view of the entire document, and the right pane lets you display specific portions of the document. Finally, Full Screen mode lets you look at your document without all the cumbersome toolbars, scroll bars, and the ruler.

Begin Guided Tour Enter Text

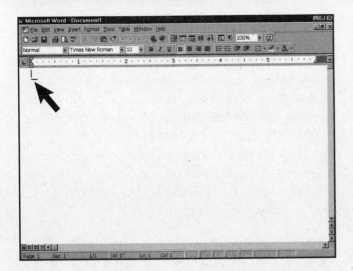

1 When you start Word, you see a new blank document on-screen with the insertion point and end of document line at the top. To begin, just start typing.

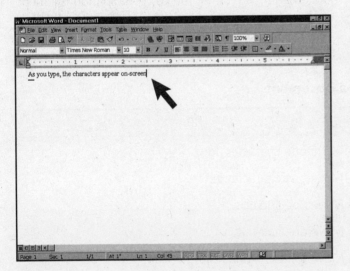

2 As you type, the characters appear on-screen and the insertion point moves to the right. If you make a mistake, press **Backspace** to delete characters to the left of the insertion point.

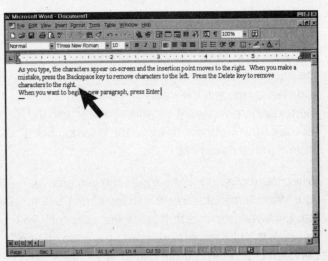

3 When you want to begin a new paragraph or insert a blank line, press **Enter**. Word inserts a hidden paragraph marker and moves the insertion point to the beginning of the next line. Continue typing your document.

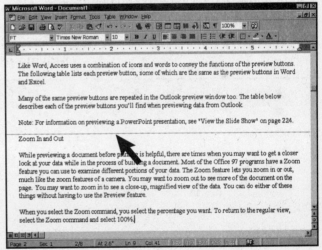

4 When a page fills up, Word inserts a break and creates a new page. The page break appears as a dotted line on-screen.

Move Around the Document

Y ou can think of the insertion point as the "You Are Here" arrow pointing out your location in the document. When you want to add or delete text, you start by moving the insertion point to the start of the text where you want to work. You can use the mouse or the keyboard to move the insertion point around in the document.

When the mouse pointer is inside the text area of your Word screen, it takes the shape of an I-beam, also known as the *cursor*. It looks like a capital I. You can click the I-beam, or cursor, into place for editing between characters, before and after words, and so on. The I-beam's shape makes it easy to do this. Anytime you move the mouse pointer outside the text area, it becomes the old pointer arrow again.

To use the mouse, point to the location where you want to move and click the mouse button. The insertion point jumps to that spot. If you can't see the place you want, you can use the scroll bar arrows to scroll to a different section or page. Click the up arrow to scroll up and the down arrow to scroll down; or drag the scroll box the relative distance you want to move. Use the horizontal scroll arrows to scroll left or right in the document. Remember that the insertion point remains at the same spot until you click to position it. If the insertion point is on page 1 and you scroll to page 3, the insertion point is still on page 1 until you click somewhere on page 3.

Sometimes, it is faster to move around the document using the keyboard, especially if you are a fast typist and don't like to take your hands away from the keyboard. You can use any of the key or key combinations listed in the table below to move around in the document. Note that if the key combination is joined with a plus sign, you must press and hold the first key and then press the second key.

Moving in a Document

Press	To Do This
→	Move one character right.
←	Move one character left.
↑	Move one line up.
↓	Move one line down.
Home	Move to the beginning of the line.
End	Move to the end of line.
Ctrl+Home	Move to the beginning of the document.
Ctrl+End	Move to the end of the document.
Ctrl+←	Move one word left.
Ctrl+→	Move one word right.
Ctrl+↓	Move one paragraph down.
Ctrl+↑	Move one paragraph up.
PgUp	Move one screen up.
PgDn	Move one screen down.

Press	To Do This
Ctrl+PgDn	Move to the bottom of screen.
Ctrl+PgUp	Move to the top of screen.
Shift+F5	Move to the last location of the insertion point. You can press Shift+F5 up to four times. The first three times, you move to theprevious three locations. The fourth time, you move back to the original location of the insertion point.
Ctrl+G	Display the Go To dialog box.

If you have not typed anything on-screen (or pressed the **Spacebar** or **Enter**), you cannot move the insertion point. Word doesn't permit the insertion point to move beyond the end of document line. Only after you enter text or spaces on-screen can you move the insertion point.

In a long document, you can quickly move to a particular page using the **Go To** command. This method is much faster than scrolling through the document. You can jump to any page in the document by typing the page number. You can access the Go To command in two ways: open the **Edit** menu and select **Go To**, or click the **Select Browse Object** button on the vertical scroll bar (the tiny button with a circle on it located between the scroll arrows at the bottom of the bar), and then click the **Go To** button. Either method opens the Find and Replace dialog box which has a **Go To** tab for quickly locating particular on-screen objects or page numbers. You'll learn how to use the Go To command in a Guided Tour below.

Begin Guided Tour   Use the Mouse

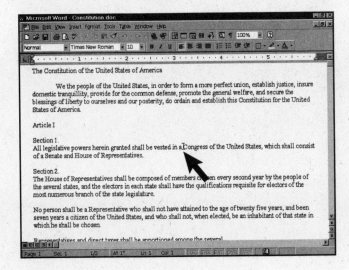

1 Point to where you want the insertion point.

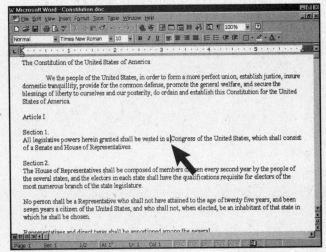

2 Click the left mouse button. The insertion point jumps to this spot.

Begin Guided Tour Use the Go To Command

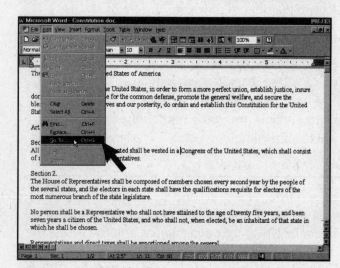

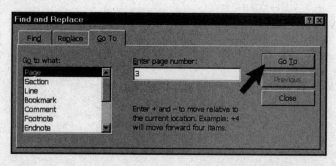

3 When you type a page number, the **Next** button changes to the **Go To** button. Click the **Go To** button. You move to that page. Word also places the insertion point at the top of the page.

1 Open the **Edit** menu and select the **Go To** command.

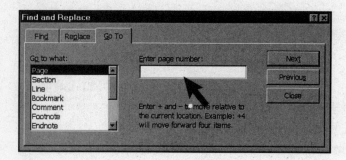

2 The Find and Replace dialog box appears on-screen. Type the page number in the **Enter Page Number** text box.

Begin Guided Tour Use the Select Browse Object Button

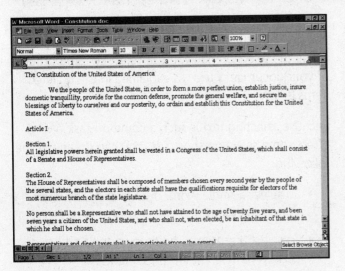

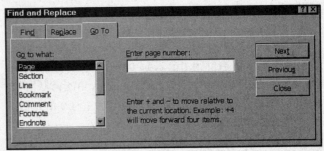

3 The Find and Replace dialog box appears on-screen. Type the page number in the **Enter Page Number** text box. When you type a page number, the **Next** button changes to the **Go To** button. Click the **Go To** button and you move to that page.

1 To access the Go To command, click the **Select Browse Object** button in the vertical scroll bar.

The Select Browse Object palette on the vertical scroll bar helps you locate specific document elements in your Word file. For example, if you're looking for a table you've inserted in a long document, you can quickly find the table using the **Select Browse Object** button, and then click the **Browse by Table** button in the palette.

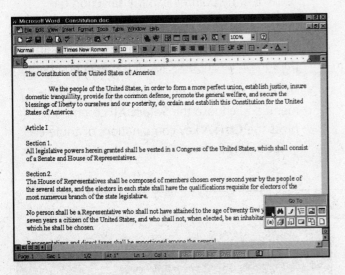

2 A palette of buttons appears. Click the **Go To** button. (When you move your mouse pointer over the button, its name appears at the top of the palette.)

Select Text

As you work with your documents, you will eventually find that you need to move, delete, or copy text. To edit in this way, you have to learn how to select text. You have to grab it somehow to manipulate it, and there's only one way to do it, and that is electronically.

You can use the mouse or the keyboard to select text. Once you select text, you can then apply all kinds of editing and formatting techniques. Selecting with the mouse is similar to dragging a highlighter pen over the text. Selected text appears highlighted on the screen in reverse type: white type on a black background instead of black text on a white background. To use the keyboard to select text, hold down the **Shift** key and use the arrow keys to highlight the text you want. When all the text you want is highlighted, release the **Shift** key.

If you select text by mistake, you can deselect it. To do so, click anywhere outside the selected text or press any arrow key. The far left side of the text area of the Word screen has an invisible selection bar. To find the selection bar, move the mouse pointer to the left of the text until the pointer takes the shape of a northeast-pointing arrow. When you click the mouse inside the selection bar, you can select certain portions of your document's text, as explained in the bulleted items below.

Because selecting text is such a common task, Word offers some selection shortcuts. You can do any of the following:

- To select a single word, double-click anywhere within the word.

- To select a sentence, hold down the **Ctrl** key and click anywhere within the sentence.

- To select a line, click once in the selection bar, the thin border to the left of the text. (You can tell when the pointer is in the selection bar because it looks like a northeast-pointing arrow.)

- To select a paragraph, click three times within the paragraph or double-click in the selection bar.

- To select the entire document, open the **Edit** menu and choose the **Select All** command, press the **Ctrl+A** key combination, or triple-click in the selection bar.

Begin Guided Tour   Select Text with the Mouse

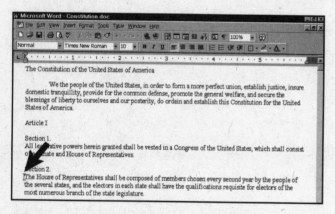

1 Point to the beginning of the text you want to select. Hold down the left mouse button and drag across the text you want to select.

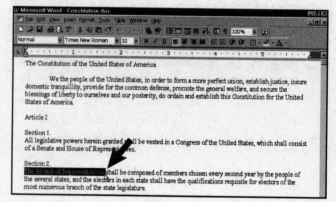

2 As you drag, the text appears white on black. After you highlight all the text you want, release the mouse button. (To deselect the text, click anywhere in the document.)

Begin Guided Tour   Select Text Using the Selection Bar

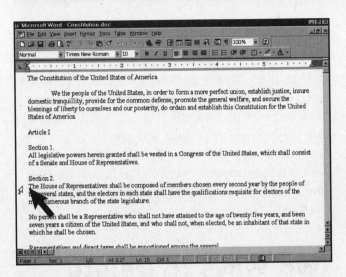

1 To select a line of text using the selection bar, first move the mouse pointer to the left of the sentence you want to select. The pointer becomes a northeast-pointing arrow.

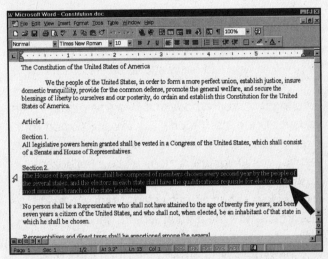

3 To select an entire paragraph, double-click in the selection bar next to the paragraph you want selected. This selects a whole block of text.

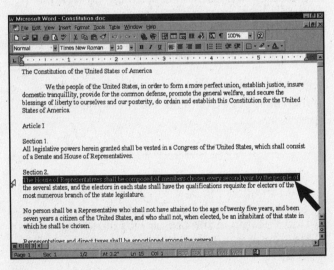

2 Click once in the selection bar and the line of text is selected.

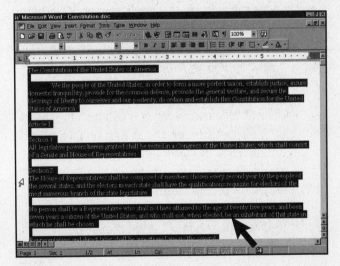

4 To select the entire document, triple-click inside the selection bar area.

Add and Delete Text

Have you ever typed a document and then remembered something you wanted to add? With Word, you can easily add or delete text from your document. Word provides two modes for entering text: *Insert mode* and *Overtype mode*. When you type using Insert mode, any existing text on your screen moves to the right to make room for the new text you're typing. Insert mode is like a bulldozer, pushing your old text out of the way to make room for the new. When you first start Word, you're in Insert mode (it's the default setting). Insert mode is ideal for inserting new words into the middle of existing sentences. In Insert mode, you can simply click the mouse into place and start typing.

When you type using Overtype mode—also called *Typeover* or *Overwrite* mode in some circles—the new text replaces the existing text you're typing. Overtype mode is like a tank that runs over all the characters that are in its way. Overtype mode is effective for deleting existing text by simply typing over it.

As I mentioned, by default, Word is set up to let you type in Insert mode. However, you can turn the Insert and Overtype modes on or off. To turn on Overtype mode, double-click the **OVR** letters in the status bar. When the Overtype mode is in effect, you'll see the bold letters OVR on the status bar (at the bottom of your screen). When you're ready to use Overtype, switch to Overtype mode, click the mouse pointer in place, and start pecking away at the keyboard. To turn the mode off again, simply double-click the **OVR** area on the status bar again. Just remember, when Overtype mode is on, that means Insert mode is off (and vice-versa).

However, you should be careful when using Overtype mode: although it works well when you want to replace text, you have to remember to turn it off when you're done so you don't accidentally replace more text than you intended. Most often, you will turn on Overtype by mistake and wonder what's happening when characters disappear when you start typing. If this happens, check the status bar for OVR. Simply double-click **OVR** on the status bar to turn Overtype off.

Two Ways to Delete

Another way of deleting text is with the **Backspace** or **Delete** keys. Backspace deletes characters to the left; Delete removes characters to the right of the insertion point. If you have a lot of text to remove, it's faster to select the text and then delete it all at once by simply pressing the **Delete** key.

You can also delete text by selecting it, and then immediately start typing the new text you want to enter.

Make a mistake? If you delete text by accident, you can undo the deletion by using the **Undo** command in the **Edit** menu or by using the **Undo** button in the toolbar. It's best to use the Undo command immediately after making the mistake.

Begin Guided Tour Add Text

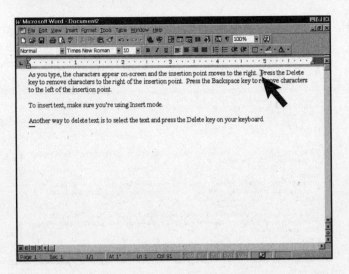

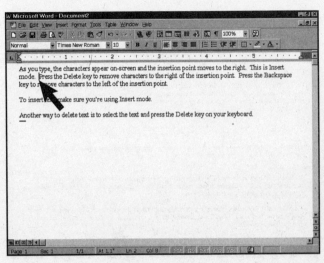

1 Move the insertion point to the spot where you want the new text. Type the new text.

2 The existing text moves over to make room.

Begin Guided Tour Delete Text

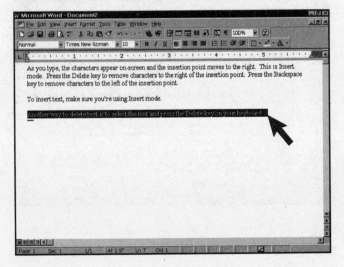

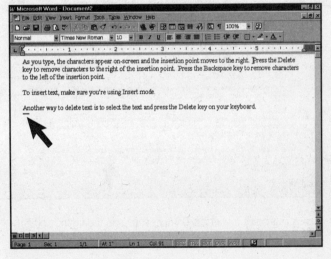

1 Select the text you want to delete and press the **Delete** key. See the preceding task for help on selecting text.

2 Word deletes the text.

Begin Guided Tour Use Overtype Mode

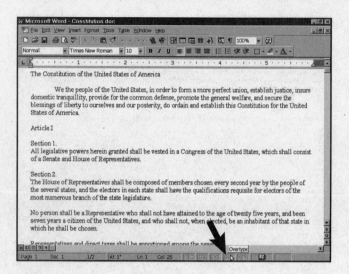

1 To type over existing text, first turn on Overtype mode. Double-click **OVR** on the status bar.

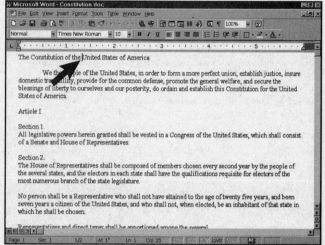

3 To type over existing text, place the insertion point where you want to start typing.

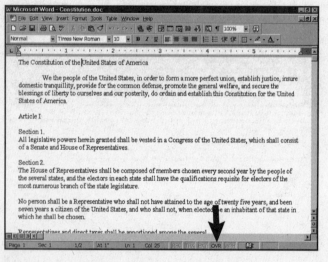

2 This bolds the letters **OVR**, as shown in the figure, and indicates that Overtype mode is now on.

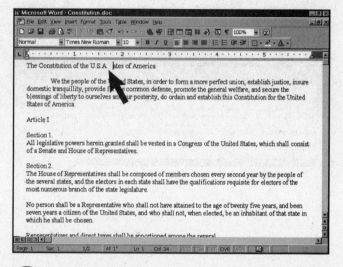

4 Start typing and the existing text is replaced with new text, as shown in this figure.

Remember to turn Overtype mode off when you're done using it. Double-click **OVR** on the status bar to return to Insert mode. When the letters **OVR** are no longer bold on the status bar, you know the feature is turned off.

Move and Copy Text

The ability to and move text from one place to another in your document can really come in handy as you edit your Word documents. One of the editing changes you may make is to change the order of the text to make the document flow more smoothly or to make the document read better. You can also save yourself time by copying text that you need to use again rather than retyping it. For example, you may want to use the same text or similar text again. You can copy the text and then modify the copy.

When you are moving or copying text, think of scissors and paste. That's the analogy used for these procedures. With a move, you cut the text from the original location using the Cut command and paste it in the new location using the Paste command. With a copy, you copy and then paste using the Copy and Paste commands. You can find these commands in the Edit menu or you can use the buttons in the toolbar or the equivalent shortcut keys.

When you cut or copy text, Word places it in the *Clipboard*, a temporary holding spot. (The Clipboard is a Windows 95 feature, which means you can copy text from one application to another. The text remains in the Clipboard until you cut or copy something else or until you exit Windows 95. That means two things. One, you can paste the text more than once. Two, you need to paste the text before you copy or cut something else; otherwise, the text is overwritten in the Clipboard with the new text.

Move and Copy by Dragging

If you want to move or copy the text a short distance, you may prefer to simply drag the text to its new location rather than use the Cut, Copy, and Paste commands. Many beginners have a hard time with dragging and dropping; it's difficult to get the pointer in just the right spot. Another common mistake is to select some text, decide to select additional text, and instead of selecting more text, you actually move the text. If this happens, click the **Undo** button on the toolbar and start over.

To move and copy by dragging, follow these steps:

1. Select the text to move or copy. Release the mouse button.

2. Point to the selected text.

3. Drag the selected text to the new location. The cursor has a small square attached to it to let you know it's moving the text. To drag a copy, hold down the **Ctrl** key as you drag.

> If dragging doesn't work, the feature may have been turned off. Pull down the **Tools** menu and select the **Options** command. Then select the **Edit** tab. Check the **Drag-and-Drop Text Editing** check box and choose **OK**.

Begin Guided Tour   Move Text

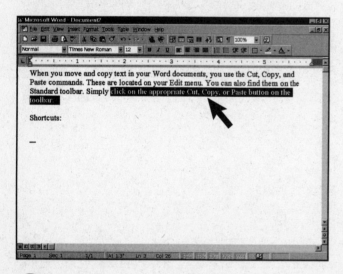

1 Select the text you want to move.

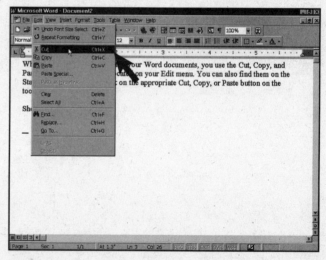

2 Open the **Edit** menu and select the **Cut** command. Word removes the text from the document and places it on the Clipboard.

Guided Tour   Move Text

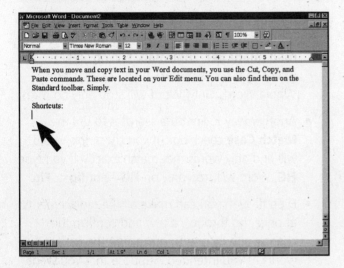
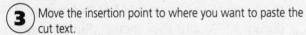

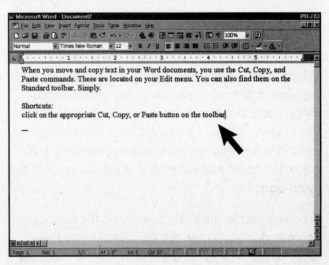

3 Move the insertion point to where you want to paste the cut text.

4 Open the **Edit** menu again, and this time select the **Paste** command. Word pastes the cut text at the new location.

Begin Guided Tour   Copy Text

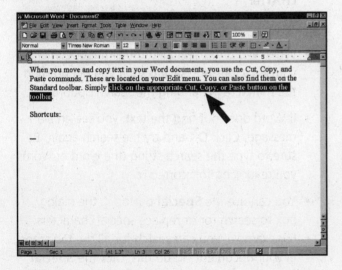

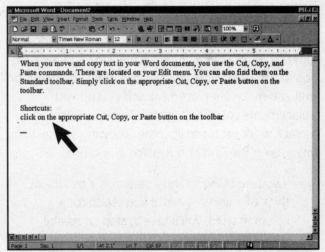

1 Select the text you want to copy. Nothing changes on-screen, but Word has placed a copy of the text in the Clipboard. Move the insertion point to where you want to paste the text.

2 Open the **Edit** menu again, and this time select the **Paste** command. Word pastes the copy at the new location.

Find and Replace Text

Sometimes, you can read a document over and over looking for a particular word or phrase. Where is it? Are you going blind? If you are looking for a particular word, phrase, or section of a document, you can move there more quickly using the **Find** command. Find is particularly useful for moving around in a long document. Imagine scanning a 20-page document looking for the one occurrence of the word **dog**.

A companion to the Find command is the Replace command. You can use this command to find one word or phrase and replace it with another. Suppose that you used the not-so-politically correct term "spokesman" in a document. You decide that "spokesperson" is a better word choice. You can look for each occurrence and replace the word manually, or you can have Word find all occurrences and make the changes for you. The latter is definitely going to save you some time and effort.

Find and Replace sound great until you search for a common letter combination such as **not** and have to stop at 15 words until you find the word you want, or until you make a replacement and end up with replacements you didn't intend. To make Find and Replace work best, consider the following suggestions when using the Find and Replace dialog box:

- If you are trying to find a section in a document, think of a unique word. If you search for a common word, you'll have to stop on several occurrences until you find the one you want. For example, suppose that you have a document describing different cooking classes offered and you want to move to the section on Italian Cooking. If you search for **cooking** or **class**, you may have to stop on several sections before you find the one you want. If you search for the word **Italian**, on the other hand, you have a better chance of moving directly to the section you want.

- Use the **Find Whole Words Only** check box when you want to stop on whole words. For example, if you type **man**, Word will stop on **man**, **manager**, **chairman**, and any other words that contain **man**. If you check Find Whole Words Only, Word will stop only on **man**.

- Another way to limit the search is to use the **Match Case** check box. If you check this, Word will find only words that match exactly. If you type **FIG**, Word will stop only on **FIG**—not **fig** or **Fig**.

- Even though you can make all the replacements at once, go through a few and confirm the change one by one to make sure the replace works as you intended. Suppose that you want to change all occurrences of **hat** to **cap** in your document. Sounds easy enough. But did you think that those three letters—**hat**—may appear in other words? If you replace without checking, you may end up with **cCAPter** instead of **cHATter**.

- To repeat a search, press **Shift+F4**.

- When Word has searched the entire document, you see a message saying so. If you did not find the match, try changing the search options.

- If Word does not find the text, you see an alert message. Click **OK** and try the search again. Be sure to type the search string (the word or words you're looking for) correctly.

- You can use the **Special** button in the dialog box to search for or replace special characters. For example, you can search for all the tab stops in your document. To do this, click the **Special** button. From the pop-up list that appears, click the item you want to find.

- You can also search for or replace formatting. To do so, click the **Format** button. From the drop-down menu that appears, click the type of formatting you want to find: Font, Paragraph, Language, or Style. Word displays the appropriate dialog box. Make selections in the dialog box and click **OK**. The next section of the book covers formatting features.

Begin Guided Tour   Find Text

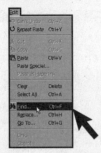

1 Open the **Edit** menu and select the **Find** command (you can also click the **Select Browse Object** button on the vertical scroll bar, then select the **Find** button from the palette.

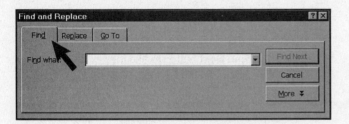

2 You see the Find and Replace dialog box with the Find tab displayed at the front of the dialog box.

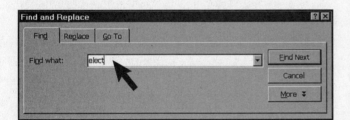

3 In the **Find What** text box, type the text you want to find. You can type as much or as little text as you want. If you have searched previously in this document, the last text you searched for appears in the **Find What** text box. Simply delete the current entry and type the new one.

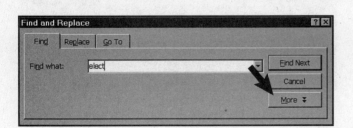

4 To add more options to your search, click the **More** button.

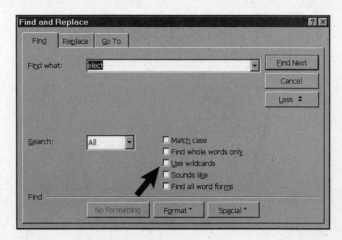

5 Set any additional search options you want to use by clicking the appropriate check boxes to select them. For example, if you want Word to match the case as you've typed it, select the **Match Case** check box. If you want Word to flag only whole words as opposed to partial words, select the **Find Whole Words Only** check box. (If no options are needed, click the **Less** button to hide the options again.)

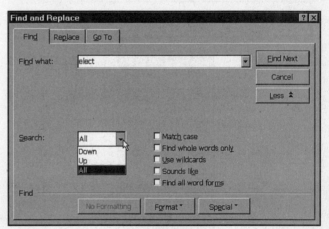

6 If necessary, use the **Search** drop-down list to choose what direction you want to conduct the search: Down, Up, or All. The default is to use the All option.

(continues)

Guided Tour   Find Text

(continued)

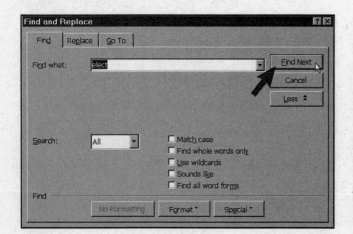

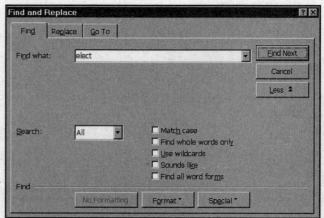

7 When you're ready to start the search, click the **Find Next** button.

8 Word moves to the first match and highlights the found word or phrase in the document. If this is the text you want, click the **Cancel** button to close the dialog box. If this isn't the text, click the **Find Next** button to find the next match. Continue to do so until you find the match you want.

Begin Guided Tour   Replace Text

1 Open the **Edit** menu and select the **Replace** command.

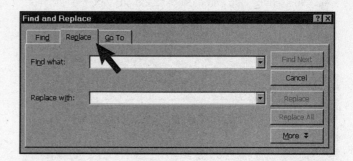

2 You see the Find and Replace dialog box. The **Replace** tab is displayed at the front of the dialog box.

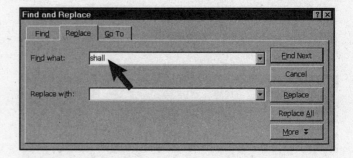

3 In the **Find What** text box, type the text you want to find.

Guided Tour Replace Text

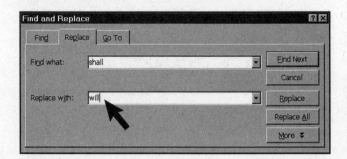

4 In the **Replace With** text box, type the text you want to insert to replace the text you typed into the **Find What** box.

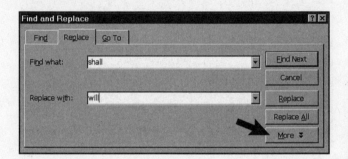

5 To select from additional search options, click the **More** button.

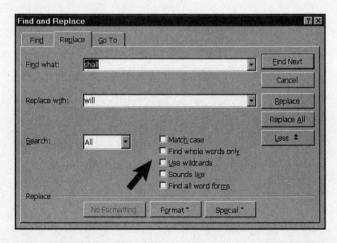

6 More search options are displayed at the bottom of the Find and Replace dialog box. Select the options you want to apply.

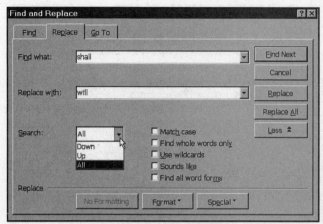

7 If necessary, use the **Search** drop-down list to choose what direction you want to conduct the search: Down, Up, or All. The default is to use the All option.

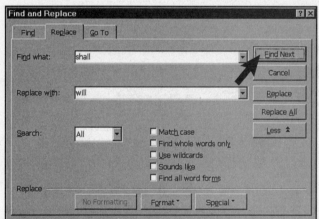

8 When you're ready to start the search, click the **Find Next** button.

(continues)

Guided Tour   Replace Text

(continued)

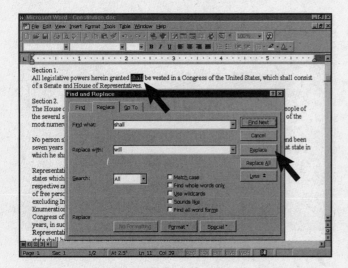

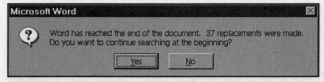

11 When Word finishes searching the document, you see an alert message. Click **Yes**.

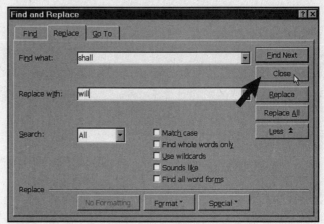

9 Word moves to the first match and highlights the found word or phrase. The dialog box remains open. If you want to make the replacement, click the **Replace** button. (To leave this text as is and move to the next match, click the **Find Next** button.)

12 Click the **Close** button to close the Replace dialog box.

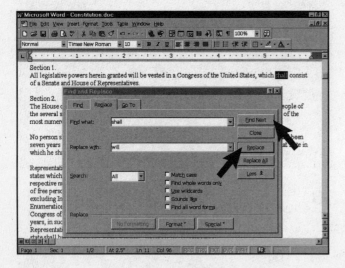

10 Word makes the replacement and moves to the next occurrence. Continue clicking **Replace** or **Find Next** until you go through each occurrence. You can also click the **Replace All** button to make all the replacements at once.

Insert the Date or Time

If you are like most people, you may not know today's date off the top of your head. Most of us have to look at a calendar (especially on Mondays). With Word, you can insert the current date quickly without having to look at a calendar or do any typing, and you can select from several different formats.

If you insert the date as text, Word inserts the current date but does not update it. Think of this as a date stamp. In some cases, you may want to update the date, as you work on the document. In this case, you can insert the date as a *field* (a database-related entry in your document), and Word will update it for you when the time comes. For example, suppose that you are working on a project that will probably take you more than two weeks. You want the current date at the top of the document. You can insert the date as a field and when you finish the document and print it,

Word will reflect the current date (not the date when you inserted the field) in the document. Pretty handy!

Because the date is not text, but a field, you cannot delete the date character by character. If you try to, Word beeps. Instead, you must drag across the entire date to select the field. Then press **Delete**.

> Word uses the date and time from your system clock. If this date or time is incorrect, you can update it using Windows' Control Panel. From the Windows Taskbar, open the **Start** menu, select **Settings**, then select **Control Panel**. Next, double-click the **Date/Time** icon. Enter a new date or time in the dialog box and then click **OK**.

Begin Guided Tour   Insert a Date or Time

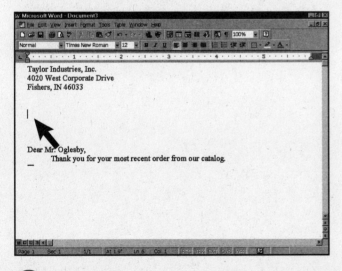

1 Place the insertion point where you want to insert the date.

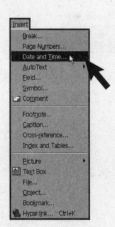

2 Open the **Insert** menu and select the **Date and Time** command.

(continues)

Guided Tour Insert a Date or Time *(continued)*

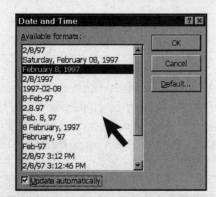

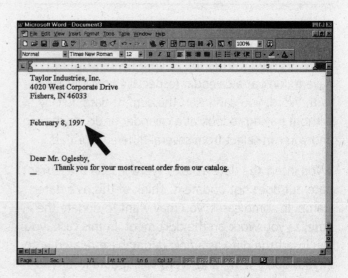

3 You see the Date and Time dialog box. Click the date or time format you want to use. To insert the entry as a field that will be updated, check the **Update Automatically** check box.

5 Word inserts the date or time in the format you selected.

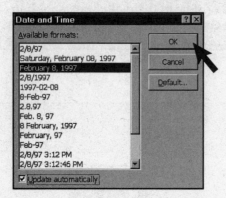

4 Click **OK** to exit the dialog box and return to the document.

Check Your Spelling and Grammar

A typo or misspelling, or even a grammatical error in an otherwise perfect document stands out like a red flag. And speaking of red flags, that's exactly what Word's Spelling and Grammar feature does. If any funny-looking wavy, red lines appear under any words that you type, don't be alarmed. That's Word's AutoCorrect feature kicking in. It automatically checks your spelling while you type, and it's turned on by default. The wavy, red line that you see under a word means one of two things:

- You've misspelled a word

- Or, the word you spelled isn't in Word's dictionary.

When you go back and correct the word, the wavy, red line disappears. If you can't tell if the word is misspelled or not, just move your mouse pointer over the word and right-click. Word recommends alternative spellings you can use. Select one from the list and the word is corrected.

If you get tired of seeing the wavy, red lines as you type, you can turn the feature off. Open the **Tools** menu and select **Options**. In the Options dialog box, click the **Spelling & Grammar** tab, then deselect the **Check Spelling As You Type** option.

If you don't see the wavy, red lines, when you're misspelled something, then the feature probably isn't turned on. Open the **Tools** menu, select **Options**, click the **Spelling & Grammar** tab, and make sure to select the **Check Spelling As You Type** check box. (Follow these same steps to turn the feature off again.)

The Spelling and Grammar Tool

Another way to be sure your document doesn't include any spelling errors is to use Word's Spell Check tool. You can start the Spell Check program at any time, either by clicking the **Spelling and Grammar** button on your toolbar, or opening the **Tools** menu and selecting **Spelling and Grammar**. As part of the Spell Check feature, Word also checks your document's grammar usage. By default, Word checks both spelling and grammar, but you can turn the grammar tool off and choose to check only the document's spelling errors.

To turn the grammar check off, make sure the **Check Grammar** box is deselected in the Spelling and Grammar dialog box.

You can start the Spelling and Grammar Check program anywhere in the document. Word will start checking from the insertion point forward and then go back to the top of the document and check the rest of the document.

If you want to check just a passage, you can select the text you want to check and then select the **Spelling and Grammar** command. Word will check the selection and then ask whether you want to check the rest of the document. Click **No**.

The Spell Check tool works by comparing words in the document to words in its dictionary. When it finds a word that's not in the dictionary, it flags it as misspelled. This doesn't necessarily mean the word is misspelled; it just means the program cannot find the word in its dictionary. For example, the Spell Check tool may flag proper names and some terminology, although they are spelled correctly. Word will also flag double words such as "the the."

The Grammar Check tool looks for grammatical problems in your document. For example, it examines each sentence and checks to see whether the text confirms to various grammar, style, usage, and punctuation rules. But like the Spell Check tool, the Grammar Check isn't foolproof. It's up to you to determine a course of action when an error is discovered.

When the Spelling and Grammar Check feature flags a word or sentence, you have several choices, which appear in a dialog box along with the flagged word(s). The choices vary, depending on the type of error—spelling or grammar. Here are several of the choices you can make:

- If it's a spelling error and if the correct word appears in the dialog box, click it in the **Suggestions** list. Click the **Change** button to change this occurrence. Click the **Change All** button to replace all occurrences of the word.

- If the word is spelled correctly, click the **Ignore** button to skip this occurrence but stop on the next one. To skip all occurrences of this word, click the **Ignore All** button.

- To disregard Word's grammar suggestion, click the **Ignore** button.

- If you accept a change by clicking the Change button, but then change your mind about your decision, you can click the **Undo** button to undo the correction.

- If the word that is flagged is a word that you use often, you can add it to the dictionary by clicking the **Add** button.

After you select an option, Word moves to the next word or sentence, until it checks the entire document.

Automatically Correct Common Misspellings

If you ever make a mistake typing and see the mistake corrected automatically on-screen, you have seen the magic of AutoCorrect at work. Word knows some common typing mistakes such as "teh" for "the." These misspellings are saved as AutoCorrect entries and are corrected automatically after you type them.

You can also add new AutoCorrect entries on-the-fly during a spelling check or by manually entering them using the Tools menu and the AutoCorrect command. For example, I often mistype "chapter" as "chatper." When I noticed that I did this consistently, I added it to the AutoCorrect entry by clicking the **AutoCorrect** button in the Spelling and Grammar dialog box and making the appropriate entries. Now when I mistype the word *chatper*, Word makes the correction automatically.

Use Word's Thesaurus

Word also has a Thesaurus you can use to look up synonyms and antonyms to replace your words with more interesting ones, without leaving the document. You might want to use the Thesaurus to find a more common word that means the same thing, so your reader can understand what you've written. You might also use the Thesaurus when you find yourself typing the same word over and over, and need to vary your text.

The Thesaurus tool is separate from Word's Spelling and Grammar feature. To access the Thesaurus, you first select the word you want to modify, then open the **Tools** menu, select **Language**, then **Thesaurus**. This opens the Thesaurus dialog box where you can make changes to the selected word, using Word's suggestions.

Begin Guided Tour Check Your Document for Spelling and Grammar Errors

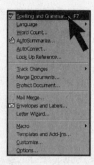

1 Open the **Tools** menu and select the **Spelling and Grammar** command.

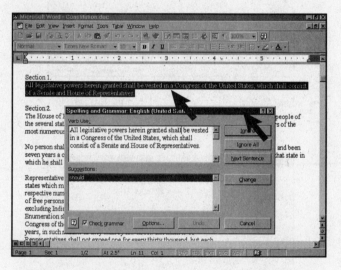

2 Word highlights any words or sentences in your text that contain potential errors and opens the Spelling and Grammar dialog box.

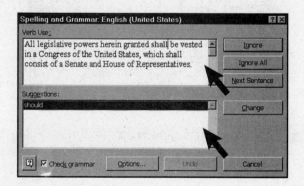

3 If you're checking grammar errors, as shown in this figure, the top portion of the dialog box describes the type of error and displays the text in question (the error is often highlighted in color). The **Suggestions** list box offers suggestions for correcting the problem.

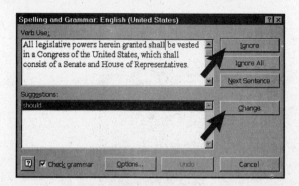

4 To accept any of Word's suggestions for fixing the problem, select the suggestion from the Suggestions list box, then click the **Change** button. If you disagree with Word's suggestion for a change in spelling or sentence structure, click the **Ignore** or **Ignore All** button.

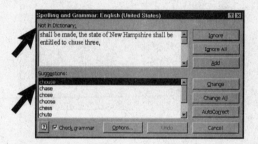

5 Word highlights the next misspelling or grammatical problem in your text. If Word spots a misspelled word, as shown in this figure, the top portion of the dialog box notes the word in question, and the **Suggestions** list box offers other spellings of the word found in Word's dictionary.

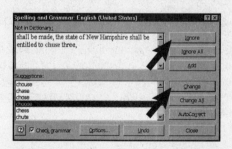

6 To use any of Word's spelling suggestions, select the new spelling from the Suggestions list box, then click the **Change** button. To ignore the word, click the **Ignore** button.

7 Continue making corrections as needed. When you see the message that the spelling and grammar check is complete, click **OK**.

Begin Guided Tour   Add an AutoCorrect Entry

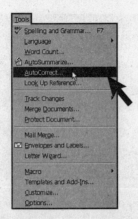

1 Open the **Tools** menu and choose **AutoCorrect**.

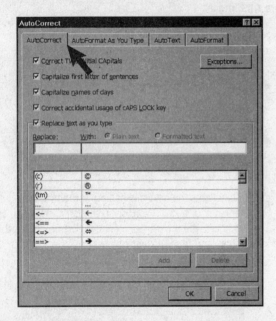

2 The AutoCorrect dialog box opens. Click the **AutoCorrect** tab to bring the options to the front of the dialog box (if they're not already showing). The AutoCorrect tab displays a list of programmed misspellings, along with options for adding your own misspellings to the list.

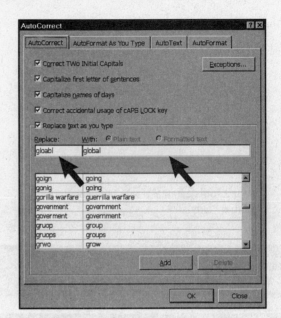

3 Type a word you often misspell into the **Replace** box; type the correct spelling in the **With** box.

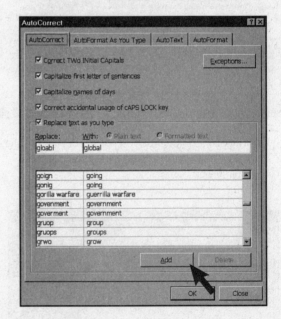

4 Click the **Add** button. This adds the word to the AutoCorrect list. Keep repeating these steps to add other common misspellings that you struggle with.

5 When you finish, click **OK** to exit the box.

Begin Guided Tour   Change a Word with the Thesaurus

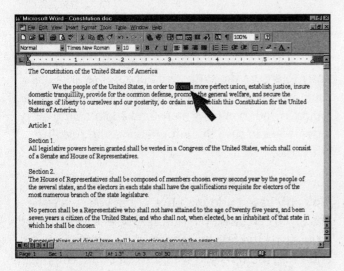

1 On the document page, select the word you want to look up or change.

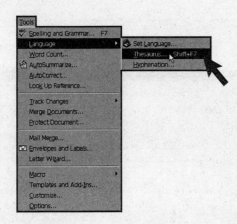

2 Open the **Tools** menu, select **Language**, then **Thesaurus**.

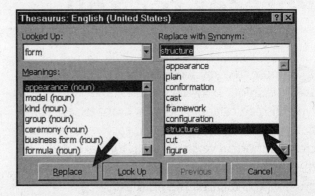

3 The Thesaurus dialog box appears. The **Looked Up** text box displays the selected word; beneath this box is a list of meanings. To the right of the Looked Up box is a list of synonyms. Select the synonym you want to use, then click the **Replace** button.

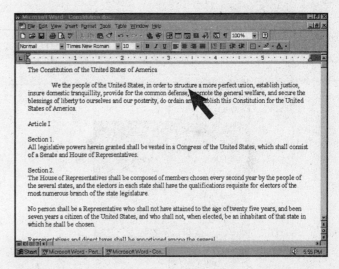

4 Word closes the dialog box and replaces the selected text with the new word.

Have Word Type Often-Used Phrases for You

Suppose that you work for the State University Division of Continuing Studies, and you have to type this particular phrase a lot. Want to save some time? Instead of typing the text each time, you can create a shortcut version, called *AutoText*. You can then type a few letters of the entry and Word prompts you to insert the AutoText.

AutoText is one of the handiest time-saving features you can use. You can use it for boilerplate phrases or paragraphs that you use again and again. For instance, you may have a paragraph that you use to describe your company. You can create an AutoText

entry to ensure the statement appears precisely the same way each time you use it. Or, maybe you tire of typing in your company name and address onto every letter. You can save this information as an AutoText entry, too.

The first step to use AutoText is to create the entry. (You only have to do this once.) After you create the entry, you can insert the AutoText whenever you need it. Just type the first few letters of the word or phrase, and Word prompts you with the rest of the entry. To use the suggested entry, just press Enter and Word inserts the AutoText word or phrase.

Begin Guided Tour   Create an AutoText Entry

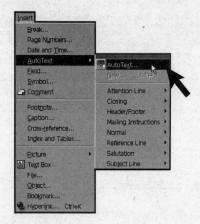

1 Open the **Insert** menu and select the **AutoText** command, then select **AutoText** again.

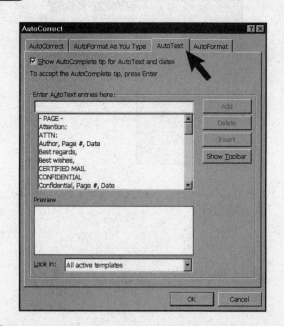

2 You see the AutoCorrect dialog box. Click the **AutoText** tab to bring it to the front of the dialog box.

Guided Tour Create an AutoText Entry

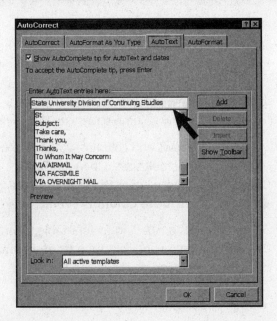

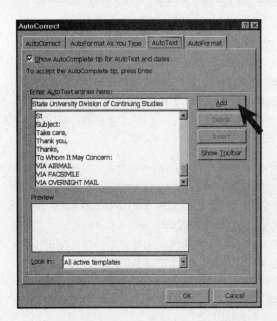

3 Type in the text you want to use as your AutoText entry in the **Enter** box.

4 Click the **Add** button. Word creates the AutoText entry. Click the **OK** button to close the dialog box. On-screen, nothing is different.

Begin Guided Tour Insert an AutoText Entry

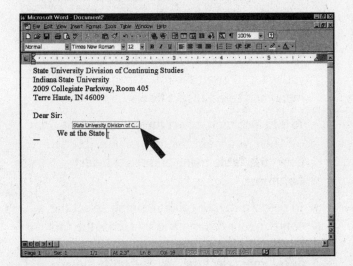

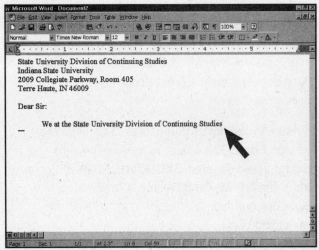

1 To insert an AutoText entry, type the first few letters of the entry and Word displays an AutoText suggestion.

2 If correct, press **Enter**. Word inserts the entry.

Set Up a Table

Forget about using a tabbed list for a grid of information (see the task "Set Tabs" on page 109 to learn more about tabs). You'll waste your time setting up the tabs, pressing Tab again and again, and working hard on aligning the columns just how you want. Instead, set up a table.

A *table* is much more flexible than a tabbed list. You set up the number of columns and rows you want and just type the entries. Word keeps each entry in its cubbyhole, called a *cell*, even if the entry is longer than one line. For longer entries, Word wraps the lines and adjusts the other table entries. You can resize the columns, insert new rows and columns, and make formatting changes (covered in the next section of the book).

The fastest way to create a table is to use the **Insert Table** button in the Standard toolbar, as described in the Guided Tour. You can create a table this way with up to five columns. You don't have to worry so much about the number of rows because you can easily add new rows as you create the table.

You type in a table just as you type in a regular document. If you press **Enter**, Word inserts a paragraph break in the cell. You can also make editing changes to the text: delete or copy text, check spelling, and so on.

To move to the next column, press **Tab**. Type that entry and press **Tab** again. To move backward through the cells, press **Shift+Tab**. When you press **Tab** in the last row and column, Word adds a new row. Continue typing until you complete all the entries you want.

Once you've created a table you can change its size, add new rows and columns, or even add fancy borders and shading:

- To resize a column, move your mouse over the gridline you want to move. The mouse pointer takes the shape of a two-sided arrow. Drag the gridline to a new position. Release the mouse button and a new column size is created.

- After resizing rows and columns, you can return them to their default sizes. Open the **Table** menu, then choose either **Distribute Rows Evenly** or **Distribute Columns Evenly**.

- To add borders or shading to your table, open the **Format** menu and select the **Borders and Shading** command. In the dialog box that appears, you can custom-tailor your table border, add background colors, and more.

- To select a column, move the cursor over the top cell's border. The cursor changes to a downward-pointing arrow. Click to select the entire column.

- To select a row, move the mouse pointer to the left of the row and outside the table until it takes the shape of a northeast-pointing arrow. Click and the row is selected.

- To add a row, place the insertion point where you want to insert the row. Open the **Table** menu and select **Insert Rows**.

- To add a column, select the column to the right of where you want the new column inserted. Open the **Table** menu and select **Insert Columns**.

- To delete a row or column, simply select the entire row or column and then click the **Cut** button. To delete only the text within a row or column, select the text and press the **Delete** key.

Begin Guided Tour Add a Table to Your Document

1 Move the insertion point to the area of the document where you want to insert a table, then click the **Insert Table** button on the Standard toolbar. Word displays a grid below the Insert Table button.

2 Highlight the number of columns and rows you want to use by moving your mouse over the appropriate number of column and row blocks on the grid. For example, to create a table with 4 columns and 3 rows, highlight the first four columns and the first three rows on the grid. Click the last row or column in the highlighted group.

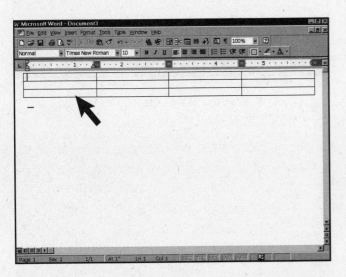

3 Word inserts a table into your document as a grid of columns and rows. The gridlines indicate the columns and rows but the gridlines themselves will not print when you print the document. Notice the insertion point is within the first table cell.

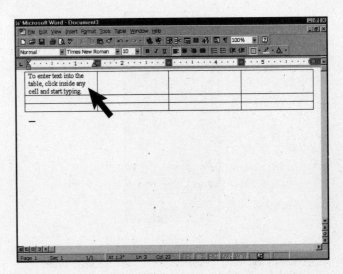

4 Type the entry in the first cell and press **Tab** to move to the next cell. You can also click the cell you want to move to, using the mouse. Continue typing entries for the row and pressing **Tab** to move from cell to cell. When you press **Tab** in the last column, you move to the next row.

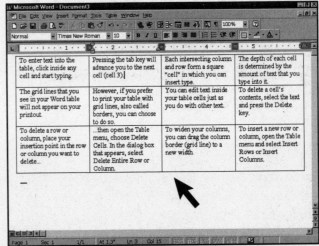

5 Continue entering the table data until you complete all the information you want your table to include (it's okay to leave some cells empty).

Begin Guided Tour   Using the Table Dialog Box to Create the Table

1 Move the insertion point to the area of the document where you want to insert a table, then open the **Table** menu and select the **Insert Table** command.

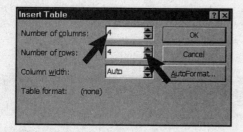

2 You see the Insert Table dialog box. In the **Number of Columns** box, enter the number of columns you want. In the **Number of Rows** box, enter the number of rows you want.

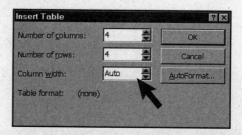

3 In the **Column Width** box, enter the column width you want for each column. If you want Word to create the column width based on the number of columns, leave **Auto** selected.

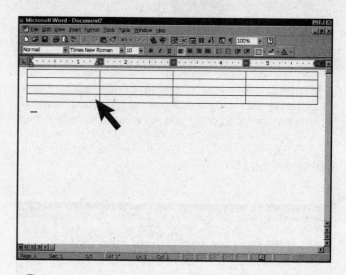

4 Click **OK**. Word inserts the table you specified into your document.

Create and Print Envelopes and Labels

When PCs first became popular, many people kept their typewriters around just for the sole task of typing envelopes. Why? Because setting up and printing an envelope using the older printers and software was more trouble than it was worth. Things have changed considerably, though, and using a laser printer (or dot-matrix or inkjet printer) and Word, you can easily print an envelope. You can also use Word to generate mailing labels.

> Your printer probably has a manual feed for envelopes. If your printer can't print envelopes, don't use the envelope feature.

If you have typed a letter in Word and want an envelope to go with it, you'll be amazed at how simple it is to create the envelope. Just select the **Envelopes and Labels** command from the **Tools** menu. Word finds the address and copies it to the Envelopes and Labels dialog box. You simply need to confirm the address, insert the envelope, and click **OK**.

In some cases, you may want to create an envelope in a document without the address. In this case, you can use the Envelopes and Labels command and type the address manually in the dialog box.

If you have a lot of mailings, you can use Word to set up and print mailing labels. This feature makes it easy to send out Christmas cards, catalogs, or other mass mailings. You can select the type of labels that you have; Word recognizes most Avery label types (a popular label company). Word sets up a document with margins, indents, and other settings appropriate for the labels you are using. The resulting document is similar to a big table; you enter the addresses in each cell in the table and then print the document using the labels.

> If you aren't sure which way to insert the labels in the printer, mark an X on a piece of paper and put it in the paper tray with the X up. Print a document. If you see the X on the printed document, you know to put the labels in face up. If the X is on the back side of the printed page, you know to put the labels in face down.

Begin Guided Tour Create and Print an Envelope

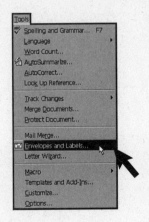

1 Open the **Tools** menu and choose the **Envelopes and Labels** command.

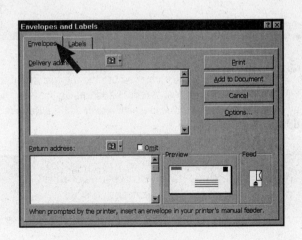

2 The Envelopes and Labels dialog box appears. If necessary, click the **Envelopes** tab to bring it to the front of the dialog box.

(continues)

Guided Tour   Create and Print an Envelope

(continued)

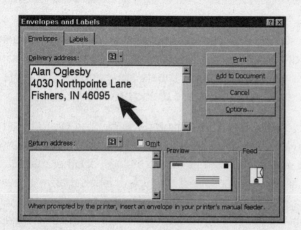

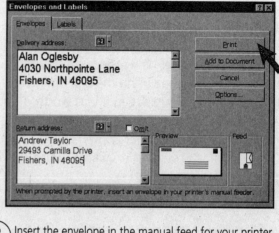

3 If your document contains an address, Word automatically displays it in the **Delivery Address** area. If not, you can enter one into the **Delivery Address** text box or make any corrections to the address that appears there.

5 Insert the envelope in the manual feed for your printer. (You'll see how to insert the envelope in the printer if you look in the Feed area of the dialog box.) Click the **Print** button. Word prints the envelope.

To add the address into your document, click the **Add to Document** button. This inserts the address in your document, which you can then save as part of the document text.

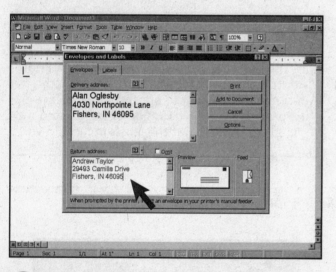

4 The **Return Address** may show just your name and company name the first time you use the command. If you have used this feature, you may see your address. Or, this area may be blank. In any case, type in an address or edit the **Return Address** area, if needed.

If your envelopes have your return address preprinted, check the **Omit** check box.

Begin Guided Tour Create Mailing Labels

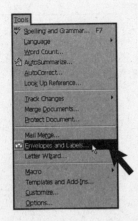

1 Open the **Tools** menu and select **Envelopes and Labels**.

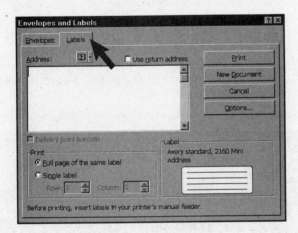

2 You see the Envelopes and Labels dialog box. Click the **Labels** tab to bring it to the front of the box.

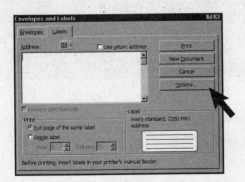

3 To select a type of label, click the **Options** button.

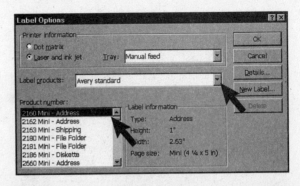

4 Word displays the Label Options dialog box. Click the down arrow next to **Label Products** and click the brand of label you are using. Then in the **Product Number** list, click the product number/name of the labels you are using. Click **OK** to return to the Envelopes and Labels dialog box.

If you've created a database of addresses with your Outlook program (another program in your Office suite), you can use the **Address Book** drop-down list to select the Outlook file to use. Simply click the **Address Book** icon above the **Delivery Address** box or the Use **Return Address** box.

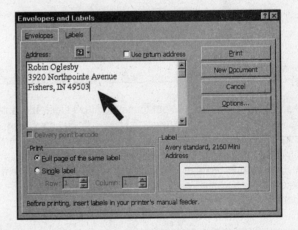

5 If you want to create a sheet of labels, all with the same address, type the address in the **Address** text box. To use your return address, check the **Use Return Address** check box. If each label will have a different address as the text on the label, leave the box blank.

(continues)

Guided Tour   Create Mailing Labels   *(continued)*

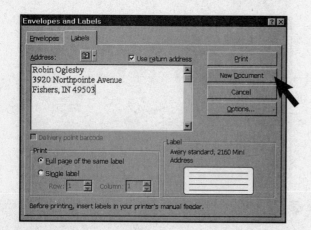

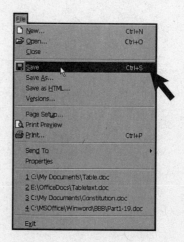

6 When you're ready to continue, click the **New Document** button.

8 When you finish typing the labels, you can save the document by pulling down the **File** menu and selecting the **Save** command. Even if you think you won't need the labels again, it's a good idea to save the document until after you print the labels. Sometimes, the labels can get jammed. You won't want to go through the process of creating the labels again if something happens during the printing process. If you don't want to save, skip to the next step.

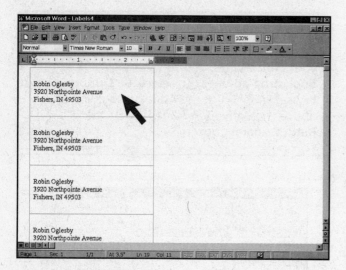

7 Word creates a document formatted into a table. The table is set up to match your selected labels. If you entered an address for step 5, all the labels display this address, and you can skip to step 9. If you did not, the labels are blank. Type the first label, pressing **Enter** to move to the next line in the label. When you complete one label, press **Tab** to go to the next label. Continue to fill in the table labels until you finish.

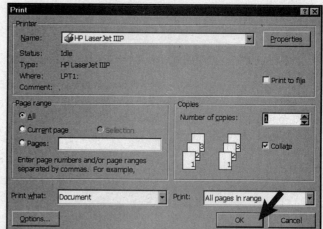

9 Insert the labels into the printer, pull down the **File** menu, select the **Print** command, and click **OK** to print the labels.

HOW TO...

Format a Word Document

In addition to the many editing features that Word provides, you can also utilize a complete toolbox of formatting features. What is formatting? Formatting is changing the appearance of the document. Why change the look? You may want to enhance the appearance of a document for many reasons: to make the document easier to read, to help clarify the meaning, or to make the document more attractive.

In this part of the book, you can find the features and the steps you need to make your document polished and professional looking.

What You Will Find in This Section

Make Text Bold, Italic, or Underline

Take a look at the following sentences:

Sign up for the **free seminar** tomorrow only.

Sign up for the free seminar **tomorrow only**.

Even though the wording of both sentences is identical, notice how the use of formatting changes the emphasis. The sentences read differently because of the font style—that is, the use of bold.

B *I* <u>U</u> As in this example, you can add emphasis to selected text by using a different font style. The three most common font styles are **bold**, *italic*, and <u>underline</u> (and various combinations of each). All three of these options are available as buttons on the Formatting toolbar (located below the Standard toolbar). When you apply a font style, you can apply the formatting to existing text, or you can apply the formatting to text you haven't even typed into your document yet.

To apply a font style to existing text, simply select the text you want to change and click the appropriate formatting button. To apply the formatting to text you are about to enter, just turn on the formatting feature you want to use before you start typing. The formatting remains in effect until you change it again.

Another formatting option you might apply to your text is *highlighting*. Word's Highlight feature lets you highlight text much like a highlighter pen. You can even select different colors to highlight with. Unfortunately, highlighting your text doesn't do much good unless you have a color printer or are networked to other computer users who can see the color highlighting in the files you send. If you do highlight text and print out to a non-color printer, you'll still see the highlighting; it will appear as shaded gray.

If you do have a color printer, you can take advantage of it using Word's Font Color command. You can use the command to add color to your document text. The **Font Color** button is located at the far right end of the Formatting toolbar. Select the text you want to color, then click the toolbar's **Font Color** arrow to reveal a palette of color choices. Select a color and Word changes the text color.

Before you go wild making all the important words in your document bold, italic, underline, or highlighted, consider these guidelines:

- Use the font styles sparingly. If every other word is bold, how is the reader to know what is really important? Too much bold makes the document look messy. Too much italic is difficult to read.

- You can combine the styles. To make text bold and italic, for example, click the **Bold** button and then click the *Italic* button.

- Underline is the least "professional" font style and is more of a carryover from the days of typewriters. Instead of underline, consider using italics.

- Some writers tend to use UPPERCASE letters as a way to emphasize a message. If you use this method, your readers are likely to feel as if you are SCREAMING AT THEM.

Begin Guided Tour Use Common Formatting Commands

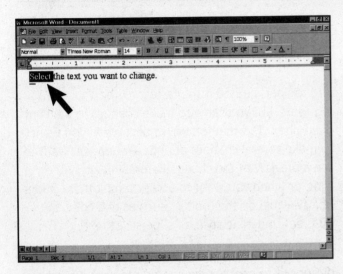

1 Select the text you want to change.

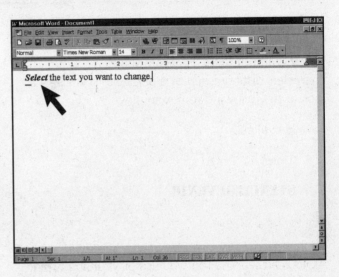

3 Word makes the change. This figure shows bold, italic text.

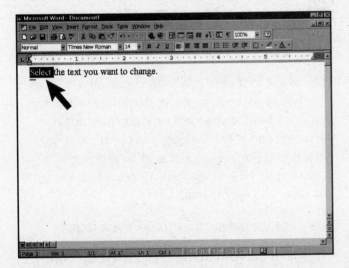

2 The text appears highlighted. Do one of the following:

Click the **Bold** button to make text bold (it looks like a bold capital **B**).

Click the **Italic** button (it looks like an italic capital **I**).

Click the **Underline** button (it looks like an underlined capital **U**).

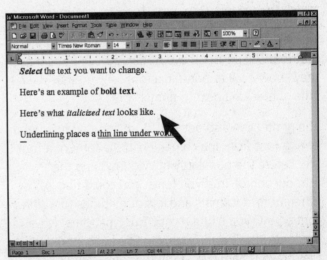

4 Here you see examples of each of the other styles (italic, underline).

To undo a style change, select the text again and click the style's button. For example, if you make text bold, you can unbold it by selecting it and clicking the **Bold** button. Doing so turns off the style.

Change the Font and Font Size

Word processing programs wouldn't be any fun without fonts. Fonts are simply a set of characters distinguished by a particular style. Take a look at the following font examples:

Helvetica

Times

STENCILOUVENIR

Shelley Volante

As you can see, the font you use plays an important part in setting the tone of the document. Some fonts are professional, some are decorative, and some are just fun. You can select from your available fonts to match the meaning you want for your document.

To use a font, the printer has to know how to print that font. All printers have certain built-in fonts that they know how to print. In a font list, you may see a little printer icon next to printer fonts.

The printer can also get the information about how to print a font from the computer, in the form of a font file. Before the popularity of Windows and the introduction of TrueType fonts, you could find lots of different font formats and lots of methods for using fonts. Now, you'll find mostly TrueType fonts, which are fonts installed through Windows and stored in files on your hard disk. **TT** in the font list indicates TrueType fonts.

Windows 95, as well as some Windows 95 programs, come with TrueType fonts. These fonts install when you install the program(s). You can also install additional fonts using the Windows 95 Control Panel.

The easiest way to change fonts is to use the Font and Font Size list boxes on the Formatting toolbar, as explained in the Guided Tour. Keep in mind that fonts are measured in points, and there are 72 points in one inch. The larger the point size, the bigger the font.

The toolbar method is the fastest method for changing fonts, but you can also make changes in the Font dialog box. This method works best when you want to make several changes at once—when you want to see a preview of the change before you apply the font, or when you want to access some other options not available on the toolbar (such as text color, a different underline style, or superscript text).

You can choose to apply a new font to existing text, or apply it to new text you enter into your document.

Change the Default Font

The default font used in all new documents is Times New Roman, 10-point type. If you don't like this font, you don't have to change it over and over again in each new document. Instead, you can select a new default font that will appear in all new documents. For example, I like to use Arial 12-point type because it is clean and easy to read.

To change the default font, follow these steps:

1. Open the **Format** menu and select the **Font** command.

2. You see the Font tab options. In the Font list, click the font you want to use as the default. In the Font Style area, click the default style you want. In the Size list, click the default font size you want.

3. Click the **Default** button.

4. You are prompted to confirm that you want to make the change. Click the **Yes** button.

Begin Guided Tour   Change the Font and Size from the Toolbar

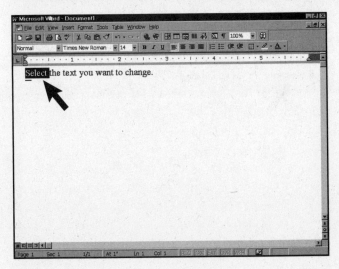

1 Select the text you want to change.

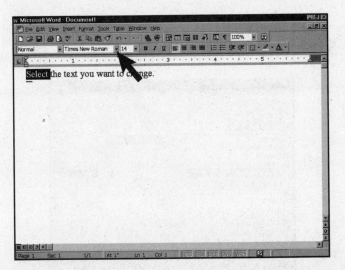

2 With the text selected, click the down arrow next to the **Font** list box on the Formatting toolbar.

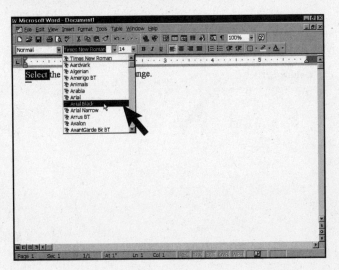

3 You see a list of fonts. Word lists the most recently used fonts at the top of the list. Click the font you want. (You may have to scroll down the list to see the one you want.) When you choose a font from the list, Word applies the font to the selected text and closes the list.

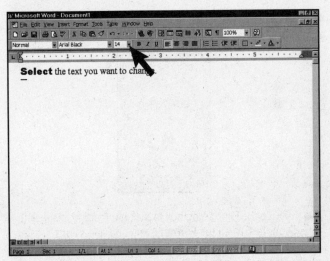

4 To change the size of the font, while text is still selected, click the down arrow next to the **Font Size** list box.

(continues)

Guided Tour Change the Font and Size from the Toolbar

(continued)

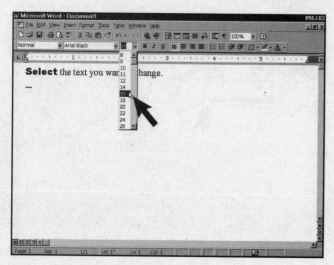

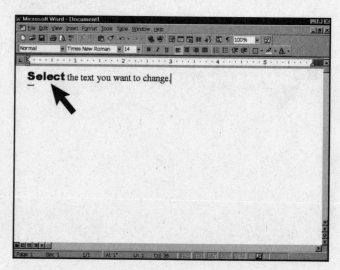

5 You see a list of font sizes. Click the size you want.

6 Word changes the font size of the selected text and closes the list. Click outside the text to deselect it.

Begin Guided Tour Changing Fonts with the Font Dialog Box

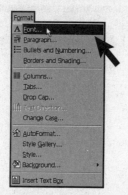

1 To use the Font dialog box to make formatting changes to your text, open the **Format** menu and select **Font**.

A quick way to summon the Font dialog box is to use the Shortcut menu. Select the text you want to edit, then right-click the text. This displays a Shortcut menu. Click the **Font** command from the menu to open the Font dialog box.

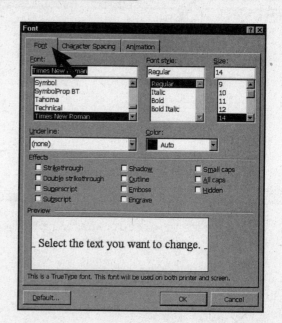

2 The Font dialog box opens onto your screen. Click the **Font** tab to bring its options to the front of the dialog box, if necessary.

Guided Tour Changing Fonts with the Font Dialog Box

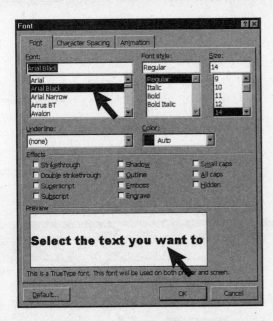

3 From the **Font** list box, scroll through the fonts and select one from the list. To select a font, click its name. To preview the font you selected, look in the **Preview** area at the bottom of the dialog box.

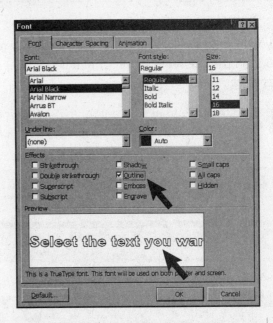

5 You can choose additional options to apply to your font, such as a color or Shadow effect. Select the appropriate options and use the **Preview** area to see how the options change the look of the text.

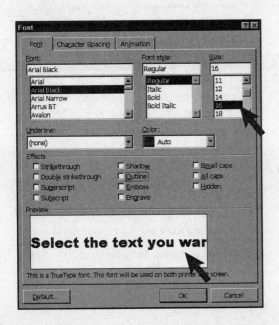

4 To change the font size, select a size from the **Size** list box. You can preview a selected size in the **Preview** area.

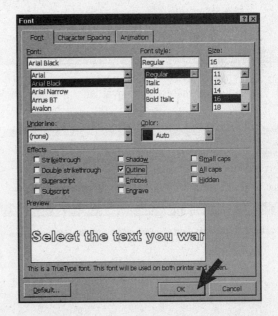

6 When finished choosing font options, click the **OK** button to exit the dialog box and apply your selections.

Copy Character Formatting

If you like the way you formatted a selection of text, you can use the same set of formatting in other areas of your document.

 You use the Format Painter tool to do this; you'll find it on the Standard toolbar. It keeps track of

the formatting options you applied to a selected portion of text and then lets you copy the same options to another portion of text. This is a lot easier than choosing the various formatting options over and over again.

Begin Guided Tour   Use the Format Painter Tool

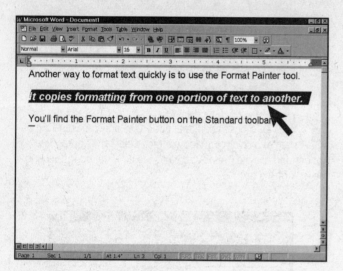

1 Select the text that has the formatting you want to copy.

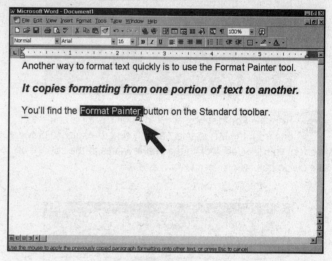

3 The mouse pointer changes to a paintbrush. Drag across the new text you want to format.

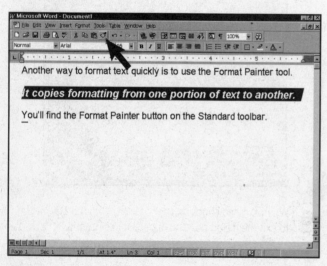

2 Click the **Format Painter** button.

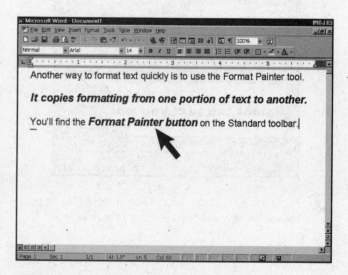

4 Word applies the formatting to the selected text.

Align Text

When you type in Word, all text is left-aligned and the right margin appears ragged. For most documents you create, this is the alignment choice that you will use; that's why it's the default. In some instances, though, you will want to choose a different alignment. For example, you may want to center text such as the title of a document, or you may want to right-align or justify text.

 Word has grouped all four of the text alignment commands together on the formatting toolbar: Left, Center, Right, and Justify. You can quickly align a new paragraph with a click of a button. The alignment features apply to the entire paragraph. Keep in mind that a paragraph is any text followed by a hard return (a press of the **Enter** key). A paragraph can be one line, one word, or several lines of text. You end one paragraph and create a new one by pressing **Enter**. When you press **Enter**, Word inserts a paragraph

marker, which is important to formatting. (The paragraph marker is hidden by default, but you can see it if you click the **Paragraph** button—it looks like a backward **P**—on the Standard toolbar.) When you make a change to the formatting, the paragraph marker stores the formatting change—tabs, indents, alignment, and so on. This concept can confuse you in two ways:

- When you format one paragraph and then press **Enter**, all the formatting continues to the next paragraph. For example, if you center a line and press **Enter**, the next line you type in will be centered, too. Just remember that the paragraph formatting is in effect until you change it.

- If you delete a paragraph maker at the end of a paragraph, the paragraph takes on the formatting of the next paragraph. You may wonder what happened to your formatting. Don't forget that the paragraph marker stores the formatting.

Begin Guided Tour   Apply Alignment

① Select the paragraph(s) you want to align. Do one of the following:

Click the **Align Left** button to the left-align text.

Click the **Center** button to center the text.

Click the **Align Right** button to right-align text.

Click the **Justify** button to justify text.

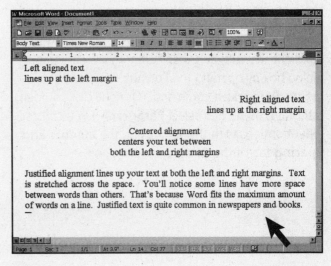

② In this figure, you can see examples of the four alignment choices. If you change your mind, you can undo the alignment or select the paragraph again and select another alignment option.

Indent Text

Indents are margins that affect individual paragraphs or lines. For example, when you start a paragraph and press the **Tab** key to move the first line over slightly, you're creating an indent. When you set a bulleted text list in the middle of a page, you have created an indent. But why use indents?

If you take a critical look at the layout of documents, you'll spot some of the techniques that the print industry uses to help make text readable and appealing to the eye. For example, when the first line of a paragraph is indented, you can easily spot the beginning of each of the paragraphs; this breaks the document text up into manageable chunks and makes it easy to follow. If a certain passage is set off from the right and left margins, your attention goes to that passage. Those are just some of the many ways indents can help a document's appearance.

When it comes to indents, Word offers several paths to choose from. Granted, pressing the **Tab** key is an easy way to indent (see the "Set Tabs" task later in this section for more information about tabs); it's rather mindless, but there are other methods you can use to indent as well—real computer-savvy methods that only smart Word users use.

To indent a block of text in the midst of your page, highlight the text, and then summon the Paragraph dialog box by opening the **Format** menu and choosing the **Paragraph** command. (Or right-click to open a shortcut menu and select **Paragraph**.) You control indent options with the settings on the **Indents and Spacing** tab of the Paragraph dialog box.

You can choose to set up indents before you type in text or apply indents to text you've already typed in. Remember, if you don't like the indent you apply, you can always set another (or click the **Undo** button).

Here are some of the indent options you can apply to your own Word documents:

- You can set *left* or *right indents* with precise measurements.

- Set a *First Line indent*, an indent that moves the first line of the paragraph over but leaves the remaining text lined up flush with the left margin.

- Set a *Hanging indent*, which leaves the first line flush at the left margin but shifts the remaining lines in the paragraph over to the right.

- For even faster indents, forego the Paragraph dialog box and use the indent buttons on the Formatting toolbar. Click the **Increase Indent** button to indent text by one tab stop. Click the **Decrease Indent** button to undo an indent.

- Also on the toolbar are buttons for creating indents for a bulleted list or numbered list. Use the **Bullet** or **Number** buttons on the Formatting toolbar. (You'll learn more about these types of lists later in this section.)

Note: You can also set indents using the Ruler. See "Use the Ruler" on page 111 for information on using this method.

Begin Guided Tour   Indent with the Paragraph Dialog Box

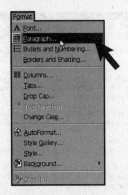

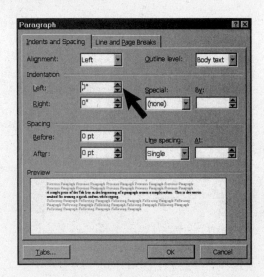

1 Move the insertion point to the beginning of the paragraph you want to indent. You can also select the entire paragraph(s) you want to indent. Open the **Format** menu and select the **Paragraph** command. This opens the Paragraph dialog box.

3 To set a left indent, enter the amount you want to indent the text in the **Left** spin box.

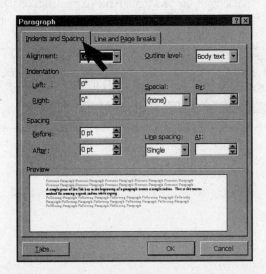

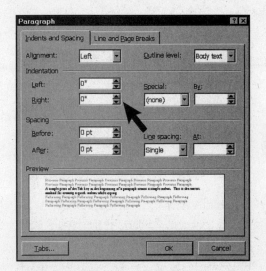

2 Click the **Indents and Spacing** tab to bring it to the front of the Paragraph dialog box.

4 To indent text from the right, type the amount or use the spin arrows to enter the amount you want in the **Right** spin box.

(continues)

Guided Tour Indent with the Paragraph Dialog Box

(continued)

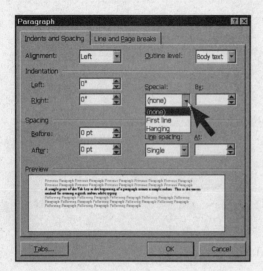

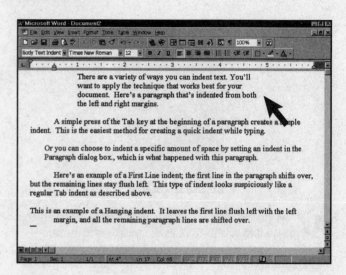

5 To create a first-line or hanging indent, display the **Special** drop-down list and choose the type of indent you want. You can enter an exact amount you want to indent in the **By** spin box.

7 Word indents the paragraph(s) per your settings. In this figure, notice the different types of indents you can create.

To quickly summon the Paragraph dialog box, right-click anywhere in the selected text and choose the **Paragraph** menu command.

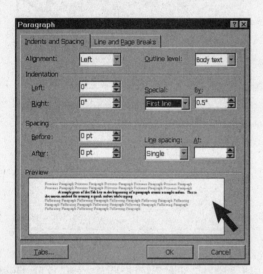

6 You see a sample of how the paragraph will look in the Preview area. Click **OK** to exit the dialog box.

Create Bulleted and Numbered Lists

Want to summarize the main points in your document? Want to enumerate a process? Then use a bulleted or numbered list. *Bulleted* lists call attention to points of equal importance, such as agenda items or performance goals. You've probably noticed several bulleted lists throughout this book. Use *numbered lists* for a series of steps or directions.

Creating either type of list is simple: select the paragraphs and click the appropriate toolbar button, as described in the Guided Tour. For bulleted lists, Word adds a bullet to each paragraph (except blank ones) and creates a hanging indent. Numbered lists appear similarly, but instead of a bullet, Word adds a number. The cool thing about numbered lists is that you can delete a paragraph or add a paragraph within the list, and Word automatically renumbers for you.

You can also choose to apply bulleted or numbered text before you start typing. Click the appropriate toolbar button, then begin typing in your text. Every time you press **Enter** to start a new bulleted or numbered item, Word adds a bullet or number to the text.

If you change your mind, you can remove the bullets or numbers the same way you add them: select the text and click the appropriate toolbar button.

You can also assign bulleted and numbered lists by opening the Bullets and Numbering dialog box found on the **Format** menu. This route gives you much more control over the options. For example, you can select the type of bullet or the style of numbering to use.

Begin Guided Tour   Create a Bulleted List

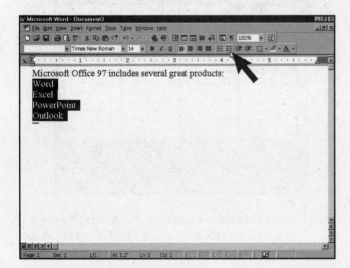

1 Select the text to which you want to add bullets and click the **Bullets** button.

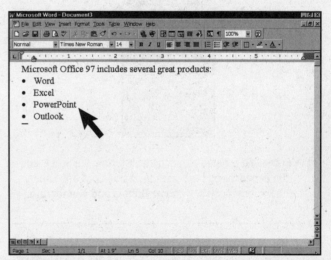

2 Word creates a bulleted list, adding bullets to each paragraph within the selection.

Begin Guided Tour Create a Numbered List

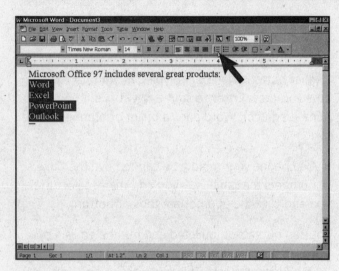

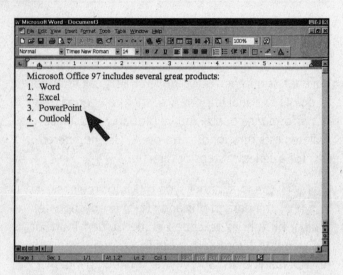

1 Select the text you want to number and click the **Numbering** button.

2 Word creates a numbered list.

Begin Guided Tour Use the Bullets and Numbering Dialog Box

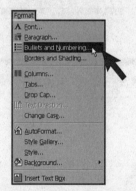

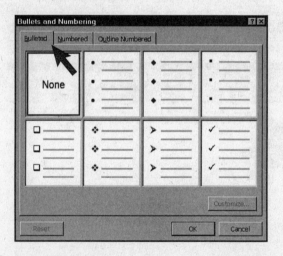

1 To create a bulleted or numbered list using the Bullets and Numbering dialog box, select the paragraphs, then open the **Format** menu and choose **Bullets and Numbering**.

To quickly summon the Bullets and Numbering dialog box, right-click anywhere in the selected text and choose the **Bullets and Numbering** menu command.

2 Click the **Bulleted** or **Numbered** tab and select the bullet or numerical style you want to use. Click **OK** to exit the box and apply the style.

Set Tabs

Tabs provide another way of strategically putting space in your document to make it look nice. Tabs come in handy when you're trying to line up columns of text in your document.

Whenever you press the **Tab** key on the keyboard, the Word cursor moves over one tab stop. By default, Word has tab stops set up at 1/2-inch intervals across the width of the document page (an increment entered as .5). These default tab stops are left-aligned tabs, which means the text lines up on the left. But you don't have to use these default tabs; you can set your own tabs.

To set your own tabs, you'll need some help from the Tabs dialog box. Open the **Format** menu and choose **Tabs**; the Tabs dialog box appears. You can also access the Tabs dialog box via the Paragraph dialog box (just click the **Tabs** button). Wait, there's more! You can also double-click any tab symbol set on your ruler to open the Tabs dialog box, too. (You'll learn how to use the ruler in "Use the Ruler" on page 111.)

If you ever get tired of the 1/2-inch default tabs, you can change them with the **Default Tab Stops** option in the **Tabs** dialog box. Click the directional arrows to select a new default setting, or type one in the **Default Tab Stops** text box. When you type in a tab measurement such as a 1-inch tab, you would enter the measurement as 1.0.

As I mentioned previously, the default tab is a left-aligned tab, which means the text lines up to the left. However, you can choose to align tabbed text differently. In the Alignment section of the Tabs dialog box, you have five tab types to choose from. If you pick **Left**, **Center**, or **Right**, the text that you tab will line up at that respective position. If you choose **Decimal**, your tab lines up the text at the decimal point. If you choose **Bar**, a vertical bar appears in your text, and your text is left-aligned to the bar (which is helpful when you're trying to separate tab columns).

The Leader section of the Tabs dialog box enables you to insert dots, dashes, or ruled lines to fill up the empty space between your tab stops. The default option is to have nothing between the stops (**None**).

Begin Guided Tour   Set a Tab with the Tabs Dialog Box

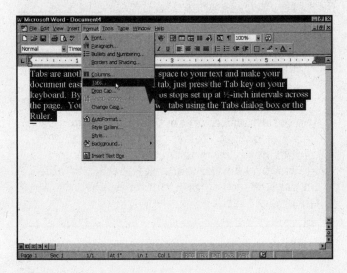

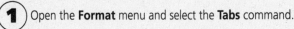

1 Open the **Format** menu and select the **Tabs** command.

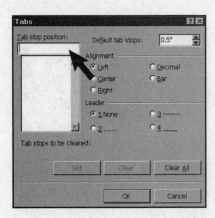

2 You see the Tabs dialog box. In the **Tab Stop Position** text box, type the position for the tab. Keep in mind that this position is measured in inches and from the left margin.

(continues)

Guided Tour Set a Tab with the Tabs Dialog Box (continued)

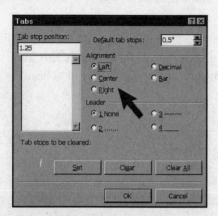

3 From the **Alignment** options, click the type of alignment you want: **Left**, **Center**, **Right**, **Decimal**, or **Bar**.

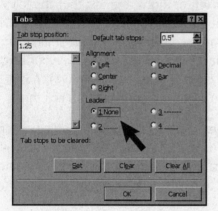

4 If you want to use a dot leader for the tab, click the leader style you want in the **Leader** area.

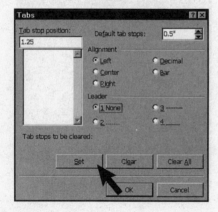

5 Click the **Set** button to set the tab position you entered.

6 Word adds the tab stop to the **Tab Stop Position** list. Follow steps 2 through 6 for each tab stop you want to create. When finished, click **OK** to exit the box.

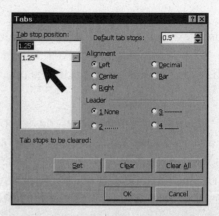

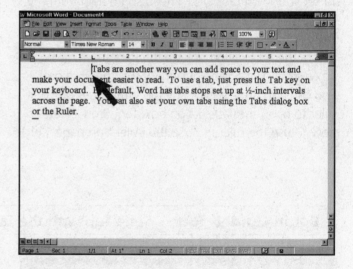

7 Word sets up the new tabs. Click the **Tab** key to insert the tab in the text. This figure shows a left tab set at the 1.25-inch mark.

The easiest way to create a tabular column of information is to create a table. Tables provide a lot of flexibility in formatting and aligning information into columns. See "Set Up a Table" on page 88 in the "How to Create a Word Document" section.

Use the Ruler

You may prefer a more visual method for formatting paragraphs (setting tabs and indenting text). In that case, you can use the Ruler. The Ruler is an on-screen formatting tool you can use to set indents, tabs, and margins. To display the ruler, open the **View** menu and select the **Ruler** command.

To use the ruler to set indents, you drag the appropriate indent marker on the ruler, as described in the Guided Tour. Be sure to drag the correct indent marker. If you don't get the results you want, check to see if you put the pointer in the right spot. You can also use the ruler to change the left margin. Again,

you have to get your pointer in the exact spot: right on the margin in the ruler.

To the far left of the ruler, you'll notice a little button that indicates the current tab type. To set a tab using the ruler, click on this button until you see the tab type that you want—left, center, right, or decimal (you cannot access the bar tab or set leader characters from the ruler). Then click on the ruler on the spot where you want to place the tab. If you don't get it exact, don't worry; you can drag the tab on the ruler to the spot you want. To remove a tab, drag it off the ruler.

Button	Tab Type	What It Does
∟	Left tab	Text starts on the marker and moves left.
⌐	Right tab	Text starts on the marker and moves right.
⊥	Center tab	Text centers on the marker.
⊥	Decimal tab	Text aligns on the decimal point.

Begin Guided Tour   Use the Ruler to Set Indents

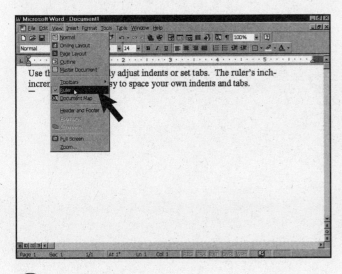

1 If your ruler doesn't appear on-screen, open the **View** menu and select the **Ruler** command to display it.

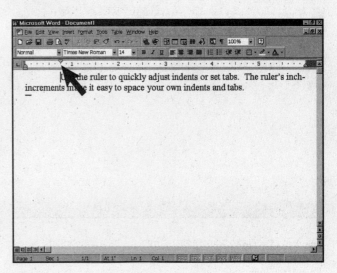

2 To set a first-line indent, drag the first line indent marker to a new location on the ruler. Be sure to click the top indent marker as shown in the figure.

(continues)

Guided Tour   Use the Ruler to Set Indents

(continued)

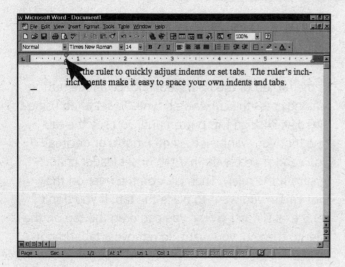

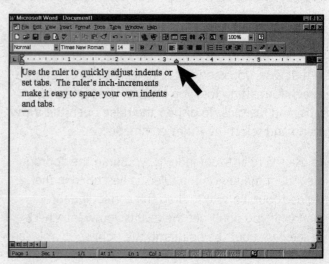

3 To set a left indent, drag the left indent marker and move it to a new location on the ruler. (The left indent marker looks like a tiny box.) When you drag a left indent, any first line indents you've set will also move.

> The Left Indent marker, when selected and repositioned, also changes the left margin of your page.

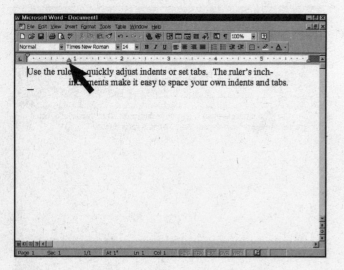

4 To create a hanging indent, drag the hanging indent marker to a new location on the ruler. Make sure you drag the correct indent marker, as indicated in the figure. When you set a hanging indent, the first line marker stays at the left.

5 To set a right indent, drag the right indent marker to a new location on the ruler.

Begin Guided Tour   Set Tabs Using the Ruler

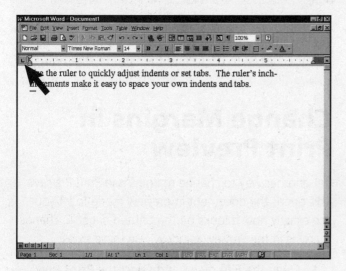

1 To select a tab style (left, center, right, or decimal), click the tab symbol box at the far left end of the ruler. Each time you click the box, a different tab style icon appears. Click as many times as needed to cycle through to the tab style you want to use.

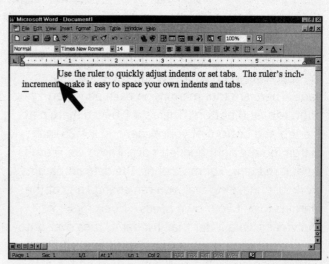

3 To use the tab, press the **Tab** key on the keyboard and the text shifts over to the tab stop location you specified.

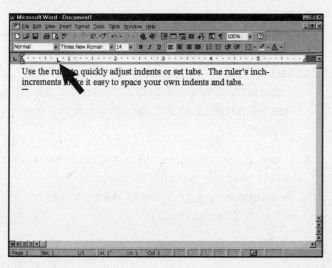

2 Click the ruler where you want the tab inserted. As soon as you click in place, a tab symbol representing the tab style you selected will appear on the ruler.

Change Margins

Yet another way to control your document's appearance is by changing margins. A *margin* is the space between your text and the edge of your page. There are four margins on each page: left, right, top, and bottom. There's a 1.0-inch margin at the top and bottom of your page, and a 1.25-inch margin on the right and left sides. Those are Word's default margins. For most of us, the default margins work just fine. However, you can change any of the margins to suit your own needs. For example, if you've written a letter that just barely runs over onto the second page, you may be able to make it fit perfectly on one page by slightly adjusting the margins. Or perhaps your company's stationery has a preprinted letterhead or logo—you may need to adjust the margins in Word to print around such items.

You can control margins using the Page Setup dialog box. To access this box, open the **File** menu and choose **Page Setup**. You will find the page margin settings in the Margins tab. You can change any of the four page margin settings and set precise measurements for the settings and even preview how your margins will look in the Preview box.

When you change the margins, you control how much of the document they affect. You can apply the new settings to your entire document, from the location of the insertion point on, or to a block of selected text. It's up to you. Just select the text and modify the margins, or place your cursor directly in the paragraph or block of text where you want the margin change to occur and then modify the margins.

Change Margins in Print Preview

Yet another way to change margins is in Print Preview. This opens the document in preview mode to let you see exactly how it looks on the printed page. To change margins in the Preview window, use these steps:

1. Open the **File** menu and select the **Print Preview** command.

2. You see a preview of the document. If the Ruler is not displayed, click the **View Ruler** button.

3. You see the ruler on-screen. To change the left and right margins, use the horizontal ruler. To change the top or bottom margins, use the vertical ruler. Put the pointer on the margin indicator and when the cursor turns to a double-headed arrow, drag the margin guide to a new location.

4. Word updates the preview of the document to reflect the new margins. When you finish making changes, click the **Close** button to return to Normal view.

Begin Guided Tour   Change the Margins with Page Setup

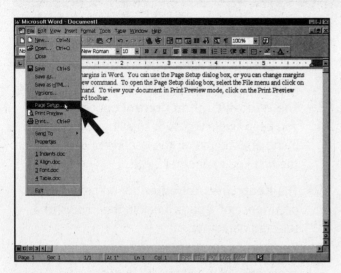

1 Open the **File** menu and select the **Page Setup** command.

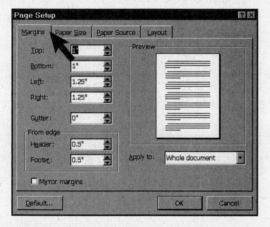

2 The Page Setup dialog box appears. Click the **Margins** tab to bring it to the front of the box, if necessary.

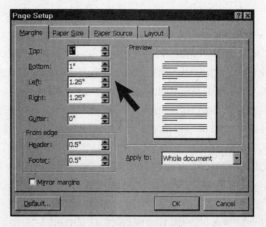

3 You can change all four page margins and the gutter (space between two side-by-side pages), as well as margins for headers and footers (see "Set Up Headers and Footers" on page 121). Click to insert the cursor in the margin text box you want to change. You can also press **Tab** to move to the different margin boxes.

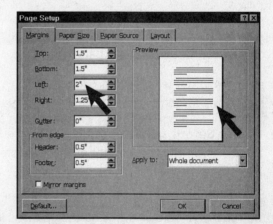

4 Enter the new margin in inches. You can delete or edit the current entry or use the spin arrows to select the value you want. Follow steps 3 and 4 for each margin you want to change.

5 The Preview area in the dialog box shows the effect of the new margins. When you finish making changes, click **OK**. Word makes the change. You won't see the effect of margins in Normal view. You can switch to Page Layout view or use the Print Preview command to preview the document to see the margin change.

Change Line and Paragraph Spacing

The Paragraph dialog box contains commands for controlling the space between lines of text and pagination (page layout). Paragraph spacing controls the amount of white space above and below a paragraph. Some people will just settle for pressing **Enter** to create white space between paragraphs. However, you can use a better method to adjust spacing. You can use paragraph spacing controls to add a set amount of space after each of your document headings, or control if single words are left floating on a line by themselves at the end of your paragraphs.

The line spacing options in the Paragraph dialog box controls the amount of space between each line, for instance, single- or double-spaced. You can also control the amount of spacing before and after paragraphs.

The pagination options in the Line and Page Breaks tab control how paragraphs and pages flow.

Here's a rundown of what you can do with the spacing commands in the Indents and Spacing tab:

- Use the **Before** and **After** settings (measured in points) to control the amount of space before and after paragraphs.

- Pull down the **Line Spacing** drop-down list to find such standard line spacing designations as single-space, double-space, and the like.

- Click the **Line and Page Breaks** tab to access the text flow options, which you use to control the flow of text from one page to another.

- The **Widow/Orphan Control** option can help you keep single words or small bits of text from being abandoned on the last line of one page or the first line of another.

- The **Keep Lines Together** option prevents the occurrence of a page break in the middle of a selected paragraph.

- The **Keep with Next** option prevents the occurrence of a page break between two designated paragraphs.

- The **Page Break Before** option places a page break before a specified paragraph instead of in the middle of it or after it.

If used effectively, all of the pagination and spacing options can help you create better looking documents that are easier to read, or at least very nicely spaced.

Press **Ctrl+1** for single-spacing, **Ctrl+5** for 1.5-inch spacing, or **Ctrl+2** for double-spacing.

Begin Guided Tour   Change Line Spacing and Pagination

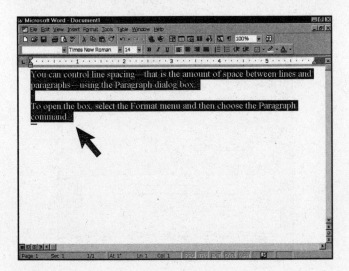

1 Select the paragraph(s) that you want to change.

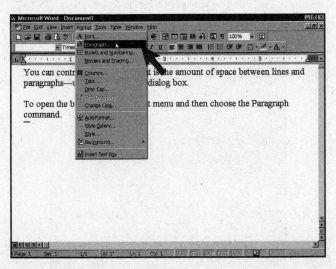

2 Open the **Format** menu and select the **Paragraph** command.

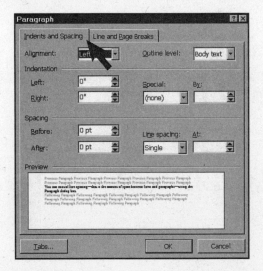

3 In the Paragraph dialog box, click the **Indents and Spacing** tab to bring the spacing controls to the front of the box, if it's not already there.

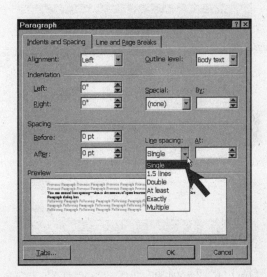

4 To set spacing between lines, click the down arrow at the end of the **Line Spacing** drop-down list box, and choose the line spacing interval you want to use.

(continues)

Guided Tour   Change Line Spacing and Pagination *(continued)*

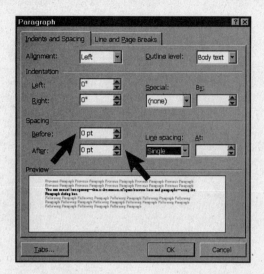

5 To add space above and below the paragraph, enter values in the **Before** or **After** spin boxes.

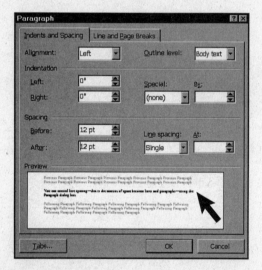

6 Check how the spacing options you select affect your document in the **Preview** area.

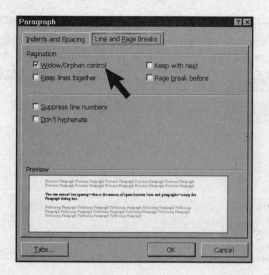

7 Click the **Line and Page Breaks** tab to bring the pagination options to the front of the box. Under the **Pagination** area, select any controls you want to apply to the ends of your paragraphs or pages.

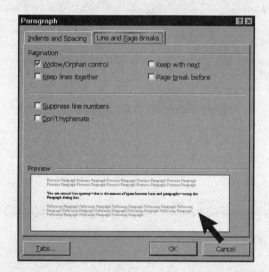

8 You can preview how the pagination options look in the **Preview** area. When finished, click **OK** to exit the box and put your changes in effect.

Number Pages

Imagine trying to find page 12 in a 20-page document you printed out if the pages weren't numbered. Imagine trying to put together a 50-page booklet without numbering the pages. Page numbers are a critical element to documents that are longer than one page. Page numbers help the reader and you keep the pages in order.

The great thing about using Word to add page numbers is that you don't have to type them on each page. You can add them once to a header (top of page) or footer (bottom of page) and Word will put them on all pages. You also don't have to worry about making sure the page numbers are correct. If you add or delete a page, Word renumbers all the page numbers.

You can add page numbers while you are creating a header or footer (covered in "Set Up Headers and Footers" on page 121), or you can add them using the **Page Numbers** command. When you use the command, Word sets up a header or footer automatically.

In addition to selecting to put the page number at the top or bottom of the document, you can select where in the header or footer to place the page number:

Left   Numbers align with the left margin.

Center   Numbers center on the page.

Right   Numbers print flush with the right margin.

Inside   Numbers print on the inside of facing pages (right-aligned on left pages and left-aligned on right pages).

Outside   Numbers print on the outside of facing pages (left-aligned on left pages and right-aligned on right pages).

Format the Page Number

The *page number* feature is a special code which updates automatically. That doesn't mean you can't delete or format the code. You can make the page number bold or italic, change the alignment, and so on by using any of the formatting features. You can also drag across the page number and press **Delete** to delete the page number on the selected page(s) or all pages.

If you don't like the numbering style used for the page numbers, you can select a different format. To do so, select **Page Numbers** from the **Insert** menu and click the **Format** button in the Page Numbers dialog box. Select the format you want. You can also enter a different starting number in this dialog box. For example, you may have broken a long document up into sections or chapters. You can start numbering the second half of the document with the appropriate number. Make your changes and click **OK**.

Begin Guided Tour   Add Page Numbers

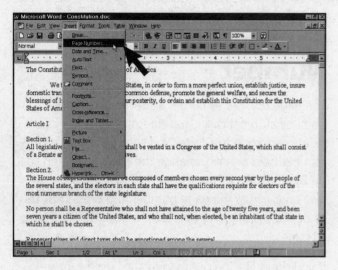

1 Open the **Insert** menu and select the **Page Numbers** command.

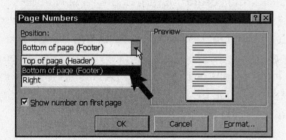

2 You see the Page Numbers dialog box. Click the down-arrow next to the **Position** drop-down list box; select **Top of Page (Header)** or **Bottom of Page (Footer)**.

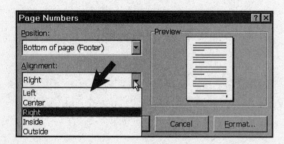

3 Click the down-arrow next to **Alignment**. You see a list of different alignment choices; click the one you want.

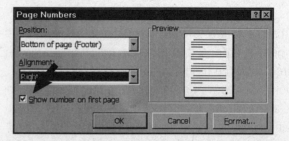

4 If you want to skip printing a page number on the first page (this is useful if the first page is a cover or title page), uncheck the **Show Number on First Page** check box. (This starts page two with a number 2.)

> If your first page is a title or cover page, and you select the **Show Number on First Page** box, no page number appears on the page. But if you want the next numbered page to start with a specific number, be sure to enter a number in the Page Numbering **Start At** box.

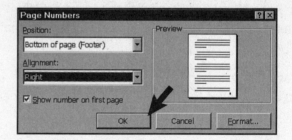

5 Take a look at the Preview area to see a preview of your page number options. Click **OK** to exit the dialog box and add page numbers to your document. On-screen, you cannot see the page numbers unless you switch over to Page Layout view (open the **View** menu and select **Page Layout**).

> If you change your mind about adding page numbers, click **Cancel** in the Page Numbers dialog box. Or click the **Undo** button on the Standard toolbar immediately.

Set Up Headers and Footers

In addition to the page number, you may want to include other identifying information on every page in your document. For example, if you are submitting the next great thriller to a publisher, you may want to include your last name at the top of each page of the document.

Text that you include at the top of each page is a *header*. Text included on the bottom of each page is a *footer*. In Word, headers and footers are separate from the regular document text and you won't be able to see them on-screen unless you're using Page Layout view (open the **View** menu and select **Page Layout**).

You insert a header or footer into your document with the Header and Footer toolbar. The following table includes the name and a short description of the buttons you can use on the toolbar.

When you create a header or footer, Word applies the header or footer style to that paragraph. Basically, this style has three tabs: a left tab, a center tab, and a right-aligned tab. That doesn't mean you are stuck with this preset formatting; you can modify any of the paragraph formatting.

You can also format the text you type into the header or footer, just as you format regular text. For example, to make the header bold, drag across it, and click the **Bold** button. The same thing works for deleting a header or footer. Drag across the text and press **Delete**.

Headers and Footers

Button	Name	Description
	Insert Page Number	Adds page numbers.
	Insert Number of Pages	Inserts the total number of pages in the document.
	Format Page Number	Opens the Page Number Format dialog box for entering formatting preferences.
	Insert Date	Adds the date to your header or footer text.
	Insert Time	Adds the current time to your header or footer text.
	Page Setup	Opens the Page Setup dialog box where you can control which pages the header or footer falls on.
	Show/Hide Document Text	Toggles between showing the text on the document page with the header/footer or just the header/footer by itself.
	Same As Previous	Creates different header or footer sections in your file.
	Switch Between Header and Footer	Lets you switch between the header and footer areas on a document.
	Show Previous	Shows the previous header or footer section of document.
	Show Next	Shows the next header or footer section of document.
Close	Close	Closes the Header and Footer toolbar.

Headers and footers will appear on every page in your document file unless you specify otherwise. You can use the Page Setup dialog box to tell Word to print headers or footers on every page, even or odd pages. You can even tell Word to start headers and footers on a different start page. Click the **Page Setup** button on the Header and Footer toolbar or open the **File** menu and select **Page Setup** to control how headers and footers print.

Begin Guided Tour   Create a Header or Footer

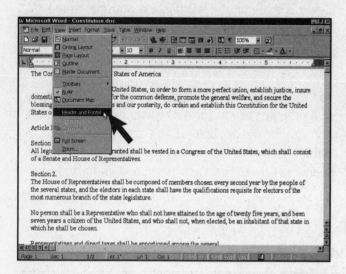

1 Open the **View** menu and select the **Header and Footer** command.

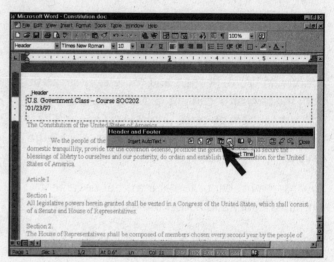

3 To add other information (such as a date) to your header or footer, click the appropriate button on the toolbar. The date is inserted automatically.

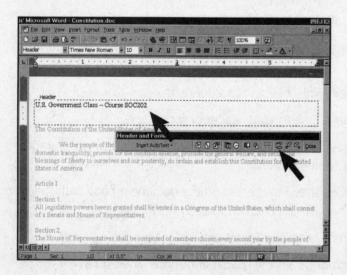

2 You see the Header and Footer toolbar on-screen and a dotted header area at the top of the page. To enter text for the header, just start typing. To create a footer, click the **Switch Between Header and Footer** button and start typing.

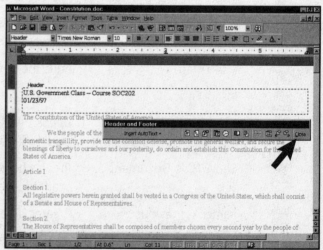

4 When the header (or footer) is complete, click the **Close** button. Word adds the header (or footer) to the document. In order to see the header on-screen, you must switch over to Page Layout view. (Simply open the **View** menu and click **Page Layout**.)

Set Up Columns

If you are an old-timer, you may remember the manual method of creating a newsletter. For my grade school paper, for example, we typed the text within narrow margins and then cut out the articles and pasted them into the semblance of a "newsletter." If only we had Word then...

Word makes it easy to set up columns, enter text, and format the columns. The easiest method is to use the toolbar button. With this method, you can select up to six columns, all of equal width. You can also set up columns using the **Columns** command. With this method, you can select different widths for the columns, create more than seven columns, and select options such as adding a line between the columns. The Guided Tour covers both methods.

> You can also create the columns using the toolbar button and then modify the formatting or column width using the **Columns** command.

You can set up your columns and then type the text for the document. Or do the reverse: type the text and then change the formatting for columns. When you type in Normal view, your text will wrap within the margins for that column, but you won't see the columns side by side. This is the fastest method for typing because Word won't continually have to adjust the line breaks and redraw the screen. If you want to see the columns side by side, you can switch to Page Layout view.

If you turn on columns and then type, Word will fill up one column and move to the next. If you want to manually end one column and move to the next, you can insert a column break. To do so, put the pointer where you want the break. Then open the **Insert** menu, choose the **Break** command, select the **Column** break option, and click **OK**.

Begin Guided Tour   Set Up Columns with the Toolbar

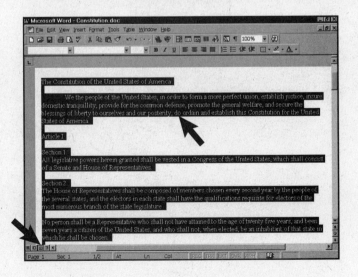

1 Place the insertion point where you want to create the columns, or if you want to turn existing text into columns, select the text. Then click the **Page Layout** view button (located to the left of the horizontal scroll bar). You must be in Page Layout view in order to see the columns of text.

(continues)

Guided Tour Set Up Columns with the Toolbar

(continued)

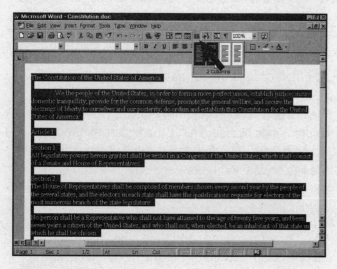

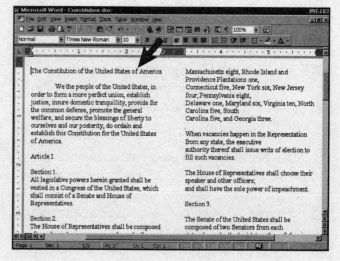

2 Click the **Columns** button on the Standard toolbar. You see a drop-down palette of columns. Click the number of columns you want to create.

3 If you're turning existing text into columns, Word reformats the text, as shown in this figure.

Begin Guided Tour Use the Columns Command

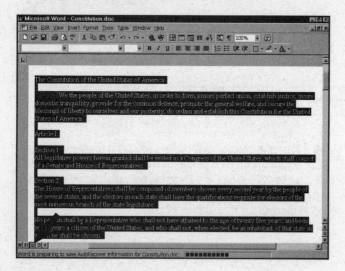

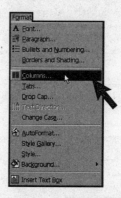

2 Next, open the **Format** menu and select the **Columns** command.

1 Place the insertion point where you want to create the columns, or if you want to turn existing text into columns, select the text. Then click the **Page Layout** view button. You must be in Page Layout view in order to see the columns of text.

Guided Tour   Use the Columns Command

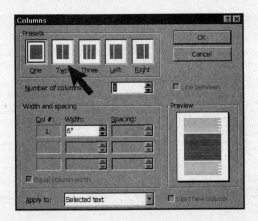

3 You see the Columns dialog box. To use one of the preset column formats, click the one you want in the **Presets** area: **One**, **Two**, **Three**, **Left**, or **Right**.

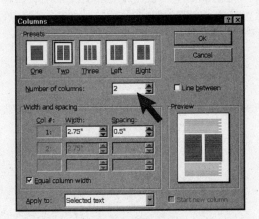

4 To set the number of columns manually, enter the number of columns you want in the **Number of Columns** spin box.

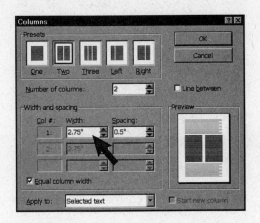

5 Depending on the number of columns you select, Word updates the **Width and Spacing** area. To change the width of all columns, enter a new width in the **Width** spin box. Word uses this width for all columns.

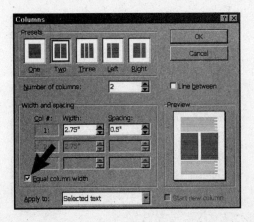

6 To create columns of unequal widths, uncheck the **Equal Column Width** check box. Then click in the **Width** spin box for the column you want to change and enter a new width. Do this for each column width you want to change.

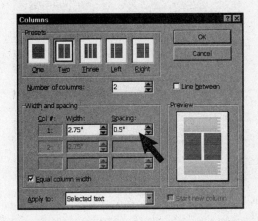

7 To change the spacing between columns, click in the **Spacing** text box for the column spacing you want to change. Then enter a new spacing. Do this for each column spacing you want to change.

(continues)

Guided Tour   Use the Columns Command   *(continued)*

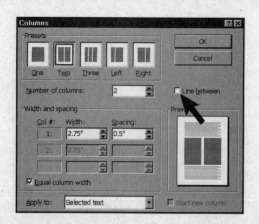

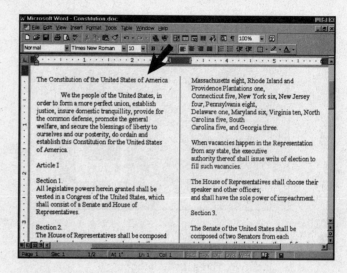

8 If you want to include a line between the columns, check the **Line between** check box.

10 Word reformats the document into the number of columns you have selected with the column width and spacing as you entered it.

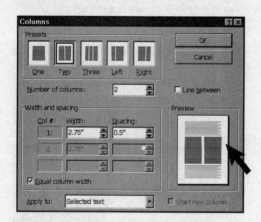

9 You see a preview of how the columns will look in the Preview area. When you finish making changes, click **OK**.

Use Templates and Wizards

If you don't want to spend your time setting up a document and messing with formatting, you may want to investigate some of Word's "auto" documents, that is, the templates and wizards provided with Word.

Both templates and wizards are preformatted, designed layouts for common document types, such as reports, press releases, memos, and faxes (although wizards are processes for building documents and not exactly documents in and of themselves). You select the one you want, and Word sets up the formatting. Most templates and wizards also include some text. For example, in the memo templates and wizards, the headings (MEMO, TO, FROM, and so on) are already entered.

The difference between a template and a wizard is the level of automation. If you select a wizard, Word leads you through the process of creating the document step by step. You make the selections you want

and when you finish, you have a completed document. All you have to do is add your own text. If you select a template, you basically just open a new document that includes appropriate formatting and text. Again, you just add your own text.

Create Your Own Template

If none of the predefined templates are what you want, you can create your own template. The template can be any type of document you choose and can include any text and formatting you want.

Remember that all new documents based on this template will include all the formatting and text you include. Therefore, include in the template only the elements you want in all documents based on this template.

Begin Guided Tour   Use a Template or Wizard

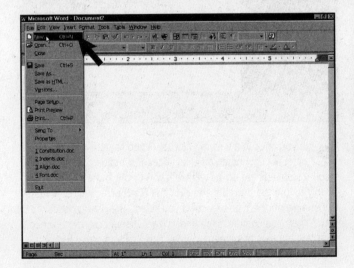

1 Open the **File** menu and select the **New** command.

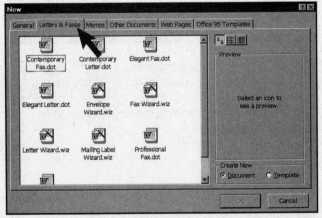

2 Word displays the New dialog box. Notice there are a variety of tabs to look through. To view the contents of each tab, simply click the tab name.

(continues)

Guided Tour   Use a Template or Wizard

(continued)

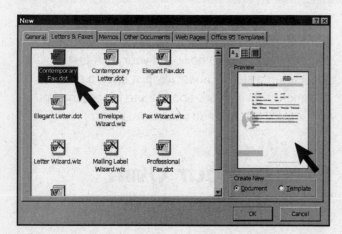

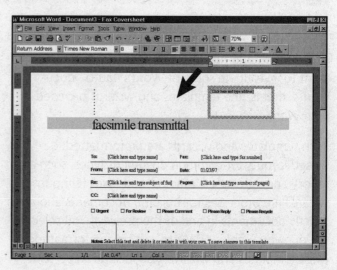

3 When you find a template or wizard you want to use, you can preview it, if applicable. Click the template, then Word displays the selected template or wizard in the Preview area.

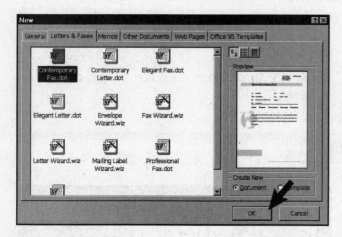

4 To select the document style, make sure it's highlighted, then click **OK**. If you choose a wizard, Word walks you through a series of dialog boxes to build the document, as shown in step 6. If you choose a template, the template appears on-screen, as explained in step 5.

5 Here's a fax form template. In many of the documents, Word inserts filler text—for example, Your Company Name. Just insert the cursor between the brackets and replace or add text, as needed, to complete your document.

6 If you choose a wizard, Word's wizard feature opens on-screen. From here you can proceed to build your document step by step—dialog boxes will walk you through the procedure. Simply follow the prompts and click the **Next** button to continue. Depending on the type of wizard you select, the dialog boxes will vary. When you complete the final wizard dialog box, the finished template appears on-screen and you can add and replace your own text as needed.

HOW TO...

Build an Excel Worksheet

The second most popular program included in Microsoft Office is Excel. To start the program, click the **Start** button on the Windows 95 taskbar; select **Programs** and **Microsoft Excel**. With Excel, you can create worksheets, for example, to total sales for your company or to track your personal expenses. You can use Excel to set up a budget or to create an invoice. You can also use Excel as a simple database program (as covered in "Create an Excel Database" on page 211) and to create charts (see "Create an Excel Chart" on page 191).

To set up a worksheet, you enter text, numbers, dates, and formulas into the grid of columns and rows in the worksheet. Excel provides many shortcuts for setting up the worksheet, as covered in this part of the book.

What You Will Find in This Section

Move Around the Worksheet

When you start Excel, you see a blank worksheet on-screen. In Excel, each individual spreadsheet is called a *worksheet*. The worksheet is a grid of rows and columns. Within each worksheet page in Excel, you can enter data, perform calculations, organize information, and more. Worksheets look like grids, with intersecting columns and rows that form little boxes, called *cells*.

You can move around an Excel worksheet using the mouse or the keyboard. As you move your mouse pointer around on-screen, you'll notice it changes shape. Sometimes, it's the arrow pointer you've come to know and love, and other times, it's a strange-looking, giant plus symbol. When the mouse pointer is inside the worksheet area of your screen, it takes the shape of a plus sign. Anytime you move the mouse pointer outside the worksheet area, it becomes the arrow-shaped pointer again.

To move from cell to cell, click the cell to which you want to move. The cell you click becomes highlighted, or selected. A dark line, called a *selector*, always surrounds a selected cell. When you select a cell, it is active and ready to accept any numbers or text you type.

You can also select more than one cell at a time. To do this, click the first cell you want to select, hold down the left mouse button, and drag over the other cells you want to select. This highlights all the cells you drag over. Let go of the mouse button and they're selected.

Sometimes, you can get lost in the vast forest of worksheet cells, so one of the first things you need to learn is how to read cell names, called *addresses*. Excel worksheets are laid out like grids, and each cell in the grid has a name or reference based on which row and column it's in.

Excel labels columns with alphabet letters, and rows with numbers. Cell names always reference the column letter first, and then the row number. For example, the cell in the top-left corner in a worksheet is A1. If you become confused about which cell you're in, look at the reference area below the menu bar, called the Name box (if you've worked with other spreadsheet programs, you may know this box as the Reference box). (You can also use the scroll bars to see other parts of the worksheet.)

You can also use the keyboard to move around in Excel. Part 4 provides a table of Excel Key combinations.

You can move to a specific cell in the worksheet by selecting the **Go To** command from the **Edit** menu. In the Reference text box that appears, type the name of the cell to which you want to move, and click **OK** or press **Enter**.

Begin Guided Tour Select a Cell

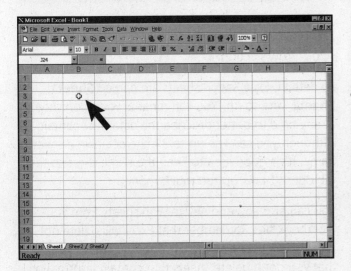

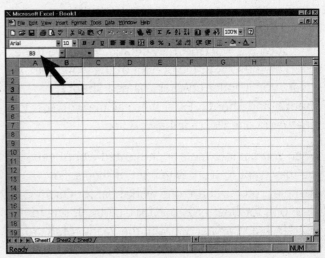

1 Point to the cell you want to select. The pointer should look like a fat plus sign.

3 The cell's address appears in the Name box on the Formula Bar.

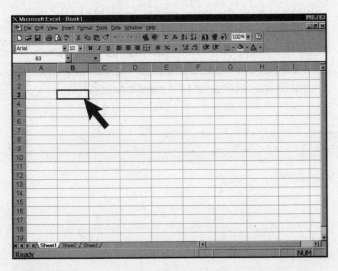

2 Click the mouse button, and Excel selects that cell. You see a thick black border around the cell.

Work with Worksheets

The grid of columns and rows that you see on-screen is a *worksheet*. By default, you have three sheets. If you look at the bottom of the worksheet screen, you'll notice little tabs named **Sheet1**, **Sheet2**, and **Sheet3**. Excel stores all the worksheets together in one file, called a *workbook*.

When you get into more sophisticated worksheets, you may want to work with a set of sheets. For example, you may have one worksheet for Quarter 1 sales, one for Quarter 2, one for Quarter 3, one for Quarter 4, and a final one with the Yearly totals. You can easily add more worksheets to your workbook, as demonstrated in a later Guided Tour.

To select a specific sheet to work with, you click the sheet tab to make it active in the worksheet window. If you've added additional worksheets, things get a little crowded when trying to read the tabs. If you want to select a worksheet that is not on-screen, you can use the scroll arrow buttons on the scroll bar to scroll through the sheet names until the one you want appears. The following table shows each worksheet scroll arrow's action:

By default, Excel's worksheets are named **Sheet1**, **Sheet2**, and so on. You can rename your worksheets at any time to better describe the data they contain. Although you can use up to 31 characters in a sheet name, it's a good idea to keep the name short so the tab doesn't take up too much room.

You can also add and delete worksheets from your workbook file. Remember that Excel will delete not only the sheet but all the data on that sheet. Be sure that you don't delete sheets that contain information you need. When Excel deletes a worksheet, it's permanently gone.

You can charge the order of the worksheet tabs by selecting a tab name and dragging it into a new location among the other tabs. You can copy your worksheets, too—press and hold the **Ctrl** key while dragging the tab name to a new location.

Click This Button	*To*
	Scroll to the first sheet in the workbook.
	Scroll to the previous sheet.
	Scroll to the next sheet.
	Scroll to the last sheet in the workbook.

Begin Guided Tour   Rename a Sheet

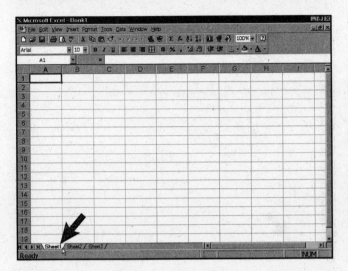

1 Right-click the sheet tab of the sheet you want to rename.

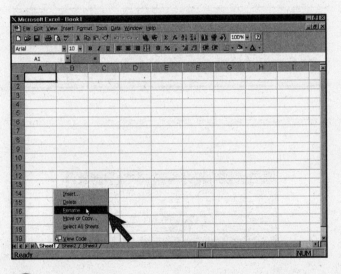

2 A shortcut menu pops up on-screen. Select the **Rename** command.

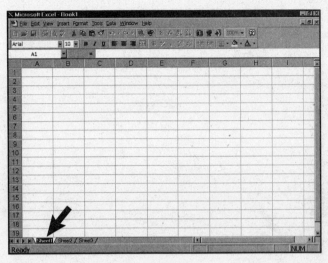

3 The sheet's tab name is highlighted. Type a new name (up to 31 characters). Press **Enter**.

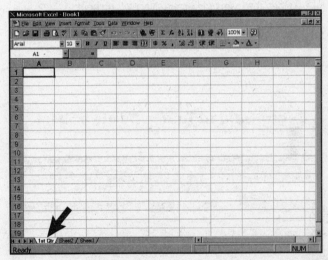

4 Excel displays the new name on the worksheet tab.

A quick way to rename a sheet is to double-click the tab and then type a new name. Press **Enter** when finished.

Begin Guided Tour   Add a Sheet

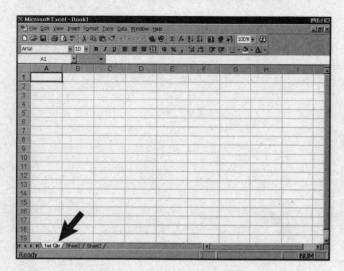

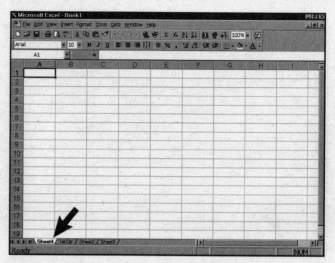

1 To add a sheet to your workbook, click the worksheet tab before which you want to insert a new sheet.

2 Open the **Insert** menu and select **Worksheet**.

3 Excel inserts a new sheet and gives it a default name.

To add a worksheet after the last sheet in your workbook, just insert a new sheet anywhere and drag it to the end of the tab display.

Begin Guided Tour   Delete a Sheet

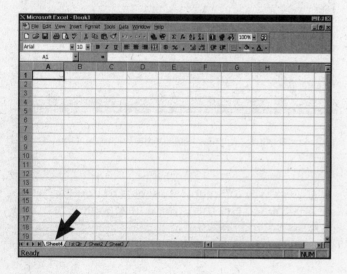

Microsoft Excel

The selected sheet(s) will be permanently deleted.

• To delete the selected sheets, click OK.
• To cancel the deletion, click Cancel.

OK   Cancel

3 You are prompted to confirm the deletion. Click **OK**. Excel deletes the worksheet and all its data. Excel does not automatically renumber existing sheet names.

Another way to delete a sheet is to right-click the sheet and choose the **Delete** command from the shortcut menu.

1 Select the sheet you want to delete.

2 Open the **Edit** menu and select the **Delete Sheet** command.

Enter Text and Numbers

A worksheet can contain three basic types of entries: *labels*, *values*, and *formulas*. (There are also *functions*, which are simply built-in formulas. You can type up to 255 characters in a cell, text, or numbers.

Excel refers to text data as a *label*; Excel cannot perform calculations on entries that are labels. For example, if you type the word **February** into a cell, you won't be able to perform a mathematical function or calculation with it—it's just a word.

Excel refers to numerical data as a *value*; Excel can calculate value entries. Values include numbers, dates, and times. For example, if you type the number 1024, you can do something with that, such as multiply or add.

The third type of data is a *formula*, which is simply an entry that tells Excel to perform calculations on the values in a cell or group of cells.

Let's say you've created a budget worksheet. In this type of worksheet, you may include a worksheet title, column labels for each month, and row labels for each expense category. All of these entries would be text (labels). Within the columns for each month, you may enter the expenses for that category. These entries would be numbers (values). For each month, you may want to calculate the total expenses. This entry would be a formula.

The rest of this task focuses on how to enter two of the basic types of entries—labels and values. Remember, labels and values include text, numbers, and dates.

Excel displays different data types in different positions in your worksheet cells. A text entry always lines up to the left side of the cell it's in. However, you can change the alignment. If the text entry is too long, it will spill over to the cells next to it, unless those cells contain data. If those cells contain data, the displayed entry will be truncated; the actual entry is still intact—you just can't see it. You need to widen the column.

Numbers always line up to the right of the cell. By default, numbers appear in the General number format (no specific number format). You can change how the numbers appear (change the alignment, use a number format such as currency, make entries bold, and more). Learn about formatting in the next section, "Format an Excel Worksheet," page 161. If you enter a number and see something strange such as **####**, it means the number is too big to fit within the cell. To fix this problem, you can change the number format or widen the column (open the **Format** menu, select **Column**, then select **AutoFit Selection**).

Using Valid and Invalid Values

When entering numbers (values), you need to know the difference between valid numbers and invalid numbers.

> Valid numbers include the numeric characters 0-9 and any of these special characters: . + - ( ) , $ %

> Invalid numbers are any characters not mentioned as valid numbers. (The letter Z, for example, would not be considered a valid number because it's a letter.)

Special characters are considered valid numbers because they are used in creating mathematical problems, equations, formulas, and so on. When you enter numeric values, you can include commas, decimal points, dollar signs, percentage signs, and parentheses.

What if you want your numbers to be treated like text? Say you want to use numbers for a ZIP Code instead of a value. To do this, you have to precede your entry with a single quotation mark (') as in '90210. The single quotation mark is an alignment prefix that tells Excel to treat the following characters as text and left-align them in the cell.

Enter a Date or Time

Another type of value you can include in a worksheet are dates and times. For example, you can use dates to keep track of when you incur an expense, when you complete a project, when you received a bill, and so on.

Excel keeps track of dates by assigning each date a serial number, starting with the first day in the century. No matter how the date appears in the cell, Excel thinks of the date as this serial number. With this tracking method, you can use a date in a calculation. For example, you can figure out how many days a bill is past due.

Excel keeps track of times by storing them as a fractional part of 24 hours (military time). For example, 8:20 P.M. is 20:20. Again, this tracking method enables you to create calculations with times.

To enter the date, use one of the following formats:

4/4/95

4-Apr-95

4-Apr (assumes current year)

Apr-4 (assumes current year)

To enter a time, type the time using one of these formats:

9:45 PM

9:45:55 PM

21:45

21:45:55

Use these steps to enter a date or time:

1. Select the cell you want.

2. To enter a date, type the date using one of the formats described in the text.

3. Press **Enter**. Excel enters the date or time.

To enter the current date in a cell, press **Ctrl+;**. To enter the current time, press **Ctrl+Shift+:**.

Use the Formula Bar

When you start typing data into a selected cell, the data immediately appears in that cell and also in the Formula Bar above the worksheet window. (You see the Formula Bar to the right of the Name box.) Three new buttons appear in the Formula Bar as you enter data:

The Formula Bar

Button	Description
✕	**Cancel** button Click it to cancel your entry.
✓	**Enter** button Click it to confirm your entry.
=	**Edit Formula** button Opens the Formula Palette to help you build a worksheet formula.

You can use the Formula Bar buttons to help you enter data. When you finish typing in data, press **Enter** or click the **Enter** button (the button with a check mark) on the Formula Bar. You can also click in the next cell in which you want to enter data. If you change your mind about the entry, click the **Cancel** button.

Begin Guided Tour   Enter Text

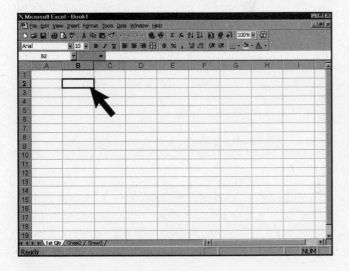

1 Select the cell you want to use.

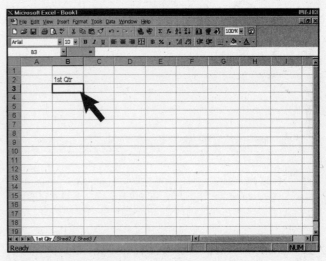

3 Excel enters the text and moves to the next cell below your entry. You can also press an arrow key to accept the entry and move the cell pointer to the next cell in the direction that the arrow key points. (Remember, text data lines up to the left of a cell.)

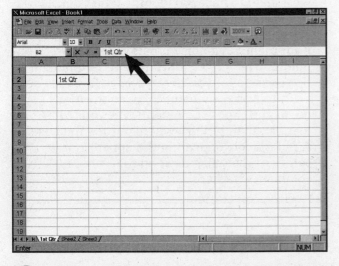

2 Start typing in your entry. As you type, take a look at the Formula Bar. Excel displays an **X** and a check mark next to the entry in the Formula Bar. Click the check mark or press **Enter** to accept the entry. Click the **X** or press **Esc** to cancel the entry.

You can edit your worksheet entries just like you edit data in any other program. Use the **Backspace** or **Delete** keys to remove characters and make corrections. You can make your edits directly in the cell or to the entry as it appears in the Formula Bar.

Begin Guided Tour Enter Numbers

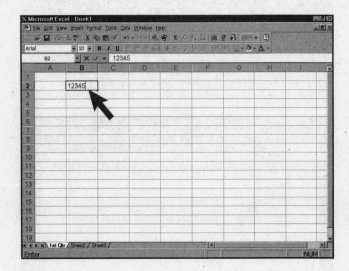

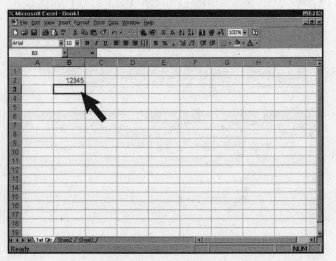

1 Select the cell you want and type the number. (To type a negative number, precede the number with a minus sign or enclose the number in parentheses.)

3 If you press **Enter**, Excel accepts the number and moves to the next cell. If you click the check mark, Excel accepts the number but the same cell remains selected. Notice the numbers are flush right in the cell. All number data aligns to the right of a cell.

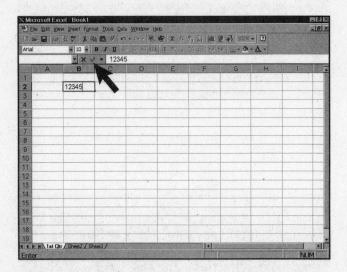

You can add comment notes to any cell in your worksheet to help you identify data or explain the contents. Any comments you add do not affect the data and do not appear when you print them. Anytime you pass your mouse pointer over a cell with comments, a comment box pops up for you to read. Select the cell you want to add a comment to, open the **Insert** menu and choose **Comment**; type your comment in, then click anywhere outside the box. A red triangle appears in the upper-right corner of the cell, indicating that it has a comment attached.

2 As you type the entry, Excel displays an **X** and a check mark next to the entry in the Formula Bar. Click the check mark or press **Enter** to accept the entry. Click the **X** or press **Esc** to cancel the entry.

Fill In Data

To make it as quick as possible to create a worksheet, Excel provides some shortcuts for entering data. One of the handiest shortcuts is the *AutoFill* feature. Excel's AutoFill lets you quickly enter a series of data into your worksheet cells or duplicate the same data as many times as necessary. A data series is any series of related information, such as days of the week, number sequences, months, etc. For example, let's say you need to enter the days of the week into your worksheet. Instead of typing each day label into its own cell, you can use the AutoFill feature to insert all seven days for you.

If you want to use the same entry data in neighboring cells, such as copy a category heading, select and drag over the cell containing the entry, then drag over the cells you want to fill. You can drag up, down, left, or right. Next, open the **Edit** menu, select **Fill**, and choose the direction you want to go (up, down, left, or right). Excel fills the cells with a copy of the original data.

To fill cells with a data series, you can use the cell's *fill handle*. Type in the first item in the data series, such as the day of the week or month, then select the cell. As you've seen previously, when you select a cell, a box appears around it—they call this the cell *selector*. In the bottom-right corner of the cell selector is the *fill handle*—a very tiny square dot. Move your mouse pointer over this handle and the pointer takes the shape of a crosshair. Drag the fill handle over the cells you want to fill, and Excel completes the data series for you.

You can use the AutoFill feature to fill a series of months (such as January, February, March), a series of numbers (such as 1, 2, 3), a series of dates (such as Monday, Tuesday, Wednesday), or a series of formulas. You simply enter the first value and let Excel fill the rest. If you're using a series of dates, all you have to type is one date to start the series. But if you're using numbers, you'll need to enter two variables to start the fill series.

The starting value determines how the fill works. If you start with a date that Excel recognizes and then drag the fill handle to extend the series, Excel fills in the cells you dragged over with a series of dates. If you start with a formula or value and then fill, Excel simply copies the formula or value.

To fill a series of numbers, you have to enter the first two values to show Excel the pattern that you want. For example, to fill a series of numbers 1, 2, 3, you would enter 1 and 2 in adjacent cells and then fill. To enter a series of numbers in increments of 10 (10, 20, 30, and so on), you would enter 10 and 20 in two cells and then fill.

If you are filling a text entry and it contains a number, Excel will increment the number in the fill. For instance, if you enter Qtr 1 and then fill a range, Excel will enter Qtr 2, Qtr 3, and so on.

Use AutoComplete

Many spreadsheet users spend a lot of time entering repetitive data, or the same labels over and over again in their columns. You can use Excel's AutoComplete feature to help you out. It works like this: Excel keeps track of your column entries for each cell. Instead of retyping an entry, you can right-click the next cell and display a list of words you've already used in previous cells. You can then just choose from the list, which is a lot faster than typing the word again.

You may notice the AutoComplete feature kicking in while you enter text. If you repeat the first few letters of a previous entry, AutoComplete guesses that you're typing in repeat information and finishes your word for you. If it's not the correct word, however, just keep typing and ignore AutoComplete.

To use the AutoComplete feature, follow these steps:

1. Type the labels in the first cells of the column.

2. When you're ready to enter a duplicate label in another cell, right-click the empty cell to open a shortcut menu.

3. Select **Pick from List**. A list of previously typed words appears beneath your cell.

4. Choose the word you want from the list and it's automatically inserted into the cell.

Begin Guided Tour   Use the AutoFill Feature

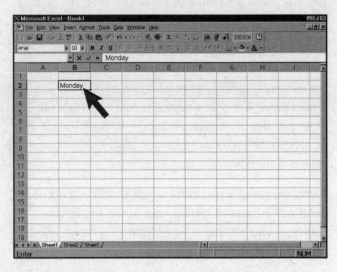

1 Type the entry into the first cell. If you want to use a number series, enter the first two values in two cells next to each other. Then select the cell or cells that contain the entry.

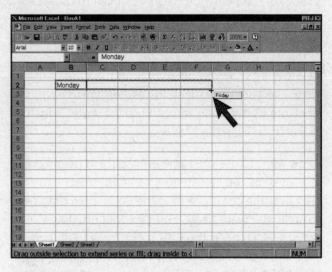

3 Drag across the range you want to fill. As you drag, you see an outline and a ScreenTip displays the value of the last cell you are currently hovering over with the mouse pointer, as shown in the example.

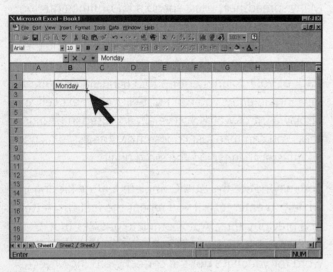

2 Put the mouse pointer on the fill handle in the lower-right corner of the cell. The pointer should look like a small crosshair.

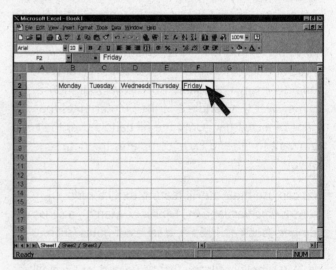

4 Release the mouse button and Excel fills the series in.

Work with Ranges

A *range* is a rectangular group of connected cells that you can connect in a column, a row, or a combination of columns and rows or even an entire worksheet. You can connect them in a number of ways, but they always have to be contiguous (next to each other in a sequence) and they must form a rectangle.

Why use ranges? Well, you can select a range and use it to format a group of cells with one simple step. You can use a range to print only a selected group of cells. Ranges are useful in formulas too. I'll explain later in the "Enter Formulas" task on page 144.

You can use the mouse (explained in the Guided Tour), or the keyboard to select a range. To use the keyboard, move to the first cell, hold down the **Shift** key, and use any of the arrow or movement keys to highlight the range. To deselect a range, click outside the selected range.

Excel indicates a range with a range reference (name), which refers to its specific anchor points: the top-left corner and the lower-right corner. A range with more than one cell uses a colon to separate the anchor points. For example, range A1:B3 would include cells A1, A2, A3, B1, B2, and B3.

You can give a range name to a single cell or a large group of cells. Once you define the name, you can use it in formulas. Range names appear in the Name Box at the top of your worksheet. When you have more than one range name in a worksheet, you can click the **Name Box** drop-down list to see a list of ranges and make your selection from the list.

The following table describes the mouse and keyboard shortcuts for selecting ranges.

Movement with the Mouse or Keyboard

To Select	Mouse Shortcut	Keyboard Shortcut
A column	Click the column letter	Press **Ctrl+Spacebar**
A row	Click the row number	Press **Shift+Spacebar**
The entire worksheet	Click the **Select All** button (the blank spot above the row numbers and to the left of the column letters)	Press **Ctrl+Shift+Spacebar**

Begin Guided Tour   Select a Range with the Mouse

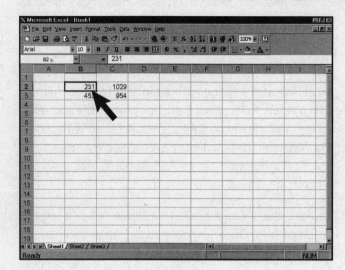

1 Click the first cell in the range.

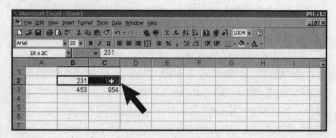

2 Hold down the mouse button and drag across the cells you want to include.

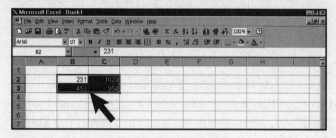

3 The range appears highlighted on-screen. When you have selected the range you want, release the mouse button.

Begin Guided Tour   Naming a Range

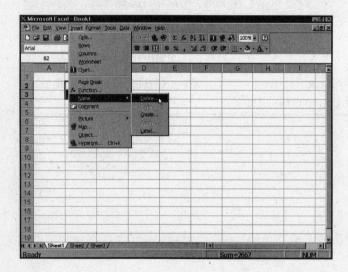

1 First select the cell or range you want to name, then open the **Insert** menu and select the **Name Define** command.

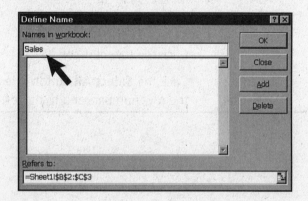

2 You see the Define Name dialog box. Type the range name you want to use. You can type up to 255 characters. Be sure not to type a name that looks like a number or cell reference. Also, you must start the name with a letter, underscore (_), or backslash (\).

Guided Tour Naming a Range

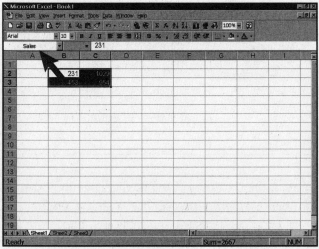

Another way to reference a range by name is to type the name directly into the Name Box at the far left end of the Formula bar. Simply click inside the box and type in a name. Press **Enter** when finished.

3 Click **OK** to exit the box. You have named the range, and the reference name appears in the Name Box at the top of your worksheet.

Enter Formulas

I once knew someone who entered all the numbers in his worksheet and then used his desk calculator to figure the totals. It kind of defeats the purpose of a computerized worksheet. In a spreadsheet program like Excel, you can use formulas to figure totals and perform all kinds of other calculations for you. *Formulas* are simply mathematical operations you can perform on the entries in your worksheet: addition, subtraction, multiplication, and division.

The real thrill of using a worksheet is seeing how quickly you can create a formula. You simply point to the values you want to use. You don't have to worry that the calculation is incorrect; Excel won't make a mistake. Also, you can change any of the values included in the formula, and Excel will update the formula automatically. Pretty cool.

A formula consists of these key elements: the equal sign (=), the values or cell references you want to calculate, and the operators (mathematical operations such as addition and multiplication). All formulas start with an equal sign. Take a look at this simple formula:

=A1+A2

This formula takes the value in cell A1 and adds it to A2. You can include more than two references, and you can use other operators, as listed in the following table.

Operator	Description
+	Addition
-	Subtraction or negation
*	Multiplication
/	Division
%	Percentage
^	Exponentiation
=	Equal
<	Less than

Operator	Description
<=	Less than or equal to
>	Greater than
>=	Greater than or equal to
<>	Not

Another thing to keep in mind when creating Excel formulas is *operator precedence*. In any given formula, Excel performs the series of operations from left to right in the following order:

1st	All operations in parentheses.
2nd	Exponential equations or operations.
3rd	Multiplication and division.
4th	Addition and subtraction.

The order of operations determines the result of your formula. For example, if you want to determine the average values in cells A1, B1, and C1, and you enter the formula =A1+B1+C1/3, you'll probably get the wrong answer. Why? Because Excel will divide the value in C1 by 3, then add that result to A1+B1. That's because division takes precedence over addition—the rule of operator precedence.

One way around this problem is to group your values in parentheses. In the previous example, =A1+B1+C1/3, enclose the values in parentheses to instruct Excel to do the addition first, then divide the result by 3. The formula looks like this now, =(A1+B1+C1)/3.

Error, error! If you get an error message after typing in a formula, check and make sure you didn't designate a blank cell, divide by zero or a blank cell, delete a cell being used in the formula, or use a range name when a single cell address is expected.

Begin Guided Tour   Enter a Formula

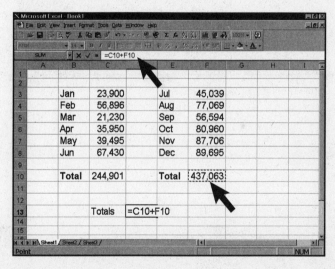

1 Select the cell that will contain the formula and type an equal (=) sign. That tells Excel you are about to enter a formula.

2 Click the first cell you want to include in the formula. (You can also directly type in the cell reference.) The cell reference appears in the active cell and in the Formula Bar.

3 Type an operator such as the + sign.

4 Click the next cell you want. Continue typing operators and selecting cells until you complete the formula.

(continues)

Guided Tour   Enter a Formula   *(continued)*

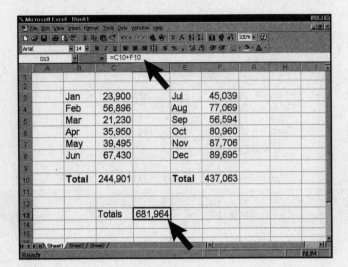

5 When you complete the formula, click the Check Mark in the Formula Bar. In the Formula Bar, you see the actual formula. The cell displays the results of the formula.

In some formulas, you may want to perform two calculations. To make sure you get the results you want, use parentheses to surround the part of the formula you want to calculate first—the rule of operator precedence. Compare these two formulas: (10*3)+5=35 and 10*(3+5)=80. See how the results differ greatly?

Use Absolute Addresses in Formulas

To make it easy to copy and move formulas, Excel uses a concept that is known as *relative addressing*. Excel doesn't think of the cells you include in the formula as a set location. Instead, Excel thinks of the cells as a relative location. Here's an example, let's say you've filled the first three cells in column A with the following data:

A1   50

A2   100

A3   =A1+A2

When you create the formula in cell A3, Excel doesn't think "Go to A1." Instead, it identifies the first cell in the formula as two above the current one. Basically, Excel thinks this: "Go up two cells, get this value, go up one cell, get this value, and add the two." Now if you move or copy the formula, the same set of instructions work. If you copied this formula to cell B3, you'd get =B1+B2. This type of referencing saves you from having to create the same formula over and over again. You can just copy it. The formula is relative to its location in the worksheet.

In some formulas, however, you may want to refer to a specific cell, that is, you don't want the formula to adjust to its location. For example, suppose that you have several columns of pricing information that refer to one discount rate, in cell A1. When you create this formula, you always want to refer to cell A1; you don't want the references to adjust. In this case, you use a different type of cell reference: an *absolute reference*. An absolute reference stays put—it doesn't change just because the formula might move to another cell.

With this type of reference, you can tell Excel to adjust the column but keep the row reference the same, or adjust the row but keep the column reference the same. To change a reference from relative to absolute, type a **$** sign before the part you want to make absolute. Here are some examples:

$A1   Refers always to column A, row will vary.

A$1   Refers always to row 1, column will vary.

A1   Refers always to cell A1.

Begin Guided Tour   Enter an Absolute Cell Reference

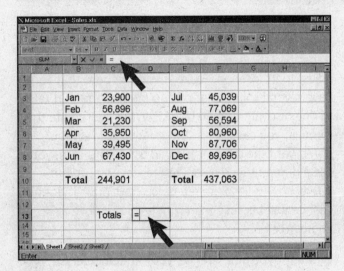

1 Select the cell that will contain the formula and type an equal (=) sign.

3 Press **F4**. Excel enters dollar signs before the column letter and row number of the cell reference.

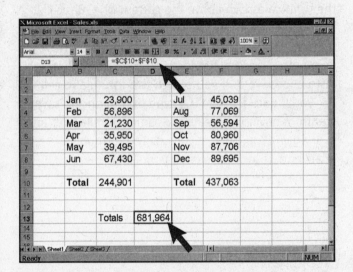

2 Click the cell reference you want to include in the formula as an absolute reference.

4 Continue building the formula until it is complete, pressing **F4** every time you want to make a cell reference absolute. When finished, click the Check Mark in the Formula Bar (or press **Enter** on the keyboard) and Excel creates the formula. When you copy a formula with an absolute reference, Excel will not update the reference.

Sum Numbers

The most common calculation used in worksheets is summing a group of numbers. To make it quick and easy to create this type of formula, use the **AutoSum** button on the toolbar. When you click this button, Excel looks around the formula cell and guesses what you want to sum.

Excel bases its guess on what you want to sum by looking up and suggesting the range above the selected cell, if those cells contain values. If the cells above the formula cell do not contain values, Excel looks to the left and suggests the range to the left of the selected cell. In many cases, Excel guesses right, but even if it doesn't, you can simply drag across the range you want to sum. Press **Enter** and you have a sum formula.

The formula that Excel creates looks something like this: =SUM(A1:B5). (The numbers inside the parentheses reflect the selected range to sum.) This formula is actually a *function*, a prebuilt formula. In addition to the SUM function, Excel includes more than 100 other special functions. The next section, "Use Functions" on page 150, covers using a function.

Use Excel's *AutoCalculate* feature to automatically sum a range of cells and display the figure on your status bar. To see it work, just highlight a cell or range of cells containing data you want summed up; then look down on your status bar for a running total.

If you right-click the status bar, you can access a shortcut menu for viewing the average of the selected cells, or you can get a count of the selected items.

Begin Guided Tour   Use AutoSum

1 Select the cell that you want to contain the sum formula. Click the **AutoSum** button.

2 Excel guesses which cells you want to sum, surrounds them with a faint line, and enters them in the Formula Bar and cell. Check that the correct range is selected. If that range is correct, skip to the next step. Otherwise, select the correct range you want to sum.

3 Press **Enter**. Excel enters the function into the cell and advances to the next cell below. In the cell in which you entered the sum formula, you see the results of the function. When the cell is selected, you see the actual function in the Formula Bar.

Use Functions

Excel provides many calculation functions for you so that you don't have to get out your slide rule and old trigonometry books. You can calculate a loan payment, find the square root of a number, calculate an average, count items in a list, and much more using one of the 100 or more Excel functions. (Part IV of this book has a list of the most common functions and what they do.)

Functions are a shorthand way for entering complex formulas. For example, the AVERAGE function condenses a longer formula into a shorthand version. Rather than have this formula

   =(A1+A2+A3+A4+A5)/5

You can use this function

   =AVERAGE(A1:A5)

Like a formula, the function starts with an equal (=) sign. The next part is the function name: usually a short, abbreviated word that indicates what the function does. After the function name, you see a set of parentheses, and inside the parentheses, you see the arguments—the values used in the calculation. Arguments can be a single value, a single cell reference, a series of cell references or values, or a range. Different functions require different arguments. Some arguments are mandatory; some are optional. You can look up the specific format or syntax for the function in online Help or in your Excel manual.

For the function to work properly, you must enter the parts in the correct order and format. You can type the function and hope you remember the right order for the arguments, or you can have Excel build the function for you using the Paste Function button on the Standard toolbar—the easier method. The Guided Tour explains how to use this feature.

Begin Guided Tour Enter a Function with the Paste Function Feature

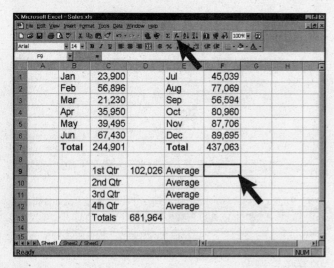

1 Select the cell you want to contain the function, and click the **Paste Function** button. You can also open the **Insert** menu and select **Function**.

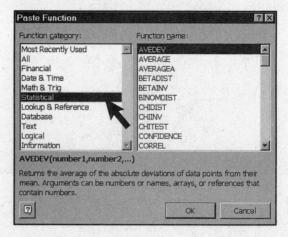

2 The Paste Function dialog box appears. This dialog box lists available Excel functions. From the **Function Category** list, select a type of function you want to use.

Guided Tour   Enter a Function with the Paste Function Feature

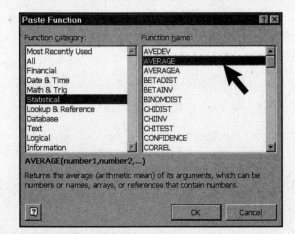

3 The **Function Name** list box lists the functions in that category. Click the function you want to use.

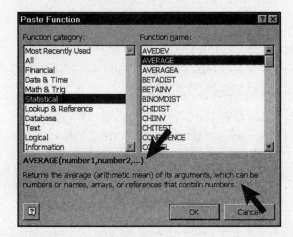

4 Excel lists the function format and a short description at the bottom of the dialog box. Click the **OK** button.

5 Another box appears. The box may vary in its appearance based on the function you selected. In this box, you enter the arguments for the function. You can enter values directly into the dialog box, or you can drag the box out of the way and make your selections on the worksheet by clicking the desired cells.

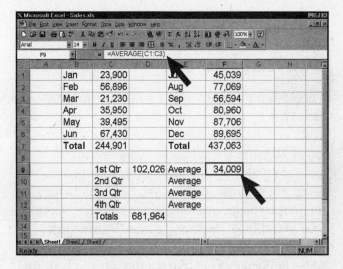

6 After you enter all the arguments, press **Enter** or click the **OK** button. Excel creates the function. Here the AVERAGE function averages each month's sales totals in a quarter.

To edit a function you created with the Paste Function feature, select the cell containing the function, open the **Insert** menu and select **Function**, or click the **Paste Function** button. This reopens the dialog box for entering the values or argument.

Edit and Delete Entries

You can easily make a change to any entries in the worksheet—text, numbers, dates, formulas. Being able to make changes to the values in your worksheet is what makes Excel such a valuable analysis tool. You can change a key value and Excel will update all the formulas. You don't have to do any recalculating.

With Excel, you can edit the entry directly in the cell as described in the Guided Tour. You can also edit directly in the Formula Bar select the cell you want to edit, press **F2** or click in the Formula Bar, make the change, and press **Enter**.

When you are editing an entry, you need to move the insertion point (the flashing vertical pointer) to the spot you want. Part 4 provides a table of keys you can use to move the inserting point.

Speculate with Scenarios

A new feature Excel 97 offers is the *Scenario Manager*. With this tool, you can plug in different sets of values into your formulas and check how the outcomes vary. This is fun to do when you want to speculate what might happen if you change a few values. For example, perhaps you want to examine different scenarios involving a loan payment. You may have a worksheet displaying a monthly mortgage amount for a $200,000 house at an interest rate of 8.5%. But what would the monthly amount be for a $150,000 house? With the Scenario Manager you can play around with the effects of different values in your formulas.

To create a scenario with Scenario Manager, follow these steps:

1. Open the worksheet containing the data you want to use to create a scenario.

2. Open the **Tools** menu and select **Scenarios**. This starts the Scenario Manager.

3. Click the **Add** button to open the Add Scenario dialog box.

4. Type a name for the scenario that describes the changes you want to enter. For example, to determine a lower interest rate on a house payment, you might name the scenario **200K@8.25%**.

5. Press the **Tab** key to move to the **Changing Cells** text box, then click the cell containing the value you want to change.

6. Click **OK**. The Scenario Values dialog box appears and displays the current values in the cells you want to change.

7. Type in the new values you want to apply, then click **OK**. The Scenario Manager displays the name of the new scenario.

8. To view a scenario, click its name and click the **Show** button. Excel replaces the cell's current values with the new values you specified for the scenario.

Begin Guided Tour   Edit Data

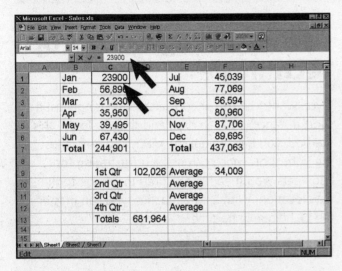

1 Double-click the cell you want to edit. The insertion point appears within the current cell. Use the arrow keys to move to the spot you want to make the change. Then make any changes and press **Enter**.

2 Excel updates the entry.

Begin Guided Tour   Edit Data

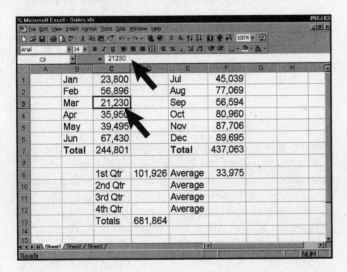

1 Select the cell or range you want to delete and press the **Del** key.

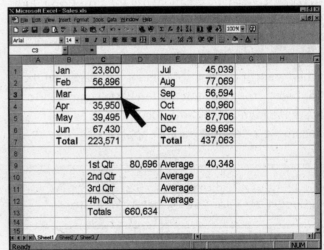

2 Excel deletes the selected cell or range. If any of the selected cells are referenced in a formula, the formula is updated, also.

Move and Copy Data

When you create a new worksheet, you should spend some time planning the layout. What is the purpose of the worksheet? Think about what information you need to enter and what information you need to calculate. Spend some time considering the best way to set up and enter the data.

Excel provides some shortcuts for entering the data, for example, the Copy command. Let's say your budgeted amounts for your categories may be the same from month to month. Rather than type them over and over again, you can copy the values. (You can also fill data as a shortcut for entering information.

If you don't get things in the right spot, you can move them. You may want to move something over to make room for something else, for instance. (You can also insert new rows and columns, as covered in "Insert and Delete Rows and Columns" on page 159.)

To copy or move information, use the **Cut, Copy**, and **Paste** commands. These commands work the same   from application to application and they all use the Windows Clipboard. When you cut or copy something, it is placed on the Clipboard. You can then use the Paste command to paste the item in the same document, in another document, or even in another application.

> Like to use keyboard shortcuts? Press **Ctrl+C** for Copy, **Ctrl+X** for Cut, or **Ctrl+V** for Paste.

Note that when you move or copy values, the values are pasted identically. Formulas are handled differently, though. What happens to the formula when you move or copy depends on the type of reference. Excel adjusts all relative references. All absolute references stay the same.

Use the Drag-and-Drop Technique

If you want to move or copy a selected range just a short distance, you can drag and drop it. To use this method, you have to get the mouse pointer in just the right spot, which can make it frustrating for beginners. You then have to drag the range to the new location. With a little practice, you can master the technique in no time.

Use these steps to drag and drop data:

1. Select the cell or range you want to move or copy.

2. Move the mouse pointer over the selection's border. The mouse pointer should change to an arrow.

3. To copy the range, hold down the **Ctrl** key. To move a range, you don't need to press any keys.

4. Drag the border. As you drag, you see an outline of the selected data. When the data is in the spot you want, release the mouse button.

> To copy the contents and formatting of cells from one worksheet to another, first click the tab for the worksheet containing the cells you want to copy. Next, hold down the **Ctrl** key and click the worksheet tab you want to copy to. Then select the cells you want to copy. Open the **Edit** menu, select **Fill**, then select **Across Worksheets**. This opens the Fill Across Worksheets box. Select **All** (to copy cell contents and formatting), **Contents** (copies contents only), or **Formats** (copies formatting only). Click **OK** and Excel copies the data.

Begin Guided Tour   Move or Copy Data

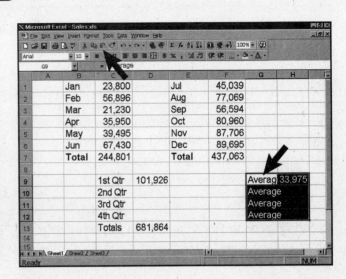

1 Select the cell or range you want to move, and click the **Cut** or Copy button.

3 Click the **Paste** button. Excel moves (or copies) the selected cell or range.

2 A message at the bottom of the screen prompts you to select a destination. Select the cell at the upper-left corner of where you want the pasted cells. Keep in mind that Excel will overwrite any cells in the destination area.

Find and Replace Data

If you have a worksheet that fits on one screen, you can quickly spot an entry. In a bigger worksheet, though, you may have to scroll and look, scroll and look to find an entry. Suppose that you keep track of customer orders in a worksheet and the worksheet contains hundreds of rows. Finding a customer by scanning would be difficult. Instead, you can use Excel's **Find** command to quickly move to the customer you want.

The companion to Find command is **Replace**. With this command, you can find and then replace a value.

For example, if you changed a product name from Widget to Wadget, you could search and replace and make the changes automatically.

If Excel can't find a match, you see a message saying so. You can try the command again and double-check your spelling. Also, check to make sure you are searching the right type of item. You can tell Excel to look in formulas, values, or notes. Be sure to choose the correct option.

Begin Guided Tour   Find Data

1 Open the **Edit** menu and select the **Find** command.

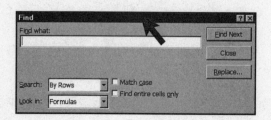

2 You see the Find dialog box. In the **Find what** text box, type the information you want to find.

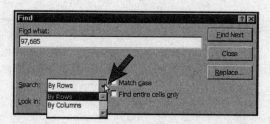

3 Select how to search by displaying the **Search** drop-down list and then choosing **By Rows** or **By Columns**.

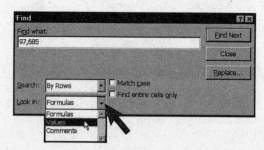

4 Select where to look by displaying the **Look in** drop-down list and clicking one of the following: **Formulas**, **Values**, or **Notes**.

Guided Tour Find Data

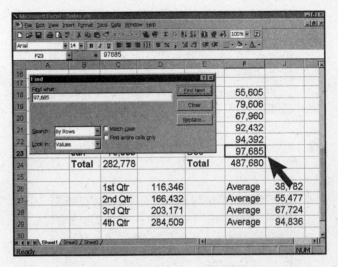

5 If you want Excel to match the case as you've typed it, check the **Match case** check box. If you want to find only entire entries (not partial entries), check the **Find entire cells only** check box.

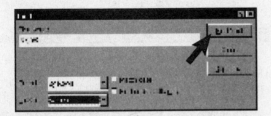

6 After you enter the text to find and select any search options, click the **Find Next** button to find the first matching entry.

7 Excel moves to and highlights the first matching entry. Continue clicking **Find Next** until you find the entry you want. Then click the **Close** button to close the dialog box.

Begin Guided Tour Replace Data

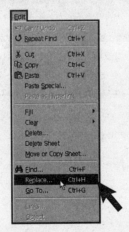

1 Open the **Edit** menu and select the **Replace** command.

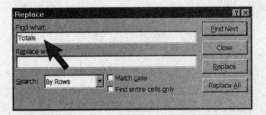

2 You see the Replace dialog box. In the **Find what** text box, type the information you want to find.

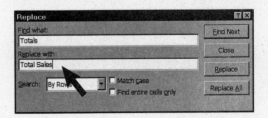

3 In the **Replace with** text box, type the entry you want to use as the replacement.

(continues)

Guided Tour Replace Data *(continued)*

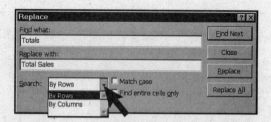

4 Select how to search by displaying the **Search** drop-down list and then choosing **By Rows** or **By Columns**.

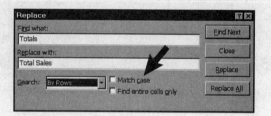

5 If you want Excel to match the case as you've typed it, check the **Match case** check box. If you want to find only entire entries (not partial entries), check the **Find entire cells only** check box.

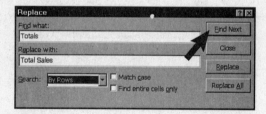

6 After you make your selections, click the **Find Next** button to find the first matching entry.

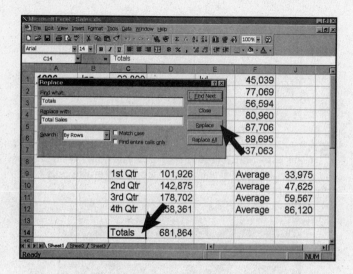

7 Excel moves to the first match; the Replace dialog box remains open. Do one of the following:

Click **Replace** to replace this occurrence and move to the next.

Click **Find Next** to skip this occurrence and move to the next.

Click **Replace All** to replace all occurrences.

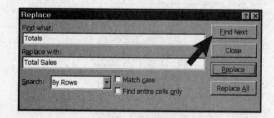

8 When all the replacements you want are made, click the **Close** button to close the dialog box.

Insert and Delete Rows and Columns

Imagine using the old paper-and-pencil method of tallying up numbers. Your budget is perfect, with all 50 categories and the totals exactly right. Then your boss asks you to add a new expense category right in the middle of the worksheet, or your boss wants you to delete an expense category. Arghhh!!! You'd have to re-enter all the data. Not with Excel. In Excel, you can easily insert and delete rows or columns.

To delete a row or column, you select the row or column that you want by clicking the row number or column letter. You can delete multiple rows or columns by dragging across them (in the number or letter area). Remember that you are not only removing the row or column from the worksheet, you are also removing all the data in that row. Be sure that's what you intend. If you make a mistake, immediately undo the deletion.

If you forget to include something in the worksheet, you can easily add a new row or column, and Excel will move existing rows down or columns over to make room. You can easily rearrange your worksheet so that you include all the data you need.

Just as with deleting, you start by selecting the column or row. If you want to insert more than one row or column, select the number you want to insert.

One thing to remember when you insert a row or column is that the new row or column does not include any formatting (styles, font sizes, and so on) you may have applied to the existing rows or columns. You'll need to format the new row or column. (You can learn more about formatting in Excel in the next section.)

Begin Guided Tour   Delete a Column or Row

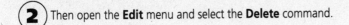

1 Select the column(s) or row(s) you want to delete.

2 Then open the **Edit** menu and select the **Delete** command.

3 Excel deletes the column(s) or row(s) and shifts the remaining cells over.

Begin Guided Tour   Insert a Column or Row

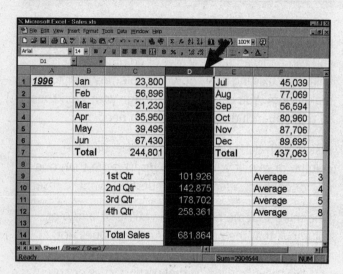

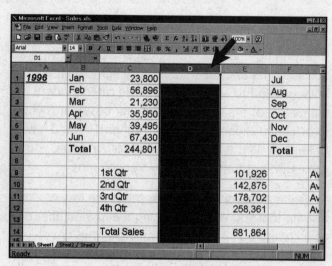

1 Select the row or column. Excel inserts new rows above the selected row. Excel inserts new columns to the left of the selected column.

3 Excel inserts the row or column and shifts the existing cells over.

2 Open the **Insert** menu and select the **Rows** command to insert a row. Select the **Columns** command to insert a column.

HOW TO...

Format an Excel Worksheet

The first task in creating a worksheet is entering the appropriate data, which is the focus of the previous section. Once you enter the data, you will probably want to spend some time enhancing the appearance of the data to make sure that the worksheet is easy to read and understand. Ask yourself these questions: Do you need to point out key factors? Do you need to clarify the numbers?

If so, you can use bold, italic, and underline to call attention to data. You can also add a border to data, shade a certain area, or change the color of a worksheet element. You can also change the number format so it is clear what the numbers represent (currency, units, or percents, for example).

Take a moment to examine how the worksheet looks on the page. Do the headings align over the columns of data or do you need to make adjustments? Does the data fit on the page or do you need to adjust the margins? If so, you can make these changes as well.

This part of the book covers all of these formatting options you can use with Excel. Use this section to make your worksheet picture perfect.

What You Will Find in This Section

Make Entries Bold, Italic, and Underline

Your worksheet is going to be a mix of information, numbers, and text. Usually, each set of numbers has a row and column heading that identifies what the data means. To make it easy to spot these headings, you may want to add emphasis; you can make them **bold**, *italic*, or underline, or apply all three styles.

You may also want to use these font styles to call attention to other data in the worksheet. For example, you may want to boldface the totals so that they are easy to see on the page, or you may want to italicize the worksheet title. Formatting is the key to making your spreadsheet data look good. Excel makes it easy to select any of these formatting styles using the toolbar.

Excel's Formatting toolbar holds many of the same buttons as the Formatting toolbar in Word, such as bold or italics. To use any of the buttons, simply click the formatting you want to apply. You can also control formatting through the Format Cells dialog box. Open the **Format** menu and select **Cells** to open the dialog box. You can easily change many of the formatting features for your data by clicking the appropriate tabs in this dialog box and selecting from the available options.

If you don't know how to format your spreadsheet, let Excel's *AutoFormat* feature give you some professional help. Simply select the data you want to format (or the whole worksheet); then open the **Format** menu and choose **AutoFormat**. A dialog box appears with options you can try. Look through the **Table Format** list to find a formatting style you want to use, and look at the sample to see if you like it. Click **OK** and Excel formats your data accordingly.

Excel provides over 15 different autoformats to choose from. The formats include preset number, border, font, patterns, alignment, column width, color, and row height selections. You simply select a style that you like, and Excel will make all the formatting changes at once.

Use the Format Painter Tool

In many cases, you will make several formatting changes to the same cell or range. For example, you may change the number format (see "Change the Number Format" on page 176 for tips about number formats) for your totals and make them bold. Once you get the range formatted the way you want it, you may like the look so much that you want to use it on other cells or ranges in the worksheet. Do you need to go through all the same formatting steps again? No. With Excel, you can copy the formatting with the **Format Painter** button on the Standard toolbar.

1. Select the cell or cells that contain the formatting you want to copy. Then click the **Format Painter** button on the toolbar (it's the one with a paint brush on the button).

2. The mouse pointer displays a little paintbrush next to the cross. Select the cells that you want to format with the same options.

3. When you release the mouse button, Excel applies the formatting to the selected range.

Begin Guided Tour   Format Data with the Toolbar

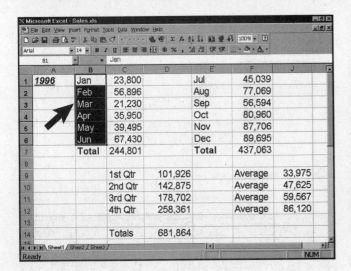

1 Select the cell or range you want to change.

3 Excel formats the selected range or cell accordingly. In the example shown, all three formatting styles are applied to the text.

You can turn off bold, italic, and underline by selecting the range and then clicking the appropriate button again.

2 Use the formatting buttons on the Formatting toolbar to do any of the following:

B Click the **Bold** button in the toolbar (it looks like a capital B) to make the entries bold.

I Click the **Italic** button in the toolbar (it looks like a capital I) to make the entries italic.

U Click the **Underline** button in the toolbar (it looks like a capital U) to underline the text in the cells.

Begin Guided Tour Use AutoFormat

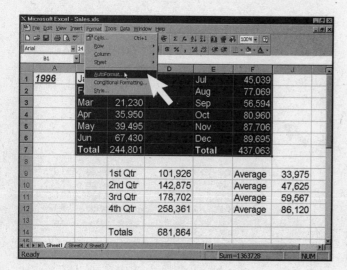

1 Select the data you want to format, open the **Format** menu, and choose **AutoFormat**.

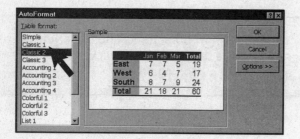

2 The AutoFormat dialog box appears with options you can try. Look through the **Table Format** list to find a formatting style you want to use. Select a style from the list.

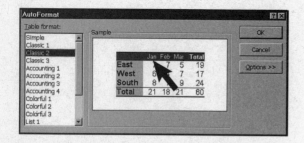

3 Look at the Sample to see if you like the style.

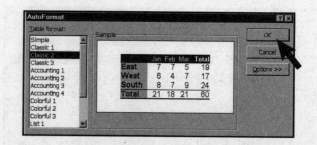

4 Click **OK** to exit the box.

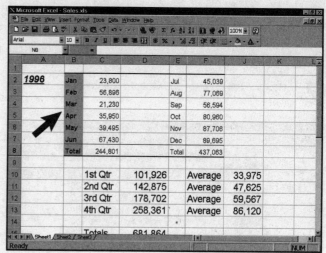

5 Excel formats your data accordingly.

Change the Font

When you create a new worksheet and enter data, Excel uses the default font and font size (Arial 10-point type). With this formatting, all the data has the same emphasis and looks the same. If you find this font is too small or if you prefer a different font, you can make a change. For example, you may want to use a large, more decorative font for your title. You may want to use a larger point size for all the entries.

With Excel, you can change the font for the entire worksheet or for only a selected cell or range. The fastest way to change the font is by using the Formatting toolbar. However, with this method, you can only make one change at a time, and you can't see a preview of the change. If you want to make several changes, you can use the Format Cells dialog box. The Guided Tour covers both methods.

If you make a change and realize immediately that you don't like it, you can click the **Undo** button on the Standard toolbar.

If you didn't undo the command immediately, you can still clear formatting by selecting the cell or range, opening the **Edit** menu, and selecting the **Clear, Formats** command. Excel clears all the applied formatting.

Begin Guided Tour Use the Toolbar to Change Fonts

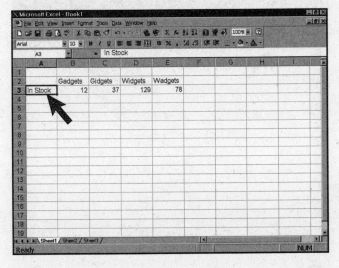

1 Select the cell or range you want to change (you can also select the entire worksheet). In this figure, a single cell is selected for change.

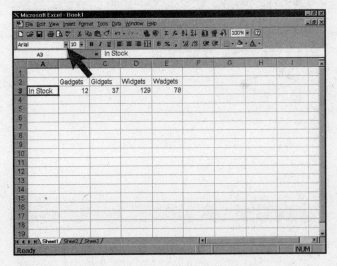

2 Next, click the down arrow next to the **Font** list.

(continues)

Guided Tour   Use the Toolbar to Change Fonts

(continued)

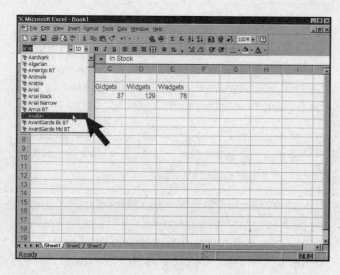

3 You see a drop-down list of font choices. Click the font you want. Excel makes the font change.

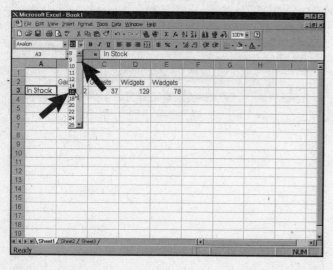

4 To change the size of the font, click the down arrow next to the **Size** list to see a list of font sizes, then click the size you want.

5 Excel formats the range with the new size (here, 16-point type). If necessary, Excel also adjusts the row height but not the column width.

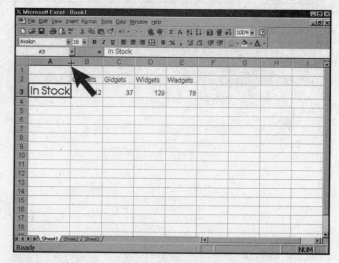

6 If you choose a font or size that makes your data wider than the existing column, you can resize the column. One way is to move the mouse pointer to the column border you want to resize until it becomes a two-sided arrow pointer. Then drag the border to a new size, as shown in this figure.

Begin Guided Tour Use the Format Cells Dialog Box

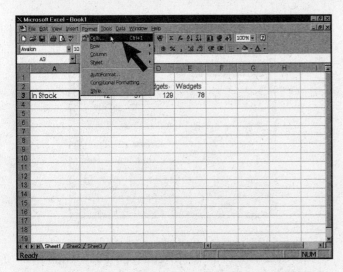

1 Select the cell or range you want to change, then open the **Format** menu and select the **Cells** command.

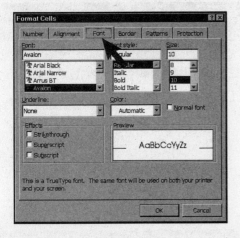

2 The Format Cells dialog box appears. If necessary, click the **Font** tab of the Format Cells dialog box to bring it to the front.

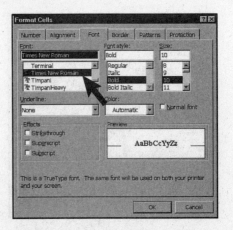

3 In the **Font** list, click the font you want.

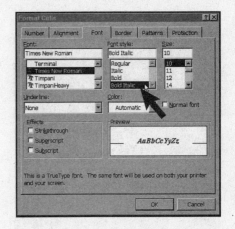

4 Select a style from the **Font Style** list. Click the size you want.

(continues)

Guided Tour Use the Format Cells Dialog Box

(continued)

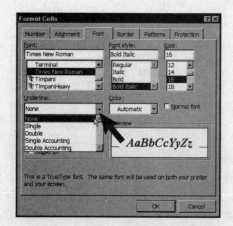

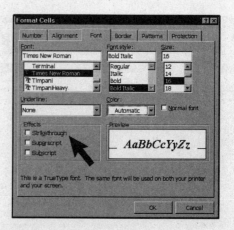

5 If you want to use a different type of underline, display the **Underline** drop-down list and click the underline style you want.

7 If you want any special effects, check the check box for any of these special effects: **Strikethrough**, **Superscript**, and **Subscript**. Look in the Preview area to see what the selected formatting looks like.

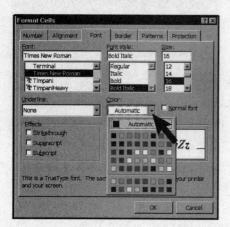

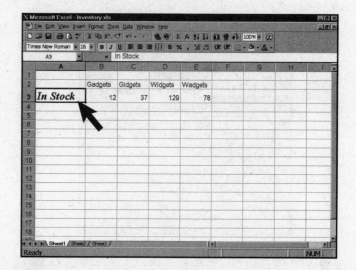

6 To add color to your data, select the **Color** drop-down box and choose a color from the list.

8 When you finish making changes, click **OK**. Excel formats the selected range with the options you selected.

Is your data too big for your column? Don't worry, you can resize the column. Turn to the task "Resize Columns and Rows" on page 182 to learn how.

Apply Conditional Formatting

nother formatting tool you can apply is *conditional formatting*. With conditional formatting, you can instruct Excel to change the formatting for a cell automatically if the cell's value changes. For example, if the value of a cell in your inventory spreadsheet falls below zero, you can instruct Excel to flag the cell with a heavy red line and shading, and boldfacing of the text. The formatting change will alert you to the cell and its contents. This is helpful when you're trying to keep an eye out for changing values.

You'll find the **Conditional Formatting** command on the **Format** menu. When the command is selected, the Conditional Formatting dialog box appears. From here you can set a cell value and specify a formatting style. You use the Conditional Formatting box to designate the condition of the argument. You can select from a variety of arguments to apply to the cell(s). For example, you can tell Excel to format the cell if its values fall between a specified range, or if

the cell's value equals a value you designate. It's up to you to define the parameters of the conditional formatting.

Like the previous task, you use a Format Cells dialog box to actually change the formatting you apply to the conditional cell. You can choose to change the font style (such as bold or italic), add a border around the cell, or change the cell's background color or pattern. Remember, in order for Excel to apply the formatting, it must first meet the criteria you establish.

When you use the Format Cells dialog box by clicking the Format button in the Conditional Formatting dialog box, only three formatting tabs appear (Font, Border, and Patterns), unlike the regular Format Cells box (open the **Format** menu and select **Cells**) which provides six tabs of formatting options.

Begin Guided Tour   Use the Conditional Formatting Feature

(1) Select the cell(s) containing the value or formula you want to format with conditional formatting.

(2) Open the **Format** menu and select **Conditional Formatting**.

(continues)

Guided Tour   Use the Conditional Formatting Feature *(continued)*

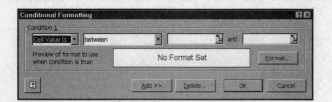

3 The Conditional Formatting dialog box appears.

4 Click the drop-down list at the far-left end of the box and choose the **Cell Value Is** option. With most scenarios that's the option you want to use (for example, if the cell's formula produces a value). However, if the cell contains a formula whose result is True or False, choose the **Formula Is** option.

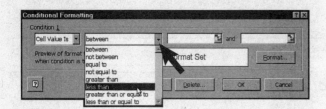

5 Click the next drop-down list to designate an argument to activate the conditional format in the cell. For example, to red flag the cell if the value falls below a particular number, select the **Less Than** option. Depending on the argument you select from the list, the remaining text boxes will vary.

6 In the remaining text boxes, finish entering in the data to complete the condition for formatting the cell. In the figure, for example, I want to flag the cell if the value falls below (less than) 105000, so I type **105000** in the next text box.

7 To specify formatting for the cell, click the **Format** button.

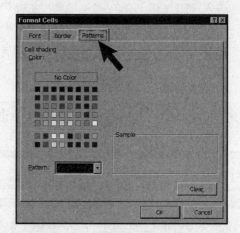

8 The Format Cells dialog box appears. Use the Font, Border, and Patterns tabs to change the formatting, such as cell shading or color. For example, if you want to format the cell with a color or pattern background, click the **Patterns** tab.

Guided Tour   Use the Conditional Formatting Feature

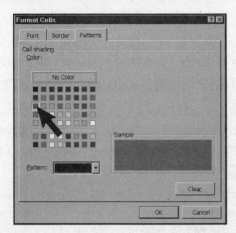

9 To choose a background color from the **Patterns** tab, simply click a color from the palette.

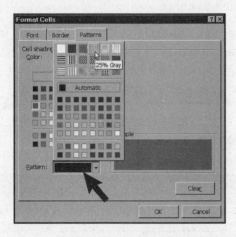

10 To choose a pattern, click the **Patterns** drop-down list and select a background pattern.

11 Select any additional formatting options you want for the cell from the Font, Border, and Patterns tabs. When finished, click the **OK** button.

12 You return to the Conditional Formatting dialog box where you can see a preview of the formatting you selected. Click **OK** to exit the dialog box.

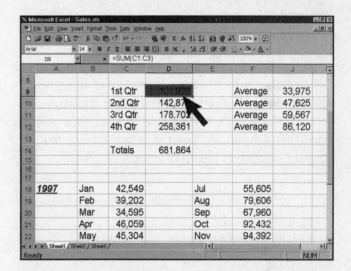

13 Anytime the cell value meets the requirements for conditional formatting, Excel applies the formatting options you selected, as shown in this figure.

To delete a conditional format, reopen the Conditional Formatting dialog box and click the **Delete** button. Then select the conditions you want to delete and click **OK**. Click **OK** again to exit the Conditional Formatting dialog box.

Change the Alignment of Entries

By default, Excel automatically aligns data as soon as you enter it into a cell. Excel aligns text on the left and numbers on the right. In addition, text and numbers are initially set flush with the bottom of the cell. After you make the entries, you may need to make some adjustments to these default alignments.

In addition to making adjustments to column headings, you may want to center your worksheet title. You can fake a centered title by using the space bar to place the title in about the center of the column, or you can have Excel center the title perfectly.

The easiest way to make any alignment changes is to use the toolbar buttons. The Formatting toolbar contains three alignment buttons you can choose from: Left, Center, and Right. You can also use the Format Cells dialog box to designate alignment.

The Alignment tab in the Format Cells dialog box has plenty of alignment options to choose from. Take a look at this list to help you decipher your choices:

- **Horizontal** options enable you to specify a left/right alignment in the cell(s). With the **Center across selection** option, you can center a title or other text inside a range of cells.

- **Vertical** options enable you to specify how you want the data aligned in relation to the top and bottom of the cell(s).

- **Orientation** options let you flip the text sideways or print it from top to bottom (as opposed to left to right).

- The **Text Control** check boxes allow you to wrap long lines of text within a cell (normally, Excel displays all text in a cell on one line), shrink text to fit inside a cell, and merge cells.

Begin Guided Tour Aligning Entries with the Toolbar

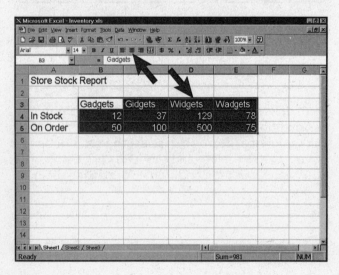

1 Select the cell or range you want to change and do one of the following:

To left-align the entry, click the **Align Left** button.

To center the entry, click the **Center** button.

To right-align the entry, click the **Align Right** button.

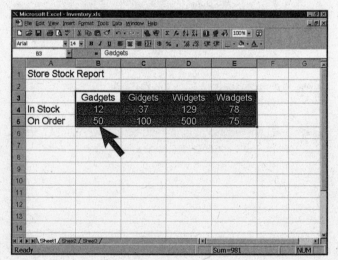

2 Excel changes the alignment of the selected cell or range. In this example, Excel centers all the text inside the range.

Begin Guided Tour Center a Heading

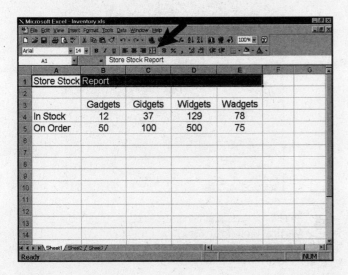

1 Select the range that contains the heading and the range that you want to center across. If you just select the cell with the entry, this feature won't work properly.

2 Click the **Merge and Center** button.

3 Excel centers the headings across the selected columns.

Even though a centered title looks as if it is in a different cell, it is still in the same cell that you originally entered it in. If you try to edit the cell and it looks blank, try selecting the first cell in the row.

Begin Guided Tour Align Entries with the Format Cells Dialog Box

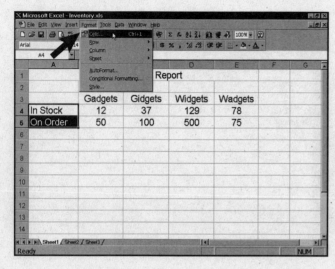

1 Select the cell or range you want to change; then open the **Format** menu and choose **Cells**.

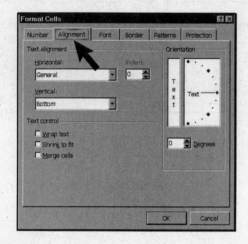

2 This opens the Format Cells dialog box. Click the **Alignment** tab to bring it to the front.

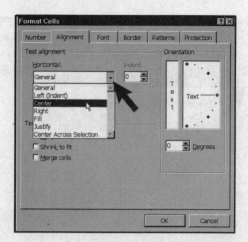

3 To change horizontal alignment, choose an option under the **Horizontal** drop-down list.

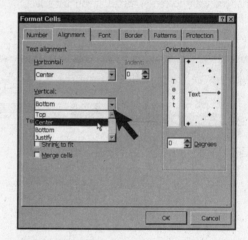

4 To change vertical alignment, select an option from the **Vertical** drop-down list.

Guided Tour Align Entries with the Format Cells Dialog Box

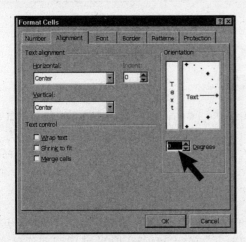

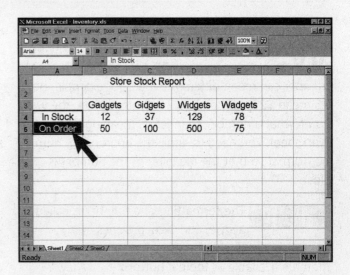

5 To change data orientation in the cell, you can use the **Orientation** dial to change data direction. Click the dial to rotate the data. Or, you can specify degrees of rotation with the **Degrees** spin box.

7 Click **OK** to exit the box and implement your alignment changes.

You can repeat an alignment format command in another cell. Just use the **Repeat Format Cells** command from the **Edit** menu.

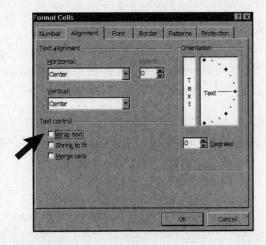

6 To wrap text onto other lines inside your cell, select the **Wrap Text** check box.

Change the Number Format

When you enter a number in Excel, it's entered as a plain number—**25**, for instance. But that number can mean different things. For example, does 25 mean $25, .25, or 25%? As you can see, the way you format a number changes its meaning. In your worksheet, you need to apply the appropriate number format so that the meaning of the number is clear.

$, % The formatting of a number is called a *style*, and Excel provides many number styles to choose from. The three most common are available as toolbar buttons (Currency, Comma, and Percent). You can also open the Format menu, select Cells, and use the Number tab to select from other available styles. The Guided Tour covers both methods.

If none of the predefined formats fits your needs, you can create your own custom format. Elect a format that's close to what you want, and then edit its code to match the custom format you want to create. To apply a custom format to other cells or ranges, display the **Number** tab in the Format Cells dialog box and click **Custom** in the Category list. The format code you defined will be listed with this category. Click it and click **OK**.

> If you see number signs (######) in a cell or range after formatting, you know the number with the new formatting is too wide to appear within the current column width. "Resize Columns and Rows," on page 182, covers how to change the column width.

Decode the Format Codes

If you use the **Format Cells** dialog box to select a number style, you'll notice that the styles aren't named, but are represented by codes. The easiest way to figure out the codes is to select a style and view the sample in the dialog box.

If you are curious or if you want to create a custom code, you can take a closer look at the parts of a number format. You can include up to four parts: a positive number format, a negative number format, a format for zeroes, and a format for text. Each part is separated by a semicolon. Within each part, a code represents digits. The following table explains the most common digits used in a style:

#	Placeholder for digits. If the digit is a nonsignificant zero, it does not appear.
0	Placeholder for digits. Zeroes appear. (For example, 9.5 in the format #.00 would display as 9.50.)
?	Placeholder for digits. Uses a space for nonsignificant zeroes.
.	Decimal point.
,	Thousands separator.
%	Percent sign. Excel multiplies entry by 100.
;	Separates positive number format from negative number format.
Underline	Skips the width of the next character. Use this to align positive numbers and negative numbers displayed in parentheses.

Begin Guided Tour Use a Number Style Button

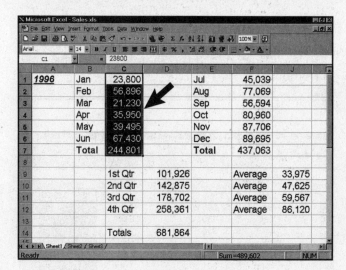

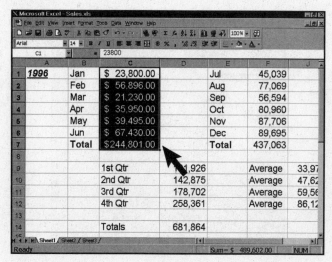

1 Select the cell or range you want to change and do one of the following:

$ To use currency style, click the **Currency Style** button.

% To use percent style, click the **Percent Style** button.

, To use comma style, click the **Comma Style** button.

2 Excel applies the style. In this example, the **Currency** style was selected; Excel added dollar signs to the numbers.

If necessary, change the number of decimals that appear by clicking the **Increase Decimal** or **Decrease Decimal** buttons on the toolbar (to the right of the Number format buttons).

Begin Guided Tour Use the Format Cells Number Tab

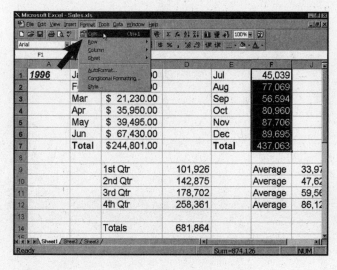

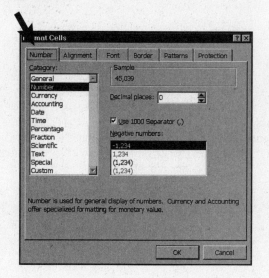

1 Select the cell or range you want to change; open the **Format** menu and select the **Cells** command.

2 Click the **Number** tab to bring it to the front.

(continues)

Guided Tour   Use the Format Cells Number Tab   *(continued)*

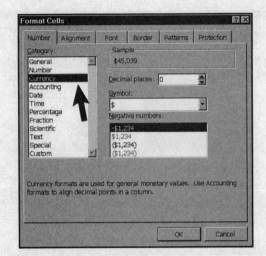

3 In the **Category** list, click the category you want.

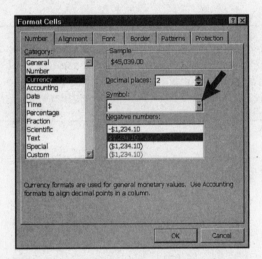

4 Excel displays the styles and options for this category. If you select a format that requires you to specify additional options, make your selections. For example, if you choose the **Currency** category, you can designate the number of decimal points to be displayed, which dollar sign symbol to use, and how you want negative numbers displayed.

You can preview what the selected number style will look like in the **Sample** area of the Number tab.

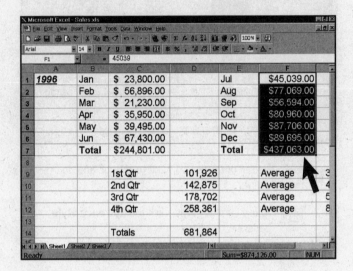

5 Click **OK** to exit the box and Excel makes the number format change.

Add Borders

You can use the **Underline** button in the toolbar to underline the entries, but if you want to underline the entire cell, you need to use a border. But why stop with underlines? You can add a complete border to any cell, or add partial borders to sides of a cell; and you can select from several line styles. For example, you can add a double-underline to your totals, or you can draw a thick outline around your headings to make them stand out.

You can do all of this with the **Borders** button on the toolbar. After you add a border, you can easily delete it at any time. To remove a border, select the range again, click the **Borders** button and click the **None** option. Excel removes the border. Remember that a cell can contain a border to the left

or right and top or bottom. If you can't find the border to turn off, try selecting the cell next to, above, or below the cell you *think* has the border.

> If you use the toolbar button to select a border, the button will reflect the last border you used. You can select a range and click the button to apply the same border to another selection.

If the **Border** button doesn't include the line style you want, you can use a different method to add a border: Use the **Border** tab of the Format Cells dialog box. The Border tab lets you control more details concerning the border.

Begin Guided Tour   Change the Border with the Toolbar

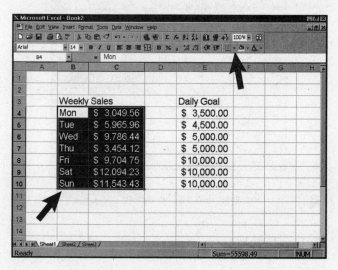

1 Select the range that you want to add a border to and click the **Border** button.

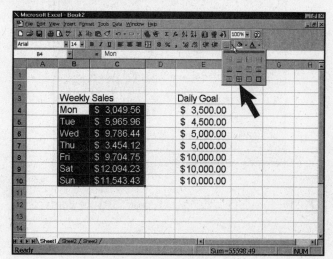

2 You see a drop-down list of common borders. Click the button that represents both the side(s) you want to border and the line style you want to use. Excel applies the border.

Begin Guided Tour   Use the Border Tab

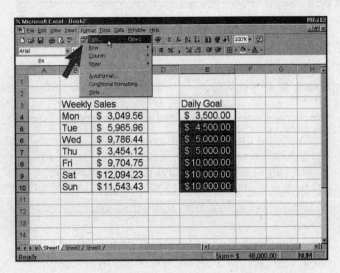

1 Select the cell or range you want to change; open the **Format** menu and select the **Cells** command.

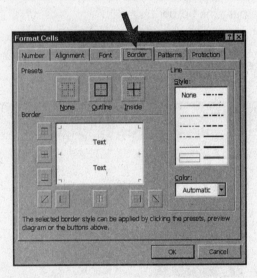

2 The Format Cells dialog box appears. Click the **Border** tab.

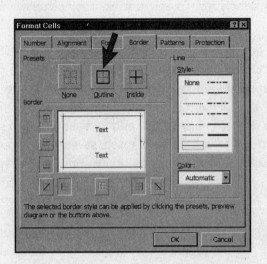

3 In the **Presets** area, click the border style you want: **None**, **Outline** (all sides), **Inside** (inside lines only).

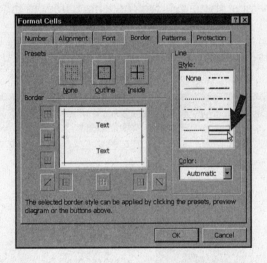

4 In the **Line** area, select a line style to use. Click the one you want.

Guided Tour Use the Border Tab

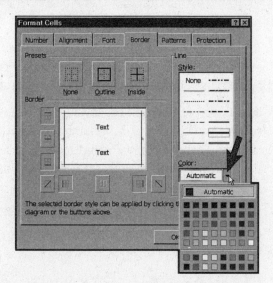

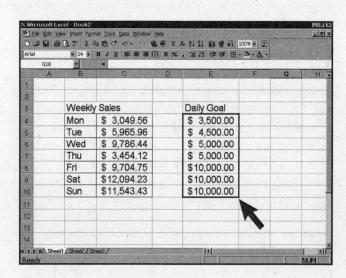

5 If you want to add color to the border, click the **Color** drop-down list and choose a color.

7 Click **OK** to exit the dialog box, and Excel applies the border.

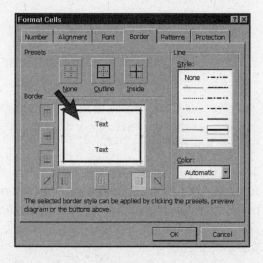

6 To customize which sides of the border are included, in the **Border** area, click the individual buttons representing the sides you want. Then preview how the border will look.

Resize Columns and Rows

In a new worksheet, all the columns are the same size. As you enter data, you'll find that this size isn't going to work for all your entries. For example, you may have an entry that is too big. With a long entry, several things can happen. For text that is too long, Excel truncates the entry. For numbers that are too long, you see the entry with nothing but **#####**. In these instances, you can widen the column to make more room for your data.

In some cases, you may have a really short column, perhaps with just two or three characters. In this case, you can narrow the column. There's no sense wasting the space.

You can manually resize a row or column by moving the mouse pointer to the row or column border heading you want to change, then drag the border to a new size. You can also specify an exact increment to widen or deepen a column or row, as explained in the following tips.

Resizing Tips

When you are resizing columns and rows, keep the following tips in mind:

- You can change the width of several columns or rows at once by selecting the ones you want to change. Then drag one border to change them all.

- To have Excel adjust the column width to fit the largest entry in that column, double-click the right column border, next to the column letter.

- If you want to enter an exact value for the column width, start in the column you want to change. Then open the **Format** menu and select the **Column Width** command. Type a value and click **OK**.

- To specify an exact row height, select the row, open the **Format** menu and choose **Row Height**. Type a value and click **OK**.

- For a shortcut, select the row or column, then right-click and choose the **Row Height** or **Column Width** from the shortcut menu and specify a measurement.

- Want Excel to fit your data into the column for you? Select the cell or column, open the **Format** menu, choose **Column**, **Autofit Selection**. Excel fits the column to the longest entry.

- You can hide a column by dragging the right border past the left. Hide a row by dragging the bottom border past the top.

- If you change the column width and then want to return to the default width, open the **Format** menu and select the **Column Standard Width** command. Click **OK**. Excel adjusts all columns in the worksheet.

Begin Guided Tour Manually Adjust Column Width

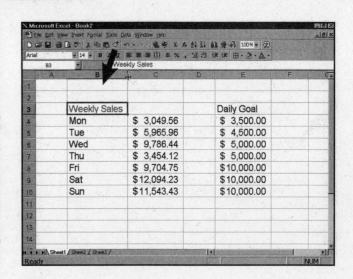

1 Point to the right column heading border. The pointer will change to a thick line with arrows on either side of it. This indicates the pointer is in the right spot.

3 When the column is as wide as you want, release the mouse button. Excel adjusts the width.

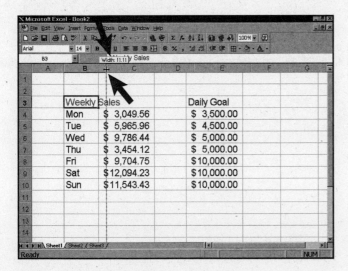

2 Hold down the mouse button and drag to a new width (expressed in points). As you drag, you see an outline of the column border. A measurement of the width appears as a ScreenTip near the pointer.

Begin Guided Tour   Change the Row Height

1 Point to the border below the row number that you want to change. The pointer will change to a thick vertical line with arrows on either side of it. This indicates the pointer is in the right spot.

3 Stop dragging the mouse and Excel adjusts the row height.

2 Drag up or down to change the height. As you drag, you see an outline of the row border. The row height appears in the reference area of the formula bar, as well as a ScreenTip next to the pointer.

Add Headers and Footers

If you print a worksheet, you see why the sheet name and page number at the top and bottom of the worksheet. This is the header and footer. You can select to use another predefined header or footer, turn off the header or footer, or create a custom header or footer.

Before you create a custom header or footer, check the ones Excel has set up for you. Excel provides combinations of the key data you are likely to want to include: Your name, page number, sheet name, workbook name, and date.

If none of the predefined headers or footers is what you need, you can create your own, as explained in the Guided Tour.

Button	Description
A	Changes the font
#	Inserts page number
⊡	Inserts number of pages (for instance, you can print Page 1 of 12 using this button and the preceding button)
🗓	Inserts the date
🕐	Inserts the time
🗐	Inserts the file name
▭	Inserts the worksheet name

Begin Guided Tour   Use a Predefined Header or Footer

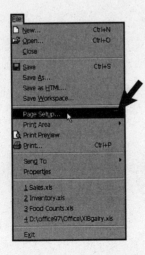

1 Open the **File** menu and select the **Page Setup** command.

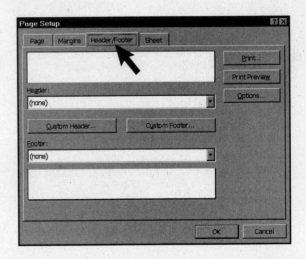

2 You see the Page Setup dialog box. Click the **Header/Footer** tab.

(continues)

Guided Tour   Use a Predefined Header or Footer   *(continued)*

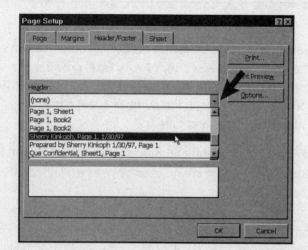

3 To use a predefined header, click the down arrow next to the **Header** drop-down list box. You see a list of predefined headers. Click the one you want.

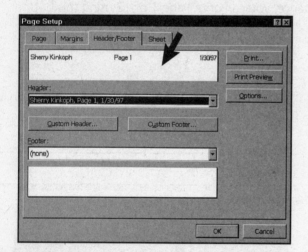

4 Excel displays a preview of the header in the dialog box. If you only want to add a header, skip to step 6.

5 To change the footer, click the down arrow next to the **Footer** drop-down list box; then click a predefined footer. Excel displays a preview of the footer in the dialog box. Click **OK** to exit the box.

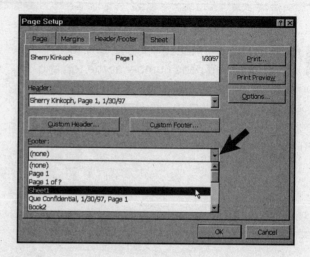

6 To see the header and footer, click the **Print Preview** button.

Guided Tour Use a Predefined Header or Footer

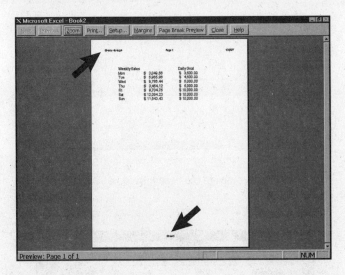

7 Excel displays the worksheet with the headers and footers you selected. (Click the **Close** button on the Preview toolbar to exit Print Preview.)

Headers are printed 1/2-inch from the top of the page, and footers 1/2-inch from the bottom. To change these margins, (see "Change Margins" on page 114).

Begin Guided Tour Create a Custom Header or Footer

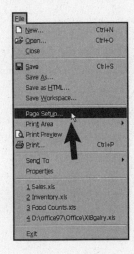

1 Open the **File** menu and select the **Page Setup** command.

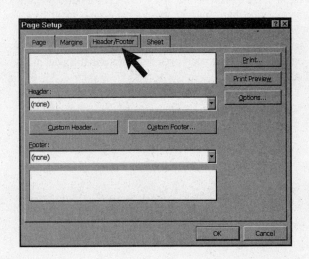

2 You see the Page Setup dialog box. Click the **Header/ Footer** tab.

(continues)

Guided Tour Use a Predefined Header or Footer *(continued)*

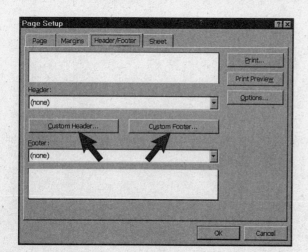

3 To create a custom header or footer, click the **Custom Header** or **Custom Footer** button.

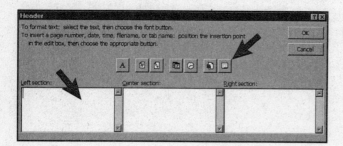

4 You see the Header or Footer dialog box, which has three sections: left, center, and right (these represent parts of the header, not the alignment of text). You also see buttons which enable you to insert special codes for the page number, date, worksheet name, and so on in the header or footer. Move to the section in which you want to enter text. Enter the text and codes you want. To insert a code, click the buttons that appear in the dialog box.

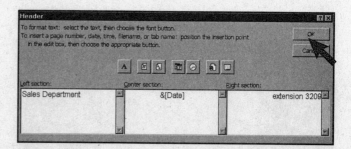

5 When you complete the header or footer, click the **OK** button.

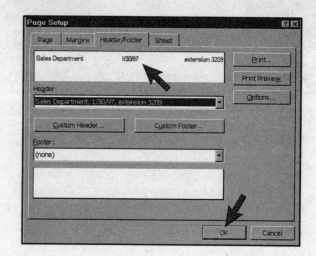

6 You return to the Page Setup dialog box, which shows your custom header and footers. Click **OK** to exit the dialog box.

Guided Tour   Create a Custom Header or Footer

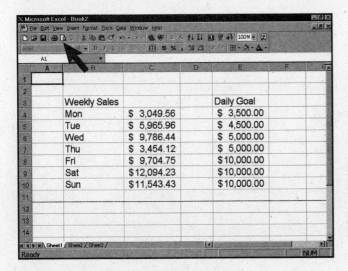

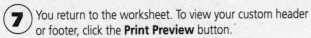

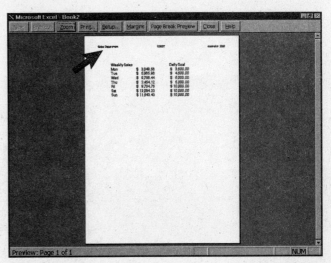

7 You return to the worksheet. To view your custom header or footer, click the **Print Preview** button.

8 Excel displays the worksheet with the custom header or footer. To exit the Print Preview feature, click the **Close** button on the Preview toolbar.

HOW TO...

Create an Excel Chart

I f you just look at the numbers in a worksheet, you may find it hard to spot trends or patterns. Also, the relationship of the numbers may not be readily apparent. To visually show trends, patterns, and relationships, you can create a chart.

Excel makes it easy to quickly create a chart from your worksheet data, and you can select from one of many different chart types to convey your message. For example, if fourth-quarter sales peak dramatically, you may want to create a bar chart. To compare product sales, you may want to create a pie chart. Interested in showing a trend over time, such as your household spending? Consider a line chart.

In addition to the features for creating a chart, Excel also provides a complete set of tools for formatting and editing a chart, as covered in this section.

What You Will Find in This Section

Create a Chart

A chart takes your data and represents it visually. You can think of a chart as a snapshot picture of your data. With this picture, you or your intended audience can more easily see the relationship among the data. For example, if you chart sales by division, you can see, at a glance, which division leads in sales. If you create a pie chart of household spending, you can easily see which area has the biggest slice of the pie. You not only can visually see the relationship, but you can see patterns and trends, and you can quickly summarize data in a chart.

To make it easy to chart your data, Excel includes the Chart Wizard. This feature leads you step by step through the process of creating a chart. You can choose to add a chart on the worksheet or as a separate sheet in the workbook. If you create a chart on the same sheet as your data, Excel prints it side-by-side with your worksheet data. If you create a chart on a separate worksheet, you can print it separately. Both types of charts link to the worksheet data that they represent, so when you change the data, Excel automatically updates the chart.

Excel also offers you great flexibility when it comes to types of charts (there are a total of 14 standard chart types you can apply). After you select the data to chart, Excel will prompt you to select the type of chart you want to create. What's the difference among the chart types? Each has a specific purpose; you can select the chart type that best conveys your message. Excel provides 14 chart types to choose from, and each chart has several subtypes, or styles, which gives you even more flexibility. The table on the following page explains each chart type.

> If you change your mind while working through the ChartWizard, click the **Back** button to go back a step. Also, if you don't like the chart type that you selected, you can change it using Chart Wizard.

As you're working with charts, you may come across charting terms that you're unfamiliar with. Here's a list of explanations for the various chart terms you'll encounter:

Data Series—A collection of related data that you want to plot on a chart. For example, if you're charting your monthly household spending, the data series would include the values (amounts) of your spending categories.

Axis—One side of an Excel chart. If you're building a two-dimensional chart, the horizontal axis is the X-axis, and the vertical axis is the Y-axis.

Legend—An information box inside the chart that defines the chart elements.

Chart Title—A name for the chart, usually describing what the chart illustrates.

> The first time you use Excel's Chart Wizard, the Office Assistant help feature will pop up and offer to help you. Click the Office Assistant's **Close** (X) button to close the feature.

Creating a Chart

Example	Chart Type	Description
	Column	This is the default chart type and is useful when you want to compare items but emphasize change over time. The values are charted vertically. You can select a 2-D, 3-D, stacked, or 100% column chart.
	Bar	Select this chart type when you want to compare items, emphasizing the comparison rather than time. The values are plotted horizontally (as opposed to a column chart where the values are plotted vertically). You can select a 3-D or 2-D chart. You can also create a stacked bar chart (values are stacked on each other) and 100% stacked (the percentage of each value is stacked).
	Line	Use this chart type when you want to show trends or emphasize change over time. You can choose to create a 2-D or 3-D line chart. You can also choose a high-low-close-open chart that is useful for charting stock prices.
	Pie	Use this chart when you want to show the relationship of the values to the whole. Select a 2-D or 3-D chart style.
	XY Scatter	This chart type is useful for charting scientific data and shows the relationship of values in several chart data series.
	Area	Use this chart when you want to show change in volume or magnitude over time. This chart type is similar to a line chart, but an area chart emphasizes the amount of change. You can select a 2-D or 3-D version of this chart.
	Doughnut	Use this chart when you want to show more than one data series and show the relationship of the values to the whole.
	Radar	Use this chart when you want to show changes relative to a center point.
	Surface	Similar to a topographical map, this chart type is useful for finding relationships that may be otherwise difficult to see.
	Bubble	Compares sets of three values, similar to a scatter chart, but with the third value displayed the size of a bubble.
	Stock	A stock market chart showing three series of values: high, low, close.
	Cylinder	A column chart with cylinder-shaped columns.
	Cone	A column chart with cone-shaped columns.
	Pyramid	A column chart with pyramid-shaped columns.

Begin Guided Tour   Make a Chart

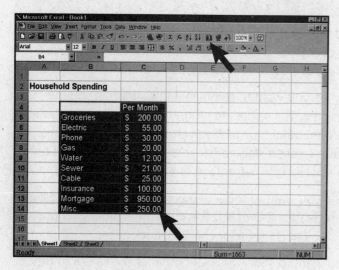

1 Select the range that you want to chart. (Keep in mind that the type of data you select affects how your chart appears.) Click the **Chart Wizard** button on the Standard toolbar.

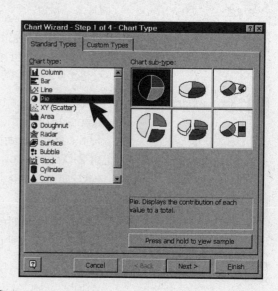

3 In the Chart Type list box, select the chart type you want to use.

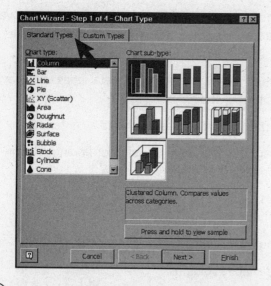

2 The Chart Wizard - Step 1 of 4 box appears. Click the **Standard Types** tab to bring it to the front of the dialog box, if necessary.

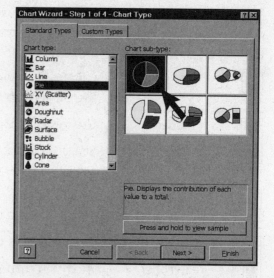

4 The Chart Sub-type area displays several renditions of the chart type you selected. Click the sub-type you want to use.

Guided Tour   Make a Chart

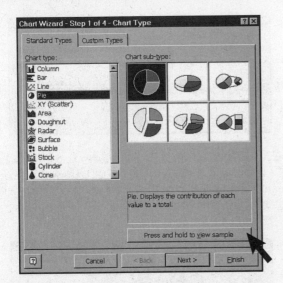

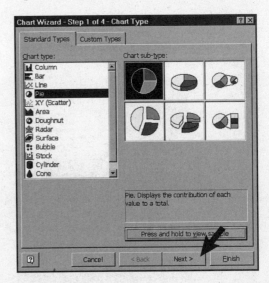

5 To preview how the chart style looks, click the **Press and Hold to View Sample** button.

7 Click the **Next** button to continue.

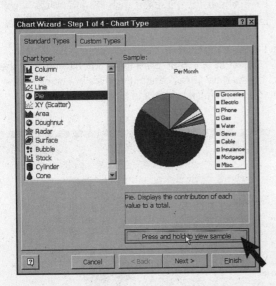

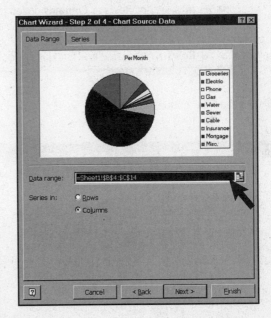

6 Press and hold the button with the mouse pointer, and you see a sample of the chart type using the worksheet data you specified. Release the button when finished viewing.

If your chart correctly graphs the worksheet data you selected, you can click the **Finish** button and Excel creates the chart for you. If you want to add more details, continue using the Chart Wizard dialog boxes to help you.

8 The Step 2 of 4 dialog box appears. In step 1, you selected the worksheet data, but this box lets you verify the information. In the **Data Range** tab, make sure the correct data range is specified. If it's not, click the **Collapse Dialog Box** button (at the far right end of the Data Range text box) and drag over the correct data in your worksheet.

(continues)

Guided Tour Make a Chart

(continued)

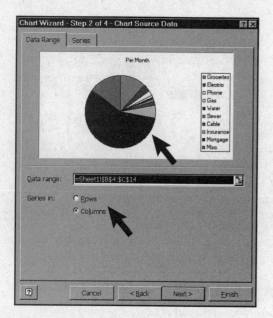

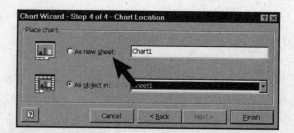

12 Click the **Next** button to continue. The Step 4 of 4 dialog box appears. In this box, you can tell Excel whether you want to insert the chart onto the current worksheet, or place the chart onto a new worksheet.

9 Under **Series In**, select the **Rows** or **Columns** option to tell Excel how you want the data charted. The preview at the top of the box will help you tell which option to select. For example, if you click **Rows** and the sample picture doesn't look like a chart, then click **Columns** instead.

10 Click the **Next** button to continue.

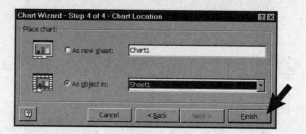

13 To place the chart on the current sheet, click the **As Object In** option. To place the chart on a new worksheet, select the **As New Sheet** option, then type in a name for the sheet. Click the **Finish** button and Excel creates the chart.

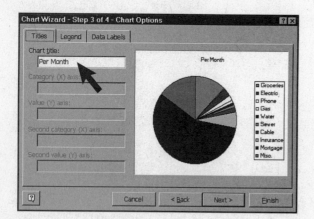

11 The Step 3 of 4 box appears. Use the tabs in this dialog box to give your chart a title, name the x- and y-axes, turn on gridlines, include a legend, and type in data labels. Depending on the chart type you've selected, fill in the appropriate preferences.

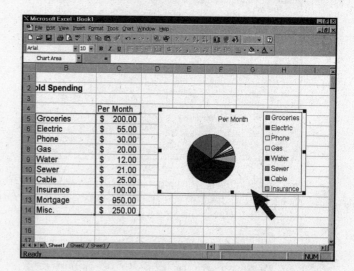

14 Depending on the choices you made with Chart Wizard, the new chart is placed on the current worksheet or in a new worksheet.

To move the chart, click it, then drag it to a new location on the worksheet.

Work with the Chart Object

You can think of the chart as an object—a Post-it Note—stuck on top of the worksheet. You can move the chart to a different spot on-screen or change the size of the chart, or you may want to delete the chart and start over. When you want to move, resize, or delete the chart, you must first select the chart object. When you want to change the appearance of items in the chart (for example, the legend or titles), you need to open the chart for editing. Once you select the chart, you can access any of the chart commands and change any of the elements in the chart.

The elements in a chart vary depending on the chart type and the options you select. When you want to make a change to the element, you can double-click it to access the commands for that element. For example, you can double-click a chart legend to change the font used in the legend or change the placement of the legend. The following table explains the most common elements you can expect to find in a chart.

If you inserted the chart as a new sheet in the workbook, you can work on the chart by simply selecting the sheet tab named **Chart1**. (You can rename the sheet with a more descriptive name by double-clicking the sheet tab, typing a new name, and pressing **Enter**.) The remaining parts of this section cover formatting.

Chart Element	Description
Data point	Each individually charted value. For example, if you chart product sales for three years, a data point would be one product's sale for one year. Think of a data point as one cell in the worksheet.
Data series	Data points are grouped together into a series. For example, you can chart one product's sale for three years as one series. In a worksheet, a series is either a row or column of data (you can select which).
Legend	The key to the chart. For some charts (such as a pie chart), the legend is often redundant and isn't included.
Axis	A 2-D chart is plotted along two axes: the Y-axis (vertical) and X-axis (horizontal). A 3-D chart has an X-, Y-, and Z-axis. The axes usually include tick marks and labels.
Plot area	The grid against which the chart is plotted. In a 3-D floor, the wall and floor provide the background for the charted data.
Title	You can include a chart title or titles for the X-axis or Y-axis.

Begin Guided Tour   Select the Chart Object

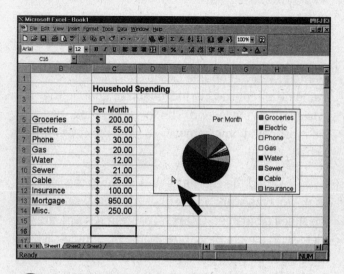

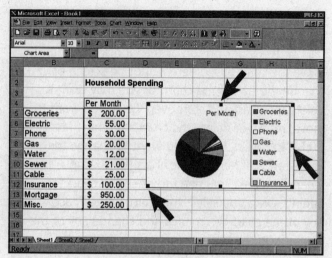

1 Point to the chart object and click once.

2 The chart object is selected. You see black selection handles around the border of the object.

Begin Guided Tour   Move a Chart

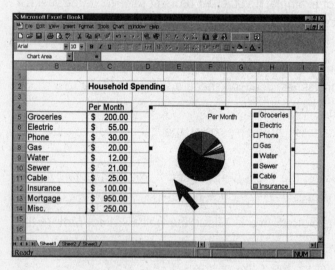

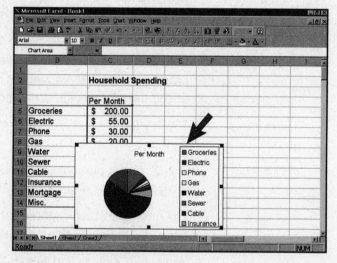

1 Click the chart once to select it. Then drag the chart to a new location on the worksheet.

2 Release the mouse button and Excel moves the chart object.

Begin Guided Tour   Resize a Chart

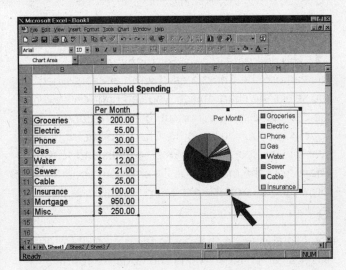

1 Click the chart once to select it.

2 Put the pointer on one of the black selection handles. The mouse pointer should look like a two-headed arrow. While still holding the mouse button down, drag to resize the chart.

3 Excel resizes the chart.

Begin Guided Tour   Delete a Chart

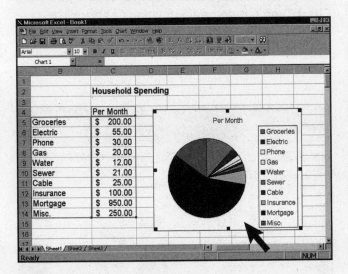

1 Click the chart once to select it.

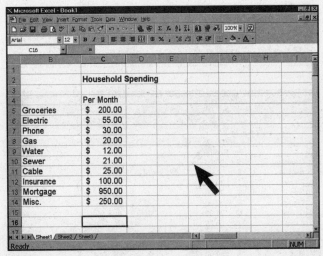

2 Press the **Delete** key and Excel deletes the chart object.

Edit the Chart Data

You can edit the data in your chart just like you edit data in cells. For formatting changes, you can use the **Chart** menu (which appears when you select the chart object), you can right-click over the chart to display a shortcut menu of editing options, or you can open the Chart toolbar (right-click over a blank space on the Excel toolbars and select **Chart** from the menu). You'll learn more about formatting chart data in the next few tasks in this section.

You can also make changes to the data content. Just like you can change a value and update a formula automatically, you can change a charted value, and the chart automatically updates to reflect the new value. The chart and worksheet data are linked. You can edit or delete data as necessary. The Guided Tour below will show you how to update the chart data.

Change the Chart Type

When you first start working with the charting features of Excel, you may not really know which chart type works best for your data. When you create the chart, you select the one you think will do, but if that type doesn't seem to work, you can select another chart type—without re-creating the chart.

One way to change the type is to reopen the Chart Wizard and go through the four dialog boxes to select a new chart style. From there you can choose from among the many chart types and make adjustments to the axes, labels, and legend. At any point during the update, you can exit the Chart Wizard by clicking the **Finish** button.

Another way to change the chart type is to open the Chart Type box, which looks similar to the first Chart Wizard box. To display this box, right-click over the selected chart, then choose the **Chart Type** command from the shortcut menu. You can also open the **Chart** menu and select **Chart Type**, or click the **Chart Type** button on the floating Chart toolbar.

Begin Guided Tour Update a Chart

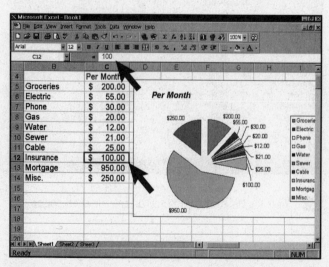

1 In the worksheet, select the cell that contains the value you want to change. Then make the change. (In this example, I'm changing 100 to 500.)

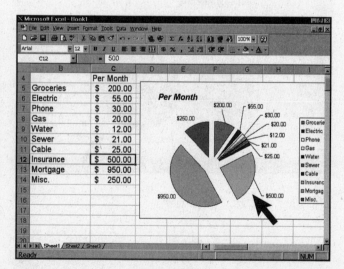

2 Excel updates the chart. Here you can see the effect of increasing a value from 100 to 500.

Begin Guided Tour Change the Chart Type

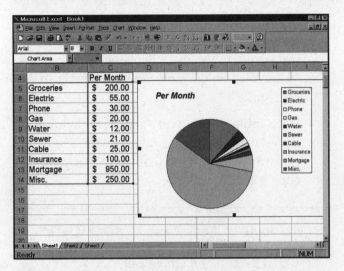

1 Select the chart, then click the **Chart Wizard** button on the Standard toolbar.

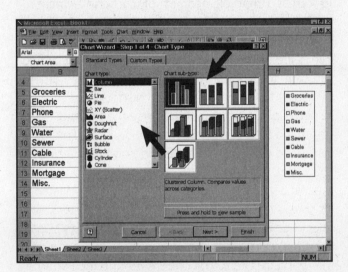

2 You see the Chart Wizard dialog box. Excel displays the available chart choices. Click the new chart type and sub-type you want.

3 If you need to make changes to chart preferences (such as labels or the legend), click the **Next** button and continue using the Chart Wizard.

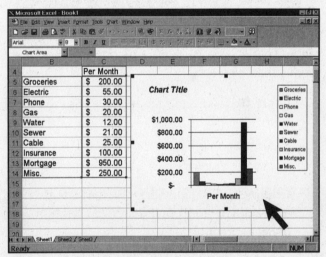

4 If the chart is ready to go, click the **Finish** button at any point among the Chart Wizard boxes and Excel inserts the new chart type onto your worksheet.

Format Chart Data

When you create a chart using the Chart Wizard, it's not always easy to know which chart preferences you may need to specify. If you skipped some of the options available, you can always add them later. On the other hand, if you specified too many options, your chart may be too crowded. You can easily go back and remove items you don't need. For example, maybe you don't really need a legend in your chart, or maybe you need to change your axis titles. Or perhaps you want to change the color of one of the bars in your bar chart. In any case, you can summon the Chart Options dialog box and the chart element formatting dialog boxes to assist you in making formatting changes.

To display the Chart Options dialog box, right-click over your chart and select **Chart Options** from the shortcut menu. (You can also open the **Chart** menu and select **Chart Options**.) You'll find six different tabs in the Chart Options dialog box representing the various chart elements. Here's a rundown of the various chart elements:

- **Chart Title**—Use this tab to add a titles to your chart.

- **Axis Titles**—Use this tab to add titles for the chart's X and Y axes.

- **Gridlines**—To change the hash marks that appear on an axis, use this tab. You can turn gridlines on or off.

- **Legend**—If you need to add a legend to your chart, click this tab and create a legend.

- **Data Labels**—Use this tab to add worksheet text entries to the chart. Remember, the more labels you add, the more crowded your chart becomes.

- **Data Table**—To turn on a data table for displaying values alongside the graph, use this tab. However, keep in mind that this makes your chart more crowded.

> If you double-click over a chart element, you'll display a dialog box with options for formatting that particular element only.

To format a chart element, simply click the element you want to change This surrounds the item with a box with selection handles (where there's room). If things are a little crowded in your chart, you may find you have to click the element a second time in order to display the selection handles. Next, right-click to display a pop-up menu and choose the **Format** command (or open the **Format** menu). The Format command name varies, depending on the chart item you select. For example, to change the color of a specific bar, select the individual bar (when selected, it's surrounded by a box with handles), right-click and select **Format Data Point**. This opens a Format Data Point dialog box with tabs and options for changing that particular item. The options include the Patterns tab which you can use to select a new color choice for the bar.

The following guided tours show you two examples of how you might use the Chart Options dialog box and a Formatting dialog box.

Use the Chart Toolbar

A great tool to help you make formatting changes to your chart is the Chart toolbar. By default, the toolbar does not appear on your worksheet unless you choose to display it. To do so, right-click a blank area of any toolbar at the top of your Excel window. This displays a menu of available Excel toolbars. Select the Chart toolbar, and it appears on-screen as a floating toolbar (which means it's not anchored to the Excel window like the Standard or Formatting toolbar).

You can move the toolbar around on-screen by dragging its title bar. The following table explains the Chart toolbar's buttons:

> To remove the Chart toolbar from your screen, click its **Close** button, or open the **View** menu, choose **Toolbars**, and deselect the **Chart** toolbar.

The Chart Toolbar

Toolbar Button	Description
Category Axis ▼	The Chart Objects drop-down list displays a list of elements found inside the chart. Choose an element from this drop-down list, then click the Format Selected Object button.
🔲	Use the Format Selected Object button to make individual formatting edits that apply only to the specified chart object.
📊▼	Click the arrow to the right of the Chart Type button and choose another chart type from the drop-down palette.
🗒	Click this button to turn the Legend on or off.
▦	Turns the data table on or off.
🗒	The By Row button selects data by row.
🎚	The By Column button selects data by column.
✎	Use the Angle Text Downward button to angle text entries so they slant down left to right.
✎	Use the Angle Text Upward button to angle text entries so they slant up from left to right.

Begin Guided Tour Add and Format a Chart Title

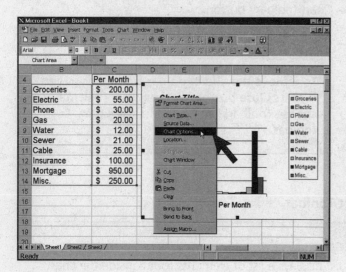

1 Right-click over the chart and select **Chart Options** from the menu, or open the **Chart** menu and choose **Chart Options**.

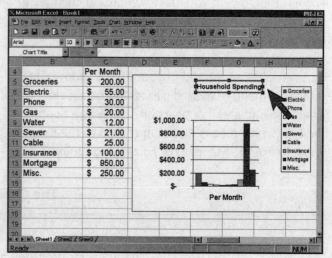

3 Click **OK** and Excel adds the title to your chart. To change the title formatting, click the title to select it.

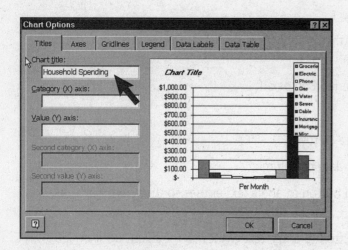

2 The Chart Options dialog box appears. With the **Titles** tab displayed, click in the **Chart Title** box and type in a title.

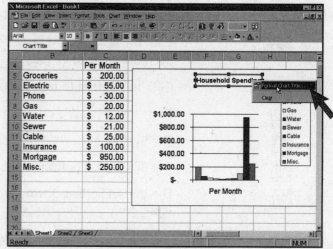

4 Right-click and select **Format Chart Title** from the menu.

Guided Tour   Add and Format a Chart Title

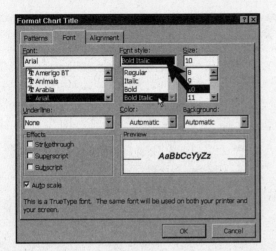

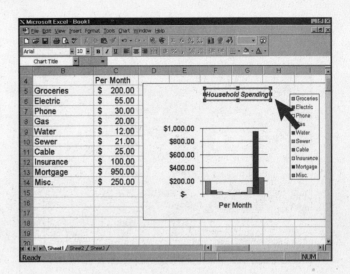

5 The Format Chart Title dialog box appears with three formatting tabs for changing the title's background pattern, alignment, or font formatting. Use the tabs and options to add formatting options to your title. For example, to make the title bold and italics, click the **Font** tab and select **Bold Italic** from the **Font Style** list.

6 Click **OK** to exit the dialog box and Excel applies the selected formatting options to your chart title.

Begin Guided Tour   Change a Data Point's Color Formatting

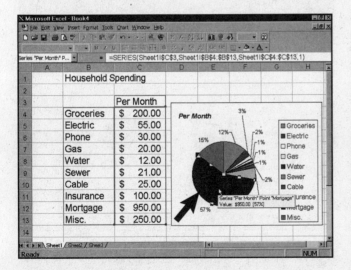

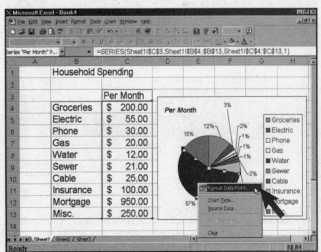

1 To change a pie chart's pie element (called a *data point*), first select the element with a click. You may need to click again to display selection handles around the item. A ScreenTip also appears next to the pointer identifying the data point.

2 Right-click over the selected item to display a shortcut menu. Click the **Format Data Point** command.

(continues)

Guided Tour   Change a Data Point's Color Formatting

(continued)

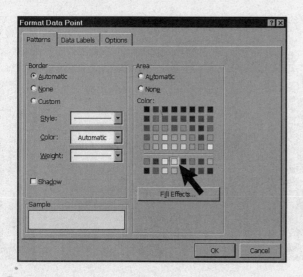

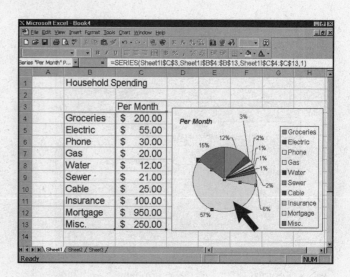

3 The Format Data Point dialog box appears. To change the data point color, click the **Patterns** tab and choose a new color in the **Area** options. In the figure shown, a light blue color is selected.

4 Click **OK** to exit the box and Excel changes the pie chart element's color.

Begin Guided Tour   Display the Chart Toolbar

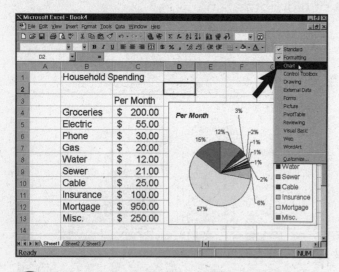

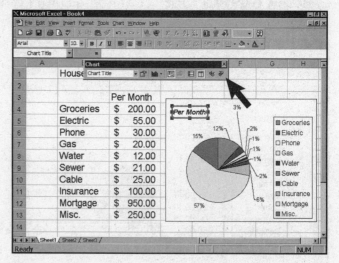

1 Right-click over any blank area on the Standard or Formatting toolbars. From the toolbar menu that appears, click **Chart**.

2 The floating Chart toolbar appears on-screen.

Format Chart Series

Excel groups each set of data points into a series, which will appear in the chart with a predefined pattern. For instance, if your chart shows quarterly sales by division, division 1 sales are one series, division 2 are another series, and so on.

By default, Excel assigns a certain pattern and color to each series and a certain width between each series. Excel charts the series in the order they appear in the worksheet. You can make changes to any of these series options. For example, if you don't like the color used, you can select a different color or pattern. Or you may want to rearrange the series so the series appears from smallest to largest. Finally, you may want to add more or less space between each series. You can easily make these changes.

When you make any change to a chart, make sure to select the correct element. You can recognize the selected element by looking for the black boxes on or around the selected object. To select the entire series (not just one point), click the series once to select it. Right-click the data and choose the **Format Data Series** command or open the **Format** menu and select the **Selected Data Series** command. The Format Data Series dialog box appears.

You can use the dialog box to change the series pattern color, series order, and more. The guided tours in this task will focus on changing the series gap and overlap, and rearranging the series order. When you change the gap, you change the space between

data marker categories. The larger the value, the greater the distance between categories. When you change the overlap, you change how much you want the data markers within a category to overlap.

Change Series Labels

When you use the Chart Wizard to create a chart, it prompts you to specify preferences such as series labels. But if you were in a hurry and skipped establishing the exact series labels you want to include in the chart, you can always go back and fix them up later. To change series labels, follow these steps:

1. Right-click over the chart and choose **Chart Options** from the pop-up menu.

2. The Chart Options dialog box appears. Click the **Data Labels** tab to bring it to the front of the Chart Options dialog box.

3. Among the **Data Labels** options, select the label you want to apply to your data series. For example, to chart the series values as a percentage, select the **Show Percent** option.

4. The preview area shows a sample of how the chart looks with the new data series labels applied. Click **OK** to exit the dialog box and apply the labels.

Begin Guided Tour   Overlap Series and Change the Gap Width

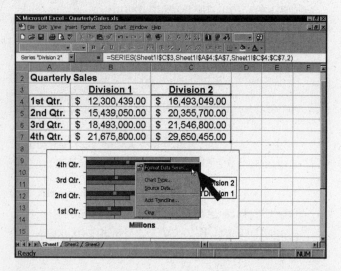

1 Select the chart data series. Handles appear on each data series element on the chart and a ScreenTip pops up.

2 Right-click over the selected data and choose **Format Data Series**.

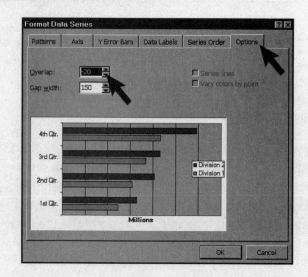

3 The Format Data Series dialog box appears. To change series overlap and gap, make sure the **Options** tab is displayed. If you want to overlap the series, type a value in the **Overlap** text box, or use the spin arrows to select a value.

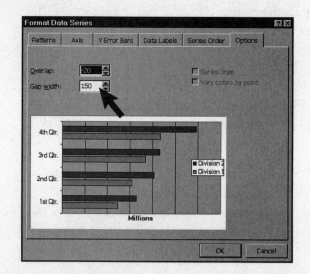

4 If you want to change the width between the data series, click the **Gap Width** text box and type a value. Or use the spin arrows to select a value.

5 You see a sample of the chart using the new gap width and overlap. Click **OK**. Excel formats the series accordingly.

Begin Guided Tour   Rearrange the Series

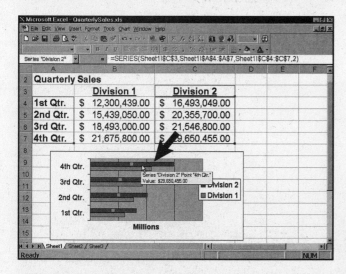

1 Select the chart data series. Handles appear on each data series element on the chart and a ScreenTip pops up.

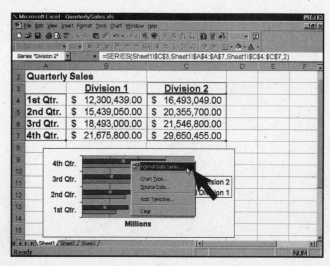

2 Right-click over the selected data and choose **Format Data Series**.

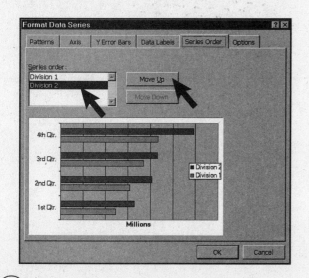

3 The Format Data Series dialog box appears. To change series order, make sure the **Series Order** tab is displayed. Click the series you want to move; click the **Move Up** or **Move Down** buttons to change the order.

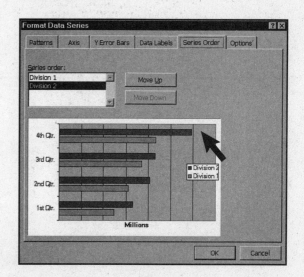

4 You see a sample of the chart using the new series order. Click **OK**. Excel rearranges the series.

HOW TO...

Create an Excel Database

I n addition to keeping track of numerical data such as budgets or expenses, you can also use Excel to keep track of lists of data. You can use Excel as a simple data management program to store information about clients, products, sales, or other information. Excel provides many tools that make it easy to enter and work with the data in a list.

Once you create an Excel database, you can easily update it as necessary. For example, if you build a database containing names, addresses, and phone numbers, it will probably require you to make changes as people move or change phone numbers.

What You Will Find in This Section

Build an Excel Database

To use any program to keep track of data, you need to have an understanding of the structure of a database. Basically, a *database* is a set of related information about a particular person, place, item, transaction, or event. For instance, you can keep a list of your clients with names, addresses, and phone information. Or you can keep your household inventory in an Excel database and include the item name, value, warranties, and so on in the list. One of the easiest databases to create is a Christmas card mailing list that contains all the names and addresses of people you send holiday cards to.

Excel stores each set of related information together in one worksheet. The categories of data you include are known as *fields*. For example, in a Christmas card database, you can have fields for the last name, first name, address, city, state, and ZIP code. You set up each field in a column and at the top of the column you include the name of the field.

One set of fields for one person or item in the database is a *record*. For example, if you have a relative named Joshua Cannon, the information (name, address, city, and so on) for this person forms one record. Excel stores each record as a row in the worksheet.

You don't have to do anything special to set up a database in Excel. Basically, you enter the field names in columns—one field name for each field you want to include. This row of field names is the *header row* and enables Excel to separate the field names from the data.

Before you start typing away, spend some time thinking about the data you want to store and then plan your fields accordingly. What fields do you need? Think about each individual piece of data you need to store and then set up fields for each. For example, you can put the address, city, and state all in one field, but then you couldn't sort by state. Instead, put each in a separate field.

Also, think about the best order to enter the data and use this order to structure the fields. For instance, think about entering a Christmas card list where the fields are in this order: City, ZIP, State, Phone, Last Name, First Name. Of course, another order would make more sense! If you are entering data from a hard copy list (an existing list you printed on paper), consider setting up the database to match the order used on the hard copy.

Finally, be sure to use unique names for each column. If you use the same name in more than one column, you will confuse Excel.

> Format your headings so they stand out. You can make them bold, add a border, or add shading. Doing so separates the headings from the data. To learn more about formatting your database, see "Format an Excel Worksheet" on page 161.

Begin Guided Tour   Build a Database

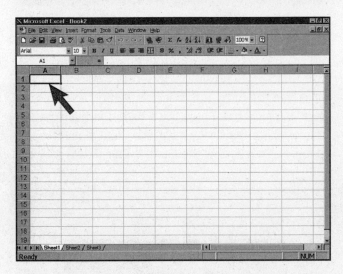

1 Start with a blank worksheet. You can include a database as part of another worksheet, but it's best to put the database on its own sheet.

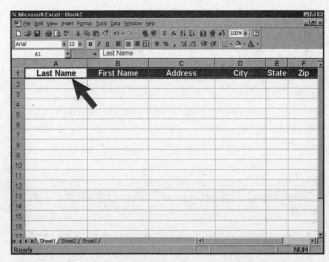

3 Continue entering each field name you want to include. You can format the headings so they stand out. You may also want to adjust the column widths, as necessary.

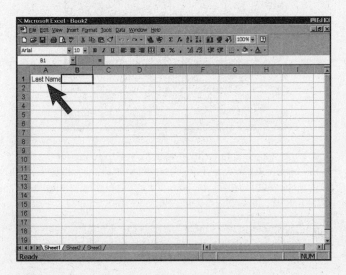

2 Type the first field name and press **Tab**. Excel enters the first field name and moves to the next column.

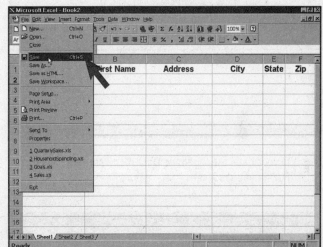

4 When you finish setting up the database, save the worksheet by opening the **File** menu and selecting the **Save** command.

Enter Data in an Excel Database

Remember: The Excel database is just a regular worksheet. You can select any cell you want and enter data or make changes. You can create formulas, make formatting changes, insert new rows, and so on. Therefore, you enter data in a database just like you do in a worksheet: Select the cell and type the entry. You can use this method to enter your records.

If you prefer to concentrate on one record at a time, you can use Excel's data form to enter data. You don't have to do anything special to set up this form; Excel will create the form automatically. With this form, you see a graphical entry box, like a fill-in-the-blank page. You complete the "page" and then add a new "page," as covered in the Guided Tour.

Begin Guided Tour   Use the Data Form

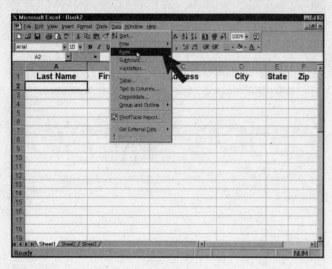

1 In your database, open the **Data** menu and select the **Form** command.

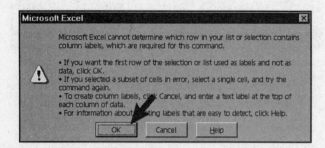

2 Excel displays a prompt box. The first bullet point in the message applies to making forms—the field names you entered in the previous task are labels. Click **OK** to continue.

3 You see the data form on-screen. Type the entry for the first field. You can type more information than the size of the field in the data form. As you type, the information scrolls to the left. When the first entry is complete, press **Tab**.

4 The insertion point moves to the next field. Type the entry for the next field and press **Tab**. Complete all the fields in the record.

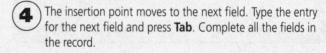

Guided Tour   Use the Data Form

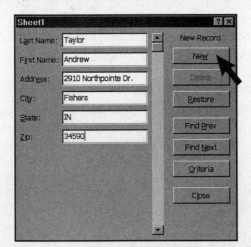

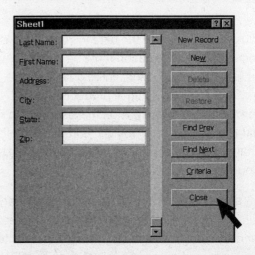

5 When the record is complete, click **New**.

7 Click **Close** when you finish.

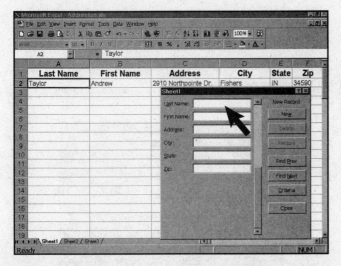

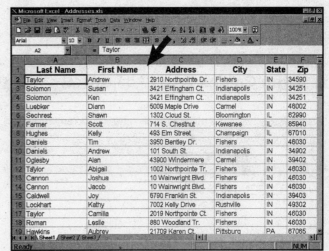

6 Excel adds the record to the worksheet and displays a blank form. Continue completing and adding records until you've added the ones you want.

8 You see the records (rows) added to the worksheet.

Add, Edit, and Delete Records

If you are going to use the data in your database effectively, the information must be current. And, as you know, things change. Prices go up. People move. Companies discontinue products and add new products. Fortunately, Excel makes it easy to keep any database up-to-date. You can edit data to reflect any changes or mistakes, you can add new records, and you can delete records you no longer need.

Again, remember that the database is an ordinary worksheet. You can edit a field directly in the record row and field column. You can insert new rows to add a new record or insert new columns to add a new field. You can delete rows (and therefore delete the record). You can copy and paste similar data. All the features you use when creating and entering a regular worksheet are available with a database worksheet.

You can also use the data form to add, edit, or delete a record, as covered in the Guided Tour.

Excel keeps track of the number of records you enter in a database. The current record number and total record number appear in the upper-right corner of the data form—for instance, 2 of 3. This information may help you find the record you want. You can also use the **Criteria** button to search for a record. See "Search the Database" on page 219.

Begin Guided Tour   Add a Record with the Data Form

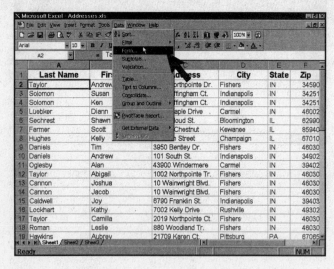

1 In your database, open the **Data** menu and select the **Form** command.

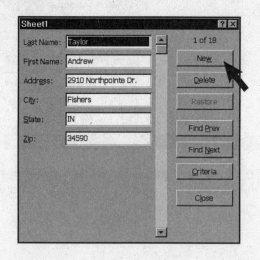

2 You see the first record in the database. Click the **New** button.

Guided Tour Add a Record with the Data Form

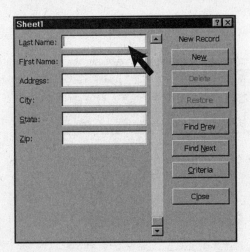

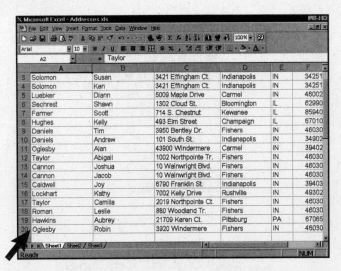

3 Excel displays a blank record. Complete the information for the new record.

5 Excel adds the new record(s) to the database at the end of the list.

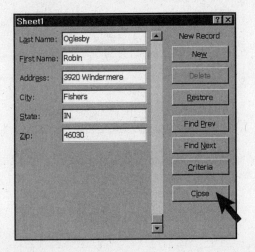

4 When the information is complete, click **New** to add another record, or click the **Close** button to close the dialog box.

Begin Guided Tour   Edit or Delete a Record

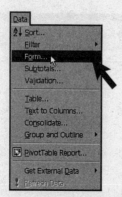

1 Open the **Data** menu and select the **Form** command.

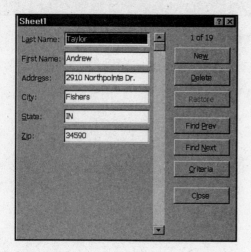

2 You see the first record in the database. Or click the **Find Prev** or **Find Next** buttons until the record appears.

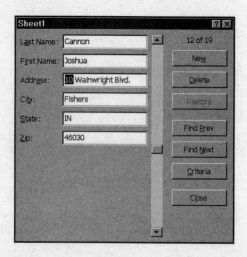

3 When the record you want appears, click the field you want to change and make any changes.

4 To delete the record displayed, click the **Delete** button.

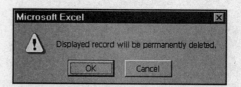

5 Excel prompts you to confirm the deletion. Click **OK**. Excel deletes the record.

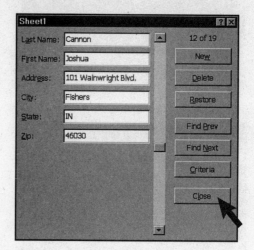

6 When the changes are complete, click **Close** to save the changes and close the data form.

Search the Database

As you continue to build your database, you'll add more and more records, possibly hundreds of records. When you are looking for information about a particular record, you can scan through the columns and rows until you see the one you want, or you can use a faster method for finding a record: the **Criteria** button.

With this button, you can quickly move to a record of interest. You can also use this command to search for and display a range of records. Clicking this button displays a form in which you enter the values you want to search for. These items are the criteria.

When you type the search criteria, you can type all or part of the value. For example, if you were searching for the name Wagner in your list and you weren't sure whether the client spelled the name Wagner or Waggoner, you could type **Wag** and search. When you type a value, Excel finds all entries that contain that value.

> If you want to display a certain group of records at once, use the **Filter** command, covered later in this section.

If Excel can't find a match, you'll hear a beep, and Excel will return to the data form. Check your spelling. Rather than typing the entire value, type a partial value or use a comparison formula.

Use Comparison Formulas

In some cases, you may want to find a range of entries in a database. For example, suppose that you want to display all sales greater than $500. In this example, you don't want to search for a particular value. Instead, you want to find a range of values. To do this, you create a comparison formula, like the following:

>= 500

This formula tells Excel to find all records that have 500 or a greater value in the Sales field. You can use the following operators in a comparison formula:

Operator	Meaning	Example
>	Greater than	>500 (Find all values greater than 500)
<	Less than	<500 (Find all values less than 500)
=	Equal to	=500 (Find all values that are exactly 500)
<=	Less than or equal to	<=500 (Find all values that are 500 or less)
>=	Greater than or equal to	>=500 (Find all values that are 500 or more)
<>	Not	<>500 (Find all values that are not 500)

Begin Guided Tour Search for Data or Values

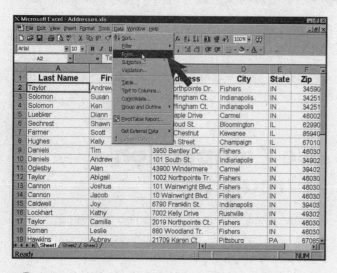

1 Open the **Data** menu and select the **Form** command.

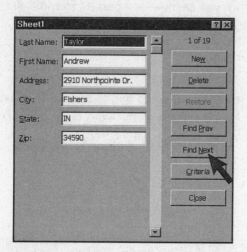

2 You see the first record in the database. Click the **Criteria** button.

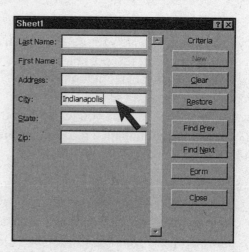

3 Excel displays a blank record on-screen. Here you enter the criteria you want to match. Click the field on which you want to search. For instance, if you are searching for a city in an address database, click the City field. Type the entry you want to find. You can type all or part of the entry. You can use more than one criteria in your search.

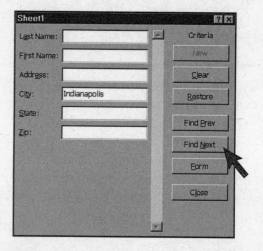

4 After you complete the criteria, click the **Find Next** button.

Guided Tour   Search for Data or Values

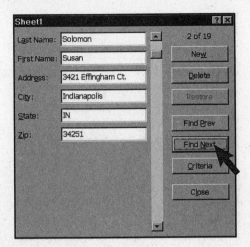

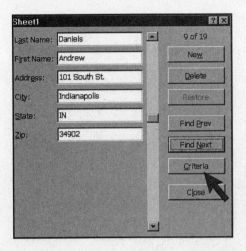

5 Excel displays the first matching record. Continue clicking the **Find Next** button until the record you want appears.

6 Click **Close** to exit the Form dialog box.

Begin Guided Tour   Search Using a Comparison Formula

1 Open the **Data** menu and select the **Form** command.

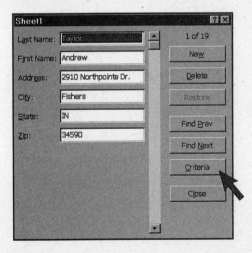

2 You see the first record in the database. Click the **Criteria** button.

(continues)

Guided Tour Search Using a Comparison Formula *(continued)*

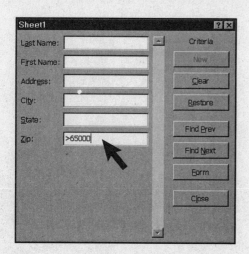

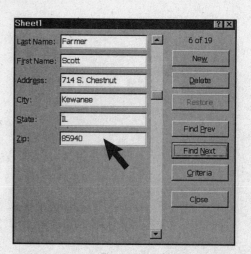

3 Excel displays a blank record on-screen. Here you enter the criteria you want to match. Click the field on which you want to search. For instance, if you are searching for ZIP codes in a certain range, click the Zip field. Type the comparison formula using the operators in the table in the text.

4 Click the **Find Next** button and Excel displays the first matching record. Continue clicking the **Find Next** button until the record you want appears. Then click **Close**.

Sort an Excel Database

One of the benefits of taking the time to enter all your data is that you can easily manipulate the data. For example, if you had a paper copy of a data list, the list would be confined to one order: the order you used to enter the records. With Excel, you can select to arrange the database in different orders by sorting. For example, in an address database, you could sort by last name, by state, or by ZIP code.

You can do a simple sort on one field or you can sort by multiple fields. For example, you may want to sort by last name and then first name. Using the Sort dialog box, you can select up to three sort fields. You can also choose to sort in ascending or descending order. When you sort fields in ascending order, the data appears alphabetically or numerically in order from top to bottom in your list (1–100 or A–Z). With descending order, the opposite occurs. Excel's sorting feature is flexible and fast.

You can also use the **Sort Ascending** or **Sort Descending** buttons in the toolbar to quickly sort on the current field.

Begin Guided Tour Sort a Database

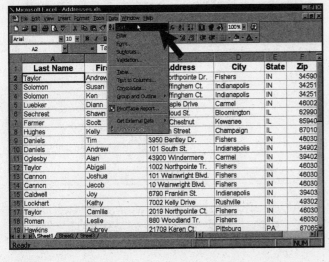

1 Open the **Data** menu and select the **Sort** command.

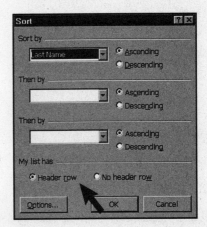

2 You see the Sort dialog box. If you select the **Header Row** option button, Excel uses the column headings as choices in the sort drop-down lists; Excel will not include this header row in the sort. If you don't have column headings, Excel will display the first value in the column in the drop-down list. If this is your case, you can click the **No Header Row** option button so that Excel will include the first row.

(continues)

Guided Tour Sort a Database *(continued)*

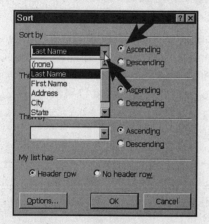

3 Display the **Sort By** drop-down list and click the column name that you want to sort by first. For instance, if you were sorting by last names, you'd select **Last Name** from this list. Click **Ascending** or **Descending** order.

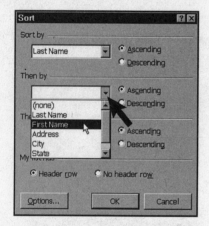

4 To sort on a second field, display the **Then By** drop-down list, click the column, and then click a sort order.

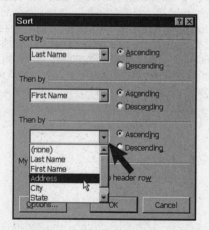

5 To sort on a third field, display the **Then By** drop-down list, click the column, and then click a sort order.

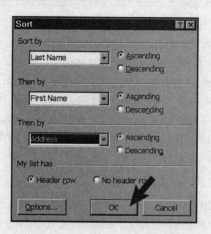

6 When you have selected all the sort fields, click **OK**.

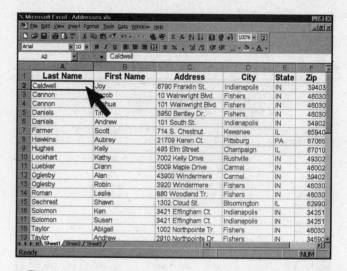

7 Excel sorts the database in the order you selected. In this example, the address database was sorted alphabetically by last names.

HOW TO...

Create and Edit a PowerPoint Presentation

Microsoft PowerPoint enables you to create beautiful, professional-looking presentations which can then be replayed before an audience, using your computer. For example, if you're a manager of a large department, you can use your presentations to help summarize departmental or company-wide changes.

When you work in a word processing program, you create a document that contains several pages of text. When you work in a presentation graphics program such as Microsoft PowerPoint, you create a *presentation* that contains information on *slides.* The data on your slides can be displayed in a wide variety of ways, such as bulleted lists, tables, charts, and graphic images (clip art, or art you draw yourself). In addition, you can add lots of visual effects (such as shading and color) to your slides to make them more eye-catching. When needed, you can add a graph to a slide to summarize your quarterly sales figures, a rise in production costs, or similar data. In addition, PowerPoint makes it easy to display the organization of your company personnel with an organization chart.

What You Will Find in This Section

Create a New Presentation

When you start PowerPoint, you see the initial PowerPoint dialog box. From this dialog box, you can open an existing presentation, or use one of the following options to create a new presentation:

AutoContent Wizard—This option leads you through the process of building a presentation by asking you pertinent questions about the topic of your presentation and the method you prefer for presenting your topic to an audience. If you want PowerPoint to do most of the work, this option is for you.

Template—This option allows you to select from several distinctive backgrounds, such as a marketing plan, or product overview. The template provides the layout of common elements, such as a bulleted list, or art work, as well as a general outline for the presentation.

Blank Presentation—This option enables you to create a presentation from scratch, designing and filling in your own information.

As you start your new presentation, PowerPoint will lead you through a series of dialog boxes appropriate for the option you choose from its initial dialog box.

Sounds simple? Well, it is. But before you begin to create a new presentation, you should determine what you intend to accomplish with the presentation. Do you want to inform the audience? Persuade the audience or teach the audience?

Next, think about the kind of information you want to convey. Do you need simple text slides? Or, do you need to convey some financial or other numerical data in the form of a graph? Do you need to show the organizational structure of the company? PowerPoint includes several different types of slides that you can select and add to your presentation.

> You can import data from the other Office programs for use in your PowerPoint presentation.

Begin Guided Tour Create a Presentation with the AutoContent Wizard

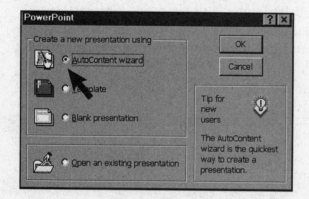

1 When you first start PowerPoint, it displays the PowerPoint dialog box. Select the AutoContent Wizard option and click **OK**. Skip to step 4.

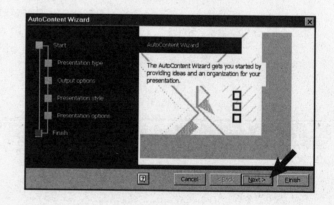

2 The opening AutoContent Wizard dialog box gives you information about what this wizard does and how it works. Notice the Start to Finish list on the left side of the dialog box; it helps you know where you are within the Wizard. Click **Next**. The Presentation Type screen appears.

Guided Tour Create a Presentation with the AutoContent Wizard

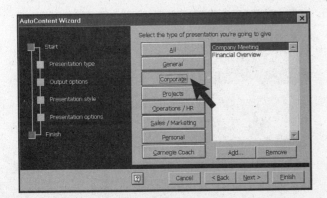

3 Click the **Category** that fits the type of presentation you want to give. For example, click the **Corporate** button. A listing of corporate-related topics appears. Click one of these topics to select it, and click **Next**.

Click the **Back** button to return to any of the earlier dialog boxes. Click the **Next** button to go forward.

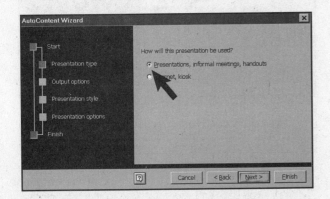

4 The Output Options screen appears. Here you select how you want to present your information. Click the **Presentations, informal meetings, handouts** option and click **Next**. (If you want your presentation to run automatically, then select **Internet, kiosk** and skip to step 7.)

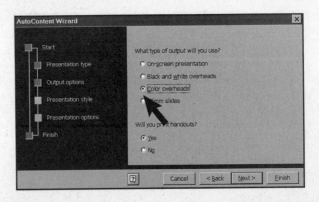

5 The Presentation Styles screen appears. Select the type of output you need for your presentation. For example, select **Color overheads**. Also, select whether you want to print handouts. Click **Next**.

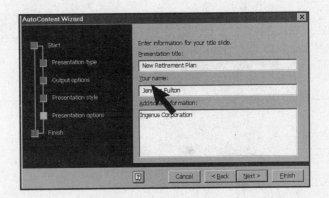

6 The Presentation Options screen appears. If you selected the Presentations, Informal Meetings, Handouts option in step 4, then your Presentation Options screen looks like this. Enter the information you want to appear on your title slide. Click each text box, delete the sample text, and type your information. Click **Next** and then skip to step 8.

(continues)

Guided Tour   Create a Presentation with the AutoContent Wizard   *(continued)*

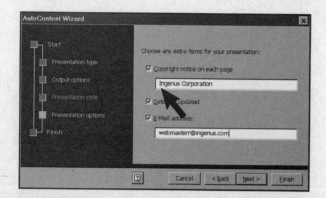

7 If you selected the Internet, Kiosk option in step 4, then the Presentation Options screen looks like this. Click an option to select it. When you're done, click **Next**.

8 Click **Finish**, and PowerPoint creates a presentation based on your responses. When PowerPoint finishes creating the presentation, you see a rough outline of your presentation on-screen.

Begin Guided Tour   Create a Presentation with a Template

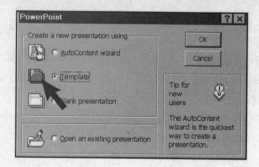

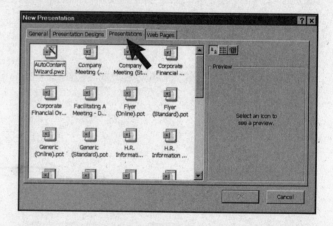

1 When you first start PowerPoint, it displays the PowerPoint dialog box. Select the **Template** option and click **OK**.

2 To select a design based on a topic, click the **Presentations** tab. (If you can't find your topic, skip to step 5 to select a generic presentation.)

Guided Tour Create a Presentation with a Template

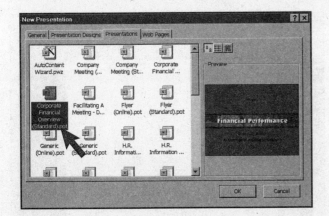

3 Click the icon for the type of presentation you want. (To present your data on the Internet or an intranet, select an *online* rather than a *standard* icon.) PowerPoint displays a preview of that presentation type on the right side of the dialog box.

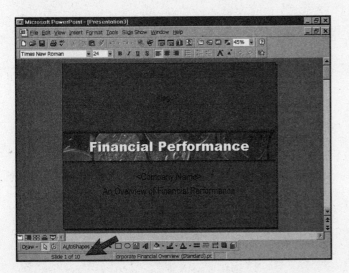

4 Click **OK** and PowerPoint presents the first slide in your presentation. Notice that for the template we selected, PowerPoint created ten slides, which follow a sample outline.

If you don't like any of the designs that are specific to a topic, you can browse through the generic presentation designs to see what they're like. Click the **Presentation Designs** tab.

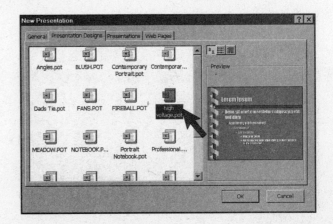

5 Click an icon. A preview of that design appears on the right. Click **OK** to choose it.

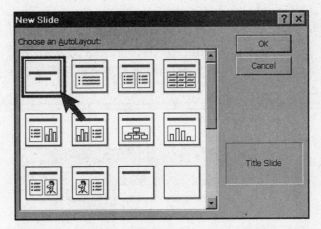

6 Select an AutoLayout (a format) for your first slide. The name of the layout you selected appears on the right side of the dialog box. Most likely, you'll want to select the **Title Slide** format. Click **OK**.

7 PowerPoint creates one slide in the format you selected. You can replace the sample text easily; see "Replace the Sample Text," page 231.

Begin Guided Tour   Create a Blank Presentation

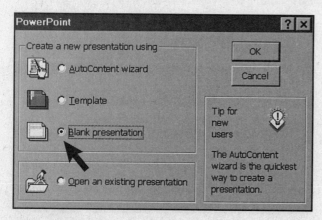

1 When you first start PowerPoint, it displays the PowerPoint dialog box. Select the **Blank Presentation** option and click **OK**.

If you clicked the **Cancel** button in the initial PowerPoint dialog box, you can also start a new presentation by clicking the **New** button on the Standard toolbar.

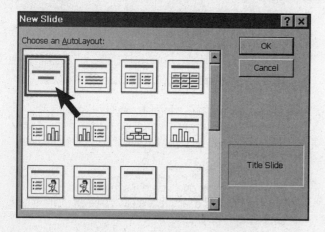

2 Select an AutoLayout (a format) for the first slide in your presentation. In most cases, you'll probably want to select the **Title Slide** format. (The name of the slide layout you select appears on the right side of the dialog box.) Click **OK**.

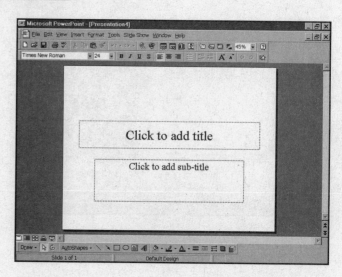

3 PowerPoint creates a slide with a blank background, in the format you selected. You can replace the sample text.

Replace the Sample Text

On each slide in a presentation, you'll see place holders for text and objects. It is a simple process to replace these placeholders (the sample text) with the actual text you want.

The AutoLayout for a slide determines the number and type of the placeholder objects. For example, the title slide includes two text placeholders: one for a title and one for a subtitle. Different slide layouts include other areas for text; a bullet slide, for instance, includes a title placeholder and text placeholder formatted with bullets. You can change the AutoLayout of a slide; see "Apply a Different AutoLayout," page 278, for help.

In this task, you'll learn how to enter text and *bulleted lists*. A bulleted list is simply a list of items, each one of which is preceded by a bullet or small icon—

typically a dot. You can change this dot to something else, such as a star, a happy face, or a hand.

> You can add additional text placeholders using the **Text Box** tool on the Drawing toolbar. See "Draw on a Slide," page 265, for more information.

You can replace your text slide-by-slide using Slide view; however, if PowerPoint created an outline for you (and thus, several slides with sample text), you may want to use Outline view instead. Outline view is the easiest view to use when you want to concentrate on the *content* of your presentation, instead of its *look*. You'll learn both methods of replacing text in this task.

Begin Guided Tour   Replace Text Using Outline View

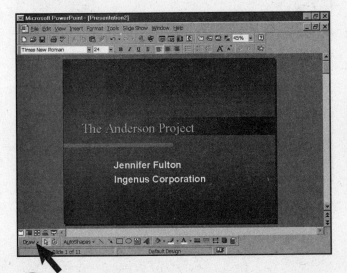

1 When you create a new presentation using the AutoContent Wizard, it displays the result in Outline view. However, if you need to switch to Outline view, click the **Outline View** button.

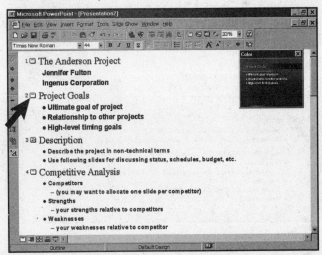

2 Click at the beginning of the text you want to replace. A view of the slide appears in the Color box.

(continues)

Guided Tour Replace Text Using Outline View *(continued)*

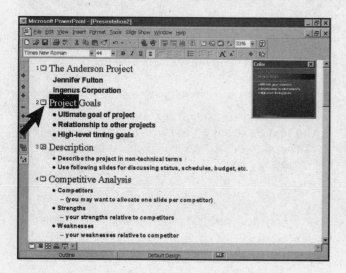

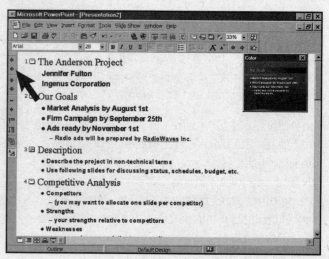

3 While holding down the mouse button, drag the pointer to the end of the text you want to replace. The text is highlighted.

4 Type the replacement text. What you type replaces the text you selected in step 3. Repeat steps 2 through 4 to replace the sample outline with your actual text.

6 To demote the text to a lower level in the outline, click the **Demote** button. For example, to indent a bulleted item in a list, click the **Demote** button. Indented bullets are preceded by a dash.

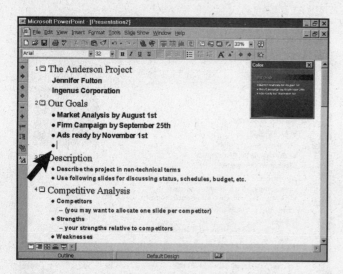

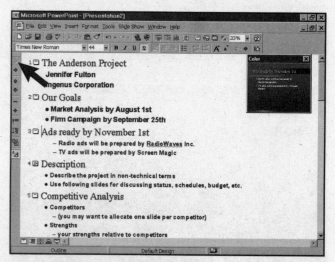

5 To insert a new line of text, click the end of the line *above* where you want to add the text and press **Enter**.

7 To promote text in an outline, click the **Promote** button. For example, to change an item in a bulleted list into a slide title, click the **Promote** button.

Begin Guided Tour Replace Text Using Slide View

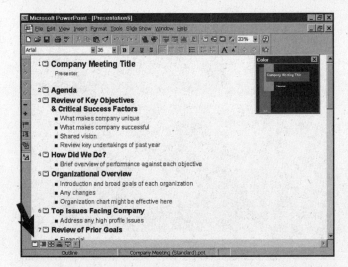

1 When you create a new presentation using a template, it displays the result in Slide view. If you created a presentation using some other method and you need to switch to Slide view now, click the **Slide View** button.

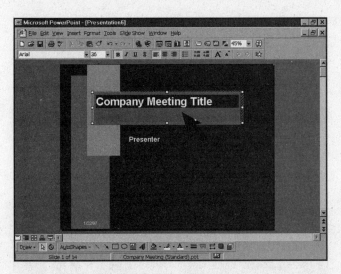

2 Click the text you want to replace. The text box is surrounded by *handles* (small boxes) to show that it is active.

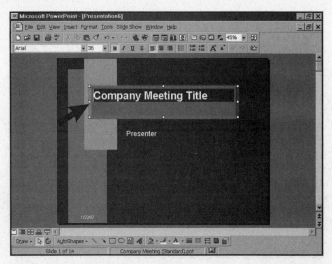

3 Click the beginning of the text you want to replace.

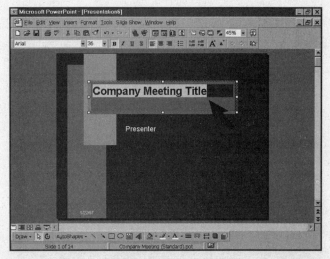

4 Hold down the mouse button and drag over the text you want to replace. The text is highlighted to show that it is selected.

(continues)

Guided Tour Replace Text Using Slide View

(continued)

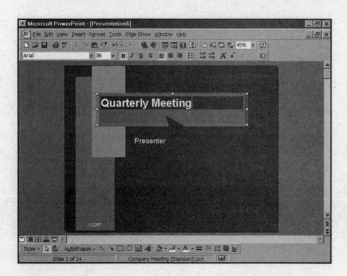

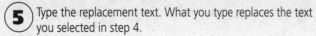

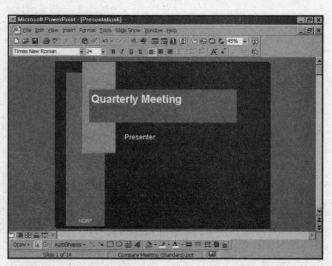

5 Type the replacement text. What you type replaces the text you selected in step 4.

6 Click anywhere outside the text box to deselect it. The handles disappear.

Begin Guided Tour Add Bulleted Text

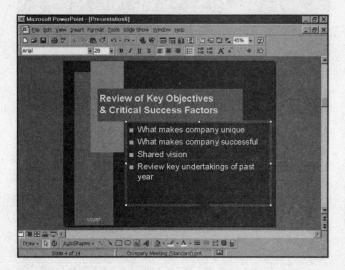

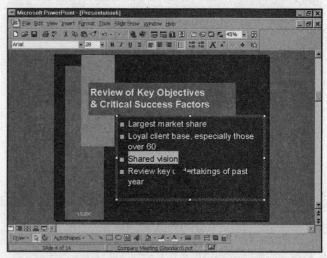

1 To add your bulleted list, click the bulleted list box. For example, in the Company Meeting presentation shown here, the third slide contains a bulleted list box whose text you can replace with your own. (To move to slide 3, click the **Next Slide** button on the vertical scroll bar twice.)

2 If the bulleted list contains sample text, select the text you want to replace by dragging over it. Type your replacement text. Repeat for each item in the list.

To delete a bulleted list item you do not need, select it and press **Delete**.

Guided Tour Add Bulleted Text

If you add a new slide that contains a bulleted list, then you don't need to select your text to replace it. Simply click the placeholder, "Click to add text," and the sample text is automatically removed for you.

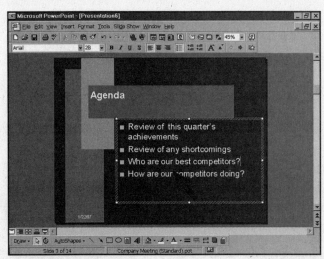

4 A new line appears after item 2. Type your new item on the inserted line.

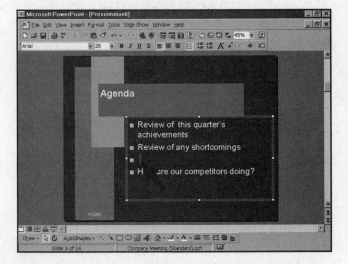

3 If you need to insert an item in the list, click at the end of the item *above* where you want to insert your new item. Then press **Enter**. For example, click the end of item 2 and press **Enter**.

Edit Text

When you look at your slides, you may find errors in your text, or you may decide you simply want to make changes to the text.

You may find that you not only want to change or edit your text, but you also want to add or delete text. For example, you might want to delete an entire section of text, or add new information to a slide. As you add or delete text on a slide, PowerPoint automatically moves your words so they wrap around at the end of each line.

> If you make a change to text that you regret, you can click the **Undo** button on the Standard toolbar, and the character reappears.

Move and Copy Text

  You can use the Cut, Copy, and Paste buttons on the Standard toolbar to move and duplicate text in your slides. When you use the Cut command, PowerPoint removes the text from its original location and places it on the Clipboard. If you use the copy command, PowerPoint makes a copy of the text and places it in the Clipboard, leaving the original text in place.

To place the cut or copied text somewhere else in your slide show, click the new location, and then click the **Paste** button. You can use the contents of the Clipboard more than once. Just click the **Paste** button to paste the same text as many times as you need. The text you cut or copy remains on the Clipboard until you use the Cut or Copy command again, or until you shut down your PC.

Use Drag and Drop

PowerPoint has a handy feature called drag and drop that enables you to use your mouse to move text from one place to another:

1. Select the text block. A hashed box appears around the text block.

2. Select the text you want to copy or move by dragging over the section you want to select. PowerPoint highlights the selected text.

3. To move the text, position the mouse pointer over the selected text and drag the text to its new location. To copy the text, press and hold the **Ctrl** key as you drag.

4. When the pointer is in the new location, release the mouse button. PowerPoint "drops" the selected text in the new location.

You can use drag and drop to copy or move text on the same slide; you can't use drag and drop to copy or move text *from one slide to another*.

> When you drag the mouse pointer during a drag-and-drop operation, you see a square under the mouse pointer that represents the text. If you copy text, you see a small plus sign under the pointer, in addition to the small square.

Begin Guided Tour Change Text

1 Click anywhere within the block that contains the text you want to change. The text block is selected (a hatched outline appears). The mouse pointer changes to an I-beam.

3 Press **Delete** to remove characters to the right of the insertion point, press **Backspace** to remove characters to the left, or simply type any text you want to add (insert). Here, I've added the letter "e" to change met to meet.

2 Move the I-beam pointer over the text you want to change and then click. The *insertion point* (a blinking vertical line) appears in the spot you selected.

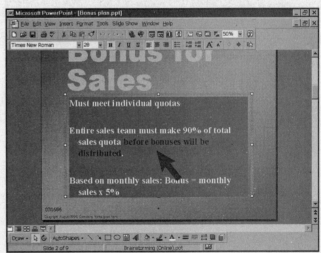

4 To replace existing text, select it and then type the new text.

5 The text you typed replaces the text you selected. After you make your changes, click outside of the selected text block or press the **Esc** key twice. The hatched outline surrounding the text block disappears, and PowerPoint returns you to the slide.

Begin Guided Tour   Delete Text

1 Click the block containing the text you want to delete. The text block is highlighted with a hatched outline.

2 Double-click the word you want to delete to select it, or drag over the words you want to delete. When you select text, its background turns to a different color.

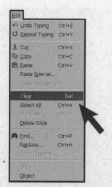

3 Press the **Delete** key, or open the **Edit** menu and select **Clear**.

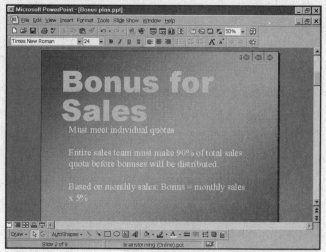

4 The selected words disappear, and PowerPoint rewraps the remaining text to fill in the spot where you deleted the word(s). Click anywhere outside the text block or press **Esc** twice to stop editing.

Begin Guided Tour   Cut (or Copy) and Paste Text

1 Select the text block by clicking it. A hashed box appears around the text block.

2 Select the text you want to move and click the **Cut** button. (To copy text, click the **Copy** button.)

If you select the wrong text, simply try to select what you want again, or click anywhere on the slide to deselect text.

3 PowerPoint places the selected text on the Clipboard and, if you're cutting (moving) text, removes it from its original location. Click the location where you want to place the cut or copied text. To move text to a different slide, click the **Next Slide** or **Previous Slide** buttons on the Vertical scroll bar.

4 Click the **Paste** button. PowerPoint inserts the text from the Clipboard at the location where you clicked. Press **Esc** twice or click outside the text box to deselect it.

Add or Delete a Slide

No matter how thoroughly you plan your presentation, you may forget an important slide and have to add it later. Or, you may even need to delete a slide or two.

PowerPoint makes it easy to add a slide to any part of the presentation and helps you choose the types of elements you want to include on your new slide by providing a series of *AutoLayouts*. The AutoLayout

determines the location of the elements on your new slide, such as the slide title, a bulleted list, a chart, or clip art.

You pick the AutoLayout that best matches the format you want, and PowerPoint then creates the slide, with the appropriate placeholders. Click or double-click the placeholder and enter your information.

Begin Guided Tour   Insert a New Slide

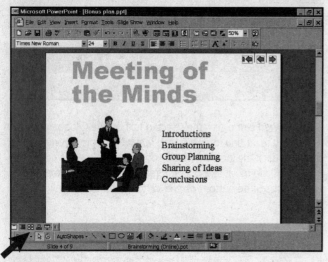

1 Switch to Slide Sorter view by clicking the **Slide Sorter View** button.

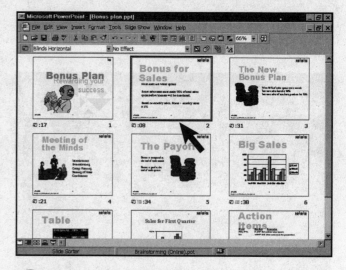

2 Click the slide located *before* the point where you want to insert a new slide. The slide you select becomes the *active* slide (it has a dark border around it).

3 Click the **New Slide** button on the Standard toolbar.

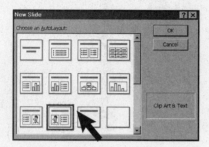

4 Choose the type of slide you want to add from the list of AutoLayouts and click **OK**.

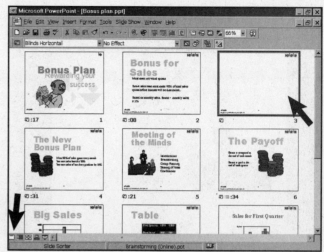

5 PowerPoint adds the new slide to your presentation just after the slide you selected in step 2. To add the slide elements, click the **Slide View** button.

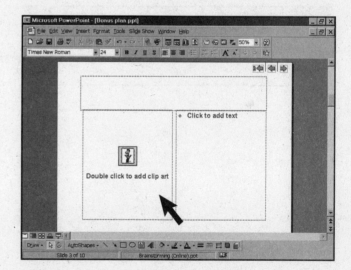

6 Placeholders appear for each element. Click or double-click the placeholder as indicated.

Begin Guided Tour   Delete a Slide

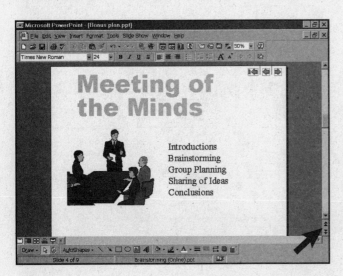

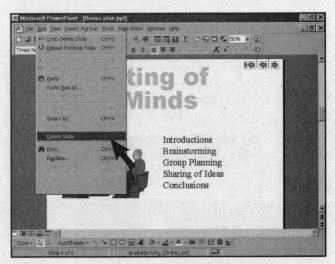

1 In Slide View or Notes Page View, display the slide you want to delete. To move from slide to slide, click the **Next Slide** or **Previous Slide** buttons on the vertical scroll bar.

2 Open the **Edit** menu and select **Delete Slide**. The slide is removed from your presentation.

You can delete a slide while in Outline or Slide Sorter view by clicking it, and completing step 2.

If you delete a slide accidentally, you can restore it by clicking the **Undo** button on the Standard toolbar.

Move from Slide to Slide

You'll often want to move from slide to slide to make changes to it. In Outline view, you simply click the slide you want within the outline. In Slide Sorter view, six slides are displayed at one time. Just click the slide you want.

However, in Slide view and in Notes Page view, only one slide is displayed at a time. (The number of the current slide appears in the Status bar.) The Guided Tour shows you how to move from slide to slide in this view.

Begin Guided Tour   Move Around in Slide or Notes Page View

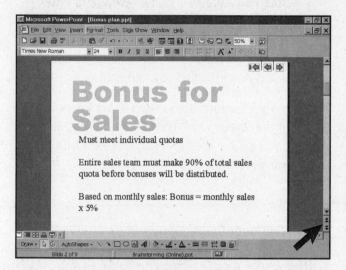

1 The steps for moving from slide to slide are the same in both Slide view and Notes Page view. Switch to either Slide or Notes Page view. To move to the next slide in the outline, click the **Next Slide** button.

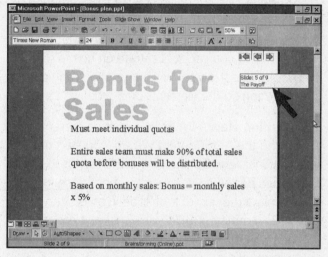

3 You can use the scroll box to move between slides. Drag the scroll box up or down until the bubble tells you that you're at the slide you want, then release the mouse button.

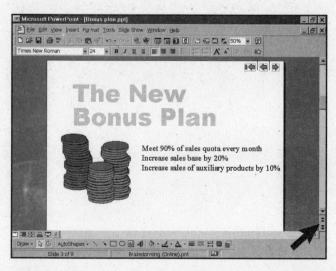

2 To move back to a previous slide, click the **Previous Slide** button.

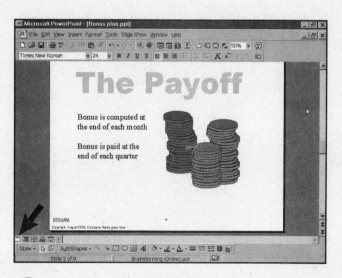

4 The slide you selected appears.

Change Views

PowerPoint has several views that enable you to see your slides using the right amount of detail. As you work, you'll often switch from one view to another, in order to find a view which suits your needs at the moment. The name of the view you are currently using appears in the Status bar.

There are four views:

Slide view—When you create a presentation using a template, you start out in Slide view. Because you can see only one slide at a time in this view, you can concentrate on how a slide looks. Use this view when inserting graphics or rearranging the elements on a slide.

Outline view—When you create a presentation using the AutoContent Wizard, you start out in Outline view. Outline view is the easiest to use when designing your presentation, since it displays the text of each slide in an easy-to-follow outline. Outline view makes it easy for you to edit, copy, or move the text on each of your slides.

Slide Sorter view—This is the view to use when you want to see an overview of your presentation. In Slide Sorter view, all your slides appear in miniature (*thumbnails*) that you can drag, in order to rearrange them within the presentation. (See "Use the Slide Sorter," page 246.)

Notes Page view—Use Notes Page to enter notes for the talk you plan to give with your presentation. In Notes Page view, only a single slide is displayed at a time. Underneath the slide is a text box in which you can enter your notes.

The Slide view buttons are located in the lower-left corner of the screen, and to change from one view to another, you simply click them. The button for the current view looks pushed in.

The last view button, Slide Show, isn't like the others, so it is not covered here. When you click the Slide Show button, your slides are displayed on-screen, one at a time, as they would appear during your presentation. See the task, "View the Slide Show," on page 285 for more information.

Begin Guided Tour   Use the Different Views

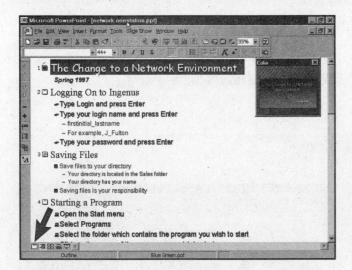

1 Typically, you begin working on your presentation in Outline view. If the icon to the left of the slide is blank, then the slide does not contain any artwork. If the slide has some art, then a small picture appears in the icon. Click the **Slide view** button to change to Slide view.

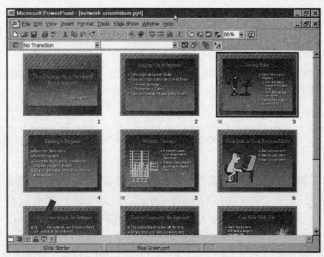

3 Slide Sorter view displays all your slides at once, in miniature. Use this view to quickly move a slide from one position in the presentation to another. Click the **Note Pages view** button to change to that view.

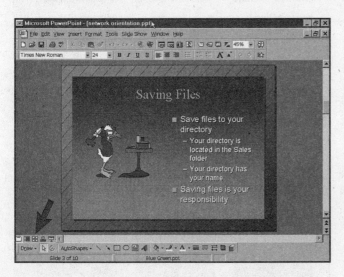

2 In Slide View, PowerPoint displays one slide at a time. This is the view to use when adding graphics, or rearranging the data on a slide. Click the **Slide Sorter view** button.

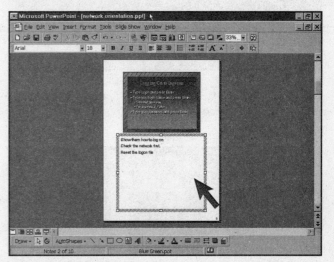

4 Notes Page view displays a miniature version of one slide per page with space for notes. Here you can add reminders about what you want to talk about when you display the slide.

Use the Slide Sorter

In Slide Sorter view, you can easily make changes to the overall presentation. For example, you might decide that moving one of the slides in your presentation will improve its flow. If you move your slides around while you're in Slide Sorter view, you can examine the thumbnails for a series of slides and see how each slide relates to the others.

Begin Guided Tour Change the Order of Slides

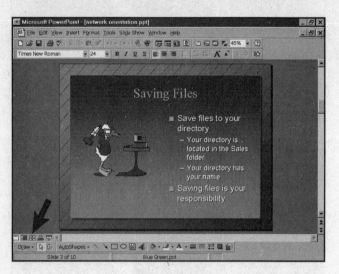

1 From any other view, click the **Slide Sorter view** button to switch to the Slide Sorter view.

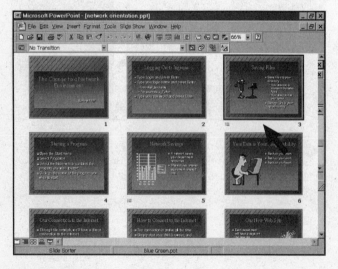

2 Click the slide you want to move. The slide appears with a dark border around it (indicating that it's selected).

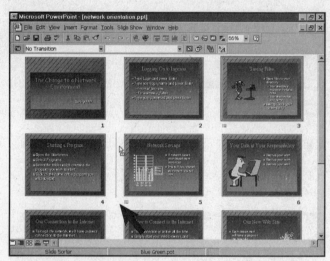

3 Drag the selected slide to its new location. The drag-and-drop mouse pointer appears (a little box is added to the pointer), and a vertical line marks the slide's new location. Release the mouse button.

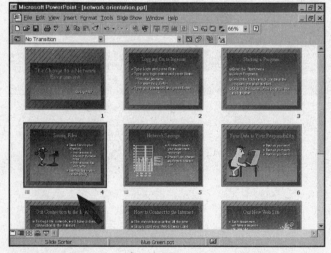

4 PowerPoint moves the slide and renumbers all the other slides accordingly.

Create a Chart (Graph)

A chart (graph) presents data in a graphical format so that people are better able to see trends in data and pick up on the point you are making. By turning numeric data into a chart, you can make the data (and your audience) come alive.

When you create a chart, you enter the chart data into a simple grid called the *datasheet*. PowerPoint then creates the chart, using the column chart type.

After completing the chart, you may find that there are several things you want to change. As you add or change data, you can switch back and forth between the datasheet and the chart to verify how your changes affect the chart.

Although PowerPoint does a terrific job of creating your chart, sometimes the text in the chart doesn't look quite the way you want it to. You can modify the fonts in the chart and their sizes. You can also change the alignment of the text from horizontal to vertical.

You can easily change the chart type and other elements of your chart as well. The *chart options* allow you to add a title to your chart, or to the value (y) axis and the category (x) axis. Adding titles helps your viewers identify what data is being charted. In addition, the chart options allow you to add gridlines to help your viewers determine the value of a particular data point. Also, you can opt to display (or not display) a legend, data labels (labels which identify each column, bar, line, and so on), or a data table (the table of data from which the chart was plotted).

Resize a Chart

You can resize a chart to make it larger or smaller. When you resize a chart, the size of its text and its other elements are also resized proportionately. Follow these steps:

1. Click the chart once to select it. Handles appear around the chart.

2. Position the mouse pointer over one of the corners of the chart so it changes to a two-headed arrow. Drag the corner outward to make the chart bigger; drag it inward to make the chart smaller. A ghostly outline of the chart follows the mouse pointer so you can see the new size.

3. Release the mouse button, and the chart is resized to fit the ghostly outline. Press **Esc** twice to return to your PowerPoint slide.

Move a Chart

You can move a chart anywhere on the slide by following these steps:

1. Click the chart to select it. Handles appear around the chart. Double-click the chart to open it. A hashed outline appears around the chart.

2. Position the mouse pointer over the chart. The mouse pointer changes to a four-headed arrow. Drag the chart to its new location. An outline of the chart follows the mouse pointer.

3. Release the mouse button, and the chart is moved to the location you indicated. Press **Esc** twice to return to your PowerPoint slide.

Begin Guided Tour Add a Chart (Graph) to a Slide

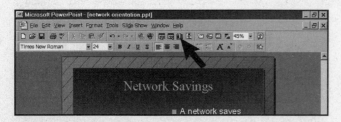

1 In Slide View, move to the slide on which you want to insert a chart. If a chart placeholder exists, then double-click it. If not, click the **Insert Chart** button on the Standard toolbar. PowerPoint opens a datasheet (table).

			A	B	C	D
			Jan	Feb	Mar	4th Qtr
1		East	20.4	27.4	90	20.4
2		West	30.6	38.6	34.6	31.6
3		North	45.9	46.9	45	43.9
4						

network orientation.ppt – Datasheet

2 The datasheet contains sample data. When you enter data into each cell (box) it replaces the sample data. Click the cell that contains the word "1st Qtr," and type the name of a category. Press the **right arrow** to move to the next cell. Continue until you've entered all your categories.

> Categories in a table typically represent units of time, such as quarters, months, or years.

			A	B	C	D
			Jan	Feb	Mar	4th Qtr
1		Indiana	20.4	27.4	90	20,4
2		Ohio	30.6	38.6	34.6	31.6
3		North	45.9	46.9	45	43.9
4						

network orientation.ppt – Datasheet

3 Click the cell that contains the word "East," and enter the name of your first data series. If your table contains more than one data series, press the **down arrow** to move to the cell that contains "West."

			A	B	C	D
			Jan	Feb	Mar	4th Qtr
1		Indiana	20.4	27.4	90	20.4
2		Ohio	30.6	38.6	34.6	31.6
3						
4						

network orientation.ppt – Datasheet

4 If any of the sample data is left after you enter your real data into the datasheet, delete it. Click the column's (or row's) header, then press **Delete**.

			A	B	C	D
			Jan	Feb	Mar	
1		Indiana	12549	11987	13445	
2		Ohio	13222	14989	15667	
3						
4						

network orientation.ppt – Datasheet

5 Enter the information for your chart. Click a cell and type the information you want there. Use the arrow keys to move from cell to cell, or you click with your mouse.

			A	B	C	D
			Jan	Feb	Mar	
1		Indiana	12549	11987	13445	
2		Ohio	13222	14989	15667	
3						
4						

network orientation.ppt – Datasheet

6 When you finish entering your data, click the **View Datasheet** button to turn it off. View Datasheet is a *toggle* button. When it's enabled (it appears to be pushed in), you see the datasheet grid. When it's not enabled, you see the chart.

Guided Tour   Add a Chart (Graph) to a Slide

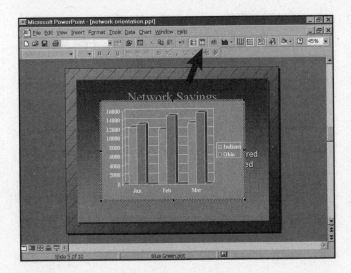

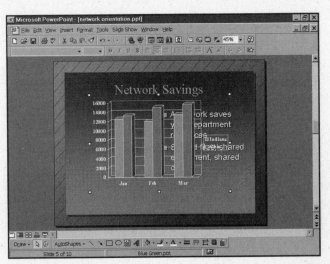

7 PowerPoint assumes that your data series were entered in rows and your categories in columns. If you entered your data series in columns, click the **By Column** button. When you switch the view, the data currently displayed on the x-axis and the legend change places.

8 Press the **Esc** key twice to return to the slide and deselect the chart.

If you add a chart to a slide that already contains data (like the one shown here) you'll probably need to resize it. See "Resize a Chart," page 247 for help.

Begin Guided Tour   Change and Add Chart Data

1 Open the chart by double-clicking it. A thatched border surrounds the chart. Click the **View Datasheet** button to switch back to the datasheet grid.

		A	B	C	D
		Jan	Feb	Mar	Apr
1	Indiana	12549	11987	13445	13098
2	Ohio	13222	14989	15667	
3					
4					

2 To change data, click the cell and type the new data. To add data, click an empty cell and type your data. You can also use the arrow keys to move from cell to cell.

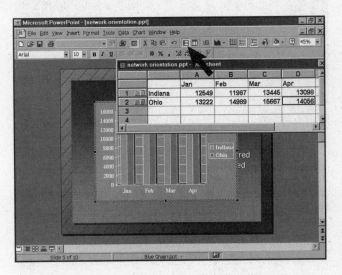

3 As you enter data, the chart under the datasheet is adjusted to reflect your changes. To remove the datasheet so you can see the chart, click the **View Datasheet** button again.

Begin Guided Tour Modify Chart Text

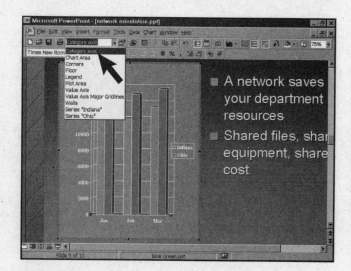

1 Double-click the chart to open it, and then click any text you want to modify. Optionally, you can select the object you want to modify from the **Chart Objects** list on the Standard toolbar. For example, you can select **Category Axis**. Handles appear at either end of the axis you select.

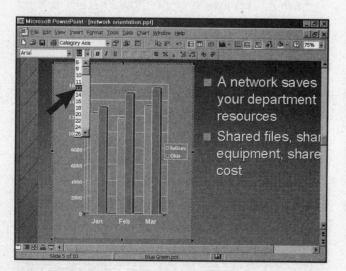

2 To change the font of the selected labels, choose a font from the **Font** list on the formatting toolbar. To change the size of the label text, choose a point size from the **Font Size** list.

Too many fonts can detract from your chart. Try to limit the number of fonts you use to two.

3 You can add bold, italic, or underline attributes to the selected labels by clicking the appropriate button on the Formatting toolbar. For example, click the **Italic** button.

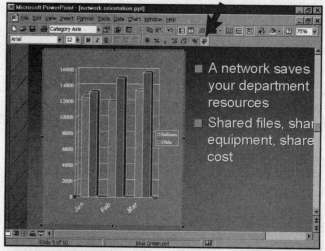

4 To change the orientation of the selected labels, click either the **Angle Text Upward** or the **Angle Text Downward** button on the Formatting toolbar.

To save space on a large chart, angle your label text.

Guided Tour Modify Chart Text

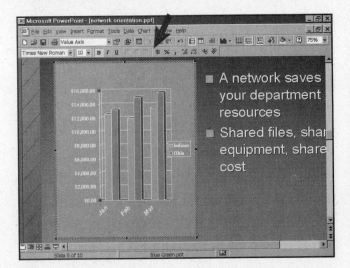

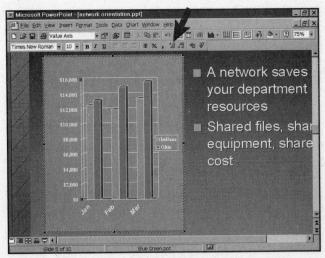

5 To change the format of the numbers of the value axis, select **Value Axis** from the Chart Objects list, then click a number style button on the Formatting toolbar, such as the **Currency Style** button, the **Percent Style** button, or the **Comma Style** button.

6 To decrease the number of decimals used in the value labels, click the **Decrease Decimal** button on the Formatting toolbar. To increase the number of decimals, click the **Increase Decimal** button instead. You can click these buttons multiple times, as needed, to display the number of decimal places you desire.

7 When you're through making changes to your chart, press **Esc** twice to return to your PowerPoint slide.

Begin Guided Tour Change the Chart Type

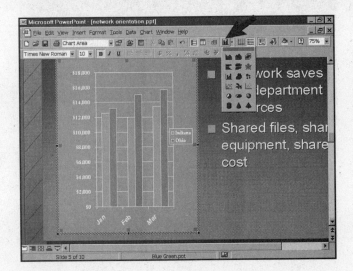

To change to the chart type shown on the Chart Type button, simply click the button itself, rather than the adjacent arrow.

(continues)

1 Double-click the chart to open it. Click the arrow next to the **Chart Type** button on the Standard toolbar. In the palette list that appears, click the chart type you want to use.

Guided Tour Change the Chart Type

(continued)

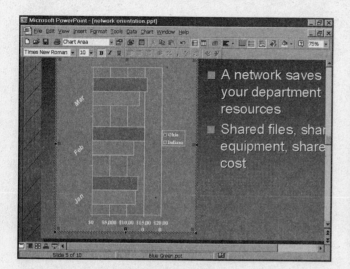

(2) PowerPoint applies the new chart type you selected to your data and displays it in the chart window.

If you select a 3-D chart from the Chart Type list, you can change how the chart looks by rotating it. By rotating the chart, you can emphasize a particular data series by making it more visible. (Likewise, you can de-emphasize a series by making it less visible.)

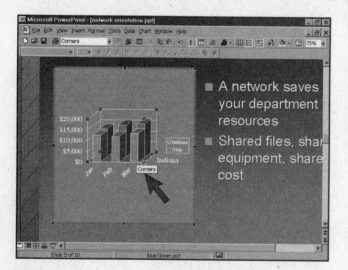

(3) If you select a 3-D chart from the Chart Type list, you can change how the chart looks by rotating it. To rotate the chart, position the mouse cursor at the lower-right corner. The handle under it turns into a "+," and the word, "Corners" appears.

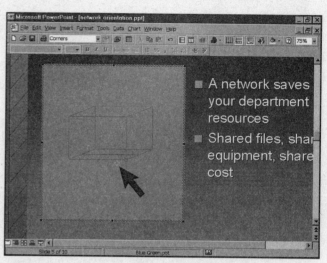

(4) Click and drag the mouse pointer. The chart disappears, and in its place you see a 3-D outline that rotates as you drag the mouse pointer.

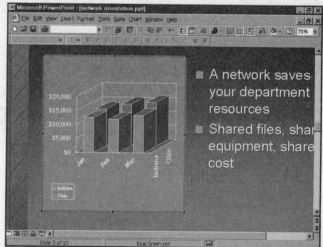

(5) Release the mouse button when you're satisfied with the chart's new position. The chart is rotated to the position you selected.

(6) Press **Esc** twice to deselect the chart.

Begin Guided Tour   Change Chart Options

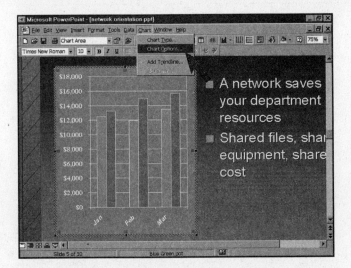

1 Double-click the chart to open it. Open the **Chart** menu and choose **Chart Options**. The Chart Options dialog box appears. Click a tab and change the options as follows:

On the **Titles** tab, you can enter a chart title (although you may already have a title on the slide), and a title for the x or y axes. As you make your changes, they're displayed in the preview area.

On the **Axes** tab, you can turn off the x or y axes labels if you like. This might be a good idea if a chart is crowded with labels and data, as the 3-D chart shown here.

> Often, the axis labels are the only thing which enable a viewer to understand your data, so be careful about turning them off.

On the **Gridlines** tab, you can add minor gridlines to the Value axis (extra lines between the major gridlines), turn off gridlines, or display gridlines from the Category (x) axis. Turn these options on or off to see which combination helps you view the data more clearly.

On the **Legend** tab, you can choose exactly where you want the legend displayed (if at all). To turn the legend display off, click the **Show legend** option to deselect it. To move the position of the legend, select an area from the placement list. On this chart, the legend appears at the top.

> A legend is important in charts with several data series, since they help the viewer identify what each series stands for.

On the **Data Labels** tab, you can add value labels (to help identify the exact value of a particular data point—handy in a pie chart like this one), or category labels (to help identify each category). If you show the legend key next to a label, the legend symbol (the color) for that data series appears next to the label.

On the **Data Table** tab, you can opt to display the datasheet (the table into which you originally entered your chart data), shown here with a column chart.

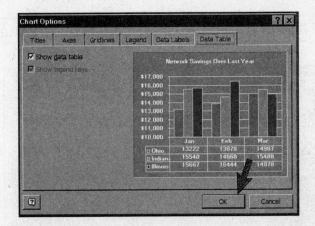

2 When you're through selecting chart options, click **OK**. The chart changes to reflect the options you selected.

Create an Organization Chart

An organization chart (or org chart) is an attractive way of presenting the relationships between people in a group. Once you create an org chart, you can add, delete, and move people within the chart as they move within your company.

PowerPoint makes it easy for you to add a new person to a group. When you add a person to an org chart, PowerPoint automatically adds the lines to connect that person to others in the group, adjusting the spacing and size of the placeholders as needed.

Each person on an org chart is represented by one of the following types:

- **Subordinate**—Reports to a Manager.
- **Coworker**—A peer; coworkers report to the same Manager.

- **Manager**—A person who has subordinates reporting to him or her.
- **Assistant**—A secretary or office assistant. An assistant reports directly to a Manager, but has no coworkers or peers.

When you move a person from one position to another on the org chart or delete a person from an org chart, PowerPoint automatically fixes the shape and appearance of the chart. PowerPoint makes sure the spacing between positions looks good and the lines connect related placeholders.

When you finish with your org chart and insert it in a slide, you can easily make the chart larger or smaller or move it to a different area of the slide. You learn how to do all these tasks in the following Guided Tours.

Begin Guided Tour   Add an Organization Chart to a Slide

1 Make sure the slide on which you want to insert the org chart is displayed on-screen. Then open the **Insert** menu, select **Picture**, then select **Organization Chart**. The Organization Chart program starts in its own window.

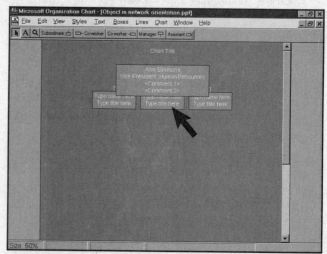

2 A placeholder with the words, Type name here appears highlighted in the highest ranking position on the chart. Type the name you want in the selected box, and press **Enter** to add a job title for that person. If you want, you can add two lines of optional comments by pressing **Enter** after the title line.

Guided Tour Add an Organization Chart to a Slide

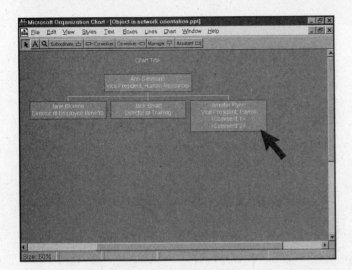

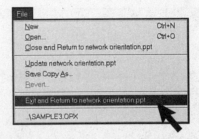

③ Click each additional placeholder that you want to replace with a name and title. Enter the appropriate information, pressing **Enter** to advance from the name to the title and comment lines.

You don't have to replace every placeholder with text. Whether you replace a placeholder or not, only the text you do type appears in the final org chart.

⑤ When you finish adding people to the org chart, you need to return to the slide. Open the **File** menu and choose **Exit and Return to** *the name of your presentation*. (The name of your presentation appears as part of the command.)

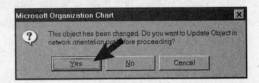

⑥ If you haven't saved your work, this dialog box is displayed. Click **Yes** to update the chart on the slide. (Alternatively, you can click **No** to keep the existing chart on the slide the way it is, or you can click **Cancel** to continue working.)

⑦ Once you return to the slide, press **Esc** twice or click an open area on the slide to deselect the org chart.

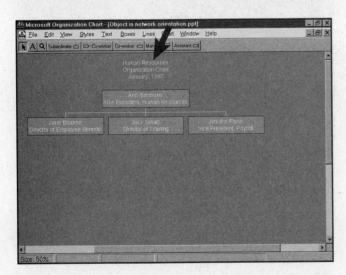

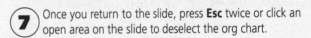

④ Highlight the **Chart Title** placeholder, and type a title for your organization chart.

Begin Guided Tour Add or Delete a Person from an Organization Chart

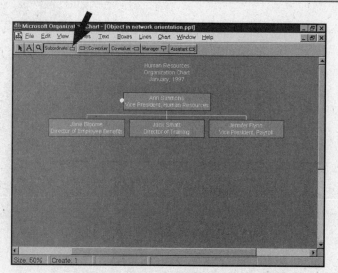

1 Double-click the org chart to open it. Then click the toolbar button for the type of position you want to add (the **Subordinate** button, for example).

Here, a subordinate works *for* someone, and a coworker works *with* someone. Generally, an assistant relieves another's responsibilities.

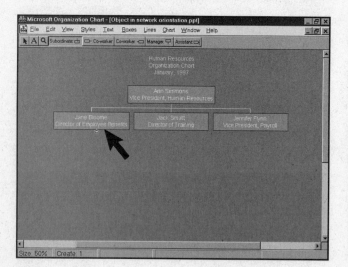

2 The mouse pointer changes to the symbol on the button you clicked. Click the placeholder box for the person in relation to whom you're adding the new position. In our example, we're adding a subordinate for Jane Bloome, so click Jane's position.

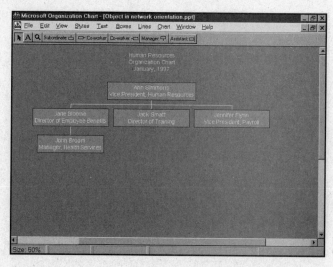

3 A placeholder appears for the new position. Type the new person's name and title and any necessary comments. Press **Enter** to move from one line of text to the next.

To return to a regular mouse pointer, click the **Select** button (the arrow).

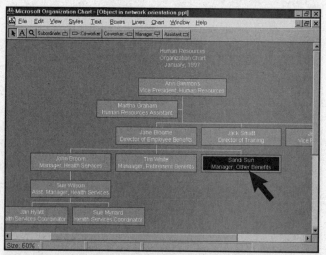

4 To remove a person from your org chart, select the position you want to delete by clicking it.

5 Open the **Edit** menu and choose **Clear**, or press the **Delete** key. The selected position is deleted.

Begin Guided Tour Move People in an Organization Chart

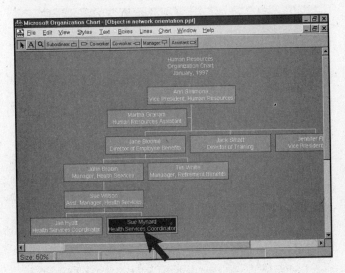 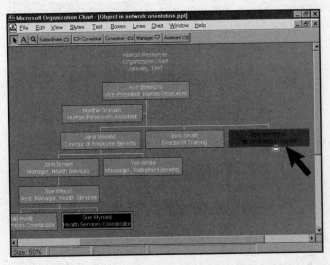

1 Double-click the org chart to open it. Then click the person you want to move and drag it on top of the placeholder for the person to whom the selected position now reports.

2 When the placeholder reaches the new location, release the mouse button. Your person is moved to his or her new location and the org chart is adjusted as necessary.

3 Press the **Esc** key or click an open area of the chart to deselect the placeholder.

Begin Guided Tour Change Relationships Within Groups

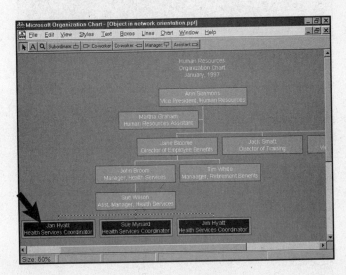 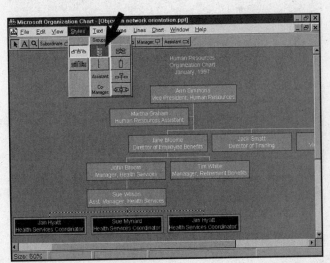

1 To change the relationship between two persons in a group (persons at the same level within a chart), double-click any member of the group. The whole group appears selected.

2 Open the **Styles** menu and choose a new group style.

3 The Microsoft Organization Chart program changes the selected group to the style you selected.

Begin Guided Tour   Move and Resize an Organization Chart

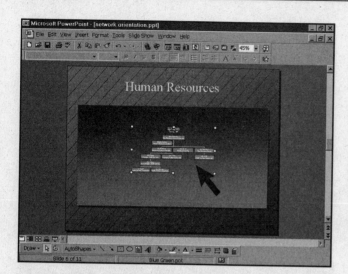

1 If needed, open the **File** menu and select **Exit and Return to** *Presentation1* to your organization chart and return to the PowerPoint window. Then, in Slide View, select the org chart by clicking it. Handles appear around the chart.

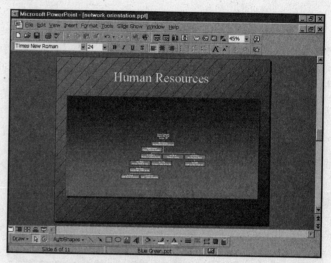

3 When you're satisfied with the chart's new location, release the mouse button. Press **Esc** to deselect the chart.

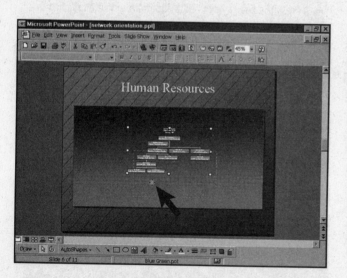

2 To move the org chart, position the mouse pointer over the chart, and the mouse pointer changes to a four-headed arrow. Click and drag the chart. An outline of the org chart's shape follows the mouse pointer as you drag.

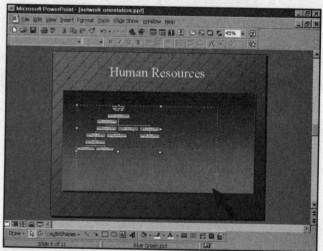

4 To resize an org chart, position the mouse pointer over a corner handle, and the pointer changes to a double-headed arrow. Click the handle and drag. An outline of the org chart moves with the mouse pointer as you drag.

5 When the outline is the size you want, release the mouse button.

Format and Run a PowerPoint Presentation

After you create a PowerPoint presentation, you will probably spend some time improving the look of the presentation. For example, you might change the font of selected text, apply a different template to your presentation, add clip art, and much more. Look to this part for help on adding the finishing touches to your presentation.

After you feel that you have a finished presentation, you'll want to preview it before you try it out on your audience. Fortunately, PowerPoint makes it easy for you to do just that. After viewing your presentation, you may decide to jazz it up by adding animated transitions between slides and to your graphics. In this part, you'll learn how to "tweak" a good presentation into a great one.

What You Will Find in This Section

Change the Look of Text

As you perfect the text in your slides, you might decide you want to emphasize some of the words. You can emphasize text by adding attributes such as boldface, italics, underlining, shadow, or color. You can also add *embossing*, which makes the text appear as if it has been raised off the slide in a kind of relief. You can add bold, italics, underlining, and shadow using buttons on the Formatting toolbar. You can change text color just as easily with the **Font Color** button on the Drawing toolbar. However, to add embossing, you must use the Font dialog box.

You might also want to change your text to a different font or to change its size. Doing so often adds emphasis to your text or helps to create a particular tone of voice (such as professional or casual) for your presentation. A *font* is a family of characters that shares a similar style and design. Characters within fonts are measured in *points*, and there are 72 points in an inch. The higher the point size, the bigger the character.

> You can combine attributes by clicking more than one button on the Formatting toolbar. For example, to make a selected word bold and italic, click both the **Bold** and the **Italic** buttons on the Formatting toolbar.

> Font sizes appear to vary from font to font. For example, 12-point Times New Roman doesn't appear to be the same size as some other 12-point fonts. If you measure the height of the characters, however, the actual point size of the fonts is the same.

Begin Guided Tour   Add Bold, Italic, Underline, or Shadow

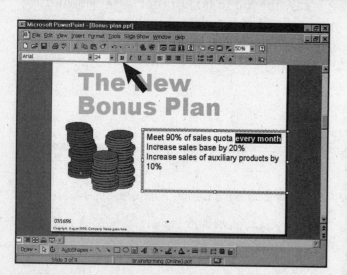

U To underline text, click the **Underline** button on the Formatting toolbar.

S To add shadow to text, lick the **Shadow** button.

1 Select the word or words you want to change and do one of the following:

B To bold text, click the **Bold** button on the Formatting toolbar.

I To italicize text, click the **Italic** button on the Formatting toolbar.

2 PowerPoint makes the change. This figure shows italicized text.

Begin Guided Tour Change Text Color

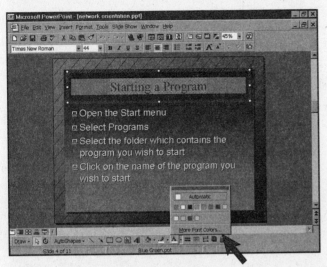

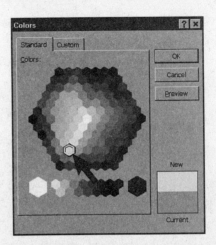

1 Select the text whose color you want to change, and then click the **Font Color** down arrow on the Drawing toolbar. Click the color you want. The Colors dialog box appears.

2 Click a color to select it, and then click **OK**. The selected text changes to the color you selected.

Begin Guided Tour Add Embossing

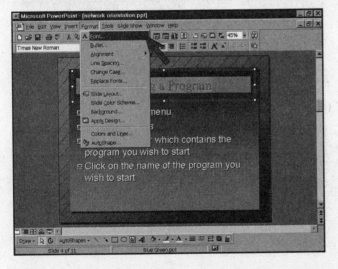

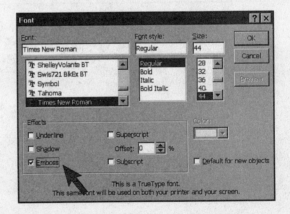

1 To add embossing (a raised relief effect), select the text you want to change and then open the **Format** menu and select **Font**. The Font dialog box appears.

2 Click the **Emboss** check box. A check mark appears to tell you that the option is selected. Click **OK**.

(continues)

Guided Tour Add Embossing

(continued)

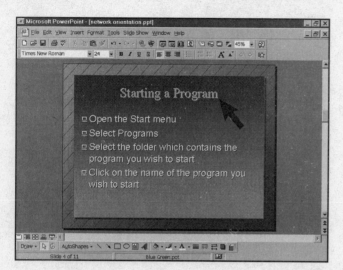

3 Embossing is added to the selected text. (Note that any color that has been added to the text is removed.)

Begin Guided Tour Change Font or Font Size of Text

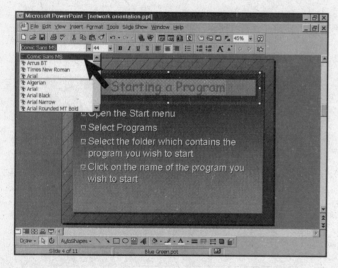

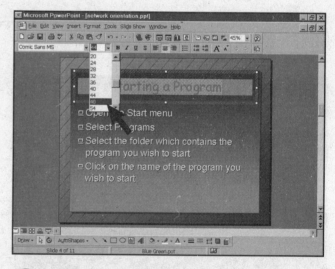

1 Select the text you want to change and then click the **Font** drop-down arrow. Click the font you want. (You'll find recently used fonts at the top of the list.)

2 You can change the font size of text by selecting it, clicking the **Font Size** drop-down arrow, and clicking the size you want.

Most computers start off with certain fonts already installed on them. As you install new programs, those programs typically add more fonts to your system. Thus, your list of fonts might look different from the one in this book.

Guided Tour Change Font or Font Size of Text

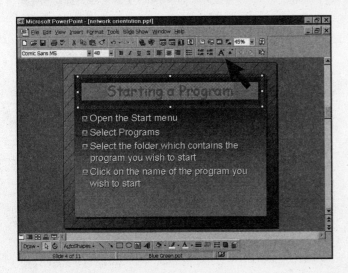

3 You can increase the point size of selected text in increments by clicking the **Increase Font Size** button. To decrease the size of text, click the **Decrease Font Size** button (just to the right of the Increase Font Size button).

Change the Alignment of Text

Part of perfecting your presentation includes making sure you line up all your text exactly the way you want it. For example, you can use text alignment to draw your audience's attention to a particular part of a slide. You can choose left, center, right, or justified alignment.

Alignment controls where the text appears within a text block. For example, *left alignment* lines up the words on the left side of the text block. *Right alignment* lines up all the words on the right side of the

text block, and *center alignment* centers the words within the text block. *Justified alignment* lines your text up on both the left and right sides of the text block, adding extra spaces as needed.

Only left, right, and center alignment have buttons on the Formatting toolbar. To select justified alignment, you have to choose the **Format, Alignment** command. This opens a submenu where you can choose from all four alignment controls.

Begin Guided Tour   Set a New Alignment

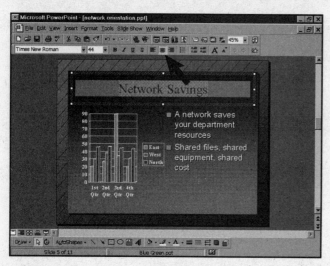

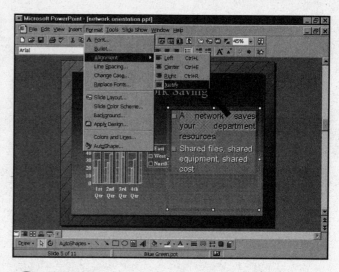

1 To change text alignment, select the text and do one of the following:

 Click the **Center Alignment** button on the Formatting toolbar. PowerPoint centers the text between the margins of the text block.

 Click the **Left Alignment** button to align text against the left margin.

 Click the **Right Alignment** button to align text against the right margin.

The figure shows text that has been centered in the selected text block.

2 You can justify text (a process which adds spaces between words in order to get the text in a paragraph to touch both the left and right margins) by opening the **Format** menu, selecting **Alignment**, then selecting **Justify**.

Draw on a Slide

When you're striving to create an effective presentation, you might want to take advantage of PowerPoint's drawing tools to highlight some information. For example, if you're using a cartoon image, you might want to add a *balloon comment* (like the bubbles that appear above cartoon character's heads). You can help the audience better understand a slide by using one of these methods.

> If the Drawing toolbar is not displayed, open the **View** menu, select **Toolbars**, and select **Drawing** to display it.

In this task, you'll get a tour of some of the various tools. To use any drawing tool, you follow the same basic steps:

1. Click the tool you want to use.

2. Click the slide and drag to create your shape.

You can change the style of the object you created by clicking it and then clicking the appropriate style button, such as **Line Style** or **Fill Color**. You can also change the style of an object *prior* to drawing it by setting the appropriate styles before you click the drawing tool you want to use. The following table identifies and explains how to use each tool.

Tool	Name	Description
 Draw ▾	Draw button	Provides access to a menu of commands that allow you to group, align, and rotate objects.
 ▧	Select Objects	Enables you to select an object so that you can move, delete, resize, or format it.
 ↺	Free Rotate	Use this tool to rotate an object.
 AutoShapes ▾	AutoShapes	Click this button to display a palette of autoshapes. Click the shape you want and then drag on the slide to draw the shape.
 ╲	Line	Use this tool to draw a line. To draw a straight line, hold down the Shift key as you drag.
 ↘	Arrow	Use this tool to draw a line with an arrowhead at one end.
 ▢	Rectangle	Use this tool to draw a rectangle. To draw a perfect square, hold down the Shift key as you draw.
 ⬭	Oval	Use this tool to draw a circle or oval. Press the Shift key as you drag to draw a circle.
 ▣	Text Box	Use this button to draw a text box on-screen. After you drag to draw the text box, type the text within the box.
 ◀	Insert WordArt	Create special text effects (such as curved and slanted text) with this button.

(continues)

Tool	Name	Description
	Fill Color	Fill the selected object with the color or pattern you choose.
	Line Color	Change the color of the selected line.
	Font Color	Change the color of selected text.
	Line Style	Change line styles.
	Dash Style	Change the style of dashed lines.
	Arrow Style	Change the style of an arrow.
	Shadow	Apply a shadow to the selected object.
	3-D	Create three-dimensional text.

Begin Guided Tour   Draw Various Objects

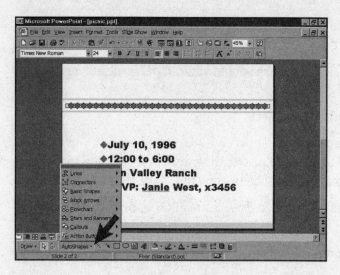

1 Select the slide you want to draw on and click one of the buttons on the Drawing toolbar. To add a banner, for example, click the **AutoShapes** button.

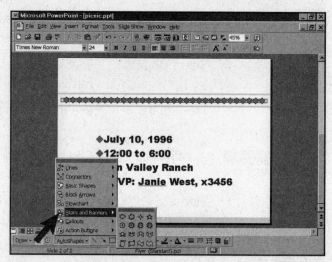

2 Select a category, then click the shape you want to use. For example, to add the banner, select the **Stars and Banners** category, then click the banner shape you like.

Guided Tour   Draw Various Objects

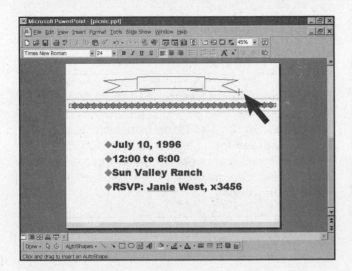

3 The mouse pointer changes to a small cross. Click the slide where you want the upper-left corner of the shape to be, and drag downward and to the right to create the shape. Release the mouse button when the shape is the size you want. Handles appear around the shape, indicating that it's selected.

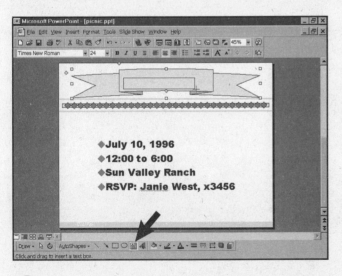

4 To add text to the banner, click the **Text Box** button. Click the banner and drag to create a text box on top of it.

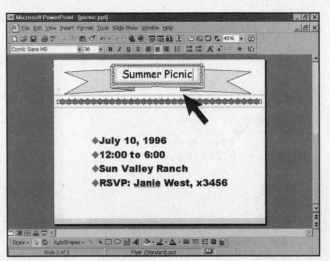

5 Type your message. You can use the buttons on the Formatting toolbar to change the font, size, or attributes of the text if you like. When you finish, click anywhere in the slide or press the **Esc** key twice to deselect the text box.

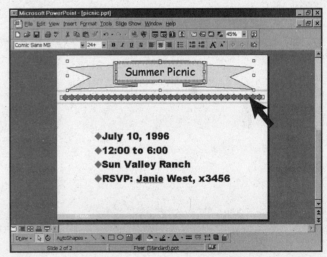

6 You can group the two objects, (the banner and the text box) together, to make positioning them on the slide a bit easier. Click the text box, and handles appear to show that it's selected. Press and hold the **Shift** key as you click the banner. Handles appear around the banner, too.

(continues)

Guided Tour Draw Various Objects

(continued)

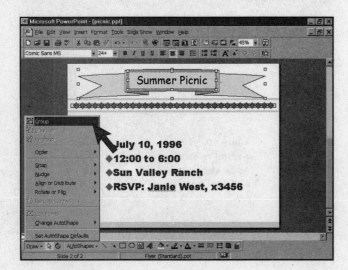

 Click the **Draw** button on the Drawing toolbar, and select **Group**.

With your two objects grouped together, they act as one unit, which you can drag to move around. You can also resize both objects at one time by dragging a handle. To ungroup the objects so you can work on them separately, click the group, then click the **Draw** button and select **Ungroup**.

Use AutoClipArt

AutoClipArt is a feature that suggests clip art images for the slides in your presentation, based on the content of those slides. After reviewing your words, AutoClipArt presents you with a selection of clip art images that echo the meaning of your slides. You then select the clip art image that you think most reflects the intent of each slide. Use AutoClipArt to avoid the hassle of reviewing every picture in the Microsoft ClipArt Gallery just to find appropriate pieces of art for your presentation.

The trick of course, is to use keywords in your presentation that can be found in the Microsoft ClipArt gallery. If, for example, the text in your presentation doesn't match the keywords for any of the art work in the Gallery, then you'll see a message telling you so. You can still insert an image on your own, however, by clicking **View Clip Art** to browse through the ClipArt Gallery images.

Begin Guided Tour   Insert Images with AutoClipArt

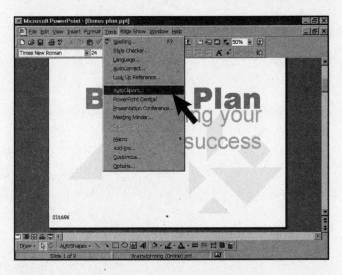

1 Open the **Tools** menu and select **AutoClipArt**. PowerPoint scans your presentation looking for keywords.

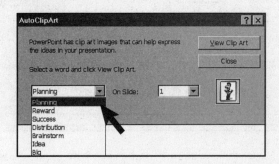

2 After AutoClipArt reviews your presentation's text, it displays the AutoClipArt dialog box. Select a key word from the first list.

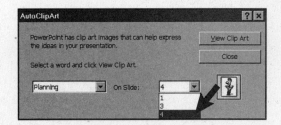

3 If the keyword you select in step 2 appears on several slides, you can choose on which slide you want to insert the clip art by selecting a slide number from the **On Slide** list. The slide you select appears under the dialog box, so you can see the text to which the key word refers.

(continues)

Guided Tour   Insert Images with AutoClipArt   *(continued)*

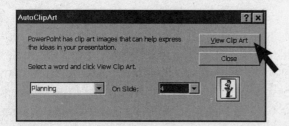

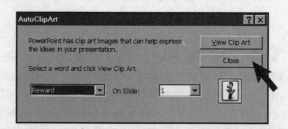

4 Click **View Clip Art**. The Microsoft Clip Gallery 3.0 dialog box appears.

6 Select another keyword if you like, and repeat steps 2 and 3 to insert an image on the same or a different slide. When you're done, click **Close** to close the AutoClipArt dialog box.

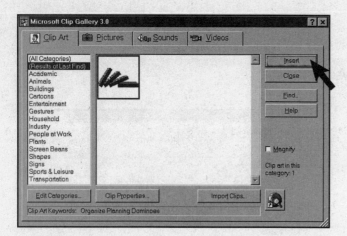

5 Scroll through the images which match the key word you selected. Click an image, then click **Insert** to add it to the slide. You're returned to the AutoClipArt dialog box.

Change the Color Scheme

Powerpoint comes with a variety of presentation designs, or *templates*. A typical design template uses one color for the background, one for the text, a set of colors for any graphs you might insert, and so on. This collection of basic colors used in a presentation is called its *color scheme*.

If you don't like the colors of your chosen presentation template, you can change each one individually, but you may spend a lot of time looking for and selecting complementary colors. As a result, you may end up with a hodgepodge of colors that do not complement your design.

An easier way is to select from a series of color palettes, each with its own set of complementary

colors. Each palette contains colors that not only look well together but that contrast well enough to make the presentation readable.

When selecting a color scheme, you can choose to apply it to the current slide only, or throughout your presentation. It is usually best to apply the same colors to every slide, because that gives your presentation a cohesive look.

If you don't like the new color scheme after you apply it, undo the change using the **Edit Undo** command or the **Undo** button on the toolbar.

Begin Guided Tour   Select a New Color Scheme

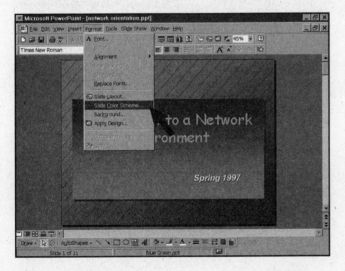

(1) If you want to change the background color of just one slide, display that slide first. Then open the **Format** menu and select **Slide Color Scheme**.

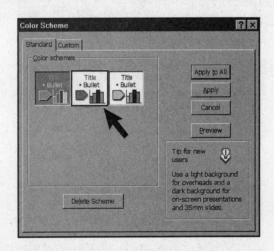

(2) PowerPoint displays the Color Scheme dialog box. Click the **Standard** tab. The Standard tab displays palettes of complementary colors that would go well with the presentation. Each example shows the colors for shadows, background, text and lines, fills, and graphs. To select a color palette, click it.

(continues)

Guided Tour Select a New Color Scheme

(continued)

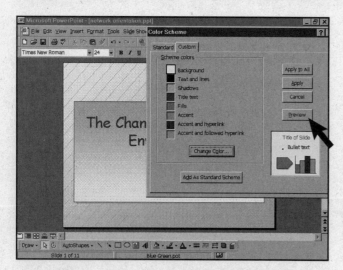 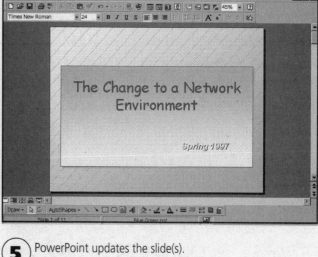

3 To preview your color scheme, click the **Preview** button and look on your slide screen to see the colors (you may have to move the dialog box out of your way to see the slide).

5 PowerPoint updates the slide(s).

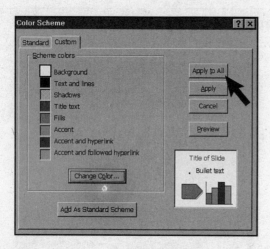

Use the Custom tab in the Color Scheme dialog box to create a customized color scheme. Click the item's current color then click the **Change Color** button. In the Color dialog box, select a new color from the palette then click **OK** to return to the Color Scheme dialog box. You can add your custom color scheme to the list of standard color palettes by clicking **Add as a Standard Scheme**.

4 Once you find the color scheme you want to use, click **Apply to All** to apply that scheme to each slide in the presentation. To apply that scheme to only the current slide, click **Apply** instead.

Customize the Background

When you change the color scheme of a presentation (as you learned to do in the previous task), you can select from several different color palettes. Each of these palettes has a distinctive, solid colored background.

Many of the templates, however, include backgrounds that contain a mix of textures, fills, and shading. As a result, the backgrounds in most of the templates are more exciting. However, you may not have based your presentation on one of these templates (you might have used the blank presentation style, for example), or the template you chose may not include a dynamic background such as those described here.

With the Fill Effects dialog box, you can choose a background that looks like marble or wood. Or you can choose two solid colors and create a unique look with a select pattern or shaded fill (called a *gradient*). You can even select a graphic image to use as your background, if you like. There is an endless variety of backgrounds you can create with the Fill Effects box.

Once you make your selection, you can apply your new background throughout your presentation or to the current slide only—whichever you want.

Begin Guided Tour   Select a New Background

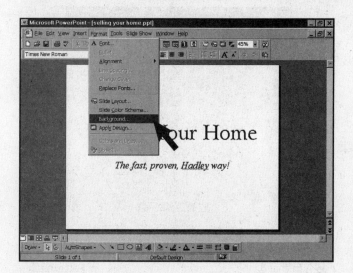

1 To change the background of only a single slide, then display it first. Open the **Format** menu and select **Background**.

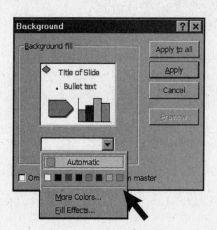

2 From the Background dialog box, you can select background colors, a shade style, a pattern, or a texture. To select a solid color background, click a new color in the drop-down list. (You can also select the **More Colors** option and choose a different color from a color dialog box.)

(continues)

Guided Tour Select a New Background

(continued)

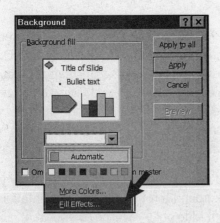

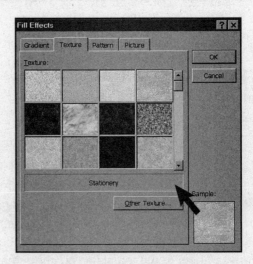

3 If you want to select a gradient, pattern, texture, or graphic picture for your background, select **Fill Effects** from the drop-down list.

5 To select a texture for the background, click the **Texture** tab. Here you can select from a variety of textures such as wood, marble, granite, and more. To select a texture, click it. Your selection appears in the Sample box. Click **OK**, and skip to step 10.

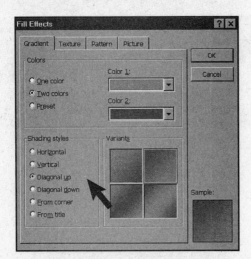

4 The Fill Effects dialog box appears. To select a gradient (shaded fill) background, click the **Gradient** tab. To blend up to two different colors, select the option you want on the left, and select the color(s) you like from the drop-down list(s) on the right. Next, select from the list of **Shading Styles**. Most styles offer several **Variants** from which you can choose and how light or dark the gradient will appear. The result of your selections appears in the Sample box. Click **OK**, and skip to step 10.

If you have a graphic which might serve as a textured background, you can import it by clicking **Other Texture.**

6 To change the background's pattern, click the **Pattern** tab. Select the two colors you want to use in your pattern from the **Foreground** and **Background** drop-down lists. Then click a pattern. Your selection appears in the Sample box. Click **OK,** and skip to step 10.

Guided Tour   Select a New Background

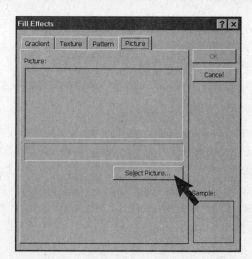

7 To use a graphic as your background, click the **Picture** tab. Then click **Select Picture** to import the graphic.

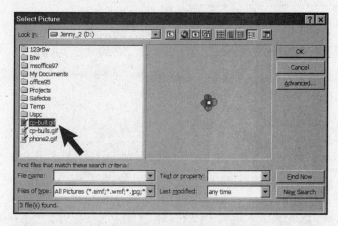

8 Change to the folder that contains the graphic you want to use as your background, select it from the list, and click **OK**.

> To see your graphic before you import it, or see what your background is going to look like, click the **Preview** button.

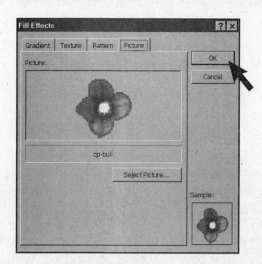

9 Click **OK**. You return to the Background dialog box.

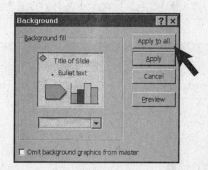

10 The gradient, texture, pattern, or picture you selected appears in the Sample box. To apply this background to the slide, click the **Apply** button. To apply the background to all slides click **Apply to All**.

11 PowerPoint formats the presentation with the new background.

Apply a Different Design Template

When you create your presentation, PowerPoint applies the preset patterns and colors of a particular design template to each slide. This gives your presentation a cohesive look.

As you've seen, PowerPoint comes with a wide variety of design templates, including generic templates, and those whose design reflects a particular topic, such as a financial report.

In any case, you can apply a different one any time you want. (The name of the current template appears on the status bar.) You might, for example, want to

use a different template that has brighter colors or simply a different design.

Changing your design template changes all the slides in your presentation. If you want to change the design for a single slide, see the tasks, "Customize the Background," page 273, and "Change the Color Scheme," page 271, for more information. To change the position and type of elements used on a single slide, see the task, "Apply a Different AutoLayout," page 278.

Begin Guided Tour Change the Template for a Presentation

1 You can perform these steps while in any view, such as Slide view, which is shown here. Click the **Apply Design** button on the Standard toolbar.

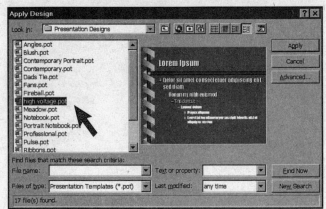

2 To select a generic template, choose **Presentation Designs** from the **Look In** list. Then click the name of a design template, and a preview of it appears in the box to the right of the list. Skip to step 4.

Guided Tour   Change the Template for a Presentation

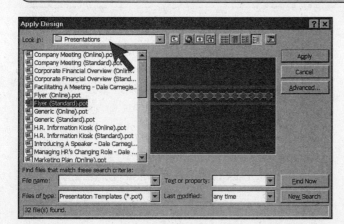

3 If you want to select a topic template, choose **Presentations** from the **Look In** list. Select a design template from the list. A preview of the design appears in the sample list.

5 PowerPoint applies the template's styles to all the slides in the presentation. (This will take a few minutes.)

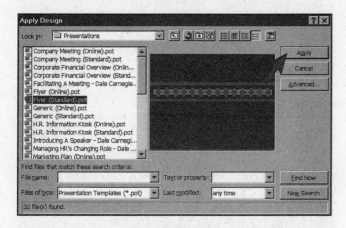

4 After selecting the template you want, click **Apply**.

Apply a Different AutoLayout

When you create a presentation with the AutoContent Wizard, or use a template, PowerPoint applies the same design template to all of your slides, providing them with the same colors, patterns, and layout.

The *layout* of a slide determines what elements it contains, such as the slide title, a chart, clip art, a bulleted list, and so on. Initially, most of the slides in your presentation will share the same layout—for example, a title at the top, followed by a bulleted list. If you want to add a new element to a particular slide such as a chart or some artwork, the simplest way to do that is to change the slide's layout.

After applying a particular layout to a slide, to add a new element, click or double-click its placeholder, as indicated.

Begin Guided Tour   Select a New AutoLayout for a Slide

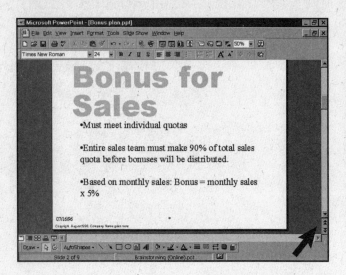

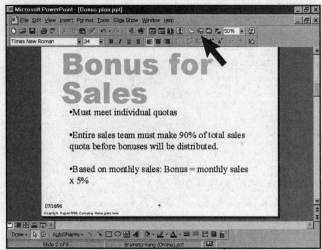

1 Change to Slide view by clicking the **Slide View** button. Click the **Previous Slide** or the **Next Slide** button on the vertical scrollbar as needed to move to the slide whose layout you want to change.

2 Click the **Slide Layout** button on the Standard toolbar.

Guided Tour Select a New AutoLayout for a Slide

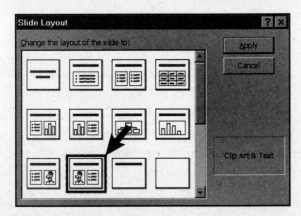

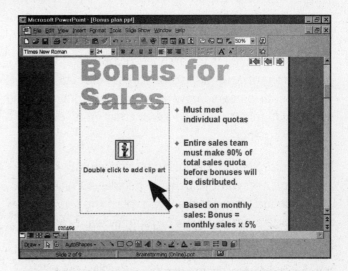

3 The Slide Layout dialog box appears. The slide's current layout is highlighted in blue. Click the layout you want to change to, and click **Apply**.

4 The slide's layout changes to the one you selected. To finish adding the new element, double-click it. For example, double-click the box which says, "Double click to add clip art."

You can also use the Slide Layout dialog box to *reapply* the current master layout of your presentation, if you want. For example, if all the slides in your presentation follow the Bulleted List layout, then click that layout and click **Reapply**.

Create Speaker Notes

Remember those mangled index cards that contained the notes for the speech you needed to give in front of your high school class? Although you're better prepared now than you were in high school, you might still need a few notes when giving your presentation.

You can use Speaker's Notes to remind you of important points you want to make or people you want to acknowledge. You may want to explain the source of financial data, for example, or you may want to be reminded to take a break at a particular point.

You can add notes as needed to any or all of the slides in your presentation. Notes, by the way, do not appear in the on-screen presentation, so your audience will not see what you enter.

After entering your notes, you may want to print them out so they can act as your script for a presentation. The notes are printed with a small thumbnail (miniature version) of the slide they relate to, so you'll always know what goes with what. You can print your notes by opening the **File** menu and selecting **Print**, then selecting **Notes Pages** from the **Print What** list, and clicking **OK**.

By default, each page of Speaker's Notes contains one slide with the notes printed beneath it. In the task, "Create Handouts," on page 282 you learn to print the Speaker's Notes in other styles to use as handouts.

Begin Guided Tour Enter Notes on a Slide

1 Select a slide on which you want to add Speaker's Notes. Then click the **Notes Page View** button. In Notes Page view, the contents of the slide appear at the top of the window, and your notes will appear at the bottom.

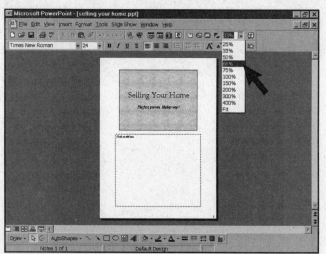

2 You will enter your notes on the lower half of the page. If the page is too small for you to see the text clearly, click the **Zoom** drop-down arrow on the Standard toolbar and select a size that is easier to read, such as 66%.

Guided Tour   Enter Notes on a Slide

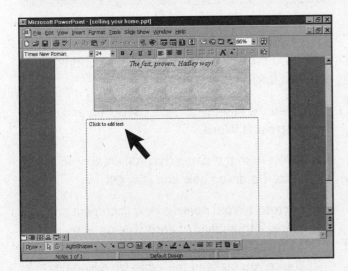

3 Click the **Click to add text** text box on the lower part of the page.

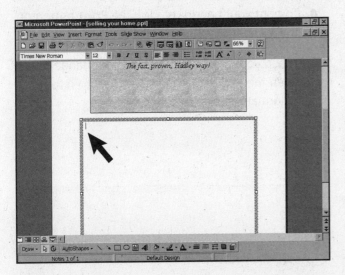

4 The words "Click to add text" disappear, and a hatched border and blinking insertion point appear. This means that the area is selected and PowerPoint is ready for you to type your notes.

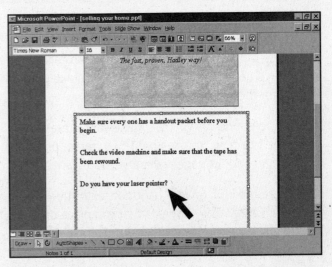

5 Type the text for your Speaker's Notes. You can select, edit, and drag-and-drop text just as you would the text in any PowerPoint slide.

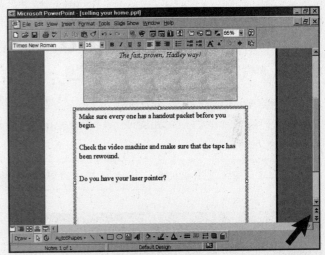

6 To add notes to another slide, click the **Next Slide** or the **Previous Slide** button. When you're through adding notes, simply select a different view, such as Slide view, by clicking the appropriate view button. PowerPoint saves your notes in the PowerPoint file; you do not have to perform additional steps to save them.

Create Handouts

In addition to Speaker Notes, you can create *handouts* from the slides in your presentation. You can pass these out to your audience so they can follow along, take notes, and have something to take with them after the presentation.

By creating handouts, you can make your presentation more effective. You can print two, three, or six slides on a handout page—whatever you want.

You create the look of your handouts with the *Handout Master*. The elements that you place on this master will appear on each handout. For example, you might add a header or a footer that will print on each handout. You can use text or graphics in the header or footer areas. For example, you may want to add your company logo, the current date, your name, the page number, or other information.

Use Microsoft Word to Create Handouts

If you have Microsoft Word installed, you can create handouts that contain miniature versions of your slides, Speaker's Notes, blank lines in which viewers can make their own notes, or a combination of any of these. You can also print an outline of your presentation. Just follow these steps:

1. Open the **File** menu, select **Send To**, and select **Microsoft Word**.

2. Select from the different configurations in the Write-Up dialog box, and click **OK**.

3. Microsoft Word opens a new document and places a thumbnail of each slide on as many pages as necessary. These pages reflect the choice you made in the Write-Up dialog box. Click the Notes area of the handout and type your comments.

4. To print your handouts, click the **Print** button on the Standard toolbar.

5. When you're through creating your handouts, open the **File** menu and select **Exit** to return to a normal view.

Begin Guided Tour   Create and Print Handouts

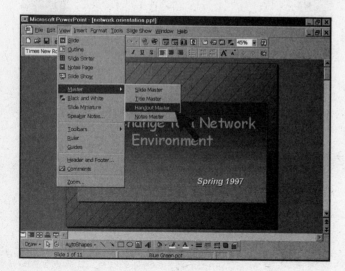

1 From any view, open the **View** menu, select **Master**, and select **Handout Master**.

You can place a graphic (such as a company logo) in the header area with the **Insert, Picture** command.

Guided Tour Create and Print Handouts

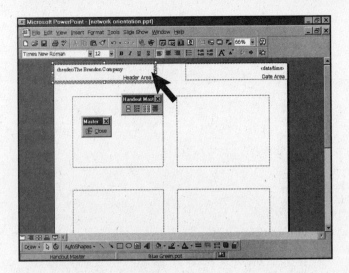

2 To add a *header*, move the cursor over the word **<header>** and click. The cursor should appear in the text box—if it does not, right-click the **Header Area** and select **Edit Text**. Then type your text.

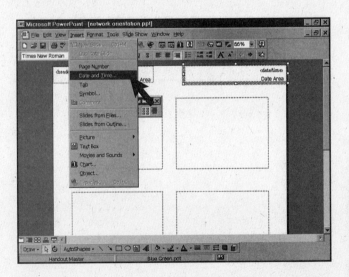

3 To add a date to your handouts, click the words, **<date/time>** in the **Date** area. The cursor should appear in the text box. If it does not, right-click the **Date** area and select **Edit Text** from the pop-up menu. Then open the **Insert** menu and select **Date and Time**. The Date and Time dialog box appears.

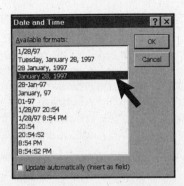

4 Select a date format and click **OK**. If you select the **Update Automatically** check box, the date is inserted as a *field*, which means that it's automatically updated whenever you save your PowerPoint file.

5 You can change the number of slides that appear on each handout, or you can choose to print an outline of the slide show by clicking the appropriate button on the Handouts Master toolbar. The view you choose *does not* determine how your handouts will print (you'll choose *that* in the Print dialog box). Changing the view with the toolbar simply lets you tell how the finished product *might* look.

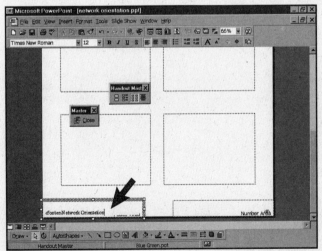

6 To add a *footer* (which will print at the bottom of every handout), click in the **Footer** area and type your text. You can add a graphic here with the **Insert**, **Picture** command. If the cursor does not appear in the **Footer** area when you click it, then right-click it and select **Edit Text** from the pop-up menu.

(continues)

Guided Tour   Create and Print Handouts

(continued)

The # symbol that appears in the Number area is the page number, which will print on each handout. You don't have to do anything here, but you can click in the Number area and add text, such as **Page**, so it will print as Page 1, Page 2, and so on. You can delete the # symbol if you don't want the page number to appear.

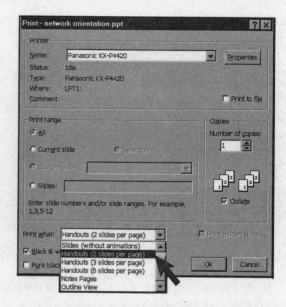

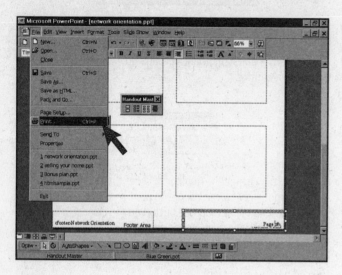

8 Open the **Print What** list box and select a handout option, such as **Handouts (2 slides per page)**. Click **OK** to print your handouts.

You can print two, three, or six slides on a handout page.

7 When you're ready to print your handouts, open the **File** menu and select **Print**. The Print dialog box appears.

View the Slide Show

After you prepare, polish, and rehearse your presentation. It's time to show your presentation to the people for whom you prepared it. There are several ways you can show your presentation. You can print out copies of your slides, make some transparencies, and use an overhead to give the presentation, or you can create slides from your printouts and use a slide projector. However, one of the best methods for giving the presentation is to use your own computer. You can display your presentation on your monitor, or you can use special equipment and the PC to display your presentation as a slide show on a larger screen.

Even if you're not a computer expert, you can easily run a professional-quality slide show with a minimal amount of effort. And you can even "write" on your slides (with the mouse) during the presentation to add emphasis to a particular point.

When you start the slide show, your first slide fills the screen, obscuring all the toolbars and window features. This first slide stays on-screen until you click a mouse button or press a key. The following table explains how to move from slide to slide in a slide show.

If you want the slide show to run unattended, it can, looping continuously until you make it stop. If you plan on talking while the slide show is running, you can enter *timings* for each slide. The timings, when present, automatically control the amount of time that each slide is displayed.

To	Do This
Display the next slide	Click anywhere on the screen or press **N**.
Display the previous slide	Press **P**.
Display a hidden slide	Press **H**.
Display the last slide	Press **End**.
Display the first slide	Press **Home**.
Stop the slide show	Press **Esc**.
Display a menu of slide show controls	Click the button in the lower-left corner of the screen.

Begin Guided Tour   Add Timings to Slides

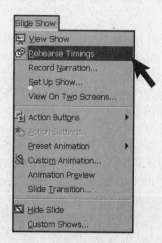

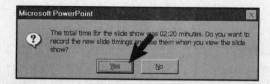

3 After you add timings to all the slides, PowerPoint shows you the total amount of time you need for the presentation. When PowerPoint asks you if you want to record the new slide timings, click **Yes**.

4 To review the timings for each slide, switch to Slide Sorter view by clicking **Yes**.

1 From any view, open the **Slide Show** menu and choose **Rehearse Timings**. (If you're in Slide Sorter view, you can click the **Rehearse Timings** button on the Slide Sorter toolbar.) The screen goes blank as PowerPoint prepares to run your show.

2 The Rehearsal dialog box appears; it keeps track of how much time you spend on each slide. As you rehearse your lines, use the VCR-like buttons in the dialog box to advance between slides. Click the **Play** button (the arrow) to advance to the next slide; click the **Pause** button (the two vertical bars) to temporarily stop the timer. If you make a mistake, click the **Repeat** button to start the timing over for that slide.

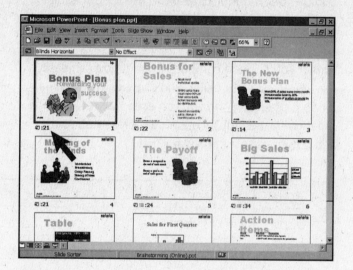

5 PowerPoint applies your new timings to the slides and returns you to Slide Sorter view. Under each slide, you see the amount of time you allotted for it.

Begin Guided Tour Set Up a Slide Show

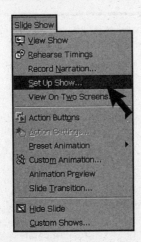

1 Before your audience arrives, set up your show by opening the **Slide Show** menu and selecting **Set Up Show**.

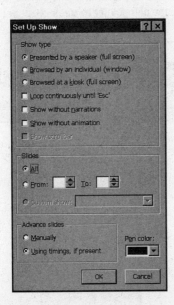

2 Under **Show Type**, select how you want to present your PowerPoint show. If you're planning on presenting the show yourself, you might want it featured in a full screen. If the show is going to run unattended at a trade show, you might want it to loop continuously.

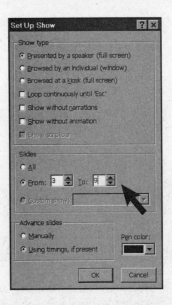

3 Under **Slides**, select which slides you want to show. Normally, all of the slides are presented, but you can select a group of slides (such as numbers 7 to 15) to show instead.

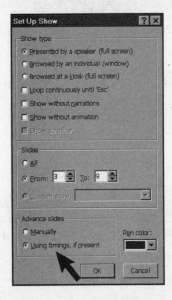

4 Under **Advance Slides**, select how you want to handle the presentation. For example, if you select **Manually**, you must advance each slide by clicking the mouse button. If you choose **Using Timings, If Present**, then the slides advance automatically.

5 Select a **Pen Color** from the drop-down list if you like. After making your selections, click **OK**.

Begin Guided Tour   Run a Slide Show

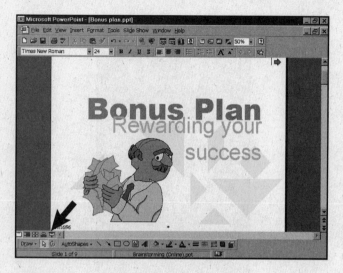

1 When you're ready to start the show, click the **Slide Show** button. The screen goes blank as PowerPoint prepares to run your presentation.

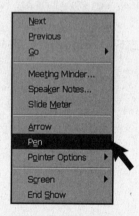

2 At any time during the slide show, you can write on a slide by right-clicking and selecting **Pen** from the shortcut menu. (You can also press **Ctrl+P** to avoid using the mouse or the shortcut menu.)

Any marks you create on a slide are temporary; they disappear when you advance to the next slide.

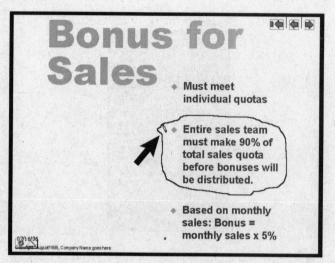

3 The mouse pointer turns into a pen. Write on a slide by dragging the pen pointer to create shapes or characters.

You can go from the pen to arrow or vice versa simply by using Ctrl+A for arrow or Ctrl+P for pen.

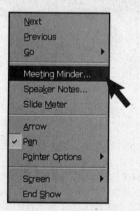

4 If you need to make a note of something during the presentation, right-click and select **Meeting Minder** from the shortcut menu.

Guided Tour   Run a Slide Show

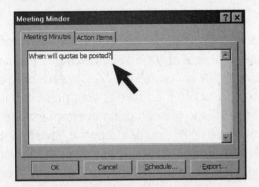

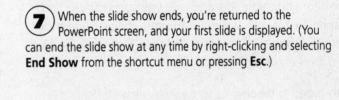

You can return to the Meeting Minder later on (with the **Tools**, **Meeting Minder** command) and either export your notes to Word for printing, and/or schedule your tasks in Outlook.

5 On the **Meeting Minder** tab, you can type in any notes you want to recall. If you need to follow up on something, click the **Action Items** tab.

7 When the slide show ends, you're returned to the PowerPoint screen, and your first slide is displayed. (You can end the slide show at any time by right-clicking and selecting **End Show** from the shortcut menu or pressing **Esc**.)

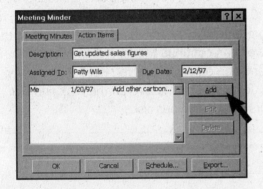

6 Enter a **Description** of your task. Enter who the task will be **Assigned To**, and a **Due Date**. Then click **Add**. Click **OK** to return to your slide show.

Use the Pack and Go Wizard

PowerPoint was designed for you to create dynamic presentations that could then be shown on your computer screen in front of an audience.

Some of us, however, live in the real world where our computer is not easily transported to a meeting room where you might want to give your presentation. In such a case, you will want to present your slide show on a portable PC, or on a desktop PC already located in a meeting room.

In order to be able to show your presentation on another PC, you would need the slide show file, of course. But you'd need other files as well: Special fonts you might have used, and graphics you might have included. And let's not forget the PowerPoint program itself, which you'd need to show your presentation.

So that you won't forget any critical file, Microsoft designed the *Pack and Go Wizard*. With it, you can tell PowerPoint to copy all the files it needs onto a disk which you can then take to your presentation site. If the PC you plan on using does not include a copy of PowerPoint, you can copy the PowerPoint Viewer to your disk as well. The Viewer is a miniature version of PowerPoint; just the parts it needs in order to show a presentation (you cannot edit a presentation with the PowerPoint Viewer).

Once you use the Pack and Go Wizard to create your presentation disk, you simply insert it into a drive on the PC you want to use, issue a few commands, and the presentation is ready to go. It's as simple as that! And you can continue to make changes to your presentation on *your* PC if you need to; however, after doing so, you must rerun the Pack and Go Wizard to update your disk.

Begin Guided Tour   Create the Presentation Disk

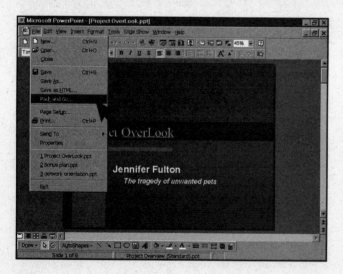

1 Open the **File** menu and select **Pack and Go**.

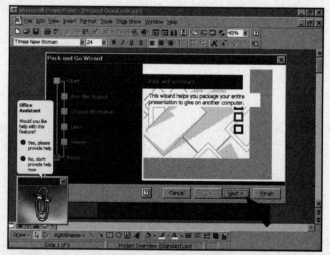

2 If you see the Office Assistant, click **No**, and follow the steps here. Read the start page of the Pack and Go Wizard, and click **Next**.

Guided Tour   Create the Presentation Disk

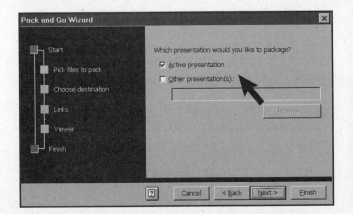

3 If you'd like to use Pack and Go on your current pre-sentation, then select the **Active presentation** option. Otherwise, select **Other Presentation(s)**, click **Browse** and select the presentation you want to pack from the list. Click **OK** to return to the Pack and Go Wizard. Click **Next** to move to the Choose Destination screen.

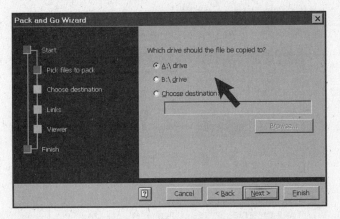

4 Select the drive to which you want your files copied, then click **Next**.

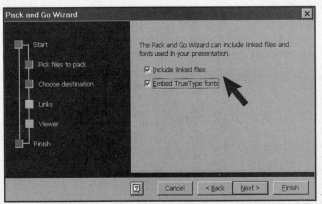

5 If you have inserted files in your presentation that are located on your hard disk or the company network, select the **Include Linked files** option. If you use special fonts (some-thing other than Times New Roman or Arial), then select the **Embed TrueType Fonts** option. Click **Next**.

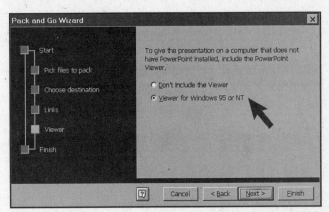

6 If the PC on which you're going to run your presentation does not have a copy of PowerPoint (and it uses Windows 95 or Windows NT), then select the **View for Windows 95 or NT** option. Click **Next**.

If the PC on which you want to run your presen-tation is using Windows 3.1, then you have to create a Viewer disk manually. After finishing with the Pack and Go Wizard, insert a new disk, and copy all the files in the **\ValuPack\ PPT4View** folder from the CD to your disk.

(continues)

Guided Tour   Create the Presentation Disk

(continued)

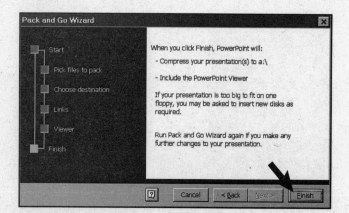

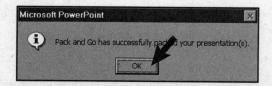

8 After the files have been copied to your disk(s), you'll see a message telling you so. Click **OK**.

7 Verify that all the options you selected are listed. Make sure a blank disk is inserted into the drive you selected; you may be asked to insert additional disks as needed. Also, if you asked for the Viewer to be copied to the disk, insert the Office 97 CD. When you're ready, click **Finish**.

Begin Guided Tour   Run the Slide Show on the Presentation PC

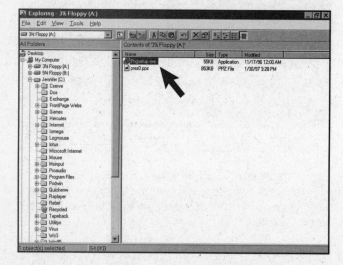

1 Insert your Pack and Go disk. Open Windows Explorer, switch to the disk drive, and double-click the **Pngsetup.exe** file.

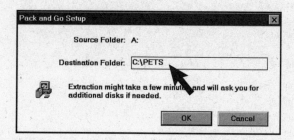

2 Type the destination drive and folder to which you want your presentation files copied. Then click **OK**.

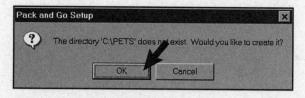

3 If the folder to which you want to copy your presentation files does not exist, you're asked if you want the folder created. Click **OK**.

Guided Tour   Run the Slide Show on the Presentation PC

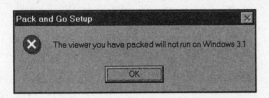

4 If you included the Presentation Viewer for Windows 95 or Windows NT, you'll see this warning. You can ignore it, as long as the PC on which you're going to run your slide show uses Windows 95 or Windows NT. Click **OK**.

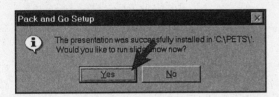

5 After the files have been copied to your PC, you'll see a message asking you if you want to run the slide show now. Click **Yes**. After the presentation starts, to move from slide to slide, click the mouse button or press the **spacebar**.

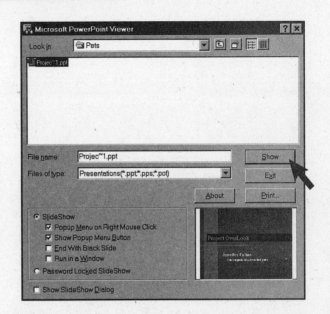

7 Click the presentation you want to run, and select any options you want. Click **Show** to start your presentation. As before, to move from slide to slide, click the mouse button or press the **spacebar**.

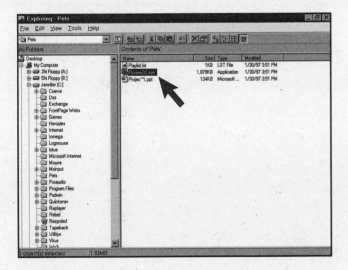

6 If you clicked **No** in step 5, you can run your slide show at a later time. To do so, open Windows Explorer, change to the folder to which you copied the presentation files, and double-click the **Ppview32** file.

HOW TO...

Use Outlook to Keep Organized

Outlook is similar to an electronic day planner. With Outlook, you can keep track of your appointments, recurring meetings, important business and personal contacts, and things to do.

You can also use Outlook to send and receive e-mail messages through all the services you use, including your office network, CompuServe, AOL, and the Internet. If an e-mail message contains an invitation to a meeting, you can use it to quickly update your Outlook Calendar. If the message is from a new contact, you can use it to update your Outlook Contacts list.

Outlook keeps all your day to day activities in one place, making it easier for you to get your work done.

What You Will Find in This Section

Get to Know the Outlook Programs

When you first start Outlook, it can be a bit confusing, since it's actually made up of several programs: Inbox, Calendar, Contacts, Tasks, Journal, and Notes. Each of these programs is represented by an icon on the *Outlook bar*, which you'll see displayed on the left side of the Outlook window.

In this task, you'll learn the purpose of each of Outlook's programs. Briefly, here is a listing of what each program is for:

- **Inbox**   An e-mail program.

- **Calendar**   An appointment, meeting, and event planner.

- **Contacts**   An address book.

- **Tasks**   A "things-to-do" organizer.

- **Journal**   A business diary.

- **Notes**   A convenient notepad.

- **Deleted Items**   Items deleted in Outlook are placed in this folder where they can be retrieved if accidentally deleted.

> If you work with Outlook in a small window (non-maximized), you might want to reduce the size of the icons on the Outlook bar so you can see more of them at once. Simply right-click an open space in the Outlook bar, and select **Small Icons**.

The Outlook bar has three buttons with which you can access other parts of Outlook: Outlook, Mail, and Other. When you click the **Outlook** button on the Outlook bar, the program icons listed above are displayed.

Click the **Mail** button and you'll find the following icons:

- **Inbox**   This icon is the same as the one in the Outlook section of the Outlook bar. It displays your incoming messages.

- **Outbox**   Here you'll find your outgoing messages.

- **Sent Items**   Once a message has been sent, it is moved to this folder.

- **Deleted Items**   This icon is the same as the one in the Outlook section. It displays recently deleted items.

Click the **Other** button to display the following icons:

- **My Computer**   This displays the contents of your PC's hard disk.

- **My Documents**   This displays the contents of the My Documents folder. Typically, the documents you create with any Office 97 program are stored in this folder.

- **Favorites**   This displays the files located in the Favorites folder. It is easy to store your most often used Office 97 documents in this folder, using the **Look in Favorites** button you'll find at the top of the Save As dialog box.

When you open Outlook, it displays the contents of the Inbox. You can set up Outlook to start with a different program instead of Inbox. Just open the **Tools** menu, select **Options**, and click the **General** tab. Then select the program you want to start with from the **Startup in this** drop-down list. For example, you might select **Calendar**. Click **OK** and you're through! The next time you start Outlook, it will start with the Calendar program (or whichever program you selected).

Begin Guided Tour   Learn What Each Outlook Program Does

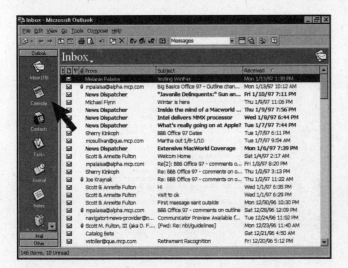

1 When you open Outlook for the first time, the Inbox is displayed. With the Inbox, you can view incoming e-mail messages, send an e-mail, or send a fax. Click the **Calendar** icon on the Outlook bar.

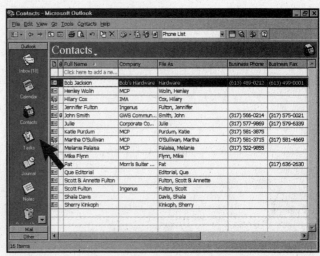

3 The Contacts list is like a big address book. Here you can keep track of business associates, family members, and friends, along with their phone numbers, fax numbers, mobile phone numbers, e-mail addresses, and more. Click the **Tasks** icon.

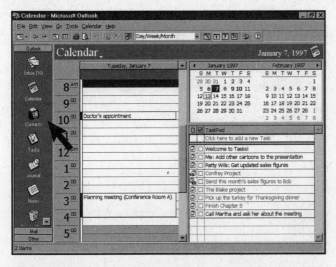

2 With the Calendar, you can track appointments and plan meetings. You can also make note of recurring events such as birthdays, anniversaries, and holidays. The Calendar can even remind you of important events, so you won't miss them. Click the **Contacts** icon.

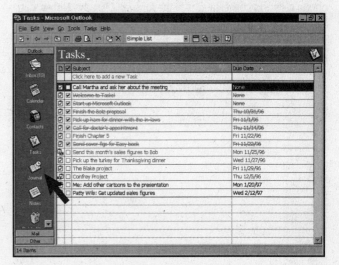

4 With the Tasks list, you can keep track of all those things you need to do. Click the **Journal** icon.

(continues)

Guided Tour   Learn What Each Outlook Program Does   *(continued)*

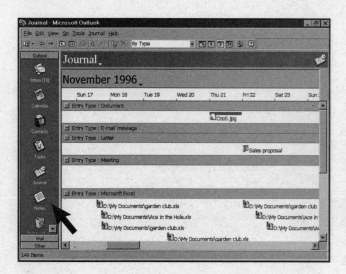

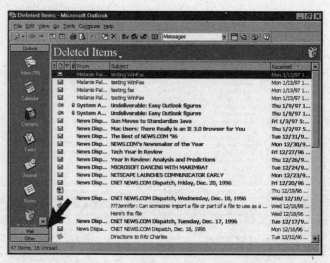

5 The Journal automatically tracks the Office documents you've worked on, and the dates on which you created or modified those documents. Thus, you can use the entries in the Journal to open recently edited Office documents without having to remember exactly where they're located. You can also track phone calls and conversations in the Journal. Click the **Notes** icon.

7 Here you'll see a listing of the items you've deleted in other parts of Outlook. Deleted items are stored temporarily (and not really deleted) until you tell Outlook to empty the contents of the Deleted Items folder. At that point, they are permanently removed from your system. Click the **Mail** button.

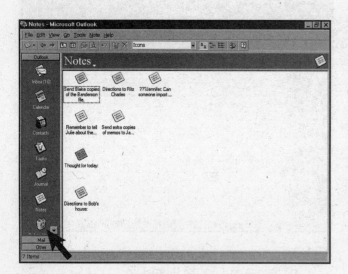

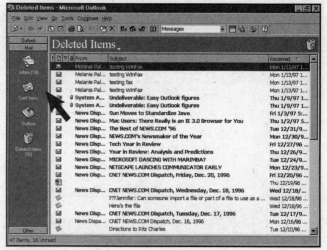

6 With Notes, you can jot down a quick thought or idea. Here you can record questions, directions to a client's office, and anything else you would normally use a sticky note for. Click the **Deleted Items** icon.

8 The icons listed in the Mail group provide access to e-mail-related activities. The Inbox and Deleted Items icon are repeated here; they act the same as they did in the Outlook group. There are some new icons here too. Click the **Sent Items** icon.

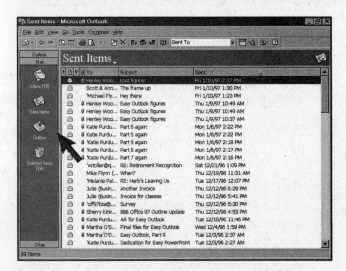

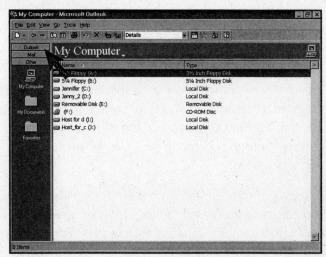

9 The Sent Items folder contains copies of e-mail messages you've sent. Click the **Outbox** icon.

11 Through the icons in the Other group, you can access the files on your computer or your company's network (through the My Computer icon). You can also access your Office Documents stored in the My Documents and Favorites folders. To redisplay the Outlook group of icons, click the **Outlook** button.

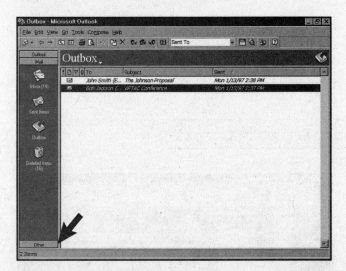

10 The Outbox contains messages waiting to be sent. Click the **Other** button at the bottom of the Outlook bar.

Switch Between the Outlook Programs

Before you can use any of the Outlook programs, you must first switch to it. When you switch to a program, the menu bar changes to display an extra menu which contains commands specific to that program. For example, when you change to the Tasks list, the Tasks menu appears on the menu bar. When you switch to the Calendar, the Calendar menu appears instead.

In addition, some of the buttons on the Standard toolbar are replaced with buttons for commands you'd use only within the current program. For example, if you switch to the Inbox, e-mail related buttons such as Reply and Forward appear on the Standard toolbar. If you then switch to the Calendar, those buttons disappear, and are replaced with calendar-related buttons such as Day, Week, and Year.

There are several methods you can use to switch from program to program in Outlook. Here's a brief description of each method:

- The *Outlook Bar* provides icons which you can click to switch to a particular program.

- The *Folder List* displays all the Outlook programs in a list, similar to the way that folders are displayed in Windows Explorer. You can switch to an Outlook program by selecting it from this list.

- The main Outlook programs are also listed on the *Go menu*. Like the Folders List, you simply select the program you want to switch to from those listed.

- The *Back and Forward* buttons on the Standard toolbar allow you to return quickly to any previously visited Outlook program.

You'll learn how to use each of these methods in this task.

Begin Guided Tour   Change from Section to Section in Outlook

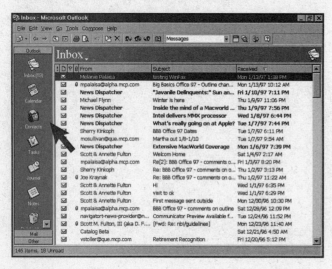

1 When you start Outlook, it starts in the Inbox. To switch to another program, click its icon in the Outlook Bar, located on the left side of the window. For example, click the **Contacts** button.

2 Another way to change from one program to another is with the Folder List. Click the **Folder List** button on the Standard toolbar. Then, to switch to a program, click its icon in the list. For example, click the **Journal** icon. To hide the list, click the **Folder List** button again.

Guided Tour Change from Section to Section in Outlook

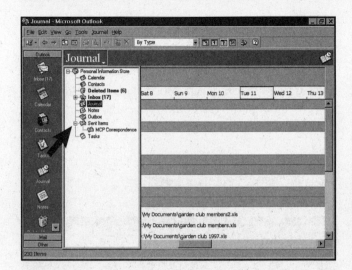

3 If a folder contains subfolders, then it's preceded by a plus sign, like the Inbox folder shown here. To display the subfolders list, click the **plus** sign. To hide them again, click the **minus** sign that appears.

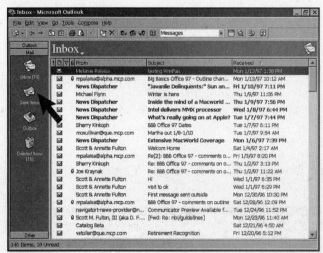

5 The Inbox displays e-mail messages you've received. To display a list of messages you've sent, click the **Mail** button at the bottom of the Outlook bar. The Mail button is moved to the top of the bar, and a list of mail-related icons is displayed. Click the **Sent Items** icon.

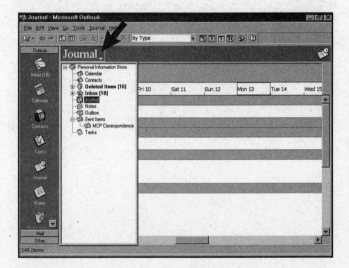

4 To display the Folder List temporarily when it is not currently displayed, click the title of the current folder. For example, click **Journal**, which appears at the top of the Journal window, and the Folder List appears. Click a folder in the list (such as the Inbox folder), and you change to that folder.

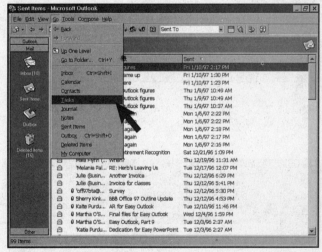

6 Another way to switch between Outlook programs is to use the **Go** menu. Click the **Go** menu to open it, then click the program you wish to change to; such as **Tasks**.

Change the View

Each of Outlook's programs displays its information in a particular way. You can change the way in which information is displayed by changing its *view*.

You can also change the order in which information is displayed. Items in each Outlook section are always

sorted in a particular order. For example, the items in the Inbox are sorted by the date they are received, from the most recent message to the oldest. You can reverse the order in which information is displayed or you can change the column by which the information is sorted.

> **Begin Guided Tour**   Change How Information Is Displayed in a Section

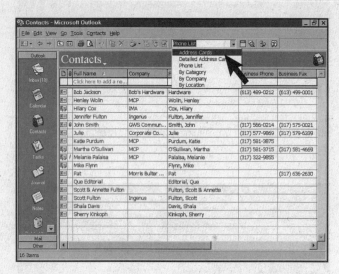

1 To change to a different view, open the **Current View** list on the Standard toolbar and select the view you want.

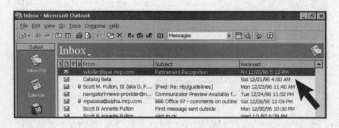

2 To reverse the order in which items are sorted, click the button marked by the arrow. In the Inbox, click the **Received** button to reverse the sort order.

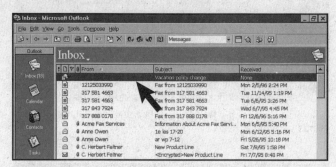

3 To sort by a different column (or field), click that column's header (title) instead.

Access Documents from Within Outlook

Since Outlook is part of your Office 97 suite, it keeps track of the Office 97 documents you create and edit. This makes it easy for you to locate the document you need, without having to remember exactly what the file is called, or where it is stored. You can even create new files with Office 97 from within Outlook.

You also can launch other programs and open documents with a simple click from within Outlook. Typically, you access your Office files through Outlook's Other group of icons. When you display the Other group on the Outlook bar, you'll find icons for My Computer, My Documents, and Favorites. Briefly, here's the purpose of each icon:

- **My Computer** This icon works similarly to the My Computer icon located on the Windows

desktop, providing access to any file on your PC's hard disk. You can also access files on your office network through the My Computer icon.

- **My Documents** Typically, Office 97 documents are stored in a special folder called My Documents. This icon provides quick access to those files.

- **Favorites** Office 97 programs allow you to quickly save often-used files in the Favorites folder, instead of the My Documents folder. Thus, this icon provides easy access to your often-used files.

Instead of using the icons in the Other group, you can access recently used Office files from within your Journal—eliminating the time it might take to locate them.

Begin Guided Tour   Open Existing Documents

1 On the Outlook bar, click the **Other** button. The Other group of icons is displayed.

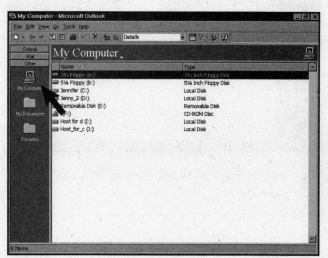

2 If the My Computer screen is not displayed, click **My Computer** button, and the contents of your PC is displayed. Select a drive from the list and double-click it to see a listing of the files on that drive. For example, double-click the **C.** drive.

(continues)

Guided Tour Open Existing Documents

(continued)

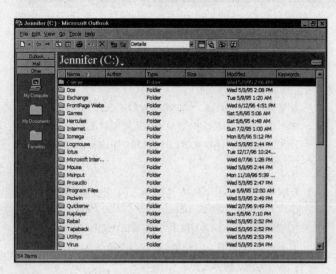

3 A listing of files and folders on the C: drive appears. Double-click the folder which contains your document.

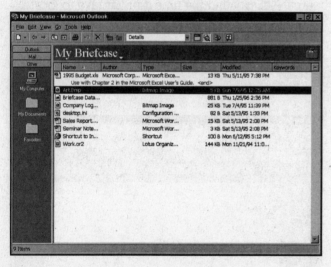

4 The contents of the folder is displayed. Double-click the file you want to edit.

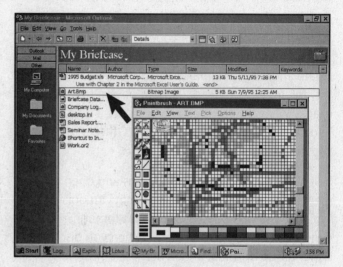

5 The program which created the file opens, displaying the contents of the file you selected. To exit the program click the close button (X).

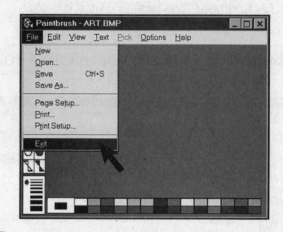

6 To return to Outlook, open the **File** menu and select **Exit**.

Begin Guided Tour   Open Existing Documents with the Journal

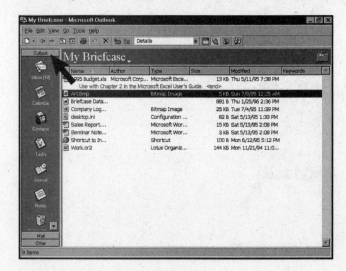

1 If the file you want to edit is an Office 97 file and you've used it recently, chances are you'll find it in the Journal. Click the **Outlook** button on the Outlook bar.

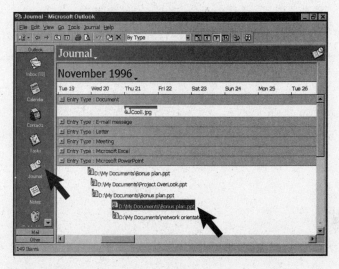

2 Click the **Journal** icon to display the contents of the Journal. Use the scrollbars to locate your file.

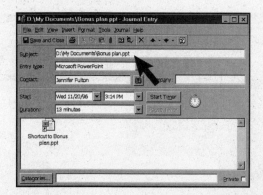

3 Double-click the file you wish to edit. A journal window opens.

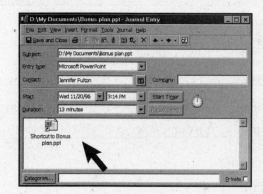

4 Double-click the shortcut icon to open the file.

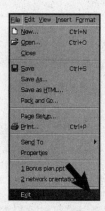

5 To exit, open the **File** menu and select **Exit** to return to Outlook.

Begin Guided Tour   Create a New Office 97 Document

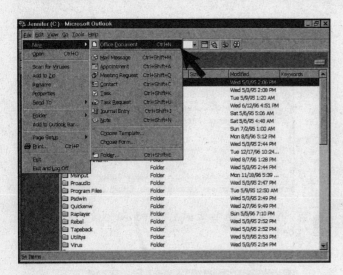

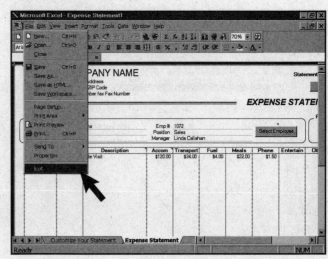

1 Instead of editing an existing document, you can start a new Office 97 document from within any part of Outlook. Just open the **File** menu, select **New**, and then select **Office Document.**

3 After completing your new document, click the **Save** button. To return to Outlook, open the **File** menu and select **Exit**.

To display the complete list of Office templates, as seen in step 2, perform this step while in My Computer.

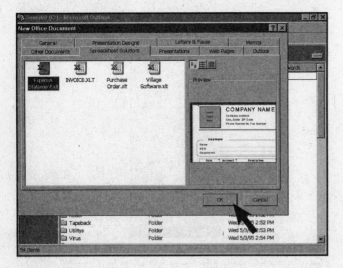

2 In the New Office Document dialog box, click the tab of the document type you want to create, then click the template you want to use. Click **OK**. The Office program associated with that template starts.

Use Categories

When you assign categories to your items, you can use these categories to help you identify items of a particular type. For example, you might want to separate your personal contacts from your business ones in the Contacts list—and you can, simply by selecting the proper category for each contact.

You can assign a category to any Outlook item, including e-mail messages and faxes, appointments and meetings, contacts, tasks, notes, and Journal entries. An item can be assigned as many categories as apply.

Outlook comes with many categories already defined for you, including:

Business	Competition	Favorites
Gifts	Goals/Objectives	Holidays
Holiday Cards	Hot Contacts	Ideas
International	Key Customers	Miscellaneous
Personal	Phone Calls	Status
Strategies	Suppliers	Time & Expense
VIP	Waiting	

If none of these categories fit your purpose, don't worry—you can easily add categories of your own.

Begin Guided Tour   Organize Items by Assigning Categories to Them

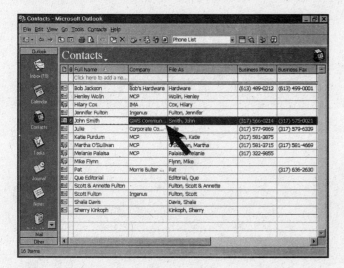

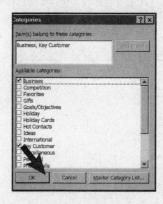

2 Click the category (or categories) you want. A check mark appears in front of the categories you select. Click **OK**.

1 Click the item to which you want to assign a category. To assign the same category to multiple items at one time, press **Ctrl** and click each of the items to select them. Open the **Edit** menu, and select **Categories**.

If the Categories field isn't visible within the Outlook window, open the **View** menu, select **Show Fields**, select **Categories**, and then click **Add**. Click **OK**.

Begin Guided Tour Create New Categories

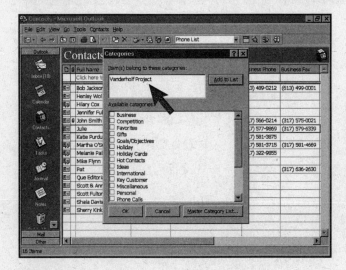

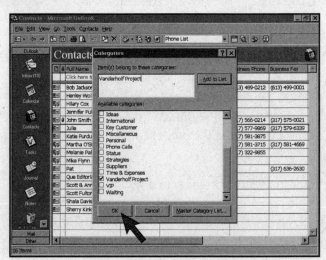

1 If you don't see a category you like, you can create a new one in the Categories dialog box. Simply type its name in the **Items belong to these categories** text box. For example, type Vanderholf Project.

3 To assign the selected items to your new category, click it within the Available Categories list. Click **OK**.

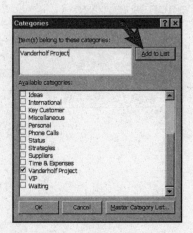

2 Click **Add to List**.

Create Folders to Organize Items

On the hard disk, you use folders to organize your files. In Outlook, you can use folders for this same purpose: to organize your Outlook items.

Outlook contains many folders already: the Inbox folder, the Contacts folder, and so on. You can organize the items in these folders by creating your own folders within them.

When you create a folder, it's placed in the current Outlook section. For example, if you're in the Sent Items folder, and you create a new folder called Faxes, then Faxes becomes a subfolder within the Sent Items folder.

Folders appear on the Outlook bar as icons. However, subfolders (the ones you create) may or may not appear on the Outlook bar. When creating a folder, you can select from these two options:

- You can create a shortcut to the new folder, making it appear as an icon on the Outlook bar. To display the items in this folder, you simply click its icon.

- You can opt not to create a shortcut. In that case, an icon for the folder will not appear on the Outlook bar. To display the contents of such a folder, open the Folder List and click its name.

> To display the Folder List, click the **Folder List** button on the Standard toolbar.

If you can want to remove a folder later on, you can use the **File**, **Folder**, **Delete Folder** command. You can also copy or move the folder, and even rename it with the commands you'll find on the File, Folder menu.

Begin Guided Tour   Create Your Own Folders

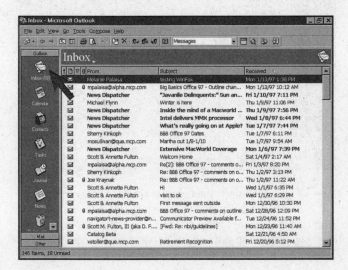

1 Change to the Outlook section in which you want to create a subfolder.

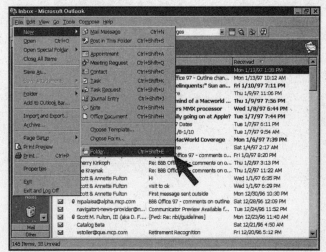

2 Open the **File** menu and select **New**. Then select **Folder** from the cascading menu that appears.

(continues)

Guided Tour   Create Your Own Folders

(continued)

You can also create a folder by selecting **Create Folder** from the **File, Folder** menu.

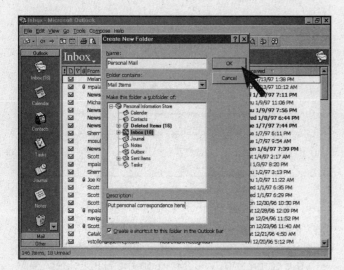

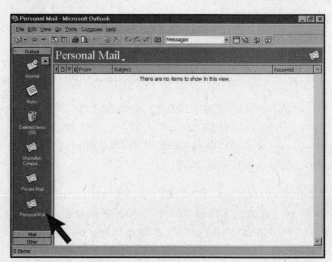

4 The new folder is added to the current Outlook folder. If you selected the option, **Create a shortcut to this folder in the Outlook Bar**, then a new icon appears on the Outlook bar. Click this icon to display the contents of the folder (which is currently empty).

3 In the Create New Folder dialog box, type a **Name** for the folder. Under **Make this folder a subfolder of**, select the folder you want to place this folder in. Type a **Description** for this new folder if you like. To access this new folder from the Outlook bar, make sure that the option, **Create a shortcut to this folder in the Outlook Bar** is selected. Click **OK**.

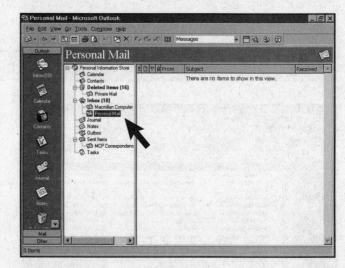

5 If you didn't select the **Create a shortcut** option, then, to display the contents of the new folder, click the **Folder List icon** on the Standard toolbar to display the folder list. For example, click **Inbox** at the top of the window. The new folder appears in the folder list. Click it to display its contents.

Copy, Move, and Delete Items

After you create a folder or two, you'll probably want to copy or move your Outlook items into these folders in order to organize them.

When you copy an item, the original item remains in its current folder, and a copy of it is placed in the folder you indicate. Refrain from making copies of items wherever possible, since doing so will waste space on your hard disk.

If you move an item, the item is removed from its current folder and then placed in the folder you indicate. Moving items allows you to keep Outlook organized without sacrificing hard disk space.

Something strange happens when you copy or move an item into an incompatible folder. For example, suppose you have a folder called Personal in the Inbox folder. If you copy or move a note into this folder, the contents of the note is placed in an e-mail message. This is because Outlook assumes that only e-mail messages belong in an Inbox subfolder.

When items are no longer needed, you can remove them from Outlook. Deleted items are not actually removed; instead they are moved to the Deleted Items folder. This allows you an opportunity to retrieve an accidentally deleted item. From time to time, you'll want to empty the contents of the Deleted Items folder to permanently delete your unused items.

Begin Guided Tour   Copy or Move Items

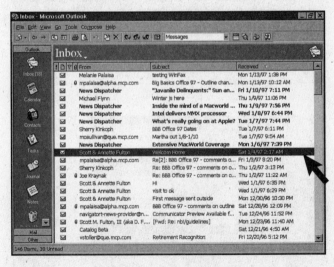

1 To copy or move an item, click to select it. You can select multiple items by pressing **Ctrl** and then clicking the items.

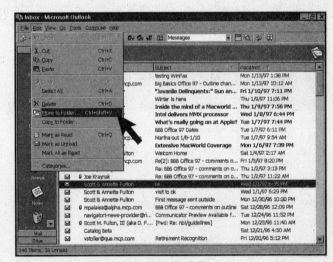

2 Open the **Edit** menu. To copy the selected items, click **Copy to Folder**. To move the items, click **Move to Folder**.

(continues)

Guided Tour Copy or Move Items

(continued)

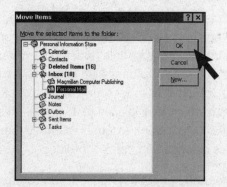

3 In the Move Items (or Copy Items) dialog box, select the folder to which you want to copy or move the selected item(s). If needed, click the **plus** sign in front of a folder to display its subfolders, then click the subfolder you want. Click **OK**.

Begin Guided Tour Delete Unwanted Items

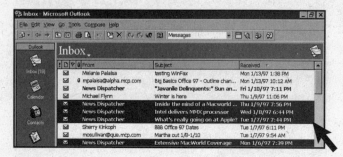

To restore an accidentally deleted item *before* you empty the Deleted items folder, right-click it and select **Move to Folder**. Select the folder in which you want the item placed, and click **OK**.

1 Select the item to be deleted by clicking it. To select multiple items, press **Ctrl** as you click them. Then click the **Delete** button on the Standard toolbar.

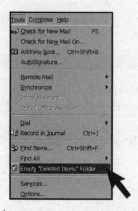

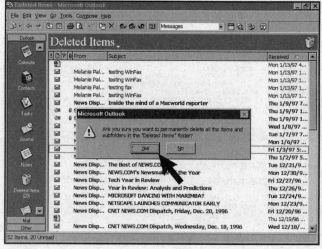

3 You'll see a message asking you if you want to empty the **Deleted Items** folder. Click **Yes**.

2 Deleted items are moved to the Deleted Items folder. To permanently remove these items, open the **Tools** menu and select **Empty "Deleted Items" Folder**.

Send, Receive, and Manage E-Mail with Outlook

One of Outlook's best features is its ability to handle your e-mail. With the Inbox, you can send and receive e-mail through a variety of services such as your company's network, the Internet, CompuServe, AOL, MSN, and so on—all in one place! The Inbox is your one-stop shopping area for all your electronic messaging needs.

In order to use the Inbox, you must install each of the messaging services you want to use, such as the Internet, MSN, and so on. If you've been using Windows Exchange, you'll find that it has already been installed for you in the Inbox, along with the services you may have been using through the Exchange, such as MSN, CompuServe, and so on. Also, the Inbox automatically imports your Exchange address lists so you don't have to reenter all those e-mail addresses.

After you've installed the messaging services you want to use, you're ready to send and receive e-mail through them. All this and more is covered in this section.

What You Will Find in This Section

Add a Messaging Service

Before you can use Inbox, you must install the messaging services you want to use. A messaging service is like an electronic version of the Post Office. For a fee, you can "drop off" your messages, and the service will deliver them. It will also accept messages for you, which you can then retrieve from the service whenever it's convenient. In other words, a messaging service collects and sends electronic mail for the users who subscribe to the service. There are a lot of different messaging services to which you can belong, including some of the following:

- The Internet (which you can access through an Internet service provider, or through your company's network Internet connection)

- The Microsoft Network (MSN)

- CompuServe

- America Online (AOL)

- Prodigy

All of these services provide more than simple message handling; so you should choose the service which best suits your needs.

In addition, if your company has a network and you use Microsoft Mail or cc:Mail, you can send your e-mail messages through Outlook.

Some messaging services are easy to add to Outlook, since support for them is included with Outlook itself. These include cc:Mail, Microsoft Network, Microsoft Mail, Microsoft Exchange Server (which handles mail on a Windows NT network), and the Microsoft at Work fax program (for sending faxes through a fax machine attached to your company's network). To add other messaging services, you'll need that service's program disks. For example, to add AOL, you'll need your AOL disks.

But even for the services which are directly supported in Outlook, there is still some setup which you'll need to complete. In this task, you'll learn how to do just that.

Begin Guided Tour   Set Up a Messaging Service

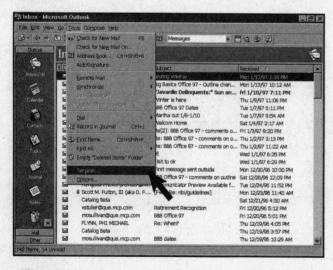

1 From within the Inbox, open the **Tools** menu and select **Services**.

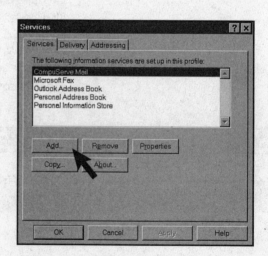

2 The services which you've already installed are listed in the Services dialog box. If you used to use Microsoft Exchange, then the services you installed there appear here automatically. To add a new service, click **Add**.

Guided Tour Set Up a Messaging Service

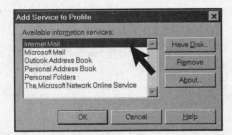

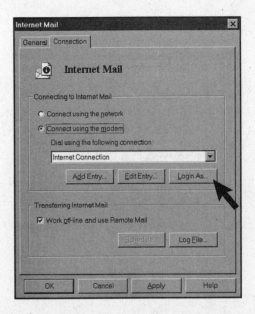

3 In the Add Service to Profile dialog box, select the service you want to use from those listed under **Available information services**, and click **OK**.

> If your service is not listed, click **Have Disk**, insert the service's setup disk, and click **OK** to install it. The service will be added to the list of those available. Select it and click **OK**.

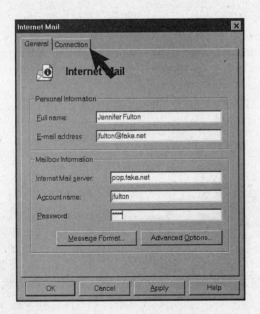

5 On the Connection tab, select how you plan to connect to the Internet: over a company network, or by modem. If you use a modem, you may want to select **Work off-line and use Remote Mail** in order to stop Outlook from trying to check for e-mail when you're not connected to the Internet. Click **Login As**.

> To set up my Internet connection, I had to click the **Advanced Options** button on the **General** tab, and enter the SMTP (Simple Mail Transfer Protocol) address of my provider's e-mail system: smtp.iquest.net. Check with your Internet provider to see if you need to do this too.

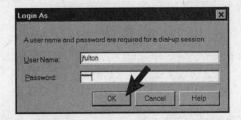

4 What you see in this step will vary based on the service you're trying to install. The figure shows how to install an Internet connection. Enter your name, e-mail address, and other information (such as the Internet mail server and password) you receive from your Internet service provider. Click the **Connection** tab.

6 Enter your login name and password. Click **OK**, and you're returned to the Internet Mail dialog box.

(continues)

Guided Tour Set Up a Messaging Service *(continued)*

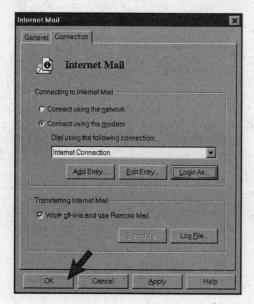

7 Click **OK** again.

8 You'll see a message telling you that you will not be able to use your new service until you restart Outlook. Click **OK**, and you're returned to the Services dialog box.

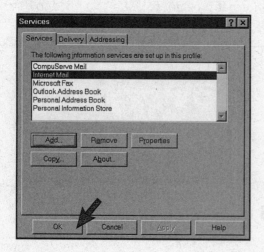

9 Click **OK**, and you're returned to Outlook.

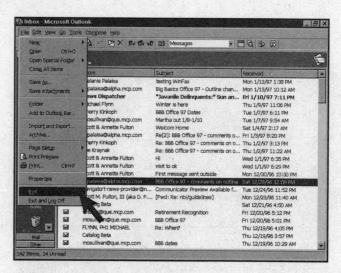

10 To restart Outlook so you can use your new service, open the **File** menu and select **Exit**.

The Exit and Log Off commands on the File menu can be used to exit Outlook and log off of a messaging service at the same time. Since you're not connected to a service at this time, you can use the Exit command instead.

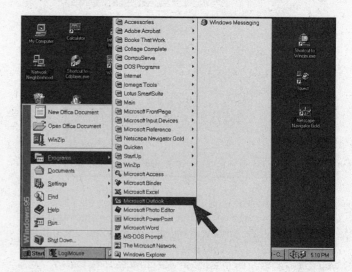

11 To restart Outlook, click the **Start** button, select **Programs**, and then select **Microsoft Outlook**.

Create and Send a Message

Electronic mail (e-mail for short) is a convenient and quick way to keep in contact with those people who are the most important to you. Unlike a letter, which make take days to reach its recipient, an e-mail message takes only minutes on a local network (or, through the Internet or some other messaging service, it might take a few hours). Also, unlike a conventional letter, an e-mail message can contain other information in the form of files: a client database, a budget spreadsheet, or a sales chart (graph). You can send e-mail messages easily with Inbox.

When creating a message, you can add flags that indicate the message's importance and sensitivity. You can also direct replies to be sent to another person. In addition, you can delay delivery of the message, and you can arrange to be notified after it's delivered or read.

To add emphasis to the words in your message, you can format the text of your message. With formatting, you can add bold, italics, or underline. In addition, you can change the font (typestyle), size, color, or alignment of your text.

Sometimes you can't say everything you need to say in an e-mail message. For example, rather than sending a message in which you try to explain how wonderfully your department has budgeted money, why not include a budget spreadsheet instead, and let your boss see for himself?

Outlook provides many options for adding a file to a message. If you *attach* the file, then the actual file is sent with the message. To be able to open the file,

the recipient must have a program similar to the one you used to create the attached file. If he doesn't have the proper program for the file, then send the file as *text only*, which will enable Outlook to display its contents. Lastly, you can add a *shortcut* to the file, which means that an icon (and not the file itself) is sent with the message. When the user double-clicks this icon, he'll connect to your system, which will open the file for him. (This option only works if both of you are connected through a network.)

In addition to being able to attach files to your messages, you can attach Outlook items as well. For example, you might attach a Journal entry, or a particular contact, or task item to share with a colleague. As with a file, the recipient must have Outlook in order to view any items you send him. If he doesn't have Outlook, you can send the contents of the item as text only. If you're both on a network, you can send a shortcut which points to the item—the recipient then double-clicks this icon, and the item is displayed using your version of Outlook.

If you need to receive a response to a message, you can attach voting buttons to it. Your recipients can then vote on various propositions, such as a salary cut, a benefits change, and so on. The buttons which appear in the message look the same as those you'd find in a dialog box. When the user opens your message, he simply clicks the button of his choice, and a reply is sent back to you. One problem: in order to use voting buttons, the recipient must also be using Outlook, and he must be located on your office network.

Begin Guided Tour Create a New E-Mail Message

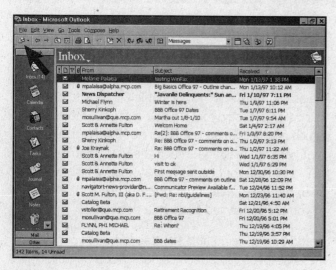

1 From the Inbox, click the **New Mail Message** button on the Standard toolbar. The Message window appears.

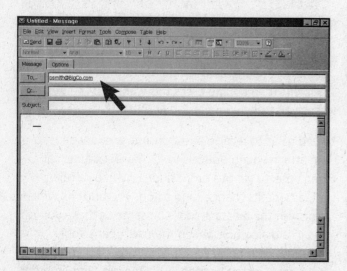

2 In the **To** text box, type the address of the person to whom you want to send your message. If you want to add a second person's name, type a semicolon first (;) and then type the additional address. To send a copy of the message to someone else, enter an address in the **Cc** text box.

You can enter addresses you use often in the Contacts list. You can then access these addresses by clicking the **To** button. See "Add a Contact," page 350, for more information.

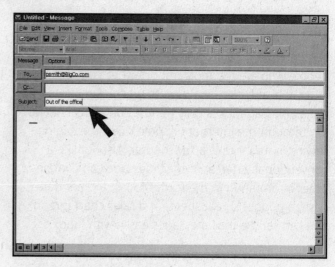

3 Click in the **Subject** box or press **Tab** to move the cursor. Type the subject of your message.

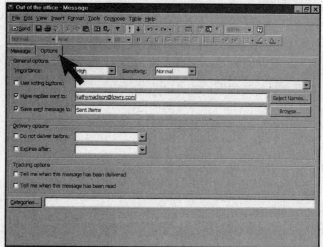

4 Click in the text box or press **Tab** to move the cursor there. Type your message in the big text box. To set options for how the message is delivered, click the **Options** tab.

Guided Tour   Create a New E-Mail Message

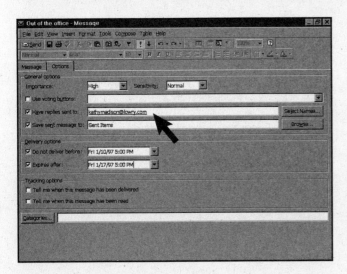

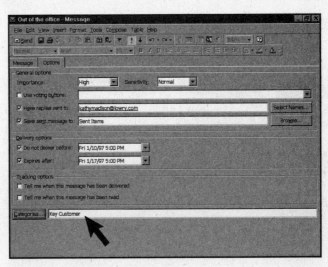

5 Within the General options section, you can set the level of importance with the Importance list. You can select the level of **Sensitivity** as well (Normal, Private, Confidential, and so on). You can have the replies to this message sent to someone else by typing his address in the **Have replies sent to** text box.

7 With the **Tracking** options, you can opt to have a message sent back to you once the message has been delivered or read. By clicking the **Categories** button, you can select a category for this message, such as Business, Personal, and so on.

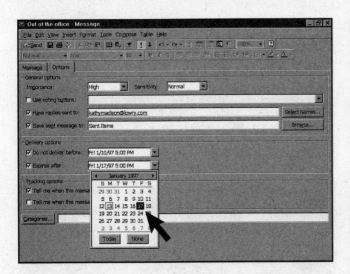

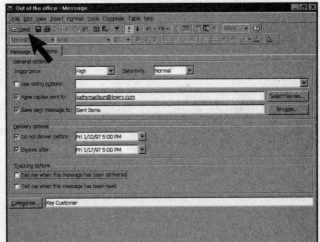

6 In the Delivery options section, you can set the date when you want the message delivered, and an expiration date as well, which will prevent the message from being delivered *after* a particular date. Click the down arrow and a calendar appears. Click the left or right arrows at the top of the calendar to move from month to month, then click the date you want.

> To select today's date, click **Today**. To remove a date selection, click **None**.

8 When you're ready to send the message, turn on your modem (if needed) and click the **Send** button. Outlook connects to your messaging service and sends the message. After a message is sent, it is placed in the Sent folder, which you can access through the Mail button on the Outlook bar.

> If your message is not yet finished but you'd like to save it to send later, open the **File** menu and select **Save**.

(continues)

Guided Tour Create a New E-Mail Message

(continued)

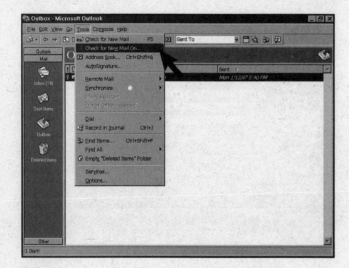

10 In the Check for New Mail On dialog box, select the services for which you want to check (or send) messages, then click **OK**. Outlook logs onto the indicated services and then sends and receives your e-mail.

9 If your message was not sent automatically, then it was placed in the Outbox folder, awaiting delivery. This can happen if you select the Remote Mail or similar option when setting up your messaging service. To send it manually, you simply check for new messages. Open the **Tools** menu and select **Check for New Mail On**.

Begin Guided Tour Attach a File to an E-Mail Message

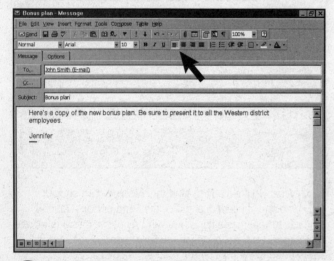

1 After you type the text for your message, click the **Insert File** button on the Standard toolbar. The Insert File dialog box appears.

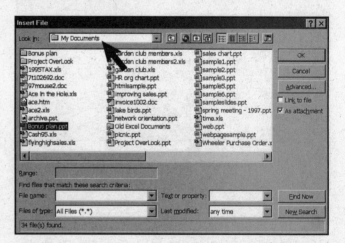

2 Locate the drive and folder in which the file exists, then double-click the folder to open it. If you need to move up one level, click the **Up One Level** button. To change to a different drive, select that drive from the **Look in** list. Once the file you want is visible, click it.

Guided Tour   Attach a File to an E-Mail Message

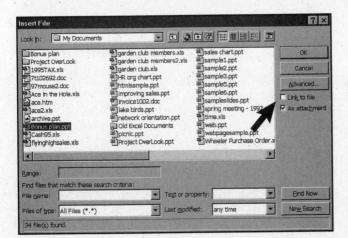

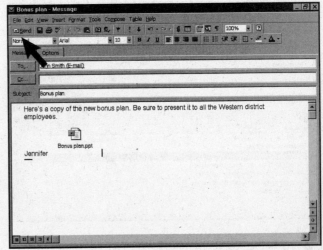

3 If you'd like to provide a link to the file (rather than the file itself), click the **Link to file** option. If you'd like to include the information as text, then select **Text only** instead. (This option may not always appear.) Otherwise, leave the Insert as option set at **As attachment**. When you're ready, click **OK** to insert the file (or the link, if you selected that option).

4 If you opted to *attach* the file to the message in step 3, then the file appears as an icon within the message. If you opted to include a *link* to the file instead, then it appears as a shortcut icon. Click **Send** to send your message.

> You can also insert a file by simply dragging it from Windows Explorer into an open message.

Begin Guided Tour   Attach an Outlook Item to a Message

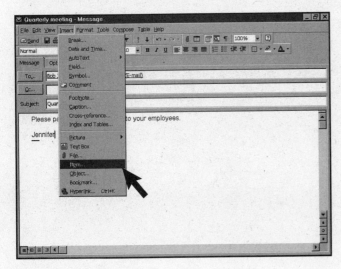

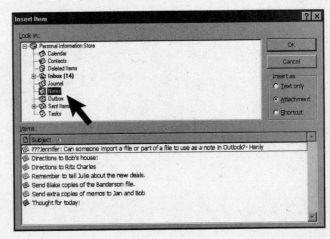

1 After you type the text for your message, open the **Insert** menu and select **Item**.

2 The Insert Item dialog box appears. In the **Look in** list, click the Outlook folder which contains the item you want to insert. The contents of that folder appears in the **Items** window below.

(continues)

Guided Tour Attach an Outlook Item to a Message

(continued)

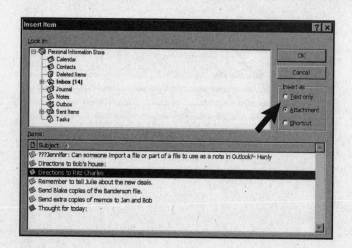

3 Click the item you want to insert. The item is attached to the message. To insert the item as text, select **Text only** from the Insert As list. To insert it as a shortcut, select the **Shortcut** option instead. When you're ready, click **OK** to insert the item.

You can also insert an item by simply dragging it into an open message, or (to create a new message) by dragging it onto the Inbox folder.

Check for Messages

People may send you e-mail messages frequently, but you'll never know it if you don't, at some time, connect to your messaging service and download (receive) your mail.

You can check for messages on all your messaging services, or just one or two. When you check for messages, if you have unsent messages in the Outbox, they are automatically sent.

If you have any new messages, Outlook places them in the Inbox and then sounds a bell to let you know. In addition, an envelope appears on the Windows 95 taskbar so that you can tell that you have unread mail. Double-click this icon to open Outlook and display the Inbox.

You can have Outlook automatically check for messages for you if you want. When setting up a messaging service (see "Add a Messaging Service," page 314), you can usually select an option which tells

Outlook to automatically check for mail. For example, when setting up an Internet connection on the **Connection** tab, you can click the **Schedule** button to schedule the frequency with which you want Outlook to check for mail.

If you're often out of the office on business, there's no reason why you can't still receive your e-mail messages. With remote e-mail, you can use your laptop to dial up your messaging service, obtain a listing of your messages, mark the ones you want to receive right now, then download (receive) the messages you marked. Of course, Outlook must be installed on your laptop, and your messaging service must be already set up (see "Add a Messaging Service," page 314).

You can use remote e-mail even if you're not out of the office. For example, if you may wish to "preview" your mail when you're busy and only download the messages you need right now.

Begin Guided Tour   Check for New Messages

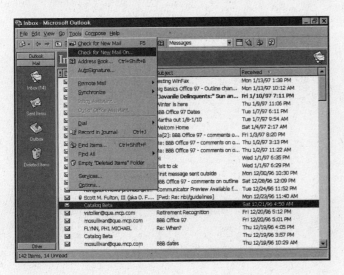

If you want to check mail on all your services, you can simply open the **Tools** menu and select **Check for new mail**.

(continues)

1 If needed, click the **Inbox** icon. Incoming mail is displayed. Open the **Tools** menu and select **Check for new mail on**.

Guided Tour   Check for New Messages

(continued)

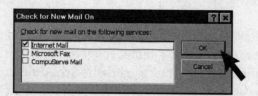

2 Click the services you want to check for messages. A check mark appears in front of the services you select. Click **OK**, and you're connected to your service. You'll see an animated dialog box depicting the sending and receiving process. After sending and receiving mail from the first service, Outlook automatically disconnects, then connects to the next service you selected.

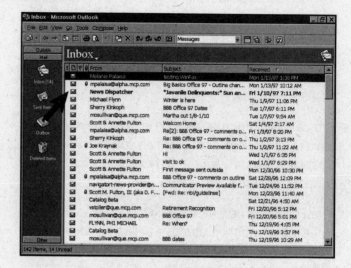

3 After messages are received, they appear in your Inbox. Since messages are normally sorted by the date in which they were received, your new messages appear at the top of the window. Unread messages are highlighted in bold text.

Read a Message

New messages, as they are received, are placed in your Inbox. Unread messages appear in bold text to distinguish them from the messages that you have already read.

In order to view the contents of a message, you must open it. When you open a message, its contents is displayed in a window so you can read it. Opening a message is as simple as double-clicking, as you'll soon learn.

Once you've read a message, you can perform the following tasks:

- You can reply to the message.

- You can forward the message to someone else.

- You can copy or move the message to a different folder.

- You can print the message.

- After reading the message, you can delete it from your system.

In order to locate a message you want to read, you may want to sort them first. Normally, locating an unread message isn't a problem, since messages are typically sorted by the date on which they were received. To sort them by the sender for example, click the **From** button at the top of the Inbox window.

Begin Guided Tour   Open a Message

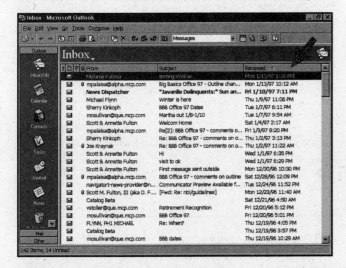

1 If needed, click the **Inbox** icon on the Outlook bar to change to the Inbox. A list of incoming messages is displayed. Unread messages appear in bold text. To open a message so you can read it, double-click the message header. The message window opens.

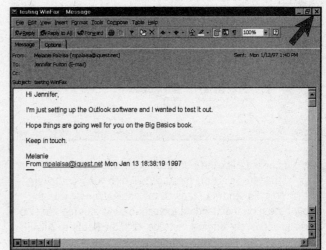

2 After reading the message, click its **Close** button, and you're returned to the Inbox.

Reply to a Message

Sometimes, in a message, a person may ask you a question, or issue a statement to which you feel you must reply. Thankfully, Outlook makes the process of replying to a message you've received simple.

When you reply to a message, the contents of the original message are copied into the text area of your reply. This helps the recipient remember exactly the words to which you are referring. However, if you don't want to include the entire contents of the original message in your reply, you can delete all or

part of it as needed. Just drag over the text you don't want in order to select it, then press **Delete** to remove it from your reply.

When sending your reply, you can send your message to only the message's originator, or to its originator and each of the recipients of the original message.

Messages to which you've already replied appear with a special icon: an open envelope with a small red arrow in front of it.

Begin Guided Tour   Respond to a Message You've Received

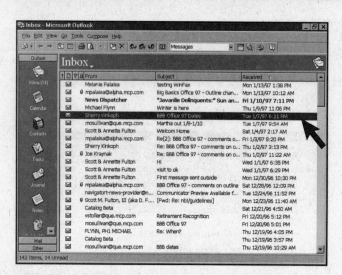

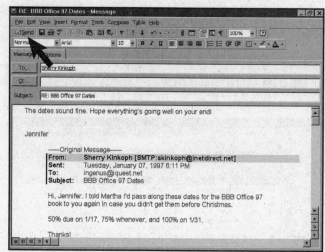

1 If needed, click the Inbox icon. Incoming messages are displayed. Select the message to which you want to reply by clicking it. To send your reply to the originator only, click the **Reply** button on the Standard toolbar. To send your reply to all of the recipients of the original message, click the **Reply to All** button instead.

2 The text of the original message appears in the message window. Type your reply above this text, then click **Send**.

You can delete some or all of the original message by selecting the text and pressing **Delete**.

Guided Tour Respond to a Message You've Received

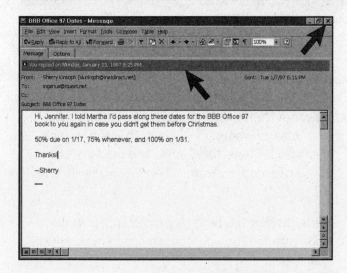

3 You're returned to the original message window. A notice appears above the text, reminding you (should you open this message again), that you've already replied to this message. Click its **Close** button to return to the Inbox.

Begin Guided Tour Replying to a Message with Voting Buttons

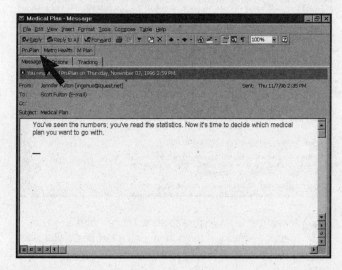

1 If you receive an e-mail message in which you're asked to respond, when you open that message by double-clicking it, you'll see voting buttons on a toolbar at the top of the window. To respond to the query, simply click the button of your choice.

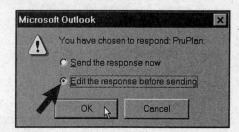

2 A dialog box appears. Click **Send the response now** to send simply your voting response. If you want to send a comment as well (in the form of an e-mail message), click **Edit the response before sending** instead. Then click **OK**.

Forward a Message

When you reply to an e-mail message, the reply is automatically addressed to the sender of the original message. When you forward a message instead, you can send it to anyone you want.

You might forward a message if it was sent to the wrong person, if the project to which it refers has been reassigned to someone else, or if you know of someone who should be made aware of its information.

When you forward a message, the original message remains on your system. A copy of the message is then sent to the persons you indicate. You can even add text to the forwarded message if you like.

You can forward multiple messages to the same people at one time, but if you do that, the messages will be sent as attachments, not as individual messages. In other words, the individual messages will appear as icons within a single message, which is forwarded to whoever you want. To select multiple messages for forwarding, press and hold the **Ctrl** key as you click each message. Then follow the steps in this task.

Messages that you have forwarded appear in the Inbox with the Forward icon: an open envelope with a small blue arrow.

> **Begin Guided Tour** Forward a Copy of a Message

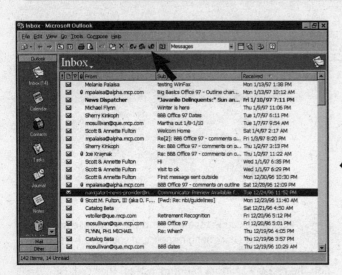

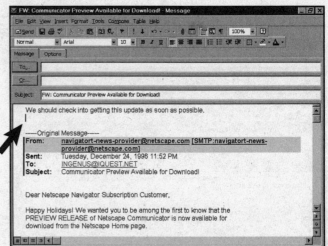

1 If needed, click the Inbox icon. Incoming messages are displayed. Select the message you want to forward by clicking it. Click the **Forward** button on the toolbar.

> You can forward multiple messages at one time. To select the messages, press **Ctrl** as you click them.

2 A new message window appears. The text of the original message appears at the bottom of the text box. If you want to add a comment to the forwarded message, type it above this text.

Guided Tour Forward a Copy of a Message

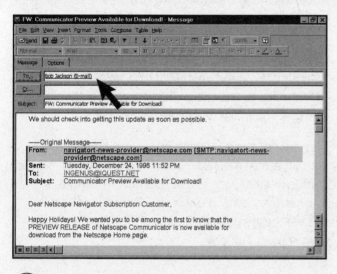

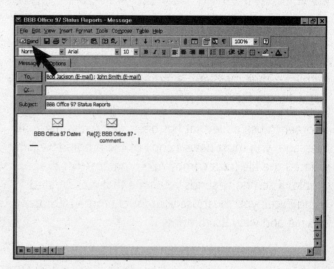

3 In the **To** text box, type the address of the person to whom you wish to send your message, or click the **To** button to select one from your address book. You can send a copy of the message to someone by including their address in the **Cc** box.

5 When you're ready, click **Send**. The message is forwarded to the indicated people.

You can forward your message to more than one person. Simply separate each address with a semicolon (;).

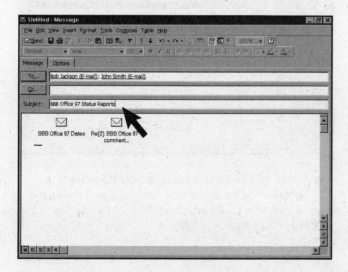

4 If you're forwarding multiple messages, a new message window appears. The messages you selected for forwarding appear as icons. Type a **Subject** for this new message.

Save an Attached File or Outlook Item

Not all the messages you receive will contain just text. Sometimes, a person will send a file along with an e-mail message, a process which is called "attaching a file."

In order to use a file that has been sent with an e-mail message, you must have a copy of the program which created the file (or a compatible program). For example, if someone sends you a file that was created using Excel, you must use your Excel program to open the file and view its contents.

Before you attempt to open the attached file, you might want to save it to your hard disk first. Although

you can open an attached file (and even make changes to it) *without saving the file to your hard disk first*, it's not a good idea. That's because if you don't save the file to your hard disk at some point, any changes you make to the file will be lost.

Files are not the only thing which can be included with an e-mail message. Users of Outlook can include Outlook items (such as a contact name, a note, a Journal entry, and so on) with a message. It's simple to save these attached Outlook items for use in your own copy of Outlook.

Begin Guided Tour   Save a File Attached to a Message

1 Messages which contain attached files appear with a paper clip icon. To save the attached file(s) to your hard disk, click the message to select it.

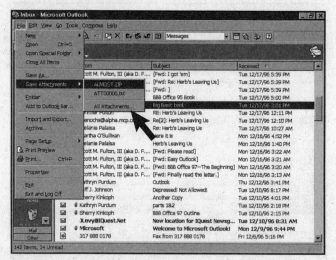

2 Open the **File** menu and select **Save Attachments**. A menu listing the attached files appears. Select the file you want to save, or select **All attachments** to save all the files attached to the selected message.

If you choose **All Attachments**, you'll be saving them all *in the same folder*. If you want to save them in different folders, or if you want to rename them, then select each one from the list separately.

Guided Tour   Save a File Attached to a Message

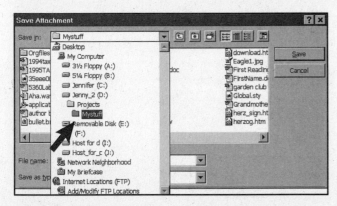

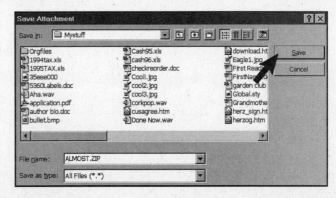

3 Select the folder in which you want to save the file. To change to a different file or drive, select it from the **Save in** list. You can rename the file as you're saving it by typing a new name for the file in the **File name** text box.

4 When you're ready to save the file to your hard disk, click **Save**. You're returned to the Inbox.

Begin Guided Tour   Save an Attached Outlook Item

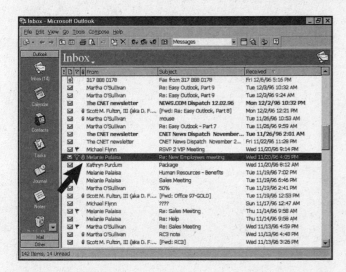

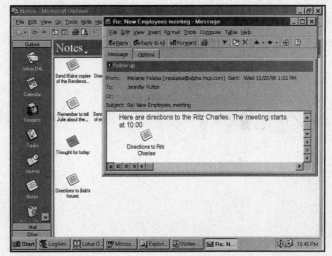

1 If a message contains an attached Outlook item, it also appears with a paper clip icon. Double-click the message to open it.

2 Resize the message window if necessary so you can see both it and the main Outlook window. Switch to the folder in which you want to save the attachment.

3 Drag the attachment into the Outlook folder and release the mouse button. Its icon appears in the folder you selected.

HOW TO...

Track Appointments, Meetings, and Other Events with Outlook

You can keep track of all the important events in your life (meetings, appointments, anniversaries, birthdays, holidays) with the Calendar.

An *appointment* is an event which does not involve inviting other people or arranging for resources such as a meeting room, slide projector, and so on. A *meeting*, on the other hand, involves sending and receiving meeting requests, and scheduling meeting resources such as a room, A/V equipment, and so on. An *event* is an activity which lasts a day or more, such as your vacation, a convention, a trade show, a birthday, anniversary, or special holiday, for example.

Besides single events, Outlook also lets you schedule recurring appointments, events, and meetings, such as haircut appointments, weekly or monthly meetings, workouts, doctor's appointments, anniversaries, and so on. In addition, you can easily move appointments, meetings, and events to keep your Calendar current.

What You Will Find in This Section

Move Around the Calendar

Initially, Calendar displays the appointments, meetings, and events you have set up for *today* only. You also see a listing of today's tasks (which are normally entered in the Tasks section of Outlook; however, they can also be entered while in Calendar). To view your appointments and tasks for a different day, you'll need to change from one day to another in Calendar.

You use the Date Navigator to move around the Calendar, as you'll learn in this task. The Date Navigator consists of two small monthly calendars, placed side by side. The calendar on the left displays the current month, and the calendar on the right displays the next month. With the Date Navigator, you can quickly display appointments, meetings, and events for any date which is visible in one of its small calendars.

If you need to see the appointments for a day in a previous month or some future month, what do you do? The answer is simple: You just change to a different month in the Date Navigator, and then select the day you want to view.

Sometimes you want to view more than a single day's appointments at the same time. In the Calendar, it's easy to view several days worth of appointments at one time, or even a whole month's worth!

In the normal Calendar view, the current appointments and tasks are displayed, along with this month's and next month's calendars. If this is not the type of information you'd like to see, you can change to one of the other Calendar views:

- **Day/Week/Month**   This is the default view; it displays today's appointments and tasks, along with this month's and next month's calendar.

- **Active Appointments**   Lists upcoming appointments.

- **Events**   Lists all events.

- **Annual Events**   Lists only yearly events such as holidays.

- **Recurring Appointments**   Lists appointments that reoccur.

- **By Category**   Lists appointments, meetings, and events by their category.

An appointment, meeting, or event does not have a category until you select one for it. See "Use Categories," page 307, for more information.

Begin Guided Tour   View a Different Day's Appointments

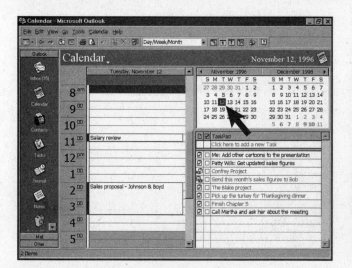

1 Click the **Calendar** button in the Outlook bar. In the upper-right corner of the Calendar window, you'll find the Date Navigator, which you use to move from one date to the next. The currently selected date appears in blue. Today's date is marked by a red outline. To move to a day which is visible in the Date Navigator, click that date. For example, click November 12.

> If a date appears in bold within the Date Navigator, then you have an appointment, meeting, or event scheduled for that day.

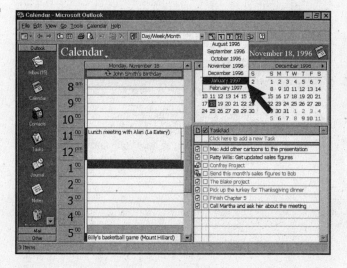

2 The Calendar for the 18th is displayed on the left. To display a date that is not visible, click either of the month labels (such as November or December) and choose the month you want from the list which appears. For example, click November and select January.

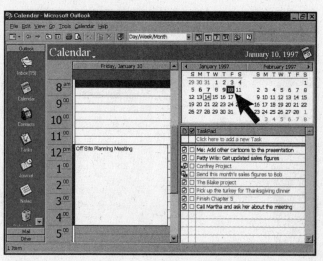

3 The Calendar for January is displayed on the left. To display the appointments for a day in January, click it. For example, click January 10th.

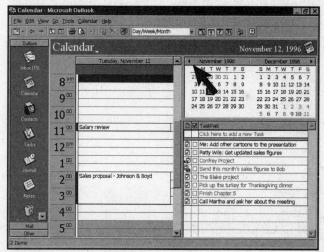

4 You can also move from month to month by clicking the left or right arrows on the Date Navigator. For example, to display November again, click the left arrow *twice* on the Navigator. Then click the date you want to display.

Begin Guided Tour Display Multiple Days' Worth of Appointments

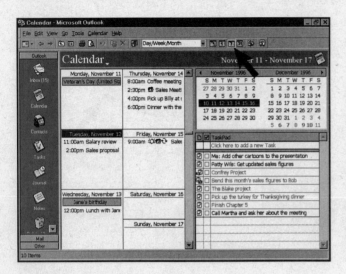

1 To view a week's worth of appointments, click the **Week** button on the Standard toolbar.

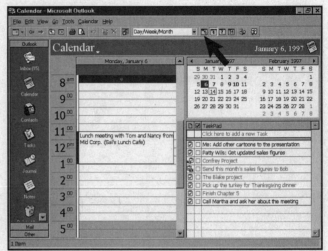

3 To view today's appointments, click the **Go to Today** button on the Standard toolbar.

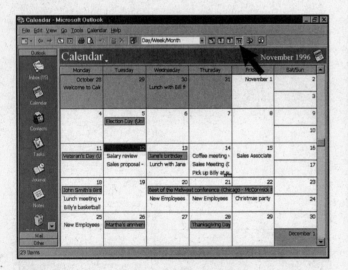

2 To view a month's worth of appointments, click the **Month** button on the Standard toolbar instead. (To return to viewing a single day, click the **Day** button.)

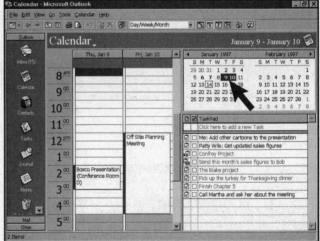

4 You don't have to view a week or a month's worth of appointments. You can view several days at once by pressing **Ctrl** and clicking the days you want to view.

Schedule an Appointment

An *appointment* is personal; it does not involve company personnel or resources, as a meeting might. You can schedule an appointment for any type of activity, such as a doctor's appointment, a lunch date, your workout, or a client meeting.

When you schedule an appointment, you block out the amount of time you need. When setting up the time for the appointment, you can select the time you want from a list, or you can use real words such as next Monday, or noon. Outlook understands what you mean and translates it into a real date such as November 11, and a real time such as 12:00 P.M. If you want to be reminded a few minutes before your upcoming appointment, you can set Outlook to beep you ahead of time.

If you're on a company-wide network, it's possible to set things up so that others can view your appointments. In such a case, you might want to add a comment to your appointments to let others know whether they are moveable or not. You can mark appointments as busy, free, tentative, or out of office. In addition, you can grant others permission to schedule appointments for you and to make changes to them. In such a case, you might mark particular appointments as "private," which means that your assistant cannot view or change them. Your coworkers can give you access to their calendars.

Outlook also lets you schedule recurring appointments such as weekly workouts, doctor's appointments, salon visits, and so on.

You can create your appointment using several methods:

- You can click the **New Appointment** button as shown in the task.

- You can change to the day on which you want the appointment to appear, *prior* to clicking the **New Appointment** button.

- You can click the start time for the appointment prior to clicking the **New Appointment** button. Or, you can drag over the time slots you want to select and then right-click and choose **New Appointment** from the pop-up menu.

- You can create a new appointment with someone by dragging their e-mail message from the Inbox to the Calendar icon on the Outlook bar. The subject of the message becomes the subject of your new appointment, and the text of the message appears in the New Appointment dialog box.

Begin Guided Tour Set Up an Appointment

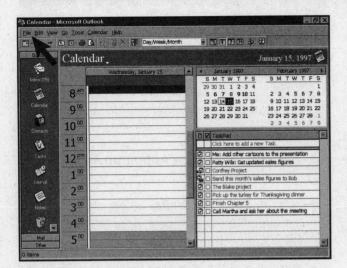

1 From within the Calendar, click the **New Appointment** button on the Standard toolbar.

2 The New Appointment dialog box appears. Type a description of the appointment in the **Subject** text box. Enter the location of the appointment in the **Location** text box.

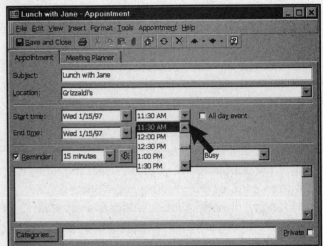

3 Enter a start date and time. To select a start date, click the down arrow on the **Start time** list to display the calendar. Then click a date. To change to a different month, click the left or right arrows at the top of the calendar window. To select a time, click the down arrow on the time list and scroll to select the time you want.

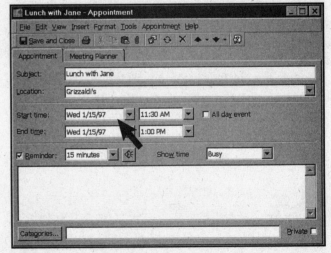

4 Enter an end date and time. If you want to block out the entire day, click **All day event**.

Guided Tour   Set Up an Appointment

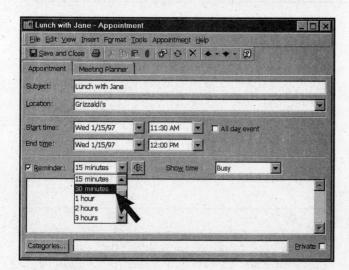

5 To be reminded of your appointment prior to its start time, click **Reminder**. Click the down arrow and select the number of minutes prior to the appointment at which you want the reminder to go off.

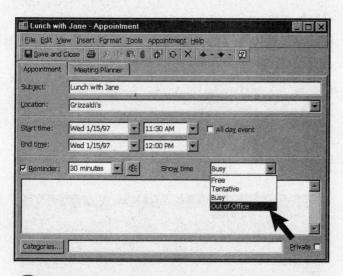

6 Click the down arrow in Show Time list and select how you want your appointment to appear to others.

If you don't want anyone to have access to the details of this appointment, click **Private** in the lower-right corner of the **Event** box.

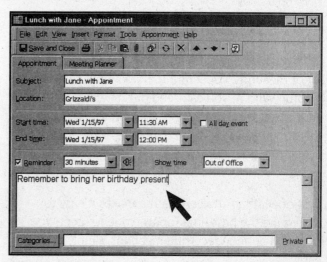

7 You can add a note to the appointment in the large text box.

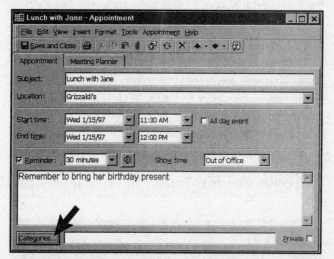

8 Click the **Categories** button to select a category for this appointment.

9 Select the categories you want to assign to this appointment and click **OK**.

10 You're returned to the New Appointment dialog box. When you're through selecting options, click **Save and Close**. Your new appointment appears in the Calendar.

Schedule a Meeting

A meeting is an appointment that involves other company personnel. If you have to schedule a lot of meetings, you'll find the Meeting Planner very helpful. With it, you can send out meeting requests to your coworkers. In addition, you can usually reserve the other resources you might need, such as a particular meeting room, a projector, and other equipment.

Best of all, the AutoPick feature makes it easy to determine the best time for everyone to meet. You can even arrange recurring meetings, simply and easily.

Here's how the AutoPick feature works: If you have access to the Calendar of the people you invited, then their free time automatically appears in the Meeting Planner. Light blue indicates that the person is tentatively free, dark blue indicates that they are busy, and purple indicates that they are out of the office. To select the next available time when everyone can meet, you simply click the **AutoPick** button in the Meeting Planner.

When you schedule a meeting, e-mail requests are sent out over your company's network, inviting the people you selected to attend. When they respond to your request, their individual responses appear as e-mail messages in your Inbox. However, if you just want to verify the number of people who plan to attend, you can access a summary of those responses through the Meeting Planner in the Calendar.

> In Outlook, you can schedule a meeting with any of your coworkers, provided that you are all connected to a company network. If you're not on a network, you can still use the meeting planner; however, meeting responses will not be automatically tabulated.

When planning a big meeting, your needs often change. That's not a problem with Calendar, which makes it easy to change not only the time of your meeting, but the day as well. You can also add more people (and delete people) from the meeting as the need arises.

Begin Guided Tour   Send Out Meeting Requests

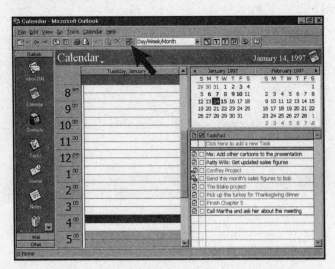

1 In the Calendar, change to the day on which you want to add the meeting. Then click the meeting's start time. Click the **Plan a Meeting** button on the Standard toolbar.

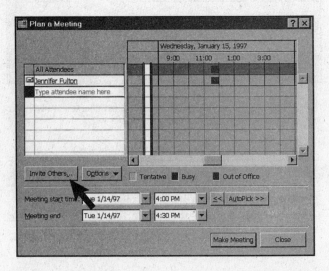

2 Click **Invite Others**.

Guided Tour Send Out Meeting Requests

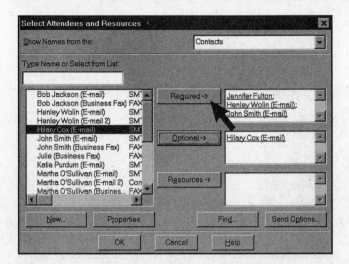

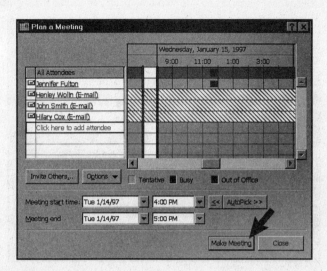

3 The Select Attendees and Resources dialog box appears. Select the address book you want to use from the **Show Names from the list**. Select a name from the list on the left by clicking it. Then click either the **Required** button (for people whose presence is required) or the **Optional** button (for people whose presence is optional). Repeat to invite additional people.

5 Select a start and end time for the meeting by selecting them from the **Meeting start time** and **Meeting end** lists. You can also drag the **meeting selection bar** along the time line to select a meeting time. Click **Make Meeting**.

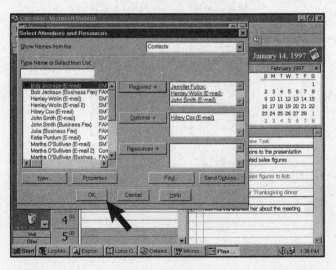

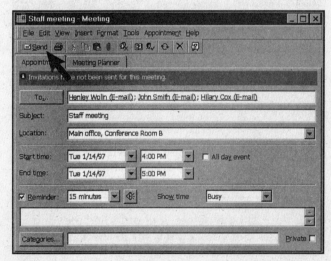

4 If you're on a company network, your network administrator may have added the names of common resources (such as meeting rooms) to your company's address list. In that case, change to your company's e-mail listing, select a resource from the list on the left and click the **Resource** button to add it. Click **OK** when all persons or resources are added.

6 An e-mail message window appears. Enter a **Subject**, **Location**, and a text message if you want. You can also select a category for the message, and attach a file (such as the agenda) to the message if you like. When you're ready, click **Send**. Invitations to attend the meeting are sent to each person listed, and the meeting appears in your calendar.

Begin Guided Tour   Cancel a Meeting

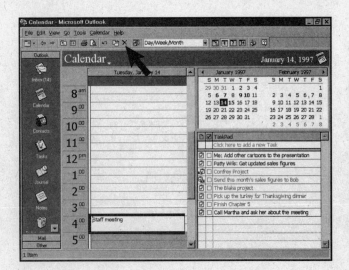

1 If you change your mind about the meeting prior to sending the invitations, click the meeting to select it. Then click the **Delete** button on the Standard toolbar.

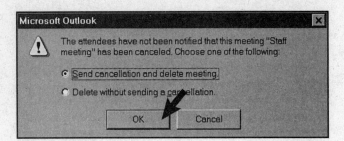

2 Since you have not yet sent your meeting requests, you can select **Delete without sending a cancellation**. Click **OK**.

Outlook should delete your outgoing meeting requests, but you might want to check and delete them manually if needed.

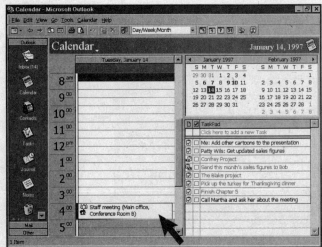

3 If you need to cancel a meeting after having sent the invitations, double-click the meeting block which appears in your Calendar.

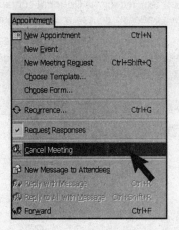

4 Open the **Appointment** menu and select **Cancel Meeting**.

Guided Tour   Cancel a Meeting

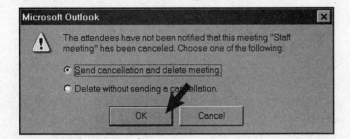

5 You can then send a message letting the attendees know about the cancellation by clicking **Send cancellation and delete meeting**. Click **OK**.

Begin Guided Tour   View Meeting Responses

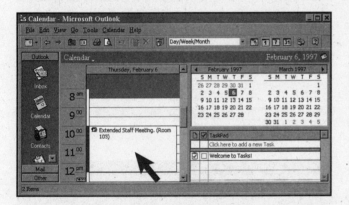

1 After attendees have responded to your meeting request, you can view their responses by double-clicking the meeting in the Calendar (provided the attendees are connected to your company's network).

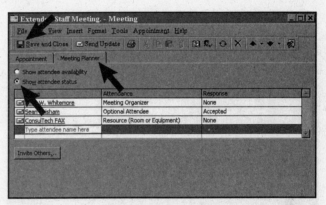

2 The Meeting window appears. Click the **Meeting Planner** tab. If needed, click **Show attendee status**, and you'll see a listing of each individual's response. Click **Save and Close** to return to the Calendar.

Schedule an Event

An *event* is an activity which often takes place over an entire day, or several days. Typical events include birthdays, anniversaries, and holidays. They also include seminars, all-day training sessions, conferences, retreats, and vacations.

Outlook supports two types of events: singular and annual. A singular event might last for a day or even several days. Singular events occur on that date (or dates) only once—for example, a convention, your vacation, a training class or seminar, and other singular events. Typical annual events include such things as anniversaries, birthdays, and special holidays.

When you schedule an event, it appears as a banner heading at the top of the day(s) in which it occurs—individual time slots are not blocked out; the

reasoning here is that often, an event (such as a birthday) does not prevent you from attending other meetings or appointments.

The handling of events is different from an appointment or a meeting, which appear within the time segments of a particular day. Also, if others have permission to view your Calendar, an appointment or a meeting will show the time as "busy," while an event will show your time as "free," unless you specify otherwise.

By the way, a particular day can contain more than one event; for example, you might be attending a conference the same day as someone's birthday. In that case, both events will appear at the top of that day's calendar.

Begin Guided Tour   Add an Event

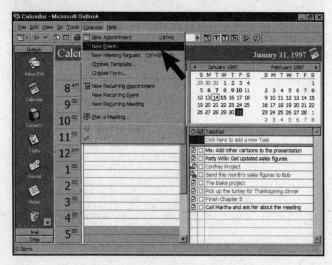

1 Switch to the date on which you want the event to occur, and then open the **Calendar** menu and select **New Event**.

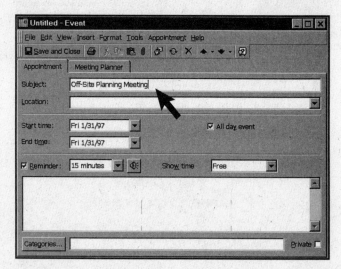

2 Type a name or description for the event in the **Subject** box.

To create an event quickly, double-click the date heading for the day on which the event will occur.

Guided Tour   Add an Event

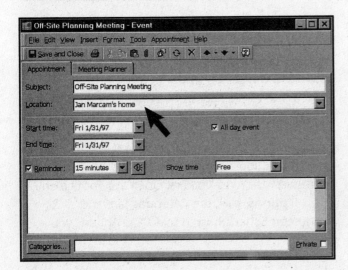

3 If there's a location associated with the event, enter it in the **Location** box.

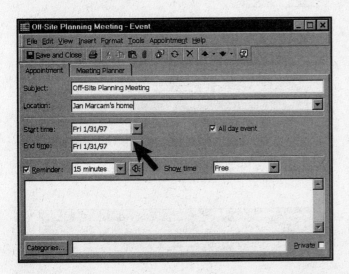

4 If the event occurs over several days, select an **End date.**

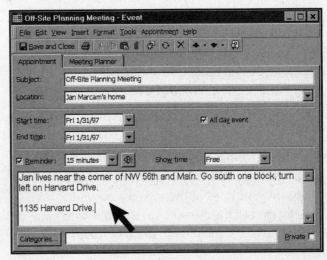

5 If you like, you can add a note in the large text box.

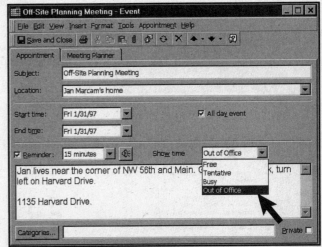

6 Normally, the time allotted to an event is shown as **Free** in your Calendar. You might want to change it to **Out of office** by selecting that option from the **Show time** list.

7 Click **Save and Close.** The name of the event appears as a heading above the time slots for the date(s) you indicated.

Responding to a Meeting Request

Obviously, if someone sends you a request for a meeting, you need to respond. When you respond, you can accept the invitation, reject it, or accept it tentatively. When you accept an invitation to attend a meeting, it's automatically added to your Calendar so you won't forget about it.

A meeting request comes to you in the form of an e-mail message. When you open the message, you'll notice three buttons at the top, just above the text. You respond to the meeting (by accepting, tentatively accepting, or declining) with these buttons.

This assumes, that the meeting request came to you from someone using Outlook, over your company's network. If the person who sent the request is not located on your company's network, then the meeting request appears as an ordinary e-mail message.

If you are on a company network, you might be able to set up Outlook to automatically respond to meeting requests from coworkers. Open the **Tools** menu, select **Options**, click the **Calendar** tab, and click **Advanced Scheduling** to select the options you want.

Begin Guided Tour   Send a Reply to a Meeting Request

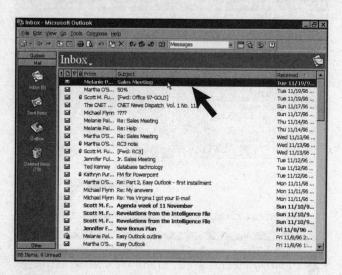

1 Switch to the Inbox and double-click the meeting request to open it.

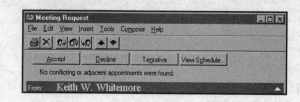

2 At the top of the message window, click **Accept**, **Tentative**, or **Decline**, depending on how you want to respond.

3 Click the **Send** icon to send your response.

If you receive a meeting cancellation, click **Remove from Calendar** to remove the meeting from your Calendar. The cancellation notification is also removed from your Inbox.

HOW TO...

Create an Outlook Contacts List

The Contact section of Outlook helps you organize phone numbers, addresses, fax numbers, mobile phone numbers, e-mail addresses, and other information about the important people in your life, both personal and business.

After entering a person into the Contacts list, you can use the information in his record to send an e-mail message, schedule an appointment, arrange a meeting, delegate a task, visit a client's Web page, and even dial the phone to call him.

With the Contacts list, there'll be no more lost phone numbers, scrambled e-mail addresses, or forgotten assistant's names. That's because everything you need to know about a personal or business contact can be entered into the Contacts list.

What You Will Find in This Section

Import an Old Address List

If you have been using another electronic day planner such as Schedule+ or Lotus Organizer prior to switching to Outlook, I have good news for you. Instead of having to retype them, you can import your old contact names, phone numbers, and addresses directly into Outlook.

Outlook can import data from several personal information manager programs, as well as many other programs, including the following:

- Schedule+ (versions 1.0 and 95)

- Microsoft Exchange

- Act! (version 2.0 for Windows)

- ECCO Pro (versions 3.0, 3.01, and 3.02)

- SideKick (versions 1.0 and 95)

- Lotus Organizer (versions 1.0, 1.1, and 2.1)

- Microsoft Excel (all versions)

- Microsoft Access (all versions)

- FoxPro (all versions)

- dBASE (all versions)

- .CSV files

- .TXT files

Some of these programs, while supported, are not immediately available to you for importing. So you may need to keep your Office 97 CD-ROM handy as you step through the following task.

Begin Guided Tour Import Old Addresses

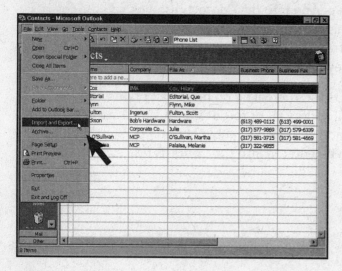
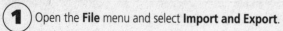

1 Open the **File** menu and select **Import and Export**.

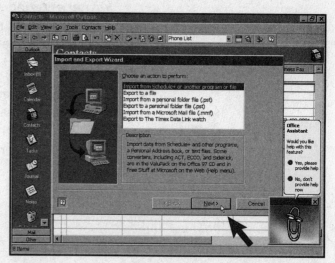

2 The Office Assistant appears. If you'd like to follow the steps here, click **No, don't provide help now**. Then, in the Import and Export Wizard dialog box, click **Import from Schedule+ or another program or file.** Then click **Next**.

Guided Tour Import Old Addresses

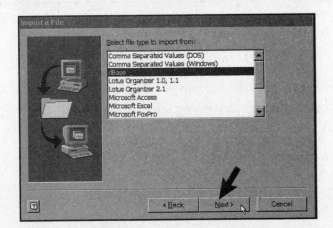

3 Select your program name in the **Select file type to import from** list. Then click **Next**.

If your program isn't listed, a file converter for the program may be contained on the Office CD-ROM. Insert the CD and click **Add/Remove Programs** to install the file converter you need.

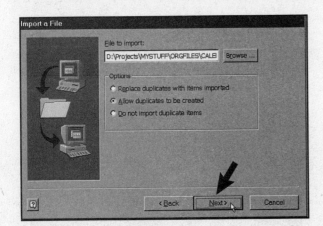

4 Type the path to the file you want to import, or click **Browse,** change to the folder in which the file is stored, select it from the list, and click **OK**. Also, choose how you want duplicates handled. When you're ready, click **Next**.

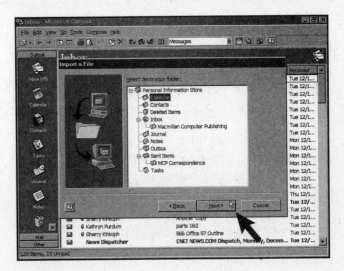

5 Select a destination folder and click **Next**.

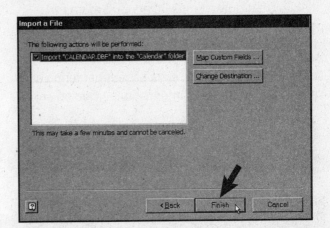

6 Click the action you want taken, and a check mark appears in front of it. Click **Finish**, and the file is imported into Outlook.

Add a Contact

Everyone has important people in their life—both business and personal. With the Contact list, you can keep track of them all easily. It offers the flexibility you need to store all the information you have on a particular contact.

In addition (and keeping with today's technology), you can enter a mobile phone number, a pager number, a fax number, and several e-mail addresses. You can even enter the address of a person's (or a company's) World Wide Web page. Then you can visit your client's Web page with the click of a mouse.

For important business contacts, you can enter the name of their assistant and their boss, the name of their company, their department, and their official title. But that doesn't mean there isn't room for personal information too, such as a contact's birthday, anniversary, nickname, and spouse's name.

Outlook has provided an extra page for entering a variety of miscellaneous information, including an

assistant's phone number, the main company number, the company's FTP site address on the Internet, a Company ID or account number, children's names, hobbies, the name of the person who referred this contact to you, and billing information.

Through the Journal, you can track conversations with a contact. Then in the Contact list, you can view the conversations and other information entered in the Journal about a particular contact. If there isn't a field for information you need to enter, you can create your own fields.

When you add a new contact, it's saved in the Contact Address Book. You may have other address books that you can access through Outlook as well.

> You can create a new contact from an e-mail message by simply dragging that message from the Inbox to the Contact icon on the Outlook bar.

Begin Guided Tour   Enter a New Contact

1 Click the **New Contact** button on the Standard toolbar.

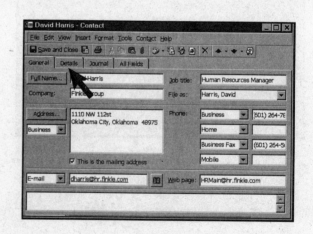

2 In the New Contact dialog box, enter the contact's name, and so on. Under **File As**, enter the text you'll use to locate this contact. Enter your contact's address, phone numbers, and e-mail address, click the **Address Book** button, select the e-mail address from the list, and click **OK**. Click the **Details** tab.

Guided Tour Enter a New Contact

To add a new contact for the same company as an existing contact, simply click the existing contact, then open the **Contacts** menu and select **New Contact from Same Company**.

If you want to enter a personal address too, just select **Personal** from the **Address** drop-down list. (The Business address will still be saved.) Also, in the phone area, you can enter additional phone numbers by selecting the type of phone number you want to enter from the **Phone** drop-down lists.

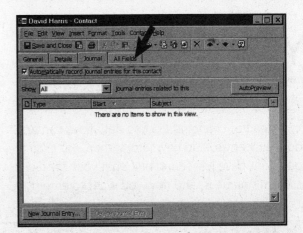

4 On the Journal page, you can track activity related to a contact. Later, you can return to this page to view that activity, all in one spot. To track activity for a contact, click the **Automatically record journal entries for this contact**. Click the **All Fields** tab.

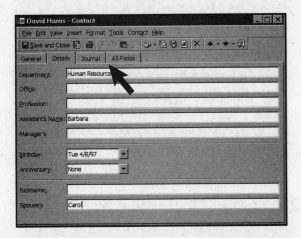

3 The Details page is displayed. Enter additional information about a contact, such as his department name, assistant's name, spouse's name, etc. To enter his birthday or anniversary, click the down arrow on the list box, and a calendar appears. Click the date you want. When you're through entering information, click the **Journal** tab.

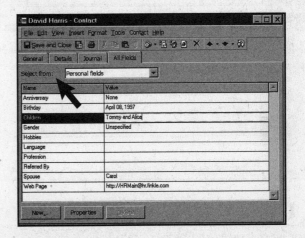

5 On the All Fields page, select the fields you want to display from the **Select from** list. For example, select Personal fields. Then click a field and type your information. For example, click the Children field and enter the names of your contact's children. When you're through, click **Save and Close**.

To enter unique information, click the **New** button, located at the bottom of the New Contact dialog box, enter a name for your new field, and click **OK**.

Change Contact Information

You may have to change a contact's information for many reasons: the contact's title and position may have changed, his company might have relocated, or his phone number might have changed.

Or, instead of changing existing data for a contact, you may want to add new information. For example, you might have just found out what your contact's assistant's name is, and now you want to enter it.

Changing (or adding) information to an existing contact is fairly simple: First, you open the contact's record, then you locate the field you want, and then you enter or change information as needed. You can delete unwanted information as well, as you'll learn to do in this Guided Tour.

Begin Guided Tour Add or Change Data on a Contact

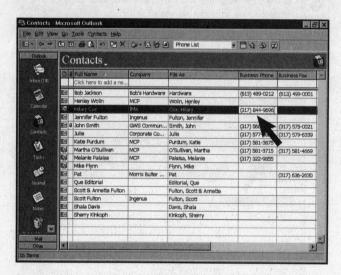

1 Click the contact you want to change. The contact is highlighted in blue to show that it's selected. To change a field which is visible (such as the contact's business phone number), just click that field. Press **Backspace** to delete characters to the left of the cursor, or **Delete** to remove characters to the right. Then type your correction. When you're through, click a different entry. Your changes are saved.

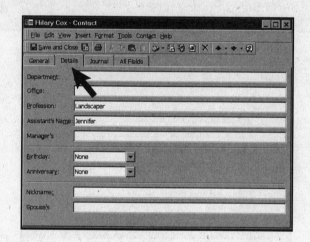

2 If the field you want to change (or add) is not visible, then double-click the contact name. The Contact dialog box appears. Click the tab which contains the field you want to change. For example, click the **Details** tab.

3 Make your changes or additions, and then click **Save and Close** to save them.

Sort Your Contacts List

Information in the Contact list can be sorted in various ways. Initially, contact information is displayed in a phone listing, with each contact appearing on a single line, and his business and personal phone numbers appearing in separate columns. This type of listing is convenient for contacting a person by phone, especially since, after selecting a contact from the list, you then can have Outlook dial the phone number for you.

The Contact list can be sorted in other ways as well. If you like the look of a conventional phone book, you can switch to the Address listing. In this view, small lettered tabs appear on the right side of the window. Click one of these tabs to view contacts whose last names begin with that letter. In this view, addresses are displayed, along with the contact's phone numbers. There's a detailed address listing as well, which displays additional information about each contact.

You can sort the Contact listing by company, which is convenient when you have several contacts at the same business. When your contacts are listed this way, a small minus sign appears next to each company's name, with the individual contacts appearing underneath. If you click the minus sign, the contact names for that particular company are temporarily hidden, and the minus sign changes to a plus. Click this plus sign, and the contact names are redisplayed.

You can also sort the Contact list by location. When you sort by location, you can again click the minus sign next to a location to hide the contacts within. Click the plus sign to redisplay the list of contact names for that location.

If you add a category (or categories) to each contact, then you can sort by it. For example, you might select the categories "Business" or "Personal" in order to arrange your business and personal contacts in different parts of the list. If the categories provided by Outlook don't help you, you can create your own categories as needed.

Also, when information is displayed using the Phone List view, you can sort by any of the visible fields, such as Company.

Begin Guided Tour   Change the View

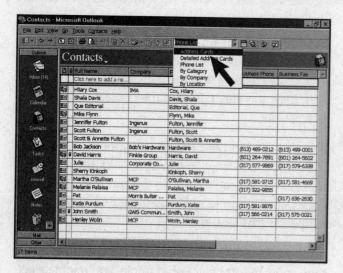

1 Initially, your Contacts are displayed in a phone listing. Here, you'll see each contact's name and phone numbers. To change to a different view, select it from the **Current View** list. For example, select **Address Cards**.

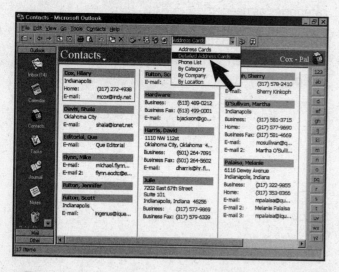

2 The Address Cards listing displays both the contact's phone numbers and his e-mail addresses. To see more information on a contact, select **Detailed Address Cards** from the **Current View** list.

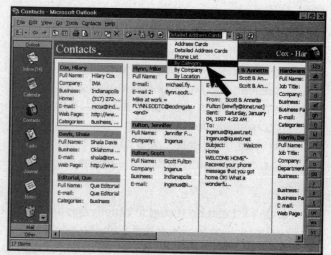

3 To locate a person quickly in either the Address Cards or Detailed Address Cards views, click the button on the right which contains the first letter of the person's last name. For example, click **wx**. To sort contact's by category, select **By Category** from the **Current View** list.

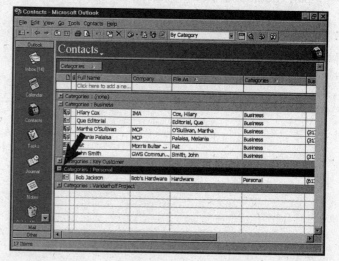

4 A plus sign in front of a category indicates that it contains entries that are not currently displayed. To display them, click the plus sign. To hide the entries again, click the minus sign that appears. Select **By Company** from the **Current View** list.

Guided Tour Change the View

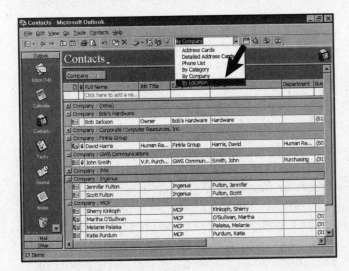

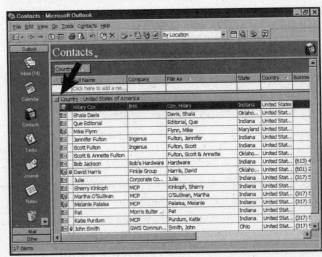

5 The company listing works in a similar manner to the category listing. To display hidden entries, click the plus sign. To hide the entries again, click the minus sign that appears. Select **By Location** from the **Current View** list.

6 The location list works just like the company and location listings. A plus sign in front of a location indicates that it contains entries that are not currently displayed. To display them, click the plus sign. To hide the entries again, click the minus sign that appears.

Begin Guided Tour Sort by a Contact Field

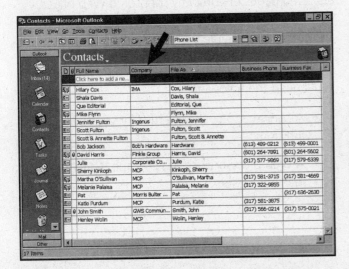

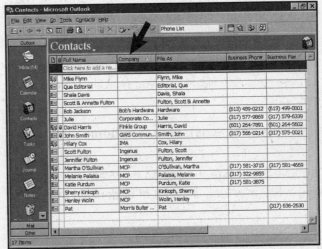

1 When using the Phone List view, you can sort by any of the displayed fields. Initially, contacts are sorted by the File As field. This arranges your contacts by their last names. To sort by another field, click its header. For example, click the Company header.

2 The field by which contacts are currently being sorted is displayed with a small triangle. If this triangle is pointing upward, then the field is being sorted alphabetically (from A to Z). To reverse the sort, click the header again. For example, click the Company header again.

Visit a Contact's World Wide Web Page

It seems that just about every business has a World Wide Web page on the Internet. What's the World Wide Web? Well, first of all, its only a part of the Internet (and not the Internet itself). The Web consists of a bunch of "pages" linked together like a gigantic book. To view these pages, you use a Web browser.

Each Web page is assigned its own address, called an URL (Uniform Resource Locator). Your Web browser uses this URL to locate the page and display it on-screen. An URL looks something like this:

http://www.indy.net/planetzero.html

The **http** part tells the Web browser that you want to view a page on the World Wide Web (as opposed to some other part of the Internet). The **www.indy.net** part is a location on the Web; specifically, it's the address of a *Web server*. The Web was created by linking together these Web server PCs all over the globe. A Web server typically stores thousands and thousands of Web pages which people can view. The last part, **planetzero.html**, is the name of a Web page.

On the Web, the *home page* is your starting point. If you use Netscape Navigator, you typically start at its main page:

http://home.netscape.com/home

To move from page to page on the Web, you click a link. A link may look like a bit of underlined text, or it may be a graphic image. No matter, since the result is the same: when you click a link, you're taken to the Web page to which it is connected. By clicking several links in succession, you can visit many pages on the Web.

So what does all this have to do with Outlook? Well, in addition to recording phone numbers and addresses on a contact, you can also record the address of a contact's Web page. Typically, background, product, and sales information are being made available on such pages. If the company of one of your contacts has a Web page, you can use Outlook to quickly connect to it.

Also, if your company has an intranet, you can connect to a coworker's Web page quickly and easily. What is an intranet? It's an inter-office network which runs Internet software. Think of an intranet as a private (company-run) Internet. On it, you can publish your own Web page. You can also visit your coworkers' Web pages or company sponsored Web pages, using the same techniques you would use to move about the World Wide Web.

Of course, in order to use this feature of Outlook, you'll need the following:

- A connection to the Internet (or your company's intranet).

- A Web browser such as Netscape Navigator or Internet Explorer.

Begin Guided Tour View the Web Page of a Contact

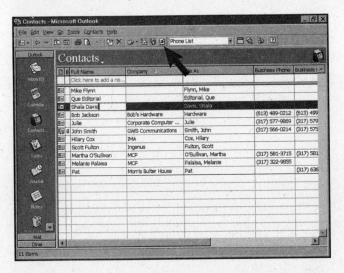

3 If you connected to the Internet via a modem, then disconnect from the Internet by clicking **Disconnect**.

When browsing a Web page, Outlook does not connect or disconnect you from the Internet, so you must do that yourself.

1 First, connect to the Internet (or log on to your company's intranet) in the usual manner. Then, open the Contacts list and click the contact whose Web page you want to visit. Click the **Explore Web Page** icon on the Standard toolbar.

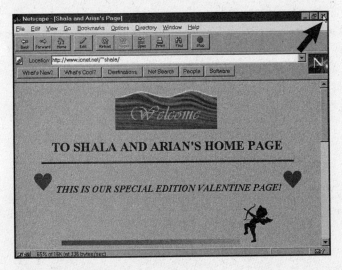

2 Outlook starts up your Web browser and connects to the Web page you selected. When you're though browsing, click the browser's **Close** button.

Use Outlook to Keep Track of Things to Do

If you have trouble keeping track of all those things you need to do, perhaps the Tasks list can help. In the Tasks list, you can enter a task, set a deadline for it, and post a reminder so you'll remember to complete the task on time.

You can enter both personal and business tasks into the Tasks list. For example, you might want to be reminded to pick up some milk on the way home or to get that birthday present by Friday. On the business side, you may have a complex project which requires several tasks to be completed. You can enter all these tasks (complete with individual deadlines) into the Tasks list. Then, as you complete each part of the project, you can track your progress. (A completed task remains on the Tasks list until you delete it. It appears in a dull gray at the top of the Tasks list, with a line through the task description.)

Outlook also helps you keep track of stray thoughts and important notes. When you find yourself reaching for one of those tiny yellow post-it pads, reach for Outlook instead. Outlook can help you organize your notes while making sure you don't lose any of them.

What You Will Find in This Section

Add a Task

If you want to keep track of something you need to remember to do, you can add it to the Tasks list. When you add the task, you can specify a due date. You can also tell Outlook to remind you when the task's due date is coming up, so you'll be able to complete the task on time.

You can add tasks directly to the TaskPad which appears in the Calendar, or you can add them through the Tasks list itself.

> You can create a task from an e-mail message by dragging the message to the Tasks icon. The message text appears in the task, so you can reference it easily.

You can prioritize your tasks when entering them by marking important tasks as "high priority," and relatively unimportant tasks as "low priority." You can then sort by the priority of the tasks to display the most important tasks at the top of the Tasks list. You can also drag tasks up and down the list, to display them exactly where you want them.

If you want to add a task that recurs, you don't have to enter it in your calendar over and over. With the Tasks list, you only need to enter a task once—and by specifying the period at which the task repeats, Outlook will enter it multiple times in the Tasks list.

If you're working on a project, the Tasks list can help you track your progress. As you complete each part of the project, you can update the percentage completed. Then, when you glance at the Tasks list, you can easily see the amount of progress you've made. You can also add notes to a task, such as "Waiting on someone else," or "Not started," to explain the amount of progress you've made (or that you haven't made).

When a task is due, it appears in the Calendar for that day. As you finish tasks during the day, you can mark them as completed.

Sometimes you won't be able to complete a task on its due date. That's all right—uncompleted tasks automatically appear on the next calendar day, so you won't forget to do them. Overdue tasks appear in red, so they stand out from other tasks which are not past their due dates.

Add a Task in Calendar

Although the Guided Tour shows you how to add a task through the Tasks list, you can also use the TaskPad in Calendar to quickly add a task.

Simply click the placeholder, **Click here to add a new task**, then type your task description and press **Enter**. Of course, using this method, you can't add other information about the task such as its due date, current status, or percentage complete.

Begin Guided Tour   Enter a New Task

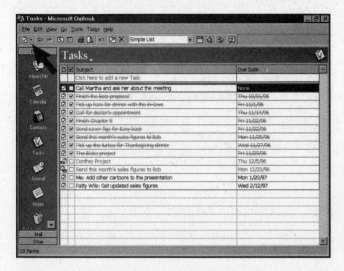

1 If you're in the Tasks list, click the **New Task** button to add your task. If you're in the Calendar, you can add a task directly to the TaskPad which appears there.

If you don't want to specify a priority or category for your task, you can click the **Click here to add a new Task** placeholder in the Tasks list to add the task quickly.

2 In the Task dialog box, type a description for the task in the **Subject** text box. Select a due date (if any) by opening the **Due** list and clicking a date. To move from month to month in the Due calendar, click the left or right arrow which appears at the top of the calendar window.

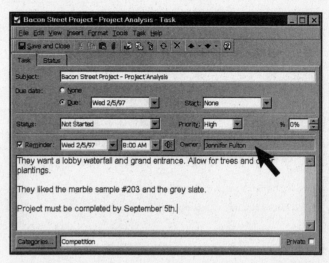

3 Select a **Priority** and a **Category** for the task if you like. If you want to add a note explaining the task, you can type it in the large text box. (You can also attach a file by clicking the **Insert File** button.)

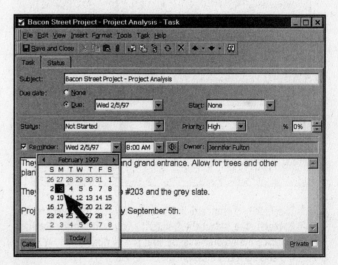

4 If you'd like to be reminded of the task's due date, click **Reminder.** Then select a date and time from the list.

You can change the sound which is played when the reminder is activated by clicking the horn button and selecting a sound file.

(continues)

Guided Tour   Enter a New Task

(continued)

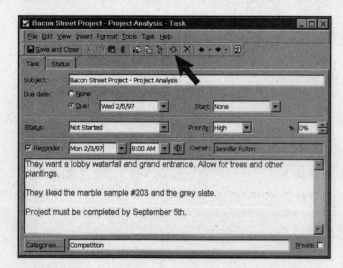

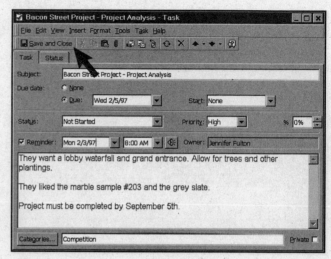

5 To make the task recur at regular intervals, click the **Recurrence** button on the Standard toolbar.

7 Click **Save and Close**. The task is added to the list.

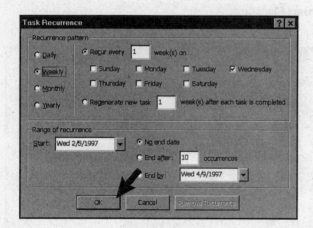

To copy the task to several dates in your Calendar, choose a **Recur Every *XX*** option. If you want the task to reappear on your Calendar only *after the original task has been completed*, then select the **Regenerate New Task** option.

6 The Task Recurrence dialog box appears. In the **Recurrence Pattern** area, select the frequency you want. In the **Range of Recurrence** area, you can set a limit to the number of times the task is copied to your Calendar. Click **OK**.

Assign a Task to Someone Else

You can assign a new or existing task in your list to someone else by sending a task request. The recipient of the request has the option of accepting the task, reassigning the task to someone else, or declining it.

> You can only reassign a task to someone located *on your company network* who is also using Outlook.

If the task is declined by the person to whom you assigned it, you can reassign it to someone else:

1. Open the task by double-clicking it.

2. Click the **Assign Task** button on the Standard toolbar.

3. Repeat the rest of the steps here to send out the new task request.

If you want to reassign a task to someone else after it was accepted, you can, as long as a copy of it still appears in your Tasks list. Just follow these steps:

1. Open the task by double-clicking it.

2. Click the **Status** tab.

3. Click **Create unassigned copy**.

4. Click **OK**. A copy of the task is created.

5. Repeat these steps given here in the Guided Tour to reassign the task to someone else.

When reassigning a task, you can opt to keep a copy of the original task in your list and receive updates on its status. These reports will update the percentage of work completed, which you can view by double-clicking the task. If you don't want to keep a copy of the original task, you can still receive a report when the task is completed.

Begin Guided Tour   Reassign a Task

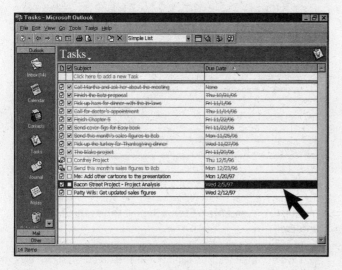

1 To create a request for a new task, click the down arrow on the **New Task** button and select **New Task Request**. Skip to step 3. If you want to reassign an *existing* task, then double-click it to open it, and continue to step 2.

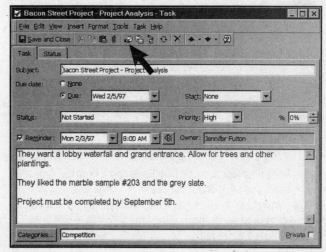

2 Click the **Assign Task** button on the Standard toolbar.

(continues)

Guided Tour Reassign a Task *(continued)*

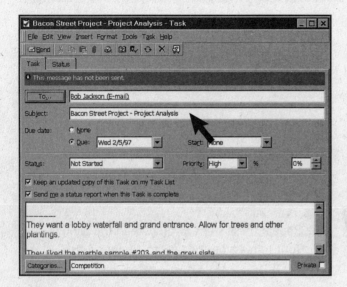

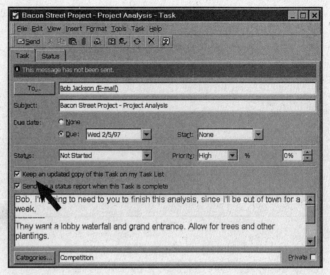

3 Type the e-mail address of the person to whom you're assigning the task in the **To** box. If you're reassigning a new task, also type a description in the **Subject** text box.

5 If you want to keep a copy of the task, select **Keep an Updated Copy of the Task on My Task List**. As progress is made on the task, Outlook will notify you automatically.

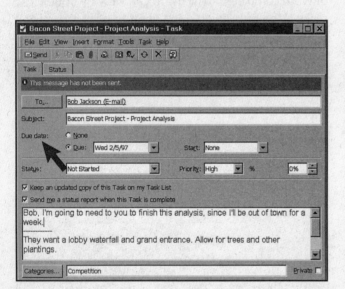

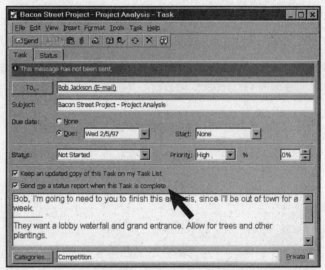

4 For a new task, select a **Due Date** and a **Priority**. Type any notes you have about the task in the large text box. If you're reassigning an existing task, you can type a note to your coworker above the original notes on the task. Make whatever other changes are needed.

6 Whether or not you kept a copy of the task, you can receive a final status report when the task is marked complete. Click **Send Me a Status Report When this Task is Complete**.

7 When you're ready to send out the task request, click **Send**.

Respond to a Task Request

When someone assigns a task to you, you can accept it, decline it, or reassign the task to someone else. If you accept the task, it is added to your task list—at that point, you're the only person who can make changes to the task or update its status.

A task which has been assigned to you appears in the Tasks list with a special icon: two small hands holding a clipboard. Tasks that you assign to someone else also use a special icon: one small hand holding a clipboard.

When you update the status of the task, a copy of it may be automatically sent to the person who originated the task (if the person who originated the task requested it). See the task, "Update the Status of a Task," page 366 for more information about how to update your progress on a task. In any case, when you complete the task, a status report is automatically sent to the task's originator.

> **Begin Guided Tour**   Send a Response to a Task Request

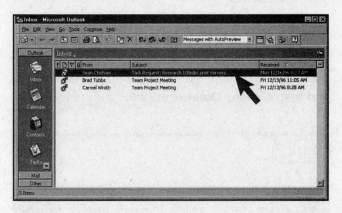

1 Double-click the message which contains the task request in order to open it.

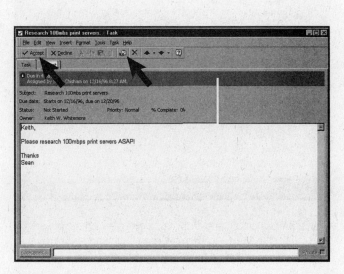

2 Click either **Accept** or **Decline**. If you want to reassign the task to someone else, click the **Assign Task** button on the Standard toolbar, enter an e-mail address in the **To** box, then click **Send**.

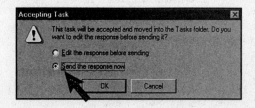

3 If you don't want to add a comment to your reply, click **Send the Response Now**. If you'd like to add a comment, click **Edit the Response Before Sending**, and type your response in the large text box. Click **Send**.

Update the Status of a Task

As you make progress on a task, you might want to update its status. If the task was assigned to you by someone else, it's important that you keep the status of the task current, because the task originator may be receiving automatic updates.

Even if the task is your own, if you update its status, you can quickly check your progress on a project by glancing at the Tasks list—that is, if you display the **% Complete** field. Here's how:

1. Open the **Current View** list on the Standard toolbar.

2. Select the **Detailed List** option.

In addition to the % Complete field, the Status and Categories fields appear.

You can forward a copy of the task (and its status) to anyone, even if the task was not assigned to you by them. Follow these steps:

1. Select the task by clicking it.

2. Open the **Tasks** menu and select **Forward**. An e-mail message window appears.

3. The task is included in the resulting e-mail message as an attachment. In the **To** box, enter the address of the person to whom you want to send a copy of the task.

4. Click **Send**.

As you mark a task as completed, keep in mind that completed tasks *are not automatically removed from the Tasks list*. To delete a task from the list, click it and then click the **Delete** button.

Begin Guided Tour   Report the Status of a Task

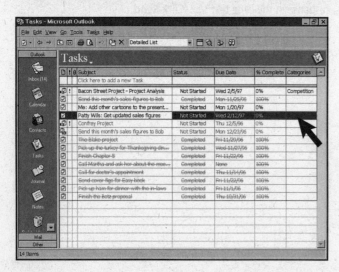

1 Double-click the task whose status you want to update. The task opens.

If you simply want to mark a task as complete, click the **Complete** box. A check mark appears, and the task is crossed out.

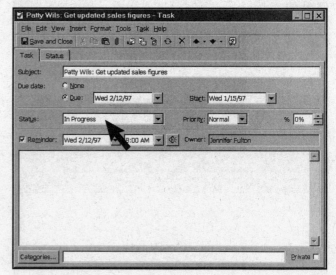

2 Select the date on which you began work on the project from the **Start** list. Then select an option under **Status**, such as In Progress or Waiting on Someone Else.

Guided Tour Report the Status of a Task

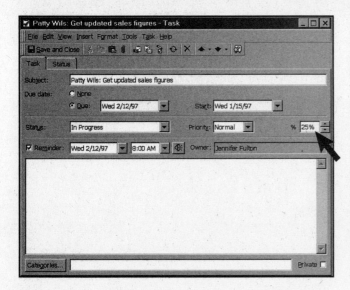

3 If you've completed a part of the task, you can mark the percentage complete with the **%** spinner. Click the **Status** tab.

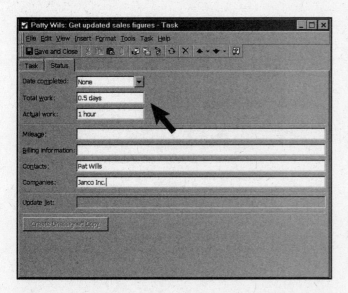

4 On the Status tab, enter the total number of hours the task is expected to take, along with the number of hours you've actually spent on it. Enter additional information which applies, such as **Mileage** and **Billing Information**.

5 If you don't want to send a status report to anyone, click **Save and Close**.

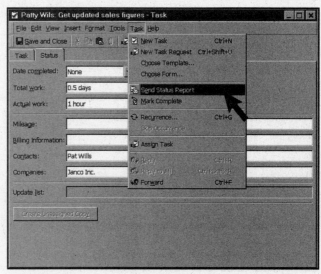

6 If you would like to send a status report, open the **Task** menu and select **Send Status Report**.

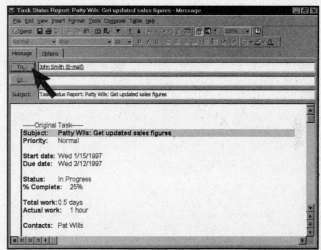

7 If the task was assigned to you, the appropriate names may already be entered in the **To** box. If not, enter the addresses to which you want the status report sent in the **To** or **Cc** boxes. Click **Send**.

HOW TO...

Create and Maintain an Outlook Journal

Y ou can use the Journal to maintain an automatic record of your activities. You select the Outlook items you want to track, and the Journal does the rest. For example, you can track all the e-mail messages, faxes, and files that you sent or received from a particular client. And so you don't clutter the Journal with information you don't need, you can specify the contacts whose activities you want the Journal to track.

Outlook also can track the work that you do with Microsoft Office. Want to know when you last updated your budget worksheet using Excel? Check the Journal. Want to see if you wrote that letter to Mr. Billings? Check the Journal. Because certain activities are recorded for you automatically, maintaining your Journal is easy.

There are some things which the Journal does not track automatically; however, you can enter this information into the Journal yourself when needed. For example, you can manually record phone calls, meeting notes, time spent on projects, and so on.

What You Will Find in This Section

Record Your Activities Automatically

Although you can record activities in the Journal manually, why not let Outlook do most of the work for you? Outlook can be made to automatically track the items you create which are related to particular contacts. Then, when you switch to the Journal, you can view all the items related to a contact in one place.

Here's a listing of items that the Journal can track per contact:

- E-mail messages sent or received from a contact
- Meeting requests sent to a contact
- Meeting responses received from a contact
- Meeting cancellations sent or received from a contact
- Task requests sent to a contact
- Task responses received from a contact

You can track activities for as many contacts as you wish. However, you must record the same activities for each contact you select.

Outlook can also track the documents you create using Microsoft Office:

- Letters, memos, and reports created with Microsoft Word
- Worksheets created with Excel
- Databases maintained in Access
- Presentations created with PowerPoint
- Complex projects created in Office Binder

Once you set up the Journal, the activities you select will be recorded *from this moment on*. To record previous activities, you must enter them into the Journal manually. See "Add Activities Manually," page 372.

Begin Guided Tour   Record Activities with a Contact

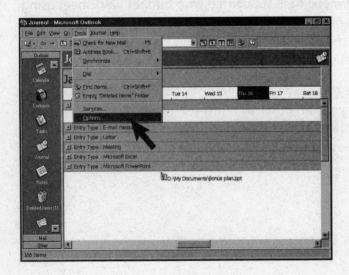

1 Switch to the Journal by clicking the **Journal** icon in the Outlook bar. Open the **Tools** menu and select **Options**.

Guided Tour   Record Activities with a Contact

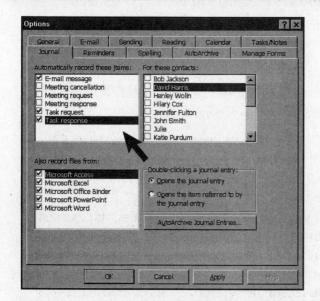

2 Under **Automatically Record These Items**, select the Outlook items you want the Journal to automatically record. The items you select appear with a check mark.

If you decide later that you no longer want to track a particular item, you can click it again to remove the check mark.

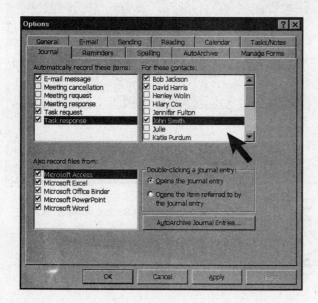

3 Select the contacts for which you want these items recorded in the **For These Contacts** box. You can select as many contacts as you want.

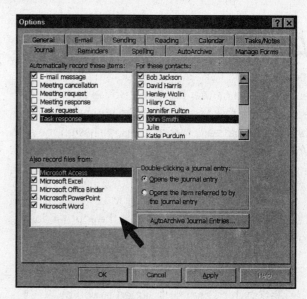

4 Under **Also Record Files From**, select the Microsoft Office programs whose activities you want automatically recorded in the Journal. Click **OK**.

Add Activities Manually

Although Outlook tracks a lot of activities for you automatically, there are many activities which it does not track. For example, appointments are not recorded, and neither are tasks. However, meeting requests and task requests sent to you by a coworker can be automatically recorded, as well as phone calls which you initiate from within Outlook. In any case, any activity which is not recorded automatically can be recorded manually.

Here's a short list of activities that the Journal does not keep track of:

- Appointments

- Tasks which are not assigned to you by someone else

- Phone calls that you initiate yourself, without Outlook's help

- Conversations in the hall, at dinner, and so on

- Faxes sent and received

- Documents created with a non-Office 97 program

- Letters sent to a client

If you'd like to track these activities, you must enter them into the Journal manually. For example, you might want to record the details of a conversation you had with a client over dinner. Or, you might want to record the details of an appointment.

Begin Guided Tour   Enter Outlook Activities Manually

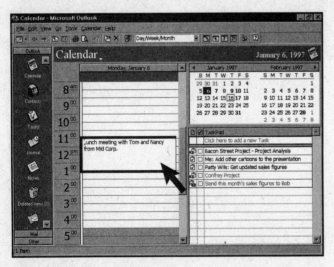

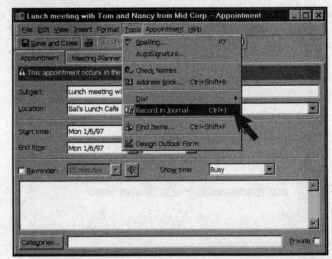

1 If the item you want to record is an Outlook item (such as an appointment or a meeting), open the item by double-clicking it.

2 Open the **Tools** menu and select **Record in Journal**.

3 If needed, you can add or change any of the information related to the activity. When you're through, click **Save and Close**.

Begin Guided Tour   Enter a Document Activity

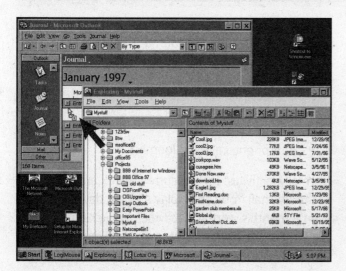

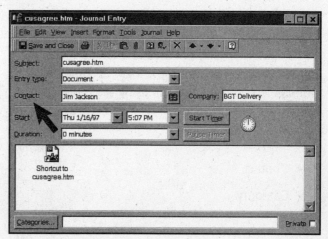

1 To record a document in the Journal, open Explorer and drag its icon into the Journal window.

2 Enter whatever additional information you need, such as a **Contact** or a **Company** name.

3 When you're through, click **Save and Close**.

Begin Guided Tour   Record Other Activities

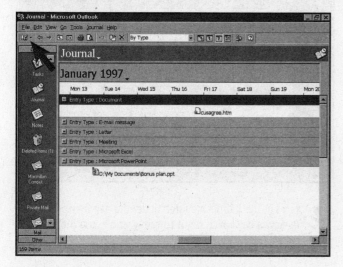

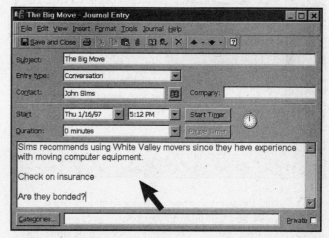

1 To record other entries in the Journal, click the **New Journal** button.

You can insert a file into the Journal entry by clicking the **Insert File** button, selecting the file, and clicking **OK**.

2 Enter a description of the activity in the **Subject** box. Select the type of entry you're recording in the **Entry Type** box. Enter other information which applies, such as a **Start** time and **Duration**. You can add a note or comment in the large text box.

3 Click **Save and Close**.

Move Through the Journal

Whether your entries are added to the Journal automatically, or whether you add them yourself, you'll want to review them at some point. Outlook lets you sort the entries by the following fields:

- Entry type
- Contact
- Category

Sorting the entries in the Journal allows you to locate the ones you want to review quickly.

In addition, you can quickly display:

- The entries for the last seven days in a long list
- Your phone calls in a long list

Normally, activities for the current week are displayed in the Journal. You can display a single day's worth, or even a month's worth of activities by clicking either the **Day** or the **Month** button on the Standard toolbar.

Begin Guided Tour   View Entries in the Journal

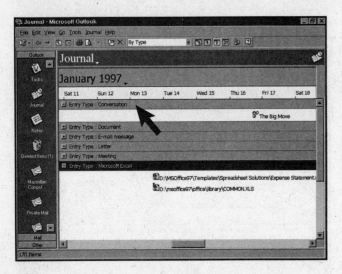

1 Initially, the Journal entries are grouped by type. For example, all your Microsoft Word documents are listed together. To display the items in a group, click its **plus sign**. The list expands to display its contents. To hide the list again, click its **minus sign.**

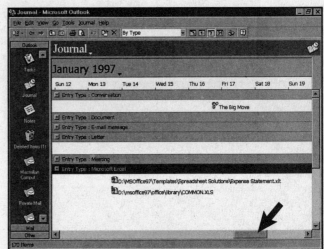

2 Items in the Journal are listed under the day they occurred. To view a day which is not currently visible, use the scroll bars.

Guided Tour View Entries in the Journal

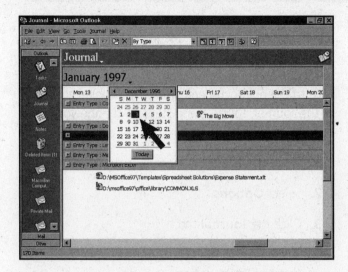

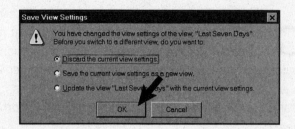

5 If you made changes to the current view, you may see a warning asking if you'd like to save them. Click **OK** to save the changes, or **Cancel** to discard them.

3 To jump directly to a particular day, click the Timeline banner (on the word **January**, for example) and a calendar appears. Click the date whose activities you want to view.

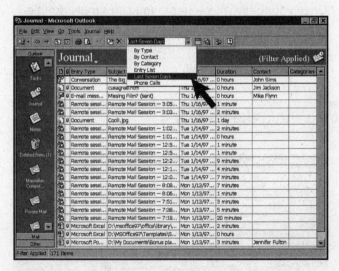

4 You can change how items are grouped and displayed by selecting a viewing option from the **Current View** list. For example, select **Last Seven Days**.

Open Files Listed in the Journal

One of the nicest features of the Journal is that it allows quick access to your files. So rather than switching from Outlook to Explorer or the Start menu to locate a recently used document, why not go straight to the Journal, and open the document from there?

Also, because the Journal maintains a record of your activities each day, you can quickly locate documents you haven't used recently. That's because the Journal not only records the fact that you made changes to a particular document on a particular day, but it also records the *location of that document*. No more searching through folders and all over your company's network to find the file you want!

Now, only Office documents are automatically listed in the Journal, although you can add other documents to the Journal by dragging them there. Doing so would give you quick access to the files you use most often.

When you double-click a document listed in the Journal, a Journal window opens. It is from there that you open the document itself. Now, if you'd like to be able to open a document simply by double-clicking it in the Journal, follow these steps to change your Journal setup:

1. Open the **Tools** menu.

2. Select **Options**.

3. Click the **Journal** tab.

4. Select the **Opens the Item Referred To by the Journal Entry** option.

5. Click **OK**.

Once you follow these steps, you can simply double-click a document file name as it appears in the Journal in order to open it, rather than following the steps given in the Guided Tour.

Begin Guided Tour　Open Documents from Within the Journal

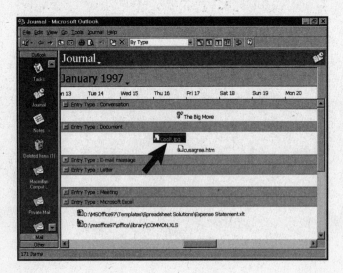

1 Double-click the document you want to open.

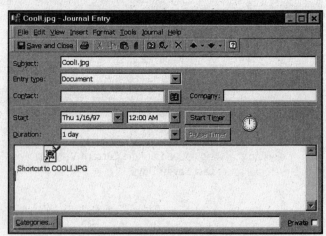

2 In the Journal window, double-click the document icon.

3 Outlook starts the related program, which opens the document. After making any changes, save them, and then click the program's **Close** button to exit the program and return to Outlook.

HOW TO...

Print Office 97 Files

The purpose of creating most documents is to print out a copy to review yourself, to give to someone else, or to distribute to a group of people. You can print a letter you created with Word, a budget you created with Excel, a database report from Access, or a presentation you created with PowerPoint. You can even print out portions of your daily schedule from Outlook. When it comes right down to it, a computer isn't much use without the ability to print out the things you create.

Printers are often a source of difficulty and aggravation among many computer users. Some people have access to two or more different printers; others have to share a printer with coworkers. People aren't the only ones confused by printers; it sometimes seems that computers themselves are a little confused by printers too. Getting your computer to send a file to your printer, and getting the printer to understand the file and print it out can sometimes become a major ordeal. Thankfully, computer hardware and software manufacturers have come a long way in making sure that computers and printers get along, electronically speaking. Printing files is easier than ever with Windows 95, as you'll see in the tasks to come.

This section of the book covers how to preview and print your Office 97 files.

What You Will Find in This Section

Preview a Document

When you are working in a file, you see only the part you are working on. You can't tell how the page numbers look, for instance, or how the document will appear on the printed page. Are the margins okay? Do you need to add a header or footer? Is the page layout pleasing to the eye? You can try and see how these features look by scrolling back and forth, but that doesn't really help. You need a way to view the entire page on your screen without wasting paper by printing out a hard copy. With the Preview feature, you can do just that.

Before you print your document, you should preview it to see how it will look when printed. This will save you time and paper because you can get an overall sense of the document, make any necessary changes, and then print. In preview mode, you see a full-page view of the document. Depending on the application, you see different on-screen tools for working with the preview.

You can click the **Print Preview** button on the toolbar to quickly preview a document.

When you preview a document in Word, you see a toolbar, and the buttons have icons or words on them. Use the buttons to perform the following tasks.

In Excel, the toolbar buttons have names, so you can easily understand them. The following table explains what each button does.

Many of the same preview buttons are repeated in the Outlook preview window too. The table below describes each of the preview buttons you'll find when previewing data from Outlook.

For information on previewing a PowerPoint presentation, see "View the Slide Show" on page 285.

The Preview Buttons

Use This Button	To
🖶	Print the document.
🔍	Magnify portions of the document. Click the button; then click the area of the document you want to get a closer look.
▫	View a single page (the default view).
▦	View multiple pages. Click the button and then drag across the number of pages in the drop-down palette.
32% ▾	Change the zoom percentage of the view. Display the drop-down list and click the zoom you want.
📐	Display horizontal and vertical rulers. You can use the rulers to change the margins.
📑	Shrink the document to fit in one window.
▢	View the document full screen; hide the menu bar and toolbar.
Close	Close the preview window. Click this button to return to the Word document window.

Use This Button	To
[?]	Get help on the different preview options.
Next	View the next page. If your worksheet uses more than one page, you can click this button to view other pages.
Previous	View the previous page. Click this button to go back and view the previous page (if your worksheet uses multiple pages).
Zoom	Zoom the preview to make it larger. You can do the same thing by clicking the mouse on the worksheet. (The pointer should look like a magnifying glass when you point to the worksheet.)
Print...	Print the worksheet.
Setup...	Display the Page Setup dialog box and make changes to the layout of the page.
Margins	Display on-screen margin indicators. You can then drag the margin indicators to change the margins.
Page Break Preview	Designate page breaks within your worksheets.
Close	Close the preview window.
Help	Display help on preview.

The Zoom Features

Use This Button	To
[↑]	Scroll up one page.
[↓]	Scroll down one page.
[🔍]	Magnify portions of the document. Click the button; then click the area of the document you want to see.
[▯]	View a single page (the default view).
[⊞]	View multiple pages. Click the button and then drag across the number of pages in the drop-down palette.
Page Setup...	Opens the Page Setup dialog box for changing page options.
Print...	Prints the data.
Close	Closes the preview window.
[?]	Accesses Microsoft's Help features.

Zoom In and Out

While previewing a document before printing is helpful, there are times when you may want to get a closer look at your data while in the process of building a document. Most of the Office 97 programs have a Zoom feature you can use to examine different portions of your data. The Zoom feature lets you zoom in or out, much like the zoom features of a camera. You may want to zoom out to see more of the document on the page. You may want to zoom in to see a close-up, magnified view of the data. You can do either of these things without having to use the Preview feature.

When you select the **Zoom** command, you select the percentage you want. To return to the regular view, select the **Zoom** command and select **100%**. You can quickly zoom a document using the **Zoom** button on the toolbar, or if you want to customize your zoom percentage, use the **View** menu to select the **Zoom** command. The fastest way to zoom a document is with the Zoom button on the toolbar.

Begin Guided Tour Preview a Document Before Printing

1 Open the **File** menu and select the **Print Preview** command or click the **Print Preview** button on the toolbar.

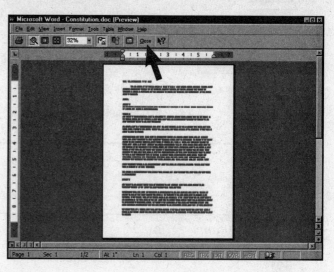

3 To exit Print Preview, click the **Close** button.

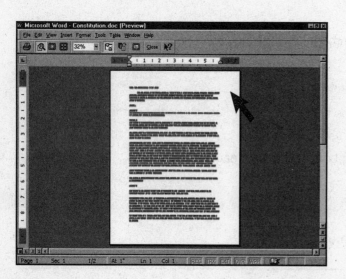

2 You see a full-page preview of the document you are working on. You can click any of the toolbar buttons on the Preview toolbar to adjust your preview of the document. See the tables on the previous pages for a description of the buttons.

Print a Document

All your hard work pays off when you can print your final document. You may want to print a copy to review and mark up editing changes, or you may print a copy to distribute to others.

> Use the **Print** button in the toolbar to print, or if you want to use a keyboard shortcut, press **Ctrl+P**.

Note that before you can print, you must set up the printer using the Windows 95 Control Panel, if you haven't done so already. Windows 95 needs to know certain information about the type of printer and fonts that you have. Once you set up the printer, it is available to all Windows 95 programs.

To print an entire file, you can simply click the **Print** button on the toolbar. To control what parts of the file are printed, and to control how the file is printed, you'll need to open the Print dialog box. You can access the box by pulling down the **File** menu and selecting **Print**. Inside the Print dialog box, you'll find all kinds of options for printing, including paper size and orientation.

In a long document, you may need to print only certain pages. Rather than waste paper, you can print just the pages you need. If you need to make several copies of a document, you should use a copier machine to avoid too much wear and tear on your printer. If you just need a couple of copies, though, you can have the application print multiple copies.

Change Your Printer Setup

Microsoft Office 97 applications always print to the default printer. In some situations, you may have more than one printer available, and you can select which printer is the default. For example, if you work in an office and are hooked up to a network, you may be able to select which network printer you want to use. If you work at home, you may have a printer and a computer fax machine. Your computer treats the fax machine like a printer; to fax something, you select the fax as a printer source.

You can control which printer you use in the Print dialog box. To access the Print dialog box, open the **File** menu and select **Print**. In this box, you'll find controls for determining which printer to use, as well as other printing options, such as controlling which pages will print from your document. The Print dialog box looks slightly different depending on which program you use.

You can also change certain default options for your printer, such as the page size and orientation. What you want to remember is that changing the printer setup this way changes the options for all documents and applications. While in the Print dialog box, you can choose the **Properties** button to change default printing options, such as page orientation. If you want to change the page orientation for just one document (for example, use landscape for a document), use the **Page Setup** command instead, covered in the "Format a Word Document" section, which starts on page 95.

Remember that once you change the default, all Microsoft Office applications will use this default printer—even if you didn't change the printer in that application.

Begin Guided Tour Print a File

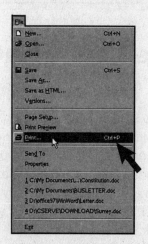

1 Open the **File** menu and choose the **Print** command.

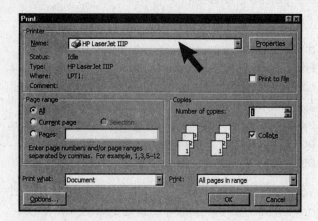

2 You see the Print dialog box. To change which printer the file is sent to, click the **Name** drop-down list under the Printer options, then select the printer from the list. If you rely on just one printer, and it's listed in the **Name** text box, you don't need to choose another printer to use.

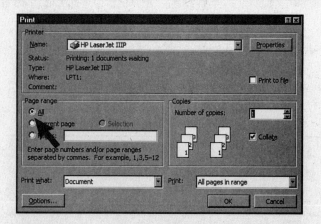

3 To print the entire file, make sure the **All** option is selected under the **Page Range** options.

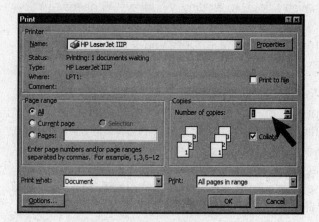

4 If you're printing just one copy of the file, make sure the **Number of copies** box under the **Copies** options says 1. If you want more than one copy, in the **Copies** spin box, type or select the number of copies you want.

Guided Tour Print a File

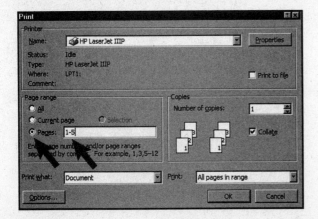 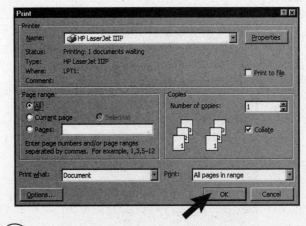

5 If you're using Word, select **Current Page** under the **Page Range** options to print the current page. To print other pages, select **Pages**, and enter the pages you want to print in the text box. If you're printing more than one page, you can use commas to separate the page numbers, such as **1,2,3**. If you're printing a range of pages, you can use a hyphen, such as **1-5**. To print just the selected text in your file, choose the **Selection** option.

6 Click the **OK** button to print out your file.

Begin Guided Tour Change Paper Size or Orientation

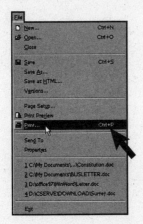 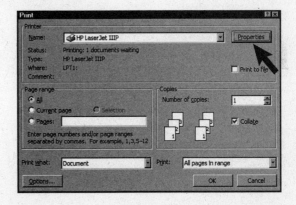

1 Open the **File** menu and choose the **Print** command.

2 You see the Print dialog box. Click the **Properties** button.

3 Click the **Paper** tab to bring it to the front of the dialog box.

(continues)

Guided Tour Change Paper Size or Orientation

(continued)

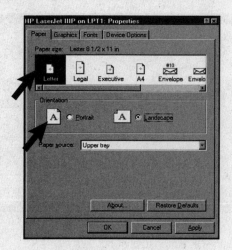

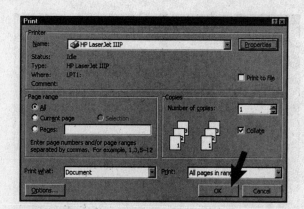

6 Click **OK** to print the file using the new paper size or orientation.

4 Under the **Paper Size** or **Orientation** options, select a new size or paper orientation.

5 Click **OK** to return to the Print dialog box.

HOW TO...

Use Office 97 on the Web

Microsoft Office has traditionally provided networking features to help people work together and share data in businesses and corporations. Office 97 has broadened its scope to help users reach out to others outside the confines of the corporation, via the Internet.

Office 97 includes Microsoft's award-winning Web browser, Internet Explorer, which you can use to view multimedia pages on the World Wide Web. You can also send and receive e-mail, and read and post newsgroup messages using Internet Mail and News. In addition, the various Office applications (Word, Excel, Power-Point, Outlook, and Access) work along with Internet Explorer to help you create your own Web pages and perform other Internet-related tasks.

This part of the book provides the basic instructions you need to connect to and wander the World Wide Web with Internet Explorer, and how to use Explorer along with the other Office 97 applications. For instructions on how to use the Office applications to create your own Web pages, see "Create Your Own Web Page," starting on page 497.

What You Will Find in This Section

Install Internet Explorer 3.0

When you installed Microsoft Office, it placed an icon on the Windows desktop for installing Internet Explorer. Before you can use Internet Explorer, you must install it on your computer. The installation program leads you through the process of setting up your Internet connection (via modem or a network cable) and setting up Internet Explorer. The Guided Tour leads you through the steps, so you will know what to expect.

After performing this one-time setup, you can run Internet Explorer by selecting it from the Start, Programs menu or by using the Web toolbar in any of the Office 97 applications.

Understand the Internet and the Web

The Internet consists of thousands of computers all over the world connected by cables and satellite. You can connect to the Internet in various ways and tap into the resources on these other computers. If the place where you work is networked and has an Internet connection, you can use that connection to access the Internet. Otherwise, you need a modem and an account with a local Internet service provider (ISP). With an Internet account, your modem dials a local number to connect with the ISP computer, which then connects you to the Internet (so you don't pay long-distance charges).

The World Wide Web (the Web, for short) is one of the major features of the Internet. The Web is like a multimedia encyclopedia, offering pages full of text, graphics, movie clips, games, audio recordings, and anything else that can be digitized. These Web pages are stored on computers all over the world, and are connected by *links* (highlighted text, pictures, or icons that you can click to go from one page to another).

Although this section of the book primarily explains how to use Internet Explorer on the Web, the Internet also offers other features, including e-mail, newsgroups (where you can read and post messages), FTP file transfers (where you can copy files), and Telnet sites (where you can use a remote computer to access information).

Because the Internet is easy to navigate and use, many companies have started using Internet technologies on their networks by setting up *intranets*. An intranet is simply an internal version of the Internet. If your company has an intranet, you can use Internet Explorer to access it, just as you use it to access the Internet.

Understand Internet Explorer

To view Web pages, you need two applications: a *TCP/IP program* (which dials in and connects your computer to the Internet) and a *Web browser*. The Web browser transforms your monitor into a sort of TV set for the Web. The browser translates all the codes that make up a Web page and then displays the Web page for you. The browser also allows you to enter addresses that tell the browser where a page is located. In short, the browser helps you navigate the Web.

There are several Web browsers that you can use, including Mosaic, Netscape, and HotJava. However, only Internet Explorer is designed to work seamlessly along with the Office 97 applications. So, if you're using Office 97 and a different Web browser, now might be a good time to switch browsers.

Begin Guided Tour   Run Internet Explorer's Installation Program

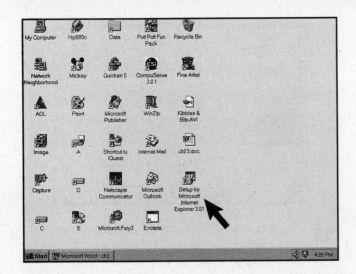

1 When you installed Microsoft Office 97, the installation program left an icon on the desktop for installing Internet Explorer. Make sure the Office 97 CD is in your computer's CD-ROM drive. Double-click the **Setup for Microsoft Internet Explorer 3.01** icon.

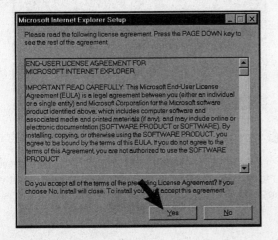

2 The Microsoft Internet Explorer Setup dialog box appears, prompting you to read the license agreement. Read the agreement, and click **Yes**.

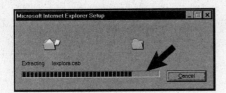

3 As the installation program extracts the files, it displays this dialog box. Wait until the process is complete.

4 The next dialog box asks if you would like to suggest which optional components to install. Click **Yes**.

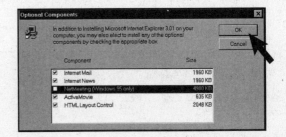

5 You will need most of the recommended components in this part and in "Create Your Own Web Page," on page 497, so keep them all selected. You can turn off NetMeeting, which is a tool that allows you to carry on telephone conversations over the Internet (or on an intranet). Click **OK**.

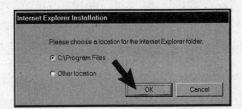

6 The next dialog box indicates that the Internet Explorer files will be placed on drive C in the Program Files folder. You can select a different folder, if desired. Click **OK** to use the default folder.

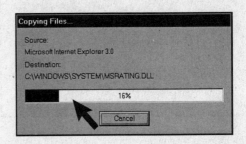

7 The Installation Status and Copying Files dialog boxes appear, showing the progress of the operation. Wait until the operation is complete.

(continues)

Guided Tour Run Internet Explorer's Installation Program

(continued)

8 When the installation is complete, you'll see a dialog box telling you so and asking if you want to restart your computer. Exit all other applications (and save any documents you haven't yet saved), and then click **Yes**.

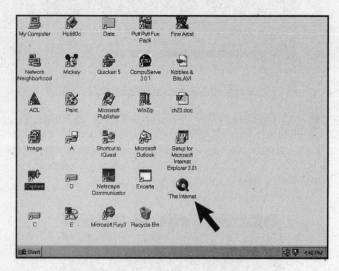

9 When the Windows 95 desktop reappears, you now have an icon called **The Internet**. Double-click it.

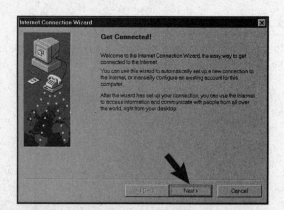

10 The Internet Connection Wizard appears. This Wizard will lead you through the process of setting up Windows to connect with your Internet Service Provider. Click the **Next>** button.

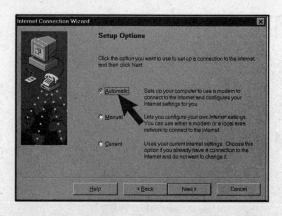

11 If you have already set up Windows 95's Dial-Up Networking to establish your Internet connection, select **Current**. Otherwise, choose **Automatic**. Click **Next>**.

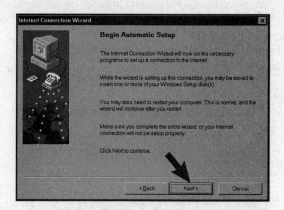

12 Continue following the Wizard's instructions until the operation is complete. (If the Wizard prompts you to enter information about your Internet connection and you don't have this information, contact your Internet service provider or network administrator for help.)

Guided Tour   Run Internet Explorer's Installation Program

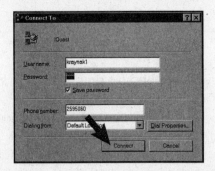

13 When the Wizard is done, it displays the Connect To dialog box, which contains information you need to establish your Internet connection. You may need to enter your password (supplied to you by the Internet service provider or your network administrator). After typing the password, click the **Connect** button.

14 The **Connecting** dialog box appears, showing the progress of the call, and indicating when you are connected.

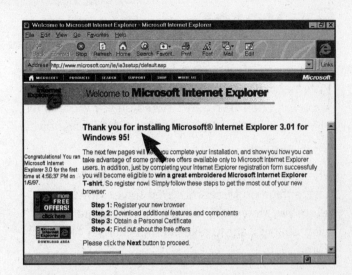

15 After the connection is established, Internet Explorer runs and displays the Welcome to Microsoft Internet Explorer page. You are now connected to Microsoft's Web server.

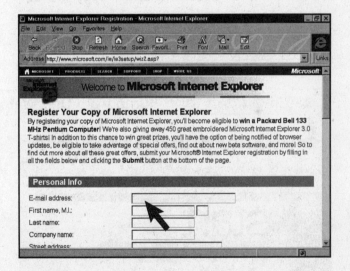

16 Read and follow the on-screen instructions to register your copy of Internet Explorer.

Navigate the Web with Internet Explorer

Internet Explorer is your key to the Internet. With it, you can open Web pages stored on any Web server anywhere in the world (provided the Web server gives you access to it).

Whenever you start Internet Explorer, it loads a startup page on Microsoft's Web server. However, before you start customizing Internet Explorer, you will probably want to take Internet Explorer for a spin on the Web.

There are a couple ways to steer on the Web. To go to a specific page, assuming you know its address, you can type the address in the Address text box at the top of the Internet Explorer window. A page address, also called an URL (Uniform Resource Locator) tells Internet Explorer where the page is located on the Web. A page address might look something like

http://www.whitehouse.gov, where *http* stands for HyperText Transport Protocol (the set of rules which govern data transfer on the Web), *www* stands for World Wide Web, *whitehouse* stands for White House (where Bill and Hillary live), and *gov* stands for government.

You can also jump from one Web page to another by clicking *links*. Links are icons, pictures, buttons, or highlighted text that point to other resources and pages on the Web. Each link has a corresponding page address that points to another resource or Web page. When you click a link, Internet Explorer automatically uses the address (which is hidden) to load the page.

The following Guided Tour shows you how to enter page addresses and use links to navigate the Web.

Begin Guided Tour   Jump from One Web Page to Another

1 Whenever you start Internet Explorer, it loads Microsoft's startup page. The address of the page that's loaded appears in the **Address** text box.

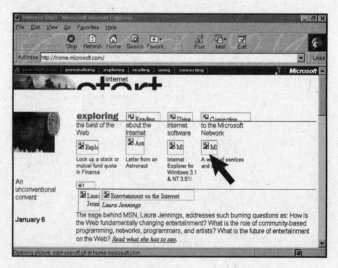

2 Internet Explorer loads the text of the page first, and displays icons in place of graphics, which it is in the process of loading. (You can click a link to go to a different page at any time; you don't have to wait for everything to load.)

Guided Tour Jump from One Web Page to Another

3 Links appear as buttons, graphics, icons, or highlighted, underlined text. When you move the mouse pointer over a link, the pointer appears as a hand. Click a link to load the corresponding page.

4 When you move forward to a page, the **Back** button becomes active. You can quickly return to the previous page by clicking the **Back** button.

5 When you back up, the **Forward** button becomes active. You can quickly move ahead to a page you've already visited (and backed up from) by clicking the **Forward** button.

6 The **Stop** button stops a page that is currently loading. The **Refresh** button reloads a page; use this button if the page only partially loads or if the transfer has been interrupted for some reason.

7 The **Home** button takes you back to the page that Internet Explorer loaded on startup.

8 The **Font** button lets you increase or decrease the size of the text on a page. You'll learn how to use the other buttons (Search, Favorites, Mail, Print, and Edit) in later Guided Tours.

9 The Links toolbar contains links to some popular sites. You can view this toolbar by dragging its slider, as shown above.

10 You can rearrange the toolbars by dragging them up or down. Here, the button bar is on top, with the Address bar below it, and the Links toolbar at the bottom.

11 If you know the address of a page you want to visit, you can go directly to that page. Click inside the **Address** text box to highlight the address of the current page.

(continues)

Guided Tour Jump from One Web Page to Another *(continued)*

12 Type the address of the page you want to visit, and press **Enter**. When you start typing, the previous address is deleted.

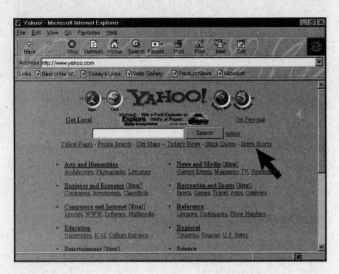

13 If all goes as planned, Internet Explorer loads the specified page.

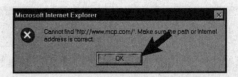

14 Errors are common on the Internet. If you receive an error message saying that the page does not exist, you may have mistyped the address, the author of the page may have moved or deleted it, the Web server on which the page is stored may be too busy to accept your request, or there may be some other reason the page is unavailable.

If you run into a problem, try retyping the address. If the page still won't load, try cropping off the right side of the address. For example, if you typed **http://www.mcp.com/ internet/explorer**, try typing just **http:// www.mcp.com**. This should get you to the home page at the site, and then you can click links to find the specific page you need.

Search the Web for Specific Information

Wandering the Web by clicking links is great when you want a Taoist experience and you want to take a few detours on the information superhighway. However, when you need to research a specific topic or you're looking for a movie or book review, skipping along with links isn't the most efficient way to get where you're going.

Fortunately, the Web has several search pages that can help you find what you're looking for. All you have to do is enter the address of a search page, type a few words that describe what you're looking for, and click a button sending the search tool on its mission. If the search tool finds Web pages (or other Internet resources) that match your search instructions, it displays a list of links you can use to access these resources. The following Guided Tour provides you with addresses of some of the more popular search pages and shows you how to perform a search.

The secret to successful searches on the Internet lies in your ability to come up with search phrases that are general enough to locate a good collection of resources, but specific enough so the list of links is not too long. As you work through the Guided Tour, you will see that some searches can find thousands of links, far too many to visit in a single session. Just keep in mind that if a search does not return the desired results, you can use the Back button to repeat the search using a different search phrase, or try a different search tool.

> You can usually omit the **http://** at the beginning of a Web page address. Internet Explorer will automatically enter **http://** for you. Try it!

Begin Guided Tour   Search the Internet

1 Yahoo! is one of the most popular search sites on the Web. To go to Yahoo!, type **www.yahoo.com** in the **Address** text box, and press **Enter**.

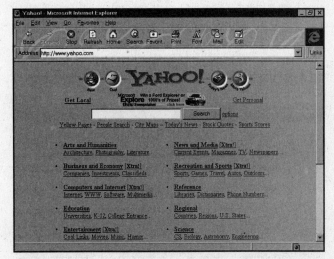

2 Yahoo!'s opening page has links to several categories of Internet resources. These categories allow you to perform a less structured search. Click a link to view subcategories.

(continues)

Guided Tour   Search the Internet   *(continued)*

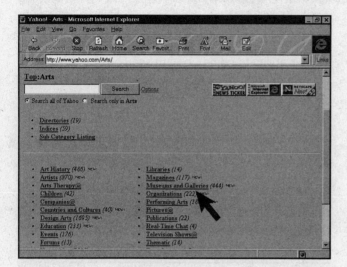

3 Follow the trail of links until you find a link to a specific Web page or other Internet resource that looks promising, and then click the link.

4 When you are done playing, return to Yahoo!'s opening page (use the **Back** button or enter its address again). To search for a specific topic, click inside the text box at the top of the page, and type two or three words describing what you are looking for. Press **Enter**.

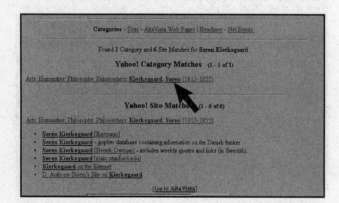

5 Yahoo! performs the search and displays a list of links that point to pages matching your search instructions. Click a link to open the corresponding page. (If the page is not what you want, use the **Back** button to return to the list of links and set out on another path.)

6 Another popular search page is AltaVista. To go there, type **www.altavista.com** in the **Address** text box, and press **Enter**.

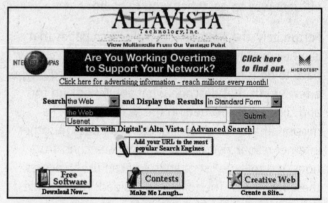

7 AltaVista lets you search the Web or newsgroups (places where people like you can post messages and read messages that others have posted). Stick with searching the Web for now.

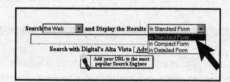

8 AltaVista can display more or less detail in the list of links it finds. Select the desired level of detail.

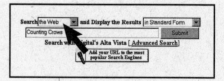

9 Click inside the bottom text box, and type two or three words that describe what you are looking for. Click the **Submit** button.

Guided Tour Search the Internet

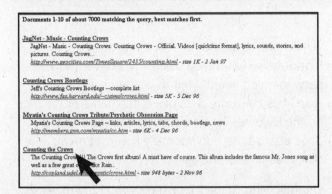

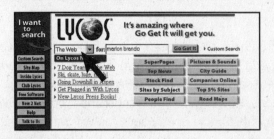

(13) Type your search phrase in the text box to the right of the list, and click the **Go Get It** button.

(10) AltaVista displays a list of links that match your search instruction. Click a link to load the corresponding page.

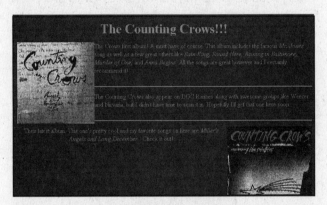

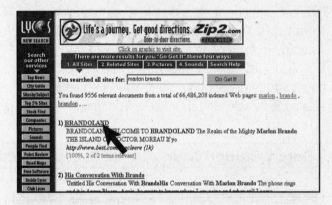

(11) Lycos is another popular site that offers a variety of search options. Type **www.lycos.com** in the **Address** text box, and press **Enter**.

(14) Lycos performs the search, and displays a list of matching pages. Click a link to load the corresponding page.

(15) Now that you know the basics, try some other search pages at the following addresses:

> **www.webcrawler.com**
> **www.infoseek.com**
> **www.excite.com**
> **www.hotbot.com**
> **www.dejanews.com (search newsgroups only)**

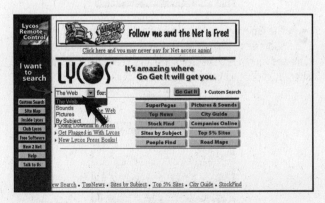

(12) At Lycos, open the drop-down list, and select the desired object (or object of your desire): The Web, Sounds, Pictures, or By Subject.

Although it's tempting to explore newsgroups at this point, fight the temptation. Because you have not yet specified a newsgroup server to use, any attempt to access newsgroups will only result in error messages. Skip ahead to "Access Internet Newsgroups," on page 410 for details.

Return to Your Favorite Web Sites

You have already seen that you can move forward and back to any pages you've opened during the current session by using the Back and Forward buttons. However, as you wander the Web, you will no doubt stumble upon pages you will want to visit again at some later date. Maybe the Nando Sports Page, Time Magazine on the Web, or the Official John Travolta Web Site.

Internet Explorer offers a couple tools that allow you to visit sites. The easiest tool to use is the *history list*. As you skip from page to page, Internet Explorer uses the history list to keep track of the addresses of the pages you have recently visited. You can then return to a page by selecting its address from the list.

A more powerful tool for revisiting pages is the Favorites list, which you create. Whenever you load a page that you might want to visit later, you simply mark it as a *favorite*. This places the name of the page on the Favorites list (or a sublist). To return to the page at any time, you open the Favorites menu and click the name of the page.

The following Guided Tour shows you how to revisit your favorite haunts using both the history list and Favorites. In addition, it teaches you how to clear the history list and manage your Favorites list to prevent it from becoming too long and cumbersome.

Begin Guided Tour   Reload Pages You Visited

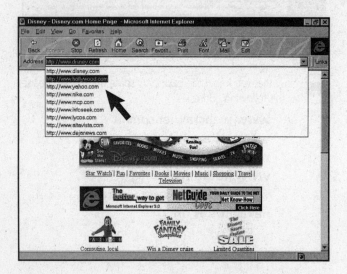

1 As you type addresses in the Address text box, Internet Explorer records the addresses. To return to a page, open the **Address** drop-down list, and select the address of the desired page. (This list does not record addresses of pages you visited by clicking links.)

2 The **Go** menu contains a similar list of page names (and addresses). Unlike the Address list, which tracks only the addresses you typed, the Go menu also keeps track of pages you visited by clicking links.

3 To view more of the history list, open the **Go** menu and select **Open History Folder**.

Guided Tour Reload Pages You Visited

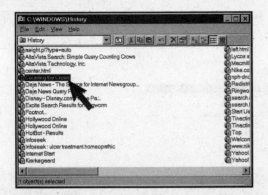

4 The history folder contains URLs for all the pages you have visited over several days. Double-click the desired icon to reopen that page.

7 A better way to revisit pages is to add a page to the **Favorites** menu. Open the page you want to mark. Open the **Favorites** menu and select **Add to Favorites**.

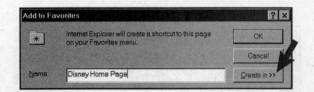

5 You can specify the number of days you want Internet Explorer to keep track of visited pages. Open the **View** menu and select **Options**.

8 Type a name for the page as you want it to appear on the Favorites menu (the page may already have a name). Click the **Create In** button, if you want to add the page name to a submenu of the Favorites menu.

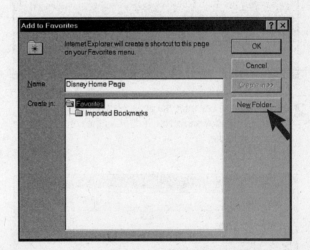

6 Click the **Navigation** tab, and use the **Number of Days** spin box to set the number of days you want Internet Explorer to keep track of pages. (The larger the number, the more disk space Internet Explorer uses for the history list.) Click **OK**.

9 To create a submenu, click the **New Folder** button, type a name for the submenu, and click **OK**. This returns you to the Add to Favorites dialog box; click **OK**.

10 Whenever you want to return to a page you marked as a favorite, open the **Favorites** menu (in the menu bar or button bar), and click the page's name.

Begin Guided Tour Maintain the Favorites Menu

1 The Favorites menu can become cluttered, so you might have to do some housekeeping. Open the **Favorites** menu, and click **Organize Favorites**.

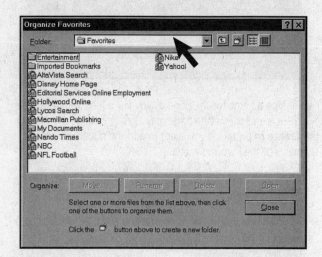

2 The Organize Favorites dialog box is similar to My Computer or Windows Explorer. It displays the contents of the Favorites folder.

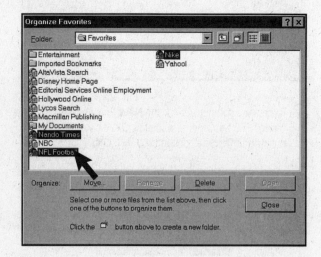

3 To change to a subfolder and display its contents, double-click it. To select a folder or a favorite inside a folder, click it. Ctrl+click any additional items to select them.

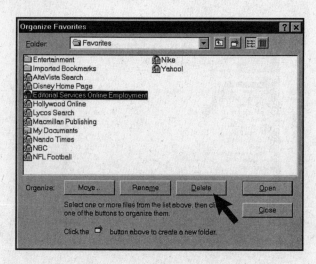

4 You can delete an item by selecting it and pressing the **Delete** button. When prompted to confirm, click **Yes**.

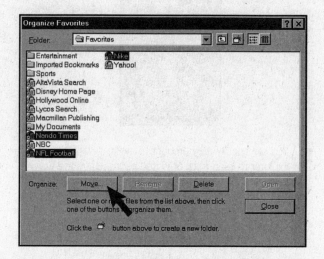

5 You can move a page name or subfolder up or down. First, select the items you want to move. Click the **Move** button. The Browse for Folder dialog box appears. Click the folder into which you want the selected items moved, and click **OK**.

Guided Tour Maintain the Favorites Menu

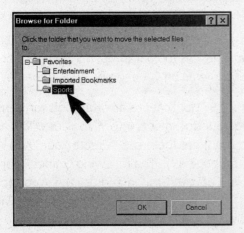

6 The Browse for Folder dialog box asks you to specify a destination for the selected folder(s) or file(s). Click the desired folder or subfolder, and click **OK**.

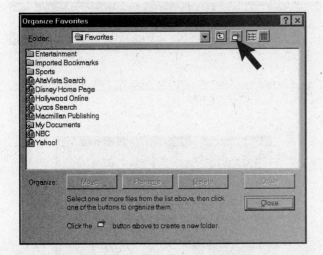

7 Every folder inside the main Favorites folder appears as a submenu. To create a new folder, first double-click the folder below which you want the new folder to appear. Click the **Create New Folder** button.

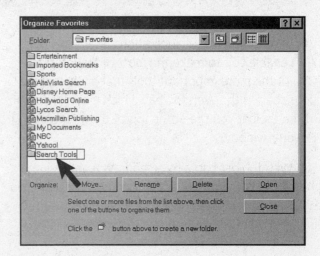

8 A new folder, cleverly named New Folder, appears. Type a name for the folder. You can now move shortcuts to this new folder, or add shortcuts to it (whenever you mark a page as a favorite).

Use the Office 97 Web Toolbar

All of the Office 97 applications offer tools that enable you to make the most of the Internet. One of the more important tools that all the applications share is the Web toolbar, which is a mini version of the toolbar you see at the top of the Internet Explorer window.

The Web toolbar contains an address text box into which you can type the address of the Web page you want to load. In addition, the toolbar contains the Back, Forward, Stop, Refresh, Home, and Search

buttons, in addition to the Favorites and Go menus. You can uses this toolbar to open Web pages or to open documents on your company's intranet.

The Office 97 applications all offer tools for transforming your documents into Web pages. To learn how to use these tools, see "Create Your Own Web Page," on page 497. The following Guided Tour shows you how to turn on and use the Web toolbar in Word. The process is the same in the other Office 97 applications.

Begin Guided Tour Turn On and Use the Web Toolbar

1 To turn on the Web toolbar, right-click any toolbar, and click **Web**.

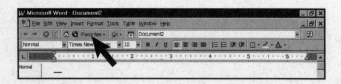

2 The Web toolbar appears just below the menu bar. You can drag the toolbar up or down to move it.

3 To open a document on the Web, type its address as shown here, and press **Enter**.

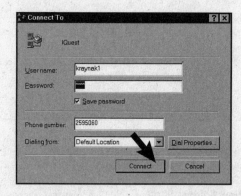

4 If your computer is not currently connected to the Internet, the Connect To dialog box appears, prompting you to establish the connection. Click the **Connect** button.

Guided Tour Turn On and Use the Web Toolbar

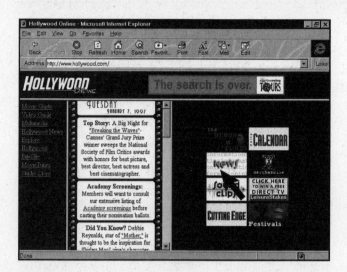

5 Once your computer is connected to the Internet, Internet Explorer runs automatically and opens the specified Web page. You can now use Internet Explorer to cruise the Web. (You can switch back to your Office 97 application at any time.)

When you open a Web Page from Word, Word closes the current document. You then must reload the document by selecting it from the File menu or by using the File Open command. If you use File Open, Word asks if you want to revert to the saved version. Select **No**.

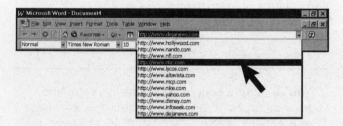

6 The Web toolbar contains a list of pages you have recently visited. To return to a page, open the address drop-down list or the **Go** menu, and select the desired page.

7 If you created a list of your favorite pages in Internet Explorer, you can access the list in your Office 97 application. Open the **Favorites** menu, and click the desired page.

8 Use the Back, Forward, Stop, Refresh, and Home buttons, just as you would use them in Internet Explorer.

Play and Save Files on the Internet

The Internet is nothing more than a huge collection of interlinked files. These files include coded Web pages, plain text, graphics, movie clips, audio recordings, interactive presentations, programs, three-dimensional virtual worlds, and much more.

As you cruise the Web, you hardly notice that Internet Explorer is playing various file types on a page, including graphics, background sounds, and small animations. Because text, graphics, video, and sound files are so expertly integrated on the Web, you see only a cool-looking page.

However, to make the most of the Web, you do need to know a little about how Internet Explorer plays special file types, and how you can copy files from the Internet to your own hard disk. The Guided Tour shows you what to expect.

Play Multimedia Files

Internet Explorer can play most of the files it encounters on the Web. It can display coded Web pages and plain text, common graphic file types (pictures), and even audio and video clips. However, there are some file types that Internet Explorer cannot handle. To play these file types, Internet Explorer may need to use additional programs. These add-on programs are called helper applications or plug-ins.

A *helper application* typically runs outside of Internet Explorer. It is a stand-alone application that Internet Explorer runs when Internet Explorer encounters a file type that it cannot run. A *plug-in* is additional computer code that adds capability to Internet Explorer. For example, a video plug-in enables Internet Explorer to play video clips.

In addition to helper applications, Internet Explorer supports ActiveX technology. *ActiveX controls* are like plug-ins; they add capability to Internet Explorer. For example, Internet Explorer comes with the ActiveX Movie control, which enables Internet Explorer to play most video file types you encounter on the Web.

If you encounter a file type that Internet Explorer cannot play, it will either prompt you to save the file to your hard drive, so you can work with it later, or prompt you to download and install the control or helper application that Internet Explorer needs to play the file. The Guided Tour shows you how to download and install helper applications, plug-ins, and ActiveX controls.

When you install a plug-in or ActiveX control, the plug-in or control becomes an integral part of Internet Explorer. When you click a link for a file that the plug-in or control is designed to play, Internet Explorer, with the help of the plug-in or control, opens the file and plays it. With helper applications, you must assign particular file types to the helper application that can play files of that type. For example, you might assign a movie player to play all files with the AVI extension. When you assign a helper application to a file type, you create a *file association*.

You can visit a couple sites that list, rate, and provide access to plug-ins, helper applications, and ActiveX controls. Try TUCOWS at **www.tucows.com** or Stroud's List at **www.stroud.com**.

Begin Guided Tour   Play Multimedia Files

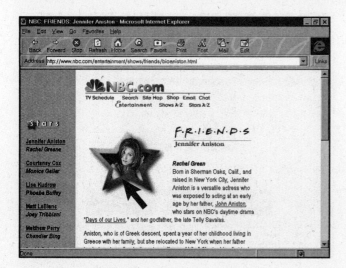

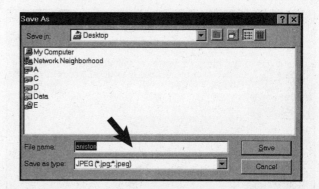

3 In the Save As dialog box, type a name for the file (if you want to give the file a different name), and select the folder in which you want the file saved. Click **Save**.

1 Many pages include embedded graphic files that Internet Explorer can play by itself. Sometimes, a page displays a thumbnail image that you can click to view the full picture.

2 In this case, Internet Explorer displays a larger version of the picture you selected. To save the picture to disk so you can view it later (or open it in another application), right-click the image, and click **Save Picture As**.

4 If you click a link for a file that requires an ActiveX control to play it, Internet Explorer may be able to get the control you need and install it. You'll see a dialog box asking for your okay. Click **Yes**.

(continues)

Guided Tour Play Multimedia Files *(continued)*

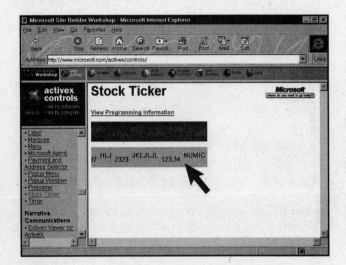

5 The ActiveX object plays right on the page. You may not even realize that it is a separate object.

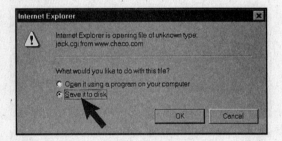

6 If you click a link that points to a file that Internet Explorer cannot play, Internet Explorer displays a dialog box asking if you want to open the file using another application or save the file to disk. For now, save the file to disk.

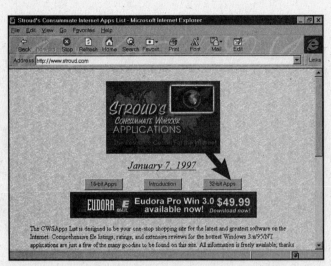

7 For files that Internet Explorer cannot play, you can find helper applications, plug-ins, and ActiveX controls on Stroud's Consummate Winsock Applications list. Visit the list at **www.stroud.com**. Assuming you are using Windows 95, click the **32-bit Apps** button.

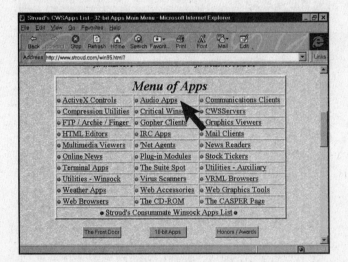

8 Scroll down the page to the **Menu of Apps**, as shown above. This displays a list of helper application categories. Click the link for the desired category.

Guided Tour Play Multimedia Files

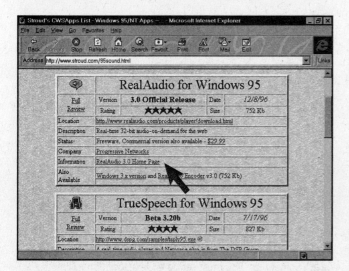

9 When you find an application that looks promising, click the link in the Information box to go to the home page for that application. (You can right-click the Location link and choose Save As, but this link commonly points to outdated files.)

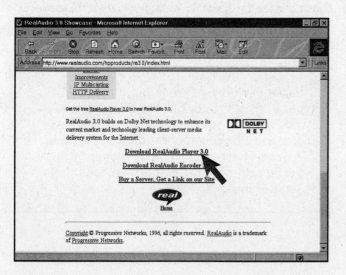

10 When you reach the application's home page, follow the trail of links to the page where you can download the file.

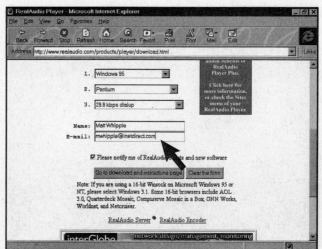

11 You might have to complete a form or select the desired application from a list.

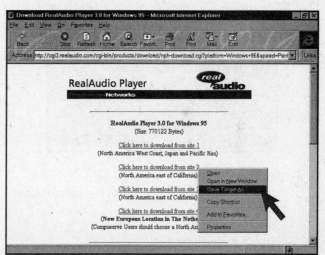

12 If you see a link for downloading the file, right-click the link, click **Save Target As**, and use the Save As dialog box to save the file to your hard drive. (If the file is large, and you have a modem connection, it may take a long time to download the file.)

(continues)

Guided Tour Play Multimedia Files *(continued)*

13 Most helper application files come as compressed executable files. To install the helper application, double-click the file you just downloaded, and then follow the installation instructions.

14 Once a helper application, plug-in, or ActiveX control is installed, Internet Explorer runs it whenever needed to play a particular file type.

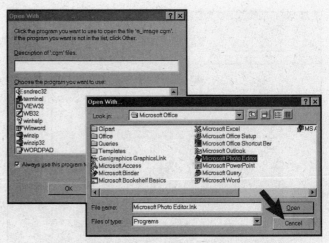

15 Sometimes, you must set up a file association to link the helper application to a particular file type. The easiest way to do this is to select the application when Internet Explorer displays the Open With dialog box. (The Open With dialog box appears if you select a file type that Internet Explorer cannot play.) If the application you want to use is not in the list, click the Other button, and use the Open With dialog box to select the application. If this doesn't work, you can manually edit and add file associations as explained in the following Guided Tour.

Internet Explorer insists on playing certain types of files, such as GIF and JPG graphics and AU audio files. You can't make Internet Explorer use a helper application to play these file types. However, you can save files of these types to your hard drive and then open them in a different application.

Begin Guided Tour Edit File Associations

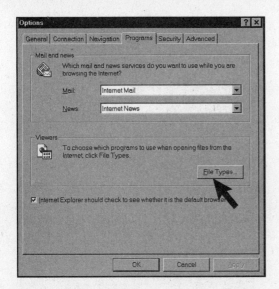

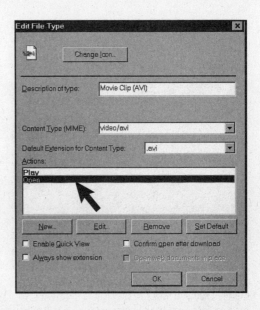

1 To set up a file association, open the **View** menu and select **Options**. In the Options dialog box, click the **Programs** tab, and then click the **File Types** button.

4 Under **Actions**, click **open**, and then click the **Edit** button.

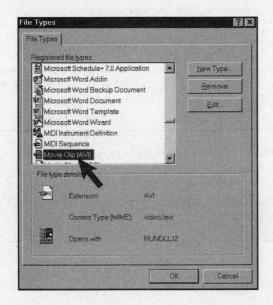

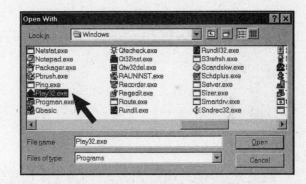

2 The File Types dialog box appears, displaying a list of file types that are associated with particular applications. Scroll through the list, until you find the file type you want to associate with another application. (If the desired file type is not in the list, skip to the next Guided Tour to learn how to add a file type.)

5 The Editing Action for Type dialog box appears. Click the Browse button, and use the **Browse** dialog box to select the application you want to use to play files of this type. Keep clicking **OK** to close all the dialog boxes and save your changes.

3 Click the file type that you want to associate with a different application, and click the **Edit** button.

Begin Guided Tour   Add a File Association

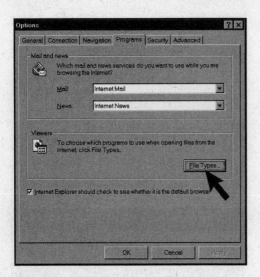

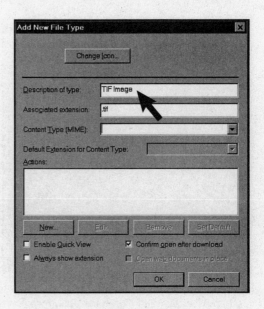

1 If a file type you want to play is not registered, you may have to associate the file type with an application manually. Open the **View** menu and select **Options**. In the Options dialog box, click the **Programs** tab, and then click the **File Types** button.

3 The Add New File Type dialog box appears. Click inside the **Description of Type** text box, and type a description of the file type. In the **Associated Extension** text box, type the file name extension that this file type commonly has.

4 Open the **Content Type (MIME)** drop-down list, and choose the MIME type (or type a new MIME type, for example, **image/tiff**). Open the **Default Extension for Content Type** drop-down list, and select the extension you want to use for this MIME type.

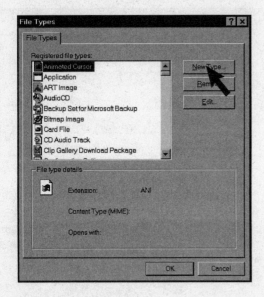

MIME stands for Multipurpose Internet Mail Extension, a coding system used to transfer files over the Internet. Internet Explorer uses the MIME type to determine which helper application or plug-in to run.

2 Click the **New Type** button.

Guided Tour   Add a File Association

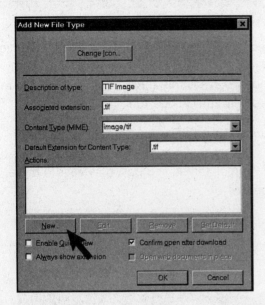

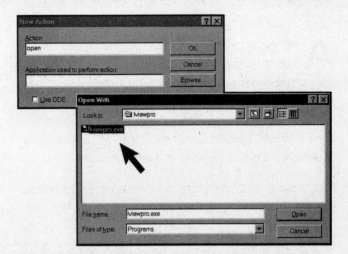

5   Under Actions, click the **New** button.

6   In the **Action** text box, type **open**, and then click the **Browse** button. Use the Browse dialog box to select the application you want to use to open and play files of this type. Click the **Open** button.

7   You return to the New Action dialog box, and the open command appears in the Actions list. Click **OK**, click **Close** twice, and click **OK** to close opened dialog boxes and save your new file association.

Access Internet Newsgroups

A newsgroup is an electronic bulletin board on which you can post messages and read messages that other people have posted. The Internet has thousands of newsgroups devoted to every topic from politics to tattooing, where people gather to express their insights, opinions, and expertise; ask and answer questions; share concerns; and debate issues.

To read and post messages in newsgroups, you need a special program called a *newsreader*. When you

installed Internet Explorer, you were given the option of installing Microsoft's newsreader, Internet News. If you chose to install this application, you're ready to proceed with the Guided Tour.

The Guided Tour shows you how to run Internet News, connect to a news server, find newsgroups that interest you, and read and post messages in those newsgroups.

Begin Guided Tour Set Up Internet News

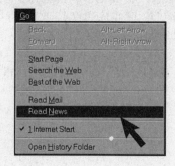

1 You can run Internet News by selecting it from the **Start**, **Programs** menu. Another way is to open Internet Explorer's **Go** menu and select **Read News**.

2 Before you can access newsgroups, you must specify a news server. Open the **News** menu and select **Options.**

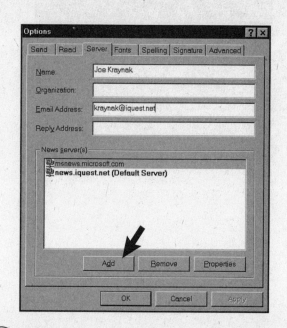

3 The Options dialog box appears. Click the **Server** tab. Type your name and e-mail address in the designated boxes, as shown above. Under **News Server(s)**, click the **Add** button.

Guided Tour Set Up Internet News

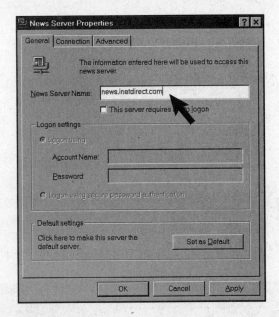

④ The News Server Properties dialog box asks you to enter the name of the server. Type the address of the news server in the **News Server Name** text box. (Get the name from your Internet service provider.)

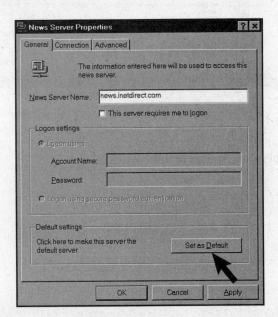

⑤ Click the **Set as Default** button, so Internet news will use this news server to access newsgroups.

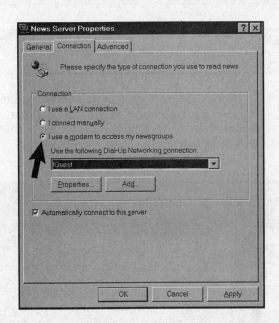

⑥ Click the **Connection** tab, and specify how you are going to connect to the news server: by using a LAN (network) connection or via modem. Click **OK** to save your changes, and then click **OK** to close the Options dialog box.

⑦ To have Internet Explorer automatically run Internet News when you click a link to a newsgroup, open the **View** menu in Internet Explorer, and click **Options**.

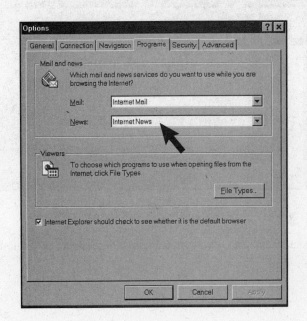

⑧ Click the **Programs** tab. In the **News** drop-down list, make sure **Internet News** is selected. Click **OK**. Now, when you click a link to a newsgroup, Internet Explorer automatically runs Internet News.

Begin Guided Tour Download a List of Newsgroups

1 The Internet has over 10,000 active newsgroups. Before you can view the messages in a newsgroup, you must download the names of the available newsgroups. Run Internet News, and click the **Newsgroups** button.

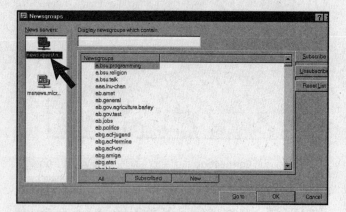

2 The Newsgroups dialog box appears. In the left pane is a list of news servers you set up. Click the desired server.

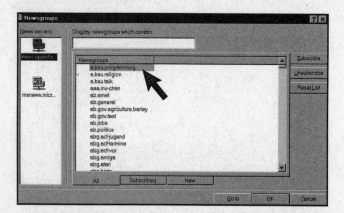

3 When you click a server, the right pane shows a list of newsgroups available on the server. If the pane is blank or you have not recently updated the list, click the **Reset List** button.

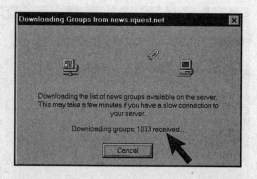

4 The Downloading Groups dialog box appears, showing the progress of the update. Because there are so many newsgroups, this may take several minutes. Wait until the operation is complete.

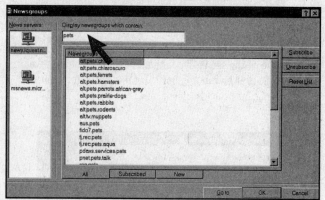

5 After Internet Explorer is done retrieving the newsgroup names, it displays them. To find a newsgroup, type some text that you think might appear in the newsgroup name in the **Display Newsgroups Which Contain** text box.

Guided Tour   Download a List of Newsgroups

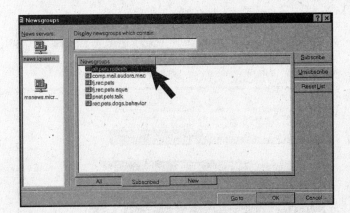

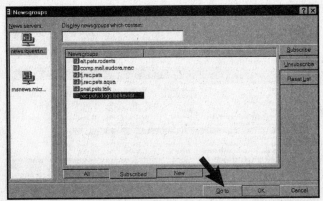

6 The list scrolls to show any names that match your entry. You can subscribe to a newsgroup by double-clicking its name. You can then view a list of only subscribed newsgroups by clicking the **Subscribed** tab.

7 To open a newsgroup and display a list of messages it might contain, click its name, and click the **Go To** button. The next Guided Tour shows you how to read messages in a newsgroup.

Begin Guided Tour   Read and Respond to Newsgroup Messages

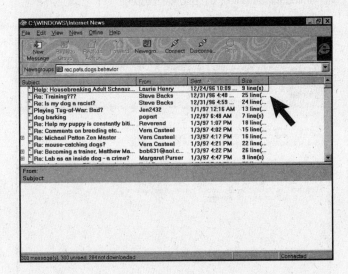

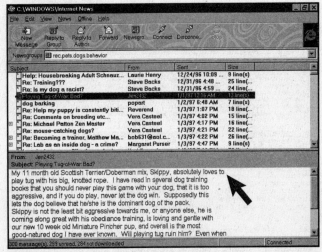

1 When you choose to Go To a newsgroup, Internet News retrieves a list of messages and displays them in the pane at the top or left side of the window. Click a message to read it.

2 Its content appears in the pane at the bottom or right side of the window, where you can read it.

(continues)

If you don't see a list of messages, you may not be connected to the news server. If the Connect button in the toolbar is grayed out, you're not connected; click the Connect button to reestablish the connection. Another reason is that the newsgroup no longer exists.

Guided Tour   Read and Respond to Newsgroup Messages

(continued)

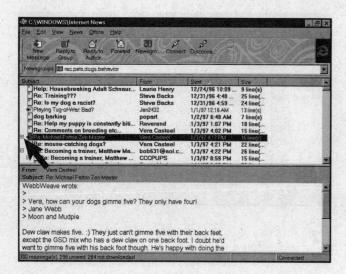

3 If someone has responded to the message, a plus sign appears next to the description of the message. Click the plus sign to view a list of replies, and then click the description of the reply to read its content.

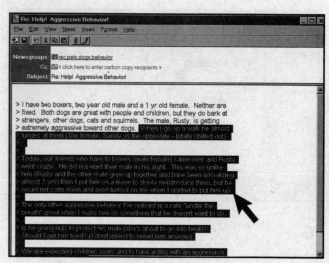

5 The reply dialog box automatically addresses the message to the group and adds a description. It also quotes the original message. Because it is impolite to quote extensively, drag over and delete most of the quoted material. Leave only enough to remind the author of the original message.

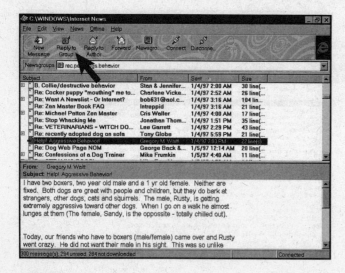

4 To reply to a message, first, click it. You can then reply to the author privately (via e-mail) or publicly by posting your reply in the newsgroup. To reply publicly, click the **Reply to Group** button.

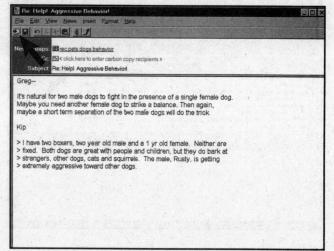

6 Type your reply at the top of the message area. Then, click on the **Post Message** button. It takes a while for the message to be posted. Check back later to see if it appears in the newsgroup and to see if anyone has replied to it.

Guided Tour Read and Respond to Newsgroup Messages

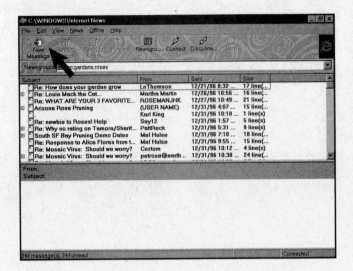

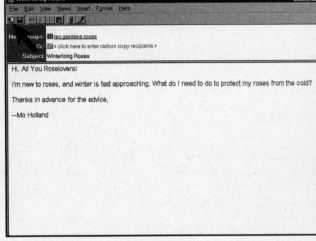

7 You can post your own message to start a conversation. Enter the newsgroup in which you want the message to appear, and then click the **New Message** button.

9 Click inside the message area at the bottom of the dialog box, and type your message. Click the **Post Message** button. Internet News posts the message, but it may not appear in the newsgroup for some time.

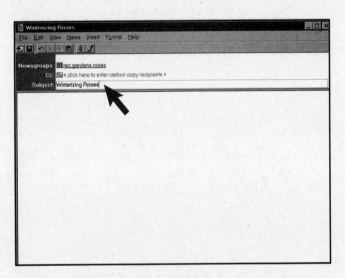

8 The New Message dialog box appears. Internet News automatically addresses the message to the current newsgroup. Click next to **Subject**, and type a brief description of the message.

HOW TO...

Share Office 97 Data

Up to this point, you have used the Office 97 applications individually, creating a PowerPoint presentation or a Word document with the help of a single application. And, except for using Outlook to contact your fellow workers and open documents, you have been doing most of your work alone, with little or no input from friends or colleagues.

Working alone with the individual Office applications is a good way to learn the basics. However, in the real world, you will rarely encounter the simplicity of being able to use a single application by yourself. Documents are usually more sophisticated, requiring you to combine text, numerical data, graphics, and other types of data. In addition, most businesses foster a team environment, which demands that you collaborate with your fellow workers, sharing documents and data.

This part of the book provides you with the opportunity to tap into the synergy of the Office 97 applications. Here, you will learn how to use the applications together to swap data between applications and collaborate on projects.

What You Will Find in This Section

Copy and Paste Data Using the Clipboard

Think of copying and pasting as using a photo copier to make a copy. With a photocopy, the original remains intact in the original location, and you have the copy. You can manipulate the copy in any way that you want. You can edit it, delete part of it, doodle on it, and so on, all without affecting the original. This method of sharing information works best when you simply want to use the same information in another document.

Here's what you need to remember about copying and pasting:

- Copying and pasting among applications works pretty much the same way as copying and pasting within a document.

- When you copy something, it is placed on the Clipboard, a temporary holding spot. The Clipboard can hold only one piece of information. If you copy something and then copy something else, the last thing that you copied is the only thing on the Clipboard.

- You can copy and paste from one document to another or from one application to another. You can paste to other Office applications and any other type of application that supports copy and paste (for example, a WordPerfect document).

- Usually, when you copy and paste without using a special command, the data is not linked or embedded. If you make a change to the original document, that change is not reflected in the pasted copy.

- The application will try to paste the data into a suitable format in the receiving document. For example, when you paste an Excel worksheet into Word, the information is formatted as a table. In some cases (when you cannot edit the information in the receiving application), the information is pasted as an embedded object; you can double-click the object to edit it in the program you used to create it.

- You can also move information from one application to another by using the Cut command.

The following Guided Tour shows you the basics of how to copy and paste data from one Microsoft Office document to another.

Begin Guided Tour   Copy and Paste Data Between Documents

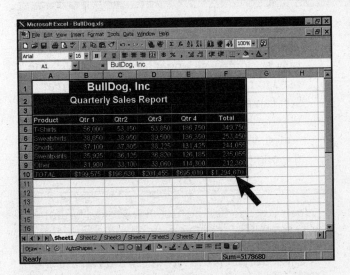

1 Start the application and open the document that contains the data you want to copy. Select the data you want to copy (refer to the other sections of this book to learn the specifics of selecting data in the application you're using.)

2 With the data selected, click the **Copy** button in the toolbar.

3 Switch to the application in which you want to paste the data. (You can click the application's name in the taskbar.)

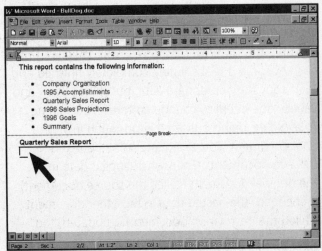

4 Open the destination document, and move the insertion point to the location where you want to paste the data.

5 Click the **Paste** button in the toolbar.

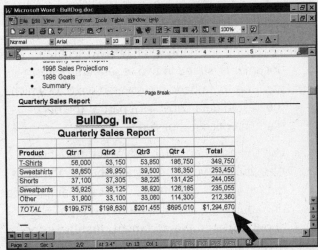

6 The data is pasted in an acceptable format (here as a table). In this example, you could use any of Word's table commands to format and edit the table. The data is not linked to the original worksheet.

Insert Copied Data as a Link

In many cases, you may be creating a document with data from several sources. You could wait until each document is absolutely, completely finished and then copy the appropriate data, but things can—and usually do—seem to change up to the last minute. To avoid including outdated information in your final document, you can create a link between the two documents. Then when copied data in the original document (called the *source document*) is changed, the pasted data in the other document (called the *destination document*) is updated, too.

Here are the key points to remember about linking data:

- You use the **Copy** command to copy the data you want to link, but you follow a different procedure for pasting the information, as covered in the Guided Tour.

- You can link data between Excel, Word, PowerPoint, and any other application that supports OLE, by using the **Paste Special** command on the **Edit** menu. If a program does not support OLE, the Paste Special command will not be available.

- When you link data, you have two separate documents, stored in two separate files. Compare this to embedding (covered next), in which the pasted data becomes a part of the document in which it is pasted.

- Use linking when you need instant updating. Also, linking works best when you use the same data in several documents. You can maintain the one source document without having to worry about updating the documents that use information from the source.

- You can link data in several formats, including RTF (rich text format), as a picture, as an object, or as unformatted text. The format you select controls how you can edit the data. For

example, in picture format, you can edit the link only by double-clicking it to run the application used to create the linked data. In RTF format, you can edit individual entries in the destination file, but if you close the file and reopen it, any edited entries revert back to the entries used in the original file.

> When you use linking, you have to be careful when moving, renaming, or deleting files. If you take any of these actions, you might break the link between the two files. You can use the **Edit, Links** command to edit the link if you move or rename the file. If you delete the file, you will have to re-create it.

Working with Linked Data

Linked data behaves in some fairly unpredictable ways. For example, if you paste data in RTF (rich text format), you can edit entries in the link without affecting the original file. However, if you close the file that contains the linked data, and then reopen it, your edits disappear. The following list will help you understand the way links behave:

- If you paste the link as a picture, you can click the link to select it. Handles (little black squares) and a border appear around the link. You can drag a handle to change the size or dimensions of the linked object, or you can drag a border to move it. To edit the link, double-click it; Windows runs the application used to create the link, allowing you to edit it.

- If you pasted the link in RTF format, you can edit individual entries in the linked object. However, editing these entries does not change the original file from which the link was copied. So, when you update the link or reopen the file that contains the link, your changes are replaced by the entries in the original file.

- You can break the link between the linked object and the file from which you copied it. The linked data then becomes a part of the host file, and you cannot edit the data by double-clicking it or by choosing a link option. To break a link, open the **Edit** menu, select **Links**, click the link you want to break, and click the **Break Link** button.

To make permanent changes to the linked data, you must edit the original file from which you copied the link. Although you can edit links by opening the **Edit** menu, selecting **Links**, and using the dialog box that appears to modify the link, there's an easier way:

1. Right-click the link you want to change. A shortcut menu appears, displaying several link options along with other options for changing the object.

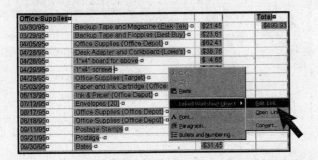

2. Point to **Linked Object**, and click **Edit Link** (the names of the link options vary depending on the application you used to create the object). Windows runs the application used to create the linked object and opens the original file.

3. Edit the data as you normally would, and then save your changes.

4. Switch back to the document that contains the linked data. The changes automatically appear in the linked object.

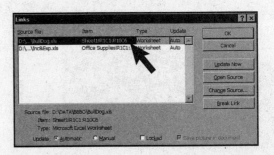

If you open the **Edit** menu and select **Links**, you'll see the dialog box shown here. You can then click a link to update it, control the way it behaves, break the link, or edit it. Think of this dialog box as control central for all your linked objects. Note the following:

- At the bottom of the dialog box are link update options. **Automatic** tells Windows to automatically update the linked object whenever the original file is changed. If you select **Manual**, you must manually update links by clicking the **Update Now** button in this dialog box. If you click **Locked**, the linked objects will not change when you edit the original file.

- To open a link in its application for editing, click the link you want to open, and then click the **Open Source** button. (This opens the original link file so you can edit it as in the previous set of steps.)

- To pick a different file as the link or to specify a different name or location for the linked file (if you moved the link file to a different drive or folder), click the **Change Source** button. A dialog box appears, allowing you to select the drive, folder, and name of the linked file.

Begin Guided Tour Paste Data as a Link for Automatic Updates

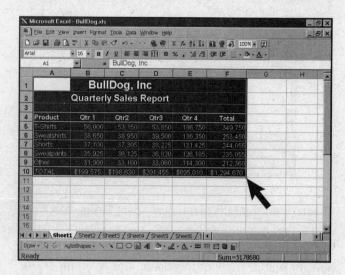

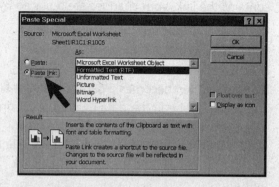

5 You see the Paste Special dialog box. In a Word document, you can paste the data as formatted text, unformatted text, a picture, or a bitmap. Select how you want the data pasted, click the **Paste Link** option button, and click **OK**.

1 Start in the application that contains the data you want to copy. Here you are starting Excel. Then select the data you want to copy.

2 With the data selected, open the **Edit** menu and choose the **Copy** command.

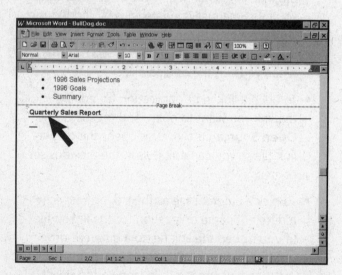

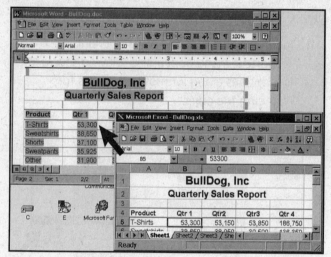

6 The data is pasted and linked to the original. If you edit the original data, the change appears automatically in the linked file. Here the Quarter 1 T-shirt sales are changed from 56,000 to 53,300 in the worksheet.

3 Switch to the application and open the document in which you want to paste the data. Move the insertion point to the location where you want the data pasted.

4 Open the **Edit** menu and choose the **Paste Special** command.

Embed Copied Data in Another Document

Linking files is great if you create large files that contain parts of documents created in several different applications. It's also great if you work on group projects and you have a single document that pulls in data from several different files maintained by your colleagues or family members.

However, linking does have two major shortcomings. First, if you want to share a file with another person, you must send that person all the linked files, as well. And when the other person places all those linked files on her computer, she'll have to update the links to make sure the central document knows where all the contributing files are located. This can be a time-consuming (and frustrating) procedure.

Second, linking allows a file's contents to be edited from more than one location. But say you want the original file to remain unchanged, and you want to modify only the data you pasted into the other document? In such a case, you want to break the link between the two files, allowing them to remain separate.

When you want to share a file with someone else or prevent an original file from being altered, you can *embed* copied information into a document. What can you do with an embedded object? How is an embedded object different than linking? Read the following list of key concepts to find out:

- When you embed an object, that object is saved with the main document. For example, if you embed part of an Excel worksheet in a Word document, the worksheet data is saved as part of the Word document (not as a separate file). Also, the embedded object is no longer connected to its original document; the embedded object becomes the sole property of the document that contains it.

- You can edit an embedded object using the original application. When you double-click an embedded object, you switch back to the application you used to create the object. (You can see both documents on the screen, but the toolbar and menu commands change for the appropriate application.) You can then use any commands to edit or format the object. Keep in mind that you must have the original application on your system.

- The major drawbacks to embedding are that you can end up with a pretty big file, and you have to manually update the data contained in this file; the data won't change automatically when you edit the original file.

- You can embed many types of objects from Office applications, from mini-applications (such as Microsoft Draw or WordArt), and from other applications that support embedding.

- You can embed a document that you have already created, or you can insert a blank embedded document (and then use its application to create it).

Work with an Embedded Object

When you insert cut or copied data as an embedded object, the data doesn't just sit inside the document like an immovable blob. You can click the object, and then move or resize it; you can even double-click the object to edit its contents. Whenever you double-click an embedded object, Windows runs the application associated with the object, allowing you to use the application's tools to modify the object.

When you select an embedded object (usually by clicking it), tiny black squares (called *handles*) appear around the object. You can then do any of the following to modify the object:

- To move the object, move the mouse pointer to a border (but not a selection handle) and drag the object to the spot where you want it.

- To resize an object, move the tip of the mouse pointer over a selection handle, and drag the handle to change the object's size or dimensions.

- To delete an object, press **Del**.

- To share the object with another document, make sure both documents are displayed on-screen. Then, drag the object from the source document into the destination document.

- Drag the object over the Windows desktop. When you release the mouse button, a scrap appears on the desktop. You can then drag the scrap into another document.

You can also call up the application you used to create the object and edit the object, as covered in the following Guided Tour.

> If you don't have the application that the object was created in, and you try to edit the object, the application you're in will try to convert the object to a format that you can use.

Begin Guided Tour   Edit an Embedded Object

1 Double-click the linked object. Windows displays the menu bar and toolbar for the application used to create the embedded object. However, you can still see the rest of the document that contains the object.

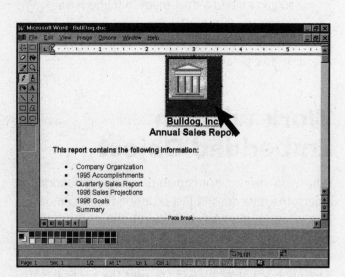

2 Modify the object as you normally would in the application you used to create it.

3 When you finish making changes, exit the application by clicking inside the main document. The object and document are updated.

Begin Guided Tour   Embed an Existing Object

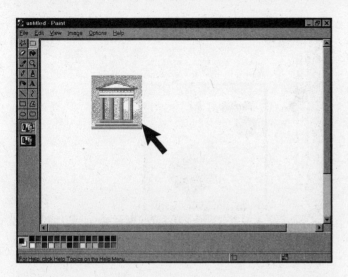

1 Start in the application that contains the data you want to embed. Here you are starting in Windows Paint. Select the data you want to copy.

2 With the data selected, open the **Edit** menu and choose the **Copy** command.

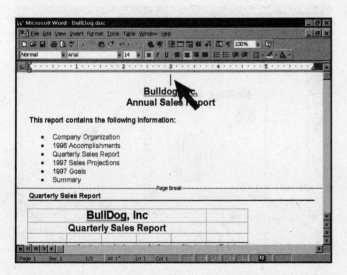

3 Switch to the application and open the document in which you want to embed the copied data. Move the insertion point to the location where you want to paste the copied data.

4 Open the **Edit** menu and select the **Paste Special** command.

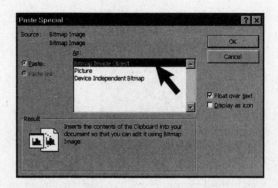

5 You see the Paste Special dialog box. In the As list, select the **Object** option. For example, if you're pasting part of a Paint drawing, click **Bitmap Image Object**. Click **OK**.

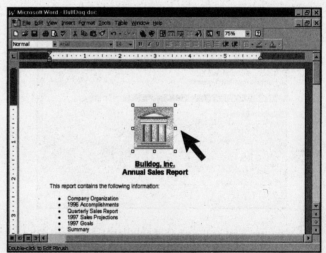

6 The data is pasted into the document as an object. Any link between the pasted picture and the original picture file is broken, but the connection between the pasted data and its application remains live. You can double-click the pasted object to open it in its application and edit it.

Begin Guided Tour Embed a New Object

1 Start in the document in which you want to embed the object (here Word). Then open the **Insert** menu and select the **Object** command. (In some applications, you open the **Edit** menu and select **Insert Object**.)

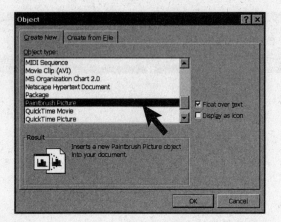

2 You see a list of the types of objects you can insert. (The dialog box looks different depending on the application.) Click the type of object you want to insert, and then click **OK**.

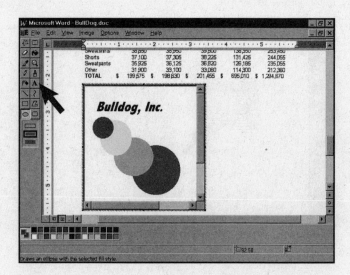

3 The application for the type of object you selected starts. You may not realize the application started, but if you look at the toolbar and menu commands, you can see that you are in a different application. Create the object using the commands and features of that application.

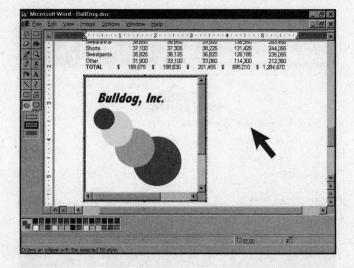

4 When you complete the object, click anywhere inside the document. This closes the application you used to create the embedded object.

5 The new object is now embedded in the document. You cannot open the embedded object as a separate file, but you can edit the object by double-clicking it.

Insert a Graph with the Graph Applet

Microsoft Office 97 includes a graph applet (a small application) that allows you to create and insert simple graphs in your Word documents, PowerPoint slides, and in other documents you may create.

When you insert a Graph object, a datasheet appears with sample data. This datasheet is similar to an Excel worksheet; it is a grid of rows and columns. You select the cell you want and then replace the existing data. You can add more data or delete sample data you don't need. You can also use the toolbar buttons and menu commands to change the chart type and make other formatting changes.

You can insert a graph in any Office application; take the Guided Tour to insert a graph into one of your Word documents.

Begin Guided Tour   Add a Graph to a Word Document

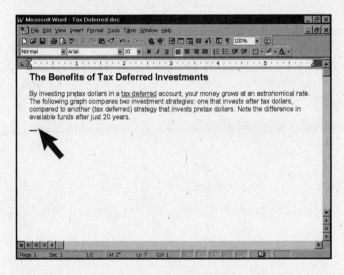

1 Open your Word document, and move the insertion point to the location where you want the graph inserted.

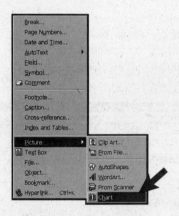

2 Open the **Insert** menu, point to **Picture**, and click **Chart**.

(continues)

Guided Tour Add a Graph to a Word Document

(continued)

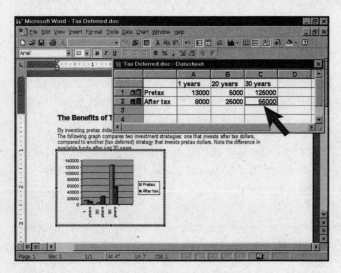

3 Graph starts, and you see the datasheet with sample data. Replace the sample data with the data you want to chart. Make any editing or formatting changes using the menu commands and toolbar buttons in Graph.

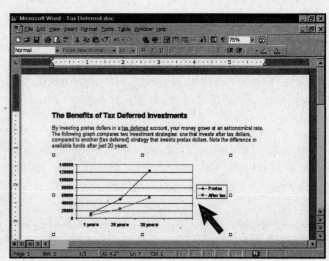

5 The new graph is inserted in the document. To move the graph, drag it. To resize the graph, drag one of its handles. To edit the graph, double-click it.

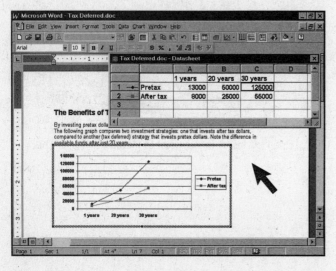

4 When you finish, click inside your Word document to return to it.

Group Related Documents with Binders

Microsoft Office has a document management tool called *Microsoft Binder* that lets you "clip" related documents together. For example, if you have a report that consists of a cover letter, one or more Excel worksheets, and a PowerPoint slide show, you can add all these files to a binder in order to work with them as a single document.

Once you've bound several documents together, Microsoft Binder allows you to rearrange the documents, number the pages, check spelling, add a header and footer, and perform other tasks to give your bound documents a consistent look and feel. You can even print all the documents with a single Print command.

To understand Microsoft Binder, take a look at this figure. Each document you add to the binder (you'll learn how to add documents later) is shown as an icon in the left pane. The icons appear in the order in which you joined the documents. When you select a document's icon, the contents of the document appear in the right pane, where you can edit the document. The toolbar and menu bar change according to the application you used to create the document.

The Guided Tour shows you how to start Microsoft Binder, create a new binder, add documents to a binder, and work on those documents as a group.

Begin Guided Tour   Organize Documents in a Binder

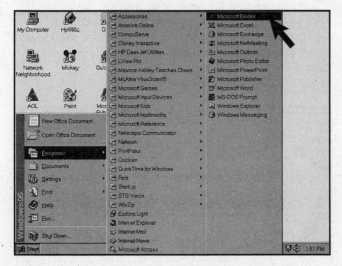

1 To run Microsoft Binder, click the **Start** button, point to **Programs**, and click **Microsoft Binder**.

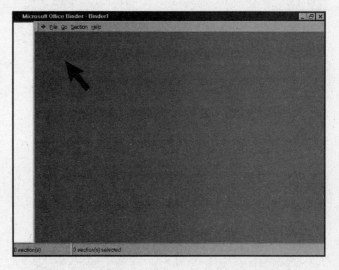

2 The Microsoft Binder window appears, as shown here. Because you haven't yet added files to the binder, it is blank.

(continues)

Guided Tour Organize Documents in a Binder

(continued)

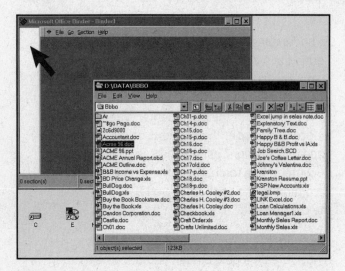

3 The easiest way to add a data file to the Binder is to run My Computer or the Windows Explorer, and drag the icon for the file into the left pane of the Binder window.

Another way to add a document is to open the **Section** menu and select **Add from File**. Use the dialog box that appears to select the file you want to add, and then click the **Add** button.

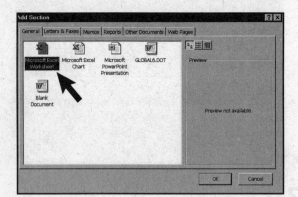

4 To add a new (empty) document, open the **Section** menu and select **Add**. A dialog box appears, asking you to specify the type of document you want to add (Excel chart or worksheet, Word document, PowerPoint presentation, whatever). Select the desired type, and click **OK**.

You can rearrange the documents in the Binder by dragging a document's icon up or down in the left pane. Release the mouse button.

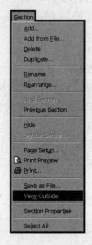

5 To work with a document in the application you used to create it (instead of in the Binder window), click its icon, and then open the **Section** menu and select **View Outside**. After editing the document, open the **File** menu and select the **Update** option. To return to the Binder, open the **File** menu and select **Close & Return to Binder**.

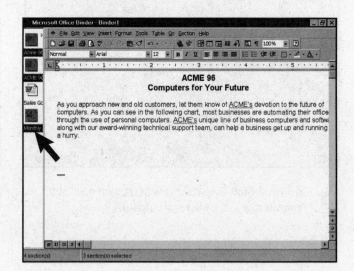

6 To perform a task (such as page numbering) on more than one document, hold down the **Ctrl** key while clicking the icon for each document you want to act on (this selects the documents). Then, perform the desired task as you normally would.

Guided Tour Organize Documents in a Binder

7 You can add a header or footer that will appear on the pages of all the documents in the binder. Open the **File** menu and select **Binder Page Setup**.

8 The Binder Page Setup dialog box appears. To insert a header or footer on all pages in the binder, select **All supported sections**. To add a header or footer only to selected sections, click **Only sections selected below** and select the sections on which you want to print headers or footers.

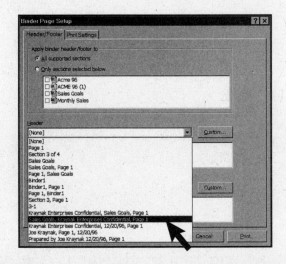

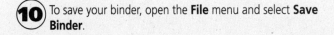

9 To add a header (text that appears at the top of every page), open the **Header** drop-down list and select the header you want to use. To add a footer, select the desired option from the **Footer** drop-down list.

10 To save your binder, open the **File** menu and select **Save Binder**.

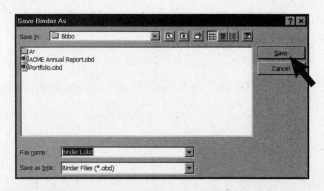

11 Use the Save Binder As dialog box to select a location and enter a name for the new binder file. Once you've saved the file for the first time and named it, you can quickly save changes by clicking the **Save** button or pressing **Ctrl+S**.

12 You can print all or some of the documents in your binder. To print selected documents, Ctrl+click each document you want to print. Open the **File** menu and select **Print Binder**.

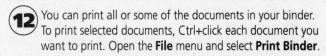

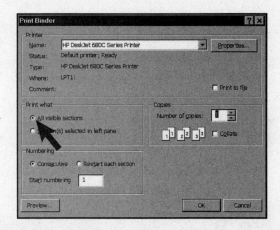

13 Under **Print What**, click **All visible sections** to print all the documents in the binder, or click **Section(s) selected in left pane** to print only those documents you selected.

(continues)

Guided Tour   Organize Documents in a Binder   *(continued)*

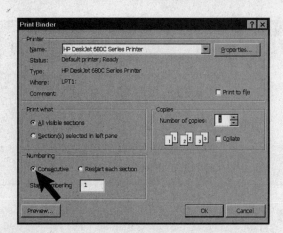

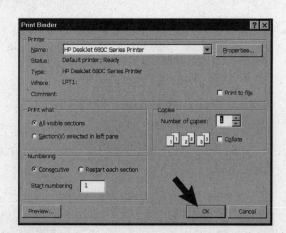

14 Under **Numbering**, select **Consecutive** to number all the pages in the binder as if they are part of a single document; or select **Restart each section** to number the pages of each document separately.

15 Enter any other printing preferences, such as the number of copies you want. To start printing, click **OK**.

Share Documents Safely with Coworkers

Y ou rarely create documents in a vacuum for your own personal gratification. You usually collaborate on a project, exchanging ideas and comments, or you at least send the completed document to someone else—your boss, a customer, or your audience.

Office 97 offers several tools to help you share your documents with others and collaborate on projects. The Office 97 applications all offer ways to e-mail a document directly from the application you used to create it, or route the document to various recipients. In addition, all the applications allow you to protect your documents with passwords, to prevent undesired changes.

For team projects, Word offers a couple of editing tools that allow you to track changes to a document and add comments (both written and spoken) to a document. With the Track Changes option on, Word uses a different color for text that you or someone else has inserted or deleted. Deleted text is displayed with a line through it, and added text appears

underlined. Any comments you or a colleague have added appear in a special window at the bottom of the screen.

The following Guided Tour shows you how to use these various collaboration and editing tools.

If you like a particular version of a file, you can save it before you start entering changes or before you review the changes that someone else has made. Just open the **File** menu and select **Versions**. Click the **Save Now** button, type a brief description of the version, and click **OK**. Whenever you open the Versions dialog box for this file, it displays a list of the saved versions. You can then click the version you want and click **Open**. To have Word automatically create a new version whenever you close the document, display the Versions dialog box and click **Automatically Save a Version on Close**.

Begin Guided Tour Protect Your Documents with Passwords

1 To add a password to a document in Word or Excel, first open the file you want to protect. Then, open the **File** menu, and select **Save As**.

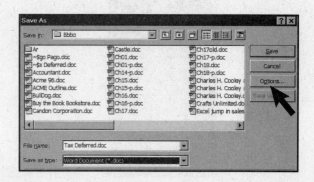

2 The Save As dialog box appears. Click the **Options** button.

(continues)

Guided Tour Protect Your Documents with Passwords

(continued)

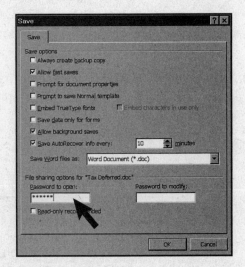

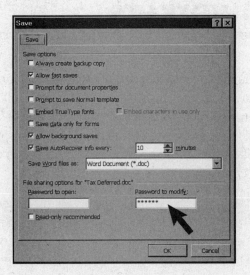

3 The Save dialog box provides you with several options, including two password options. To prevent users from accessing the file without your permission, type a password in the **Password to open** text box. As you type, the password appears as a series of asterisks, so nobody can sneak a peek while you're typing.

4 To allow users to open the file but prevent them from changing its contents without your permission, leave the Password to Open option blank and type a password in the **Password to modify** text box.

5 Click **OK** to return to the Save As dialog box, and then save the file. (Keep a list of your document names and the passwords you use to protect them. Without these passwords, you won't be able to open or edit your files.)

Begin Guided Tour Track Changes to Your Word Documents

1 Run Word, and open the document in which you want your changes displayed.

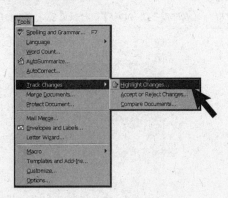

2 Open the **Tools** menu, point to **Track Changes**, and click **Highlight Changes**.

Guided Tour Track Changes to Your Word Documents

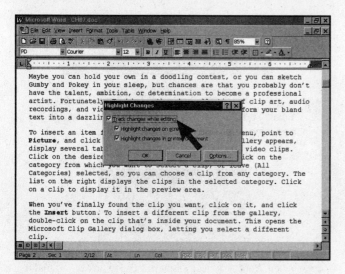

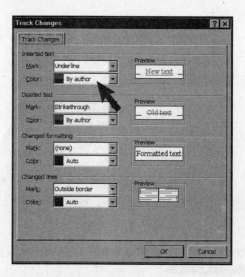

3 The Highlight Changes dialog box appears. Click **Track changes while editing** to turn the option on.

4 The other two options specify whether you want changes to be displayed on-screen, in the printed document, or both. Make the desired selections.

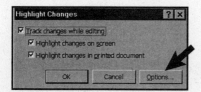

5 To control the way Word displays inserted or deleted text, click the **Options** button.

6 The Track Changes dialog box appears. Use the drop-down lists to specify how you want your changes marked. (In the **Color** drop-down lists for **Inserted** and **Deleted** text, leave **By Author** selected to have each person's changes displayed in a different color.)

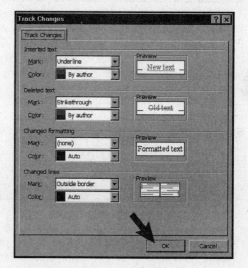

7 Click **OK**. This returns you to the Highlight Changes dialog box. Click **OK**. Now, as you enter changes, Word displays them in the selected color.

(continues)

Guided Tour Track Changes to Your Word Documents *(continued)*

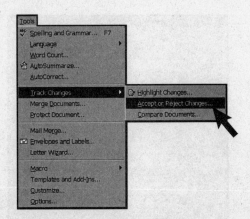

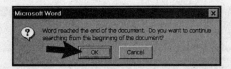

8 To review changes and accept or reject them, open the **Tools** menu, point to **Track Changes**, and click **Accept or Reject Changes**.

11 When Word reaches the end of the document, it displays a dialog box asking if you want to continue from the beginning. Click **OK**.

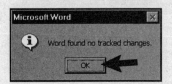

9 The Accept or Reject Changes dialog box appears, and Word highlights the first change in the document. Click **Accept** to make the requested change, or click **Reject** to return the text to its original form. (You can use the **Find** buttons to review changes without acting on them.)

12 When Word is done, it displays a dialog box saying that it found no more tracked changes. Click **OK**.

A quick way to add or edit comments or to review the changes made to a document is to use the Reviewing toolbar. To turn it on, right-click any toolbar and select **Reviewing**.

10 Word carries out your command and highlights the next change. You can click **Accept All** or **Reject All**, if you are certain that you want to accept or reject all the recommended changes.

Begin Guided Tour Add Comments to a Word Document

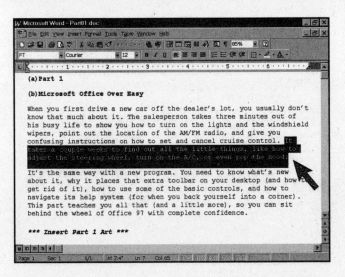

1 To suggest changes to a document without changing the actual content of the document, you can add comments. Drag over the text on which you want to comment.

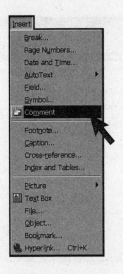

2 Open the **Insert** menu and click **Comment**.

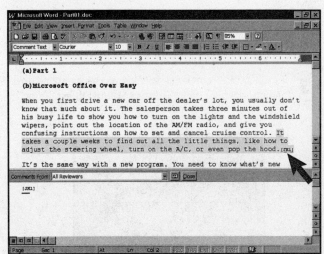

3 The selected text appears highlighted in neon yellow, and a comment pane appears at the bottom of the document window.

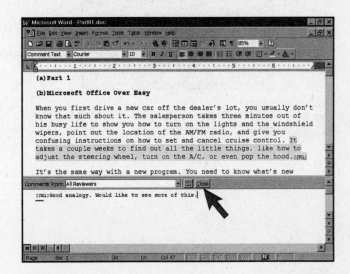

4 To add a typed comment, type your comment, and click the **Close** button.

(continues)

Guided Tour Add Comments to a Word Document

(continued)

5 To add a voice comment (assuming you have a sound card and microphone), click the **Insert Sound Object** button.

6 The Windows Sound Recorder window appears. Click the **Record** button, and start talking into the microphone.

7 When you are finished recording, click the **Stop** button, and then exit Sound Recorder.

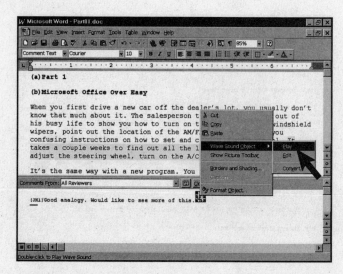

8 This places a speaker icon in the Comments pane. To play your recorded message, right-click the speaker icon, point to **Wave Sound Object**, and click **Play**.

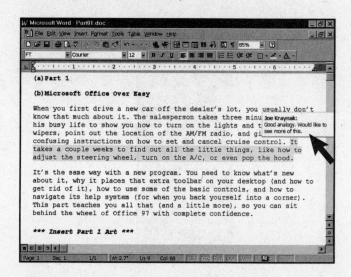

9 To display a typed comment, simply rest your mouse pointer anywhere on top of the highlighted text. To display the Comment pane (for example, to add a reply), double-click the text. (You can delete a comment by deleting the bracketed initials next to the highlighted text.)

Begin Guided Tour   Route a Document Through E-Mail

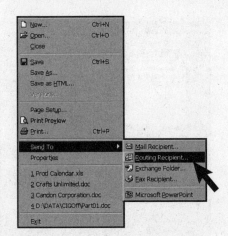

1 You may have to route your document through various team members for their approval. Open the **File** menu, point to **Send To**, and click **Routing Recipient**.

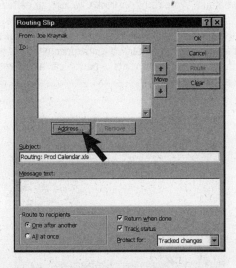

2 The Routing Slip dialog box appears, prompting you to enter the e-mail addresses of the desired recipients. Click the **Address** button.

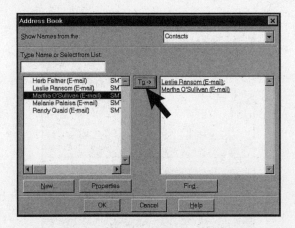

3 The Address Book dialog box appears, prompting you to enter an e-mail address. Click the recipient's name in the list, and click the **To** button.

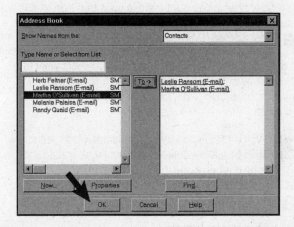

4 Repeat step 3 for each person to whom you wish to send the document. Click **OK**.

(continues)

Guided Tour   Route a Document Through E-Mail   *(continued)*

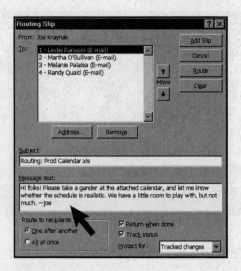

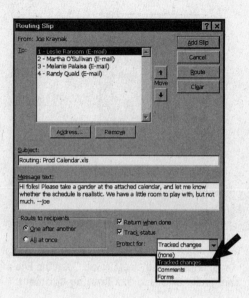

5 You are returned to the Routing Slip dialog box. Click in the **Message text** text box, and type a brief message telling the recipients what you want them to do with the attached file.

6 Under Route to Recipients, click the desired routing option: **One after another** (to send the document to each person on the list in succession) or **All at once**. (You might want to send a message to routing recipients one after another, if you want subsequent recipients to see the previous recipients' comments.)

7 If you want the document automatically returned to you when people are done entering changes, make sure **Return when done** is checked.

8 To be notified via e-mail whenever a person has entered his or her changes and then closed the document, make sure **Track status** is checked.

9 By default, Word turns on Track Changes, so each person's changes will appear highlighted. You can choose a different option from the **Protect for** drop-down list to further restrict what another person can do to the document. For example, if you choose **Comments**, a person can add comments but not edit the document.

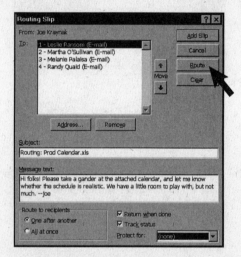

10 To route the document now, click the **Route** button. To route the document later, click **Add Slip**; then whenever you decide to route the document, open the **File** menu, point to **Send To**, and click **Next Routing Recipient**.

PART 2

Do It Yourself

You've mastered the basics of using Excel, Word, PowerPoint, Access, and Outlook. You can create your own workbooks, documents, and presentations, and you may be well on your way to organizing your life with Outlook. But now that you know your way around the Microsoft Office suite, you'd probably like to explore a little and see how you can put these applications to some practical use.

In this part, you'll apply the basics you've learned to actual projects. You'll learn how to create a multimedia, interactive résumé in PowerPoint, how to reconcile your checking account with an Excel worksheet, and even how to create a quarterly report that updates itself. In this part, you'll get hands on experience using the Microsoft Office applications separately and together to make the most of your new investment, and to have some fun in the process.

So, stretch your fingers, and check out the following project sections:

What You Will Find in This Part

DO IT YOURSELF

Combine Excel Data and Charts with Your Word Documents

Now that you are comfortable using the Microsoft Word and Excel products, you are probably using Excel for the worksheets and Word for text creation. That's good, and that's the strength of each product. But what if you need to convey both text information and worksheet information? Do you always have to worry about creating and managing two separate documents, one in Word and the other in Excel? Why not combine the advantages of Word and Excel into your single creation? This section describes projects you can perform that mix and match the strengths of each product into a single document or worksheet.

The projects in this section assume that the Microsoft Office Shortcut Bar is on, and that you added buttons for running Excel, Word, and PowerPoint. If this is not the case, see "Use the Office Shortcut Bar," on page 25 for details.

What You Will Find in This Section

Insert an Income Statement into Your Monthly Business Report

Business reports are more effective if they include data, but typing in numbers and trying to align them in columns can be a real pain. It also can be redundant work—you probably already have that data stored in an Excel worksheet, because it's the best tool for handling figures.

Why not combine the best of both worlds? You can insert an Excel worksheet directly into your report in Word. There is no limit to the number of worksheets you can include with your document. For example, you can include an accounting worksheet for each department itemized in a single auditing report. You can create business inventory reports more easily by simply including the inventory worksheet portions directly on the business report.

To do the task shown here, you'll need to create a document in Word and create a worksheet in Excel. Review the "Create a Word Document" section starting on page 59 and "Build an Excel Worksheet" section starting on page 129 if you need help doing this.

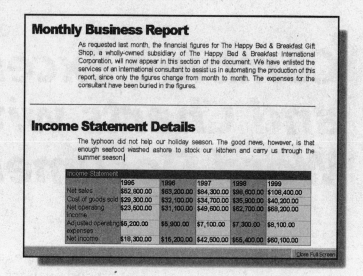

Begin Do It Yourself Paste Excel Worksheet Data into a Word Document

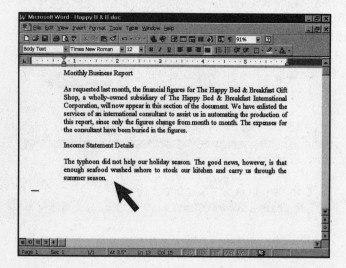

1 Prepare the text for your report in Word. Don't worry about the formatting for now. We will use the report template and automatic formatting capabilities of Word to improve the appearance. Save the report.

2 Open the **Format** menu, and select the **AutoFormat** command.

Do It Yourself Paste Excel Worksheet Data into a Word Document

3 The AutoFormat dialog box asks if you will want to review the changes it makes to your document. Click **AutoFormat and Review Each Change**, and then click **OK**.

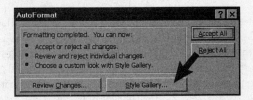

4 The AutoFormat feature improves the appearance of your report and a different AutoFormat dialog box appears so that you can accept or reject the changes. If you like this format, you can click **Accept All** and save your report. To find out how much better your report can look, click the **Style Gallery** button.

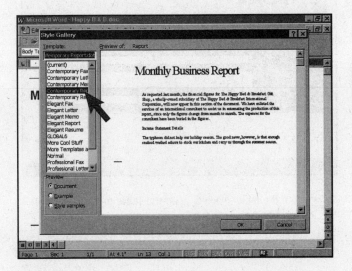

5 Here is the preview of the format chosen by Word. To choose a different format or template, click inside of the Template scroll box on the left. Scroll through the available templates until you find the one you want. Click the template to select it. For this example, click the **Contemporary Report** template.

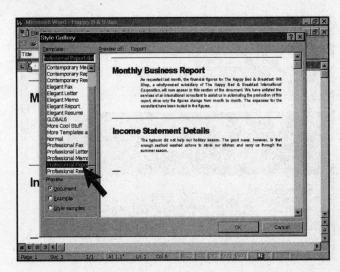

6 The preview shows the template you selected applied to your text. If you don't like the way the template looks, repeat step 5. When you find a template you like, click **OK**.

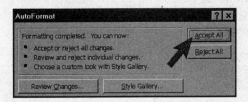

7 You are returned to the AutoFormat dialog box. Click **Accept All** to apply the template you selected (Professional Report in the example) to your text. Save your report.

8 Review your report in Word and decide where you want to place the data from your Excel worksheet. Then open Excel and locate the file containing the data you want. If it does not yet exist, you can create it now.

(continues)

Do It Yourself   Paste Excel Worksheet Data into a Word Document   *(continued)*

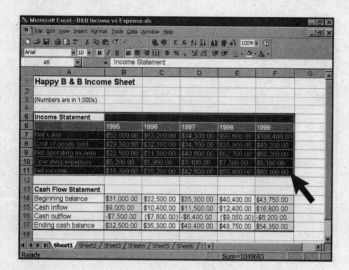

9 When you locate or create the data, select only the data you want to appear in your report by clicking and dragging with the left mouse button to capture all of the data.

10 A selection border and a frame will appear around the object, indicating that you have selected it. To copy the selected data, open the **Edit** menu and click **Copy**.

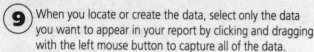

11 Switch back to Word by clicking the **Word** button in the Microsoft Office Shortcut Bar.

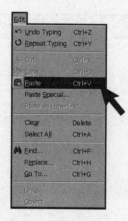

12 Move the insertion point to the location where you want the data inserted. Open the **Edit** menu, and select the **Paste** command.

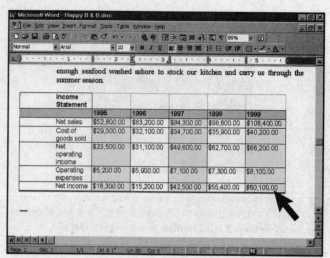

13 The Excel data appears as a table in your report. Although the worksheet formatting carries over from Excel, you can change the format by using Word's table-formatting features. To add a border or color to the table, first select the table by clicking and dragging with the left mouse button to capture the entire table.

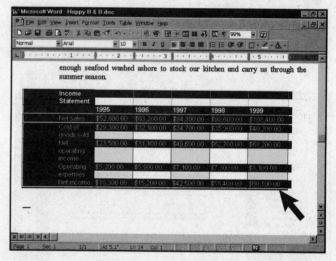

14 With the table selected, open the **Table** menu (or right-click anywhere inside the table) and select the **Table AutoFormat** command.

Do It Yourself   Paste Excel Worksheet Data into a Word Document

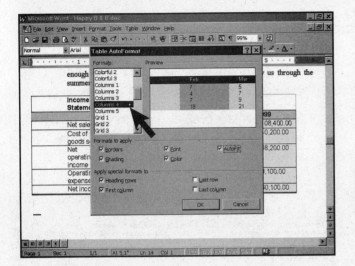

15 The Table AutoFormat dialog box appears and provides you with a large variety of options. For this example, click inside of the Formats scroll box and select **Columns 4**. A preview of your table will appear with the selected formatting options. Click **OK**.

If you are interested in actually linking an Excel worksheet into your report, review the next Do It Yourself called "Create a Quarterly Report that Updates Itself" on page 448.

...review the next Do It Yourself called "Create a Quarterly Report that Updates Itself" on page 448.

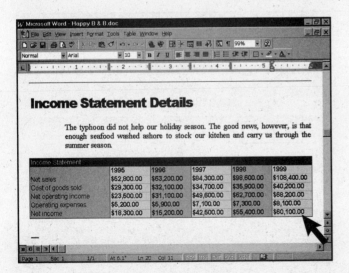

16 The report and formatted data table are now complete. Save your work by using the **File, Save** command. The formatted table is now a permanent addition to your report. You can edit the material in this pasted Excel table just as you would a Word table. Try it yourself by clicking a cell and changing something.

The Excel table you pasted into your Word document really is a Word table now, and that should be a warning: don't expect to change numbers and have things add up like an Excel worksheet. Each table cell is independent.

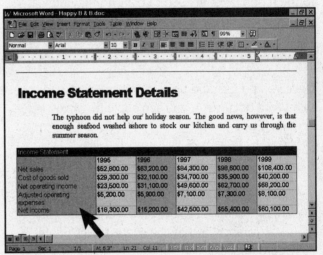

17 Here the text cell entry **Operating expenses** has been selected and changed to **Adjusted operating expenses**. Click anywhere outside of the table to return to editing your report.

Create a Quarterly Report that Updates Itself

When you create a status report, you usually maintain the structure from the last status report and update the data. If you use Excel data in the status report, you can save yourself some time by linking the data to the report once instead of copying the data each time you need to update the report. That way, when you change to the data in the Excel worksheet, that change will appear in the status report in Word.

Once you understand how to link an Excel worksheet to a Word document, you can apply that knowledge in many ways:

- You can automate the monthly creation of a status report that contains a summary chart from a company data worksheet. If anyone makes changes to the data worksheet, your status report includes the latest sales figures automatically.

- You can create a memo that informs team members of project status and link the memo to

a schedule you have created in Excel, so that the memo contains the latest mission-critical dates.

- You can create business inventory reports by including the inventory worksheet portions directly on the business report.

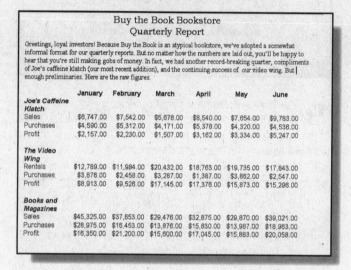

Begin Do It Yourself Paste Worksheet Data so It Updates Itself

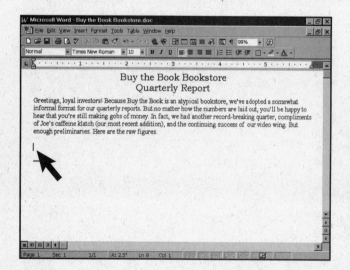

1 Prepare your report in Word and move the insertion point to where you want to insert your worksheet data.

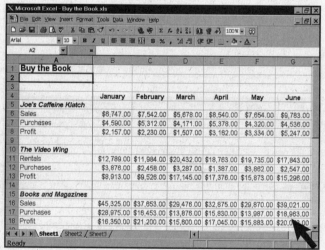

2 Switch to Excel, and open or create the worksheet from which you want to copy the data.

Begin Do It Yourself Paste Worksheet Data so It Updates Itself

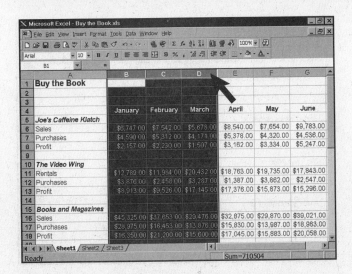

3 In this case, we want to present the income and expenses for only the second quarter. To hide the first quarter numbers, drag over the column letters B, C, and D at the top of the worksheet.

4 To hide the selected columns, open the **Format** menu, point to **Column**, and click **Hide**.

6 Switch back to your Word document. Open the **Edit** menu and select **Paste Special**, so you can insert the copied worksheet data as a link.

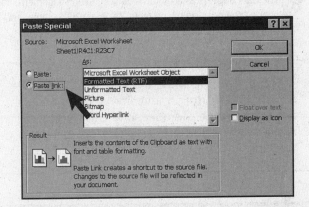

7 The Paste Special dialog box asks how you want the copied data pasted. Click the desired format (usually RTF) in the As list, and then click the **Paste Link** option. Click **OK**.

> RTF (rich text format) inserts the Excel data as formatted text. Microsoft Excel Worksheet Object inserts the data as a picture, making it a little less manageable.

5 Excel hides the selected columns, so you can copy the data in columns A, E, F, and G as a single unit. Drag over the data you want to copy. Open the **Edit** menu and select **Copy**, or click the **Copy** button in the toolbar.

(continues)

Do It Yourself Paste Worksheet Data so It Updates Itself (continued)

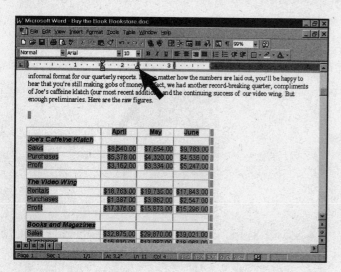

8 The data appears as a table inside your Word document. To change the position of the table, click inside the table, and drag the margin and column width markers, as desired.

You can quickly change the look of your table by using the AutoFormat command. Right-click anywhere inside the table, and click **Table AutoFormat.** You can then pick from a list of table designs.

10 Switch back to the table in your Word document, and look at the number you changed in your Excel worksheet. The new entry is automatically inserted into the table.

If you hid columns as shown in the Do It Yourself section, and then you unhide the columns, you might run into trouble if you update the link later. When you update the link (using Edit Update Link), Word assumes that you want the hidden columns inserted, as well.

9 Switch back to your Excel worksheet, and change one of the numbers. Here, the Video Wing June purchase amount was changed from 2547 to 2397. Be sure to press **Enter** after typing your change, or the link will not update.

Copy an Analysis Chart into a Letter to Prospective Investors

Sometimes, numbers alone are overwhelming, and many times, we need to create documents that contain a large amount of raw data. The visual impact of a simple but professional chart can catch the attention of your reader and at the same time make your numbers easier to understand.

Adding Excel charts to Word documents can improve the visual quality of your information. Think about receiving a letter from the lottery commissioner that details your winning. You have to decide if you want the money monthly, quarterly, or annually. What are the tax implications? Three charts could replace pages of data and make you smile even more.

You can include as many charts in a single letter as you want. You can mix and match the different types of charts—you are limited only by your imagination.

Once you know how to include charts from Excel into your Word document, your documents can be much more visually stimulating. Here are some ideas to get you started:

- To convince one of your kids (or someone else's kids) to save money, create a graph showing that if the kid sets aside so much money per month, he will have some incredible amount when it's time to leave home.

- You can send a letter requesting a raise to your boss that includes a multiline chart showing the increasing Consumer Price Index and the inflation rate graphed against your meager salary increases.

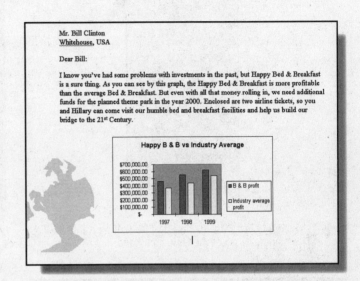

- To convince your spouse to spend less in a particular category, create a pie chart of your monthly budget. When he sees how big that slice of the pie is, he may think twice when making the next purchase.

- To explain to your IRA representative why you are transferring money out of a fund, you can send a letter with a graph that shows the declining performance of the fund next to the strong performance of the new fund you are considering.

If you need a refresher on charting in Excel, turn back to the "Create an Excel Chart" section on page 191.

Begin Do It Yourself Insert an Excel Chart into a Word Letter

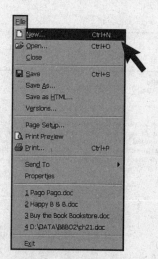

1 First, create the letter you want to send. In Word, open the **File** menu and select the **New** command.

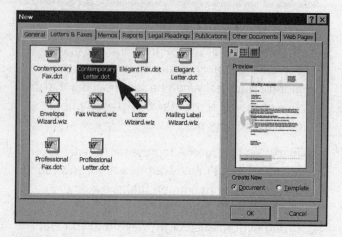

2 The New dialog box appears. Click the **Letters & Faxes** tab, and then click **Contemporary Letter**. Click **OK** to continue.

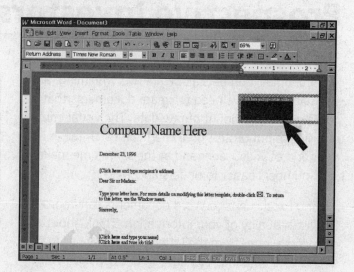

3 The template for creating a letter is ready for you. Simply click an item (as instructed in the template), and then type your entry. To change the sample text, drag over it and type your new text. Save your letter.

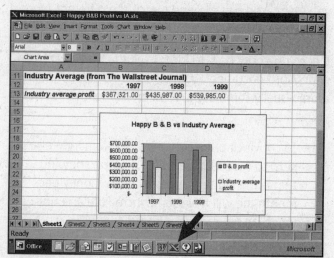

4 Now, display the Excel chart you want to copy. Open Excel by clicking its icon in the Microsoft Office Shortcut Bar and locate the file containing the chart you want. If it does not yet exist, you can create it now. When you have located or created the chart, click it to select it.

Do It Yourself Insert an Excel Chart into a Word Letter

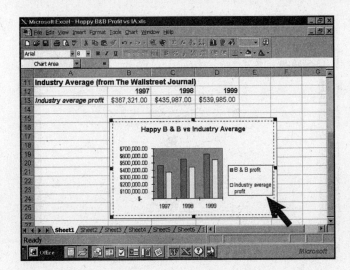

5 Selection handles and a frame appear around the object, indicating that you selected it. If selection handles do not appear around the entire chart, as shown, click outside the chart, and then click it again.

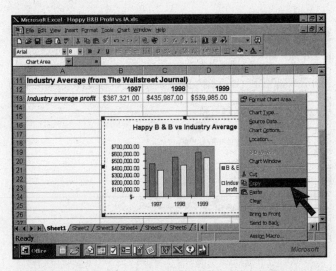

6 Click the right mouse button once anywhere inside the selected chart, and then select **Copy** from the shortcut menu.

7 Switch back to Word by clicking the **Word** button in the Microsoft Office Shortcut Bar or in the taskbar.

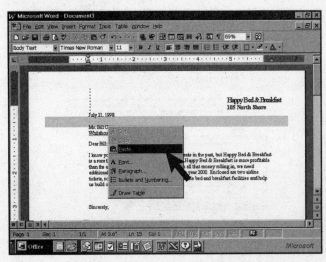

8 In your letter, click where you want the Excel chart inserted. Right-click the same spot, and then select **Paste** from the shortcut menu.

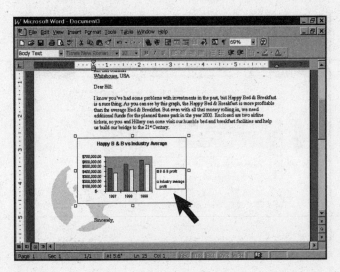

9 You now have a full-featured Excel chart embedded into your Word letter. Existing text moves to accommodate the space taken up by the addition of this new chart. Prove to yourself that it's no ordinary picture by double-clicking the chart.

(continues)

Do It Yourself   Insert an Excel Chart into a Word Letter   *(continued)*

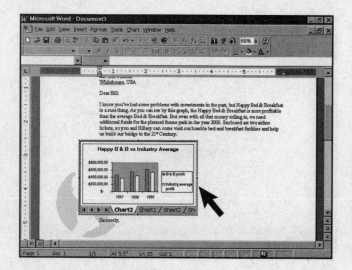

10 The Excel worksheet grid appears around your chart. Notice also that Excel's menus and toolbars are available to edit your chart.

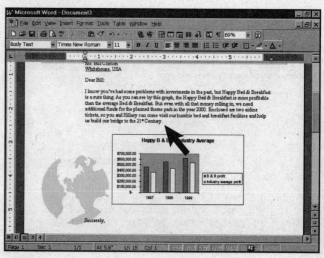

12 The standard Word editing menus reappear. You can now continue with your letter. Remember that this simple pasting of the chart from Excel does not contain a link to the original source document. You can observe this yourself by clicking the **Excel** button in the Microsoft Office Shortcut Bar.

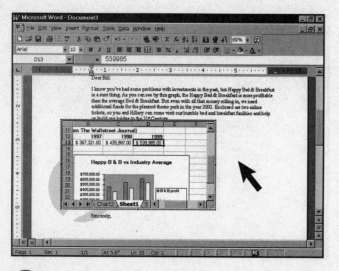

11 After making changes, click the chart inside your worksheet to select it. Now click anywhere on your original document in Word.

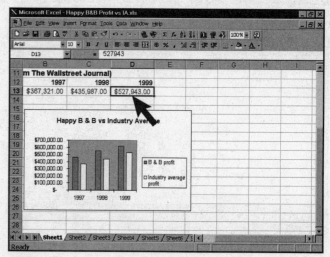

13 Excel will be open with the original chart selected, but your changes after pasting were not reflected back in this source.

DO IT YOURSELF

Find a Job with Microsoft Office

I n today's competitive job market, searching for a job takes more than just typing a resume and mailing it to a few select personnel departments. You usually have to develop a strategy, research several companies, and (most important) organize the material you need to effectively market yourself. You have to prepare a resume find a list of companies and people to send your resume to and pull together all of your records (transcripts, references, evaluations, samples of your work, and so on).

In addition, job seeking has become much more automated. Many employers might ask you to e-mail your resume or fax it. In many computer-related industries, you can make a big impression by sending a multimedia resume—a resume done as a slide show in PowerPoint or as a Word document with icons linking to pictures, sounds, and other documents. And if you're connected to an online service, you can even use your computer to search for potential openings by checking professional bulletin board systems and online want ads.

In this project section, you'll learn how to use Microsoft Office to hone your job search strategies for the '90s.

What You Will Find in This Section

Create a Resume in Word

The easiest way to create a cover letter and resume in Word is to use the Resume Wizard. To use the wizard, open Word's **File** menu and click **New**. Click the **Other Documents** tab, and click **Resume Wizard**. When you click **OK**, Word starts the Wizard, which leads you through the process of creating a resume (and optional cover letter). To learn more about using Word's templates and wizards, see "Use Templates and Wizards" on page 127.

This project shows a different approach to creating resumes...an approach that uses Word's table feature. The table feature allows you to create resumes that are easy to customize. And, once you create your basic paper resume, the project shows you how to transform it into an interactive multimedia resume, complete with links to sounds, pictures, worksheet data, and graphs.

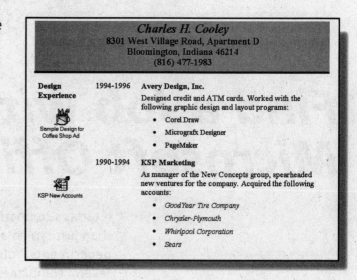

Create a Multimedia Resume

If you are submitting your resume specifically for a job that requires you to use Microsoft Office, or if you know that the person looking at the resume uses Microsoft Office, you might be able to impress the person by adding icon links to your resume. For example, you can add an icon that opens a document showing one of your writing samples. Another icon can link to an Excel worksheet that shows your salary history. You can even include an icon that stores an introductory voice recording or a photo of you.

When inserting icons, take the following two precautions:

- Paste data as an object (not as a link). If you create a link to the data, you'll have to send the person all the files that act as links, and the person will have to place those files in the same folders you used.

- Do not use data from any program that the person viewing your resume may not have. For example, if you include a video clip file, and the person does not have a program that can play video clips, the video clip won't run.

To add an icon to your resume, copy the data you want to insert as an icon, and then use the **Edit, Paste Special** command to paste the data where you want the icon to appear. In the Paste Special dialog box, make sure **Display as Icon** is selected. Enter any other paste preferences, and click **OK**.

Begin Do It Yourself   Create a Resume

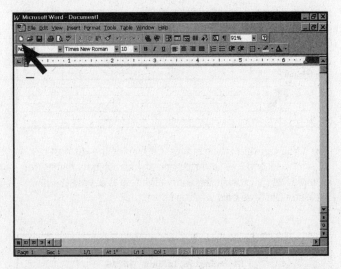

1 In Word, click the **New** button in the toolbar to create a new, blank document. (To work on the document in Page Layout view, open the **View** menu and click **Page Layout**.)

3 When you release the mouse button, the blank table appears. Now, merge the three cells at the top of the table to create a single cell. Drag over the cells, open the **Table** menu, and select **Merge Cells**.

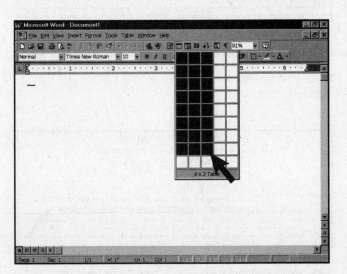

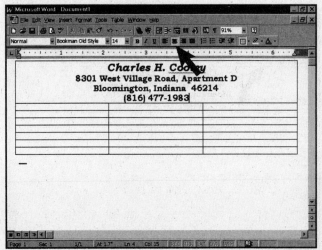

2 To create a three-column table, click the **Insert Table** button, and drag over the drop-down grid that appears until you have a table that's three columns wide and seven to eight rows long (you can insert rows later).

4 Click the **Center** button in the Formatting toolbar, and type your name, address, and phone number, pressing **Enter** at the end of each line. Format the text as desired. The text shown here is in Bookman Old Style (18-point bold italic for the name, and 14-point bold for the address and phone number).

For details on pasting data between Office documents, see "Share Office 97 Data," starting on page 417. For a more interactive and animated resume, see "Create an Electronic Resume in PowerPoint" on page 467.

(continues)

Do It Yourself   Create a Resume   *(continued)*

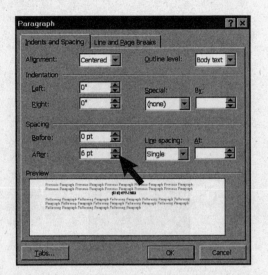

5 To insert some space after the phone number paragraph, highlight the phone number, open the **Format** menu, and select **Paragraph**. Click the up arrow in the **Spacing After** spin box once to add six points after the paragraph. Click **OK**.

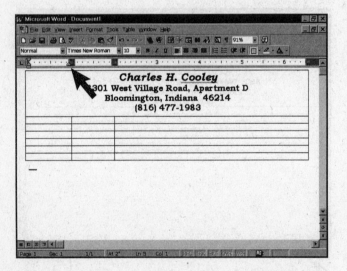

6 Now, set the column widths for the rest of the table. Click inside any cell below the topmost cell. Hold down the **Ctrl** key and drag the left column marker to the 1-inch mark on the ruler, and the right column marker to the 2-inch mark. This makes the two left columns 1-inch wide, and the rightmost column 4.5 inches wide. (See "Set Up a Table" on page 88 for more information about working with columns.)

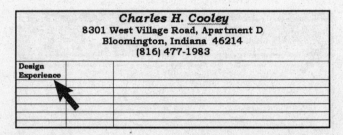

7 You can start typing entries. Click inside the leftmost cell in the second row, and type one of your category names (for example Design Experience). Format the text as desired (11-point Bookman Old Style bold was used here).

8 Click inside the middle cell and type the appropriate date or date range for the time you held your current job. (You typically list work experience in reverse order, starting with the most recent position.)

9 In the rightmost cell in row 2, type the name of the company and a brief description of your position. Format the text as desired. The text shown here is in 12-point Bookman Old Style. The Company name is bold.

Do It Yourself   Create a Resume

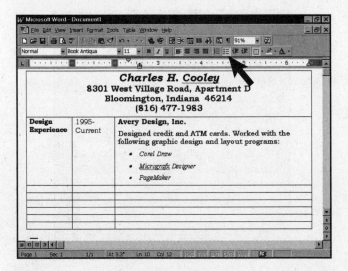

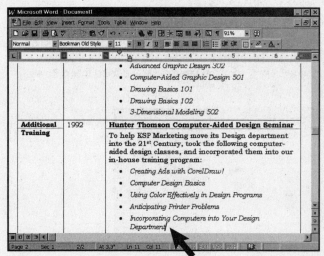

12 When you finish typing your work experience entries, click inside the leftmost cell in the next row down to begin typing your entries for the next category. Type the next category's name (for example, **Education**). Format the text as desired (11-point Bookman Old Style bold was used here).

10 Press **Enter**, and type a bulleted list of job responsibilities or key projects. To create the bulleted list, click the **Bullets** button. Before you start typing, change the font to 11-point Bookman Old Style italic using the Formatting toolbar.

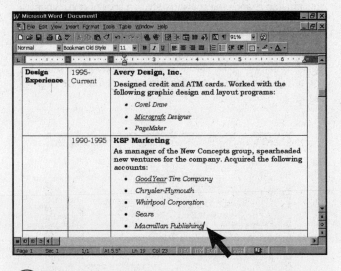

13 Continue typing dates and entries for the various categories, as shown here. You might have categories such as Education, Training, Skills, Awards, Professional Organizations, Special Interests, and Community Service.

(continues)

11 If you have another job to list under **Work Experience**, type the date and job description in the middle and right cells of the next row down. Because you are still in Work Experience, you don't have to retype the category name.

Do It Yourself Create a Resume *(continued)*

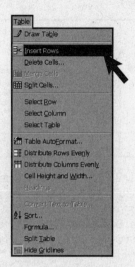

14 If you see that you will need additional rows, it's best to insert rows before you type inside the last row because rows are inserted above the selected row. Click in the selection area to the left of the row above which you want the new row inserted. Then, open the **Table** menu and select **Insert Rows**.

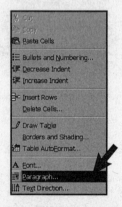

15 When you finish, you might notice that some text is awkwardly spaced. It may be too close or too far away from a cell border. To change the spacing, drag over the text that is awkwardly spaced, and then right-click it and select **Paragraph**.

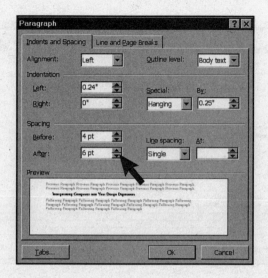

16 The Paragraph dialog box allows you to change the layout of your paragraphs. In tables, you can change the space between text and a top or bottom cell border by changing the **Spacing Before** and **After** settings, which affect the spacing between paragraphs. Usually a 4–6-point change will do the trick. You can also change the spacing between lines of text. When you've made your changes, click **OK**.

17 If your resume runs long or short, you can adjust it with the formatting tools. (You typically want a resume that runs one or two full pages.) Open the **File** menu and choose **Page Setup**.

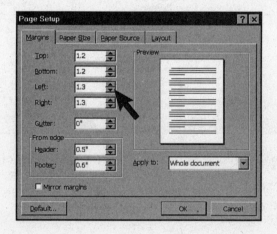

18 The Page Setup dialog box appears. Try changing the top, bottom, right, and left margins and then click **OK**.

Do It Yourself   Create a Resume

You can change the font size and type by selecting text and choosing new fonts and sizes from the formatting toolbar. You can also right-click the paragraph and choose Font to display the Font dialog box, which gives you a wider range of options and a preview window to try out changes before they get applied to your resume.

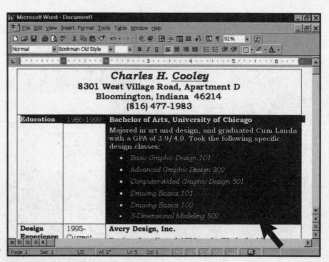

20 When you release the mouse button, the selected rows move up or down in the table.

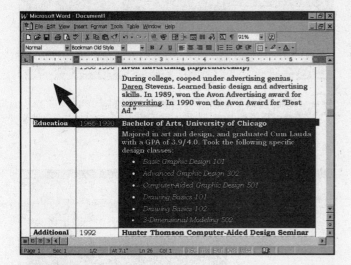

19 Experts suggest that you tailor each resume you send to make it more appealing to each prospective employer. For example, your education may be more important for one job, whereas your work experience is more important for another. In a table, you can quickly move rows. Drag in the selection area to select the rows you want to move; then, position the mouse pointer over any of the selected text, and drag it up or down.

21 The standard lines that Word uses to define a table and its cells only get in the way. To turn them off, first select the entire table; open the **Table** menu and click **Select Table**.

22 The entire table is highlighted. Open the **Format** menu, and select **Borders and Shading**.

(continues)

Do It Yourself Create a Resume *(continued)*

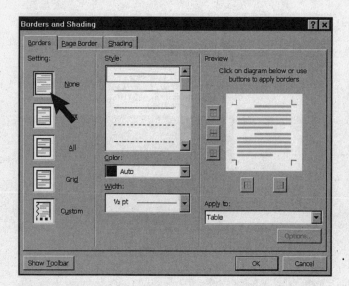

23 The Borders and Shading dialog box appears. Under **Setting**, click **None**. Click **OK**. The lines that define the table and cells are removed.

24 Now you can insert a few lines to accent your resume. Click inside the cell that contains your name, address, and phone number. Open the **Format** menu, and select **Borders and Shading**.

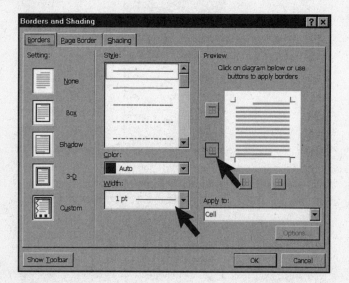

25 The Borders and Shading dialog box appears again. Open the **Width** drop down list, and select the **1 pt** line. Under **Preview**, click the **Bottom Border** button. Make sure **Cell** is selected in the **Apply To** drop-down list.

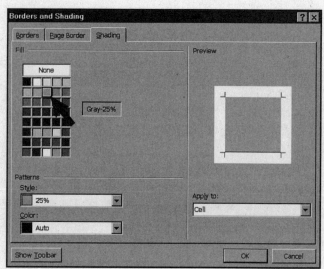

26 Now, shade this cell. Click the **Shading** tab, and click the **Gray-25%** button. Make sure **Cell** is selected in the **Apply To** drop-down list. Click **OK**.

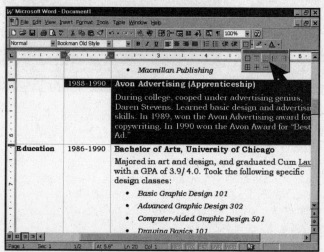

27 You should also add lines to separate the various sections of your resume. Drag over the cells that contain the last date and job description entries. Open the **Borders** drop-down list in the Formatting toolbar, and click the **Bottom Border** button to add a line that separates this category from the next one.

Do It Yourself Create a Resume

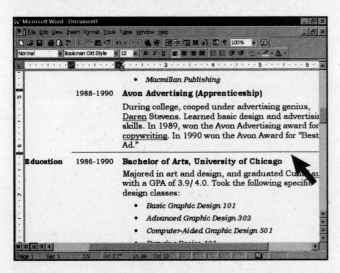

28 The new line provides a visual break. Save your work. Before sending the resume, be sure to spell check it (as explained on page 81).

Fax Your Resume to a Prospective Employer

Most employers want you to mail your resume and cover letter the old-fashioned way in an envelope. However, more and more employers are asking applicants to submit resumes via e-mail or fax. In fact, if a headhunter contacts you, chances are the headhunter will want a copy pronto, usually by fax. If you can supply your resume quickly, and in the form that the employer requests, your chances of landing an interview are better than those of another person who is working through the U.S. Postal Service.

This project contains brief instructions on how you can use Word along with Microsoft Fax (which comes with Windows 95) to quickly fax your resume to an employment service or personnel office. Keep in mind that the receiving fax machine will probably print your resume in black and white (so don't bother with fancy color formatting or graphics), and that the text may be a little more blurry than what you see on-screen. You might want to bump up the point size of your text or use a font that's slightly thinner.

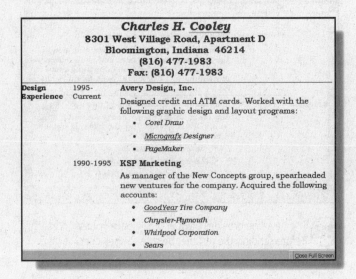

If you need to send your resume via e-mail, the process is even easier. You simply open your resume in Word, and then open the **File** menu, point to **Send To**, and click **Mail Recipient**. The Message dialog box appears, inserting your resume as an attachment. All you have to do is type the person's e-mail address and type a brief message describing the attachment.

Begin Do It Yourself Fax Your Resume

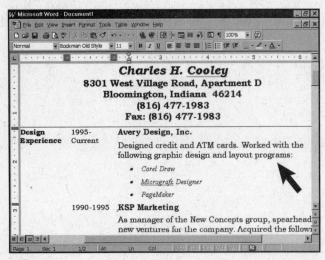

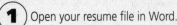

1 Open your resume file in Word.

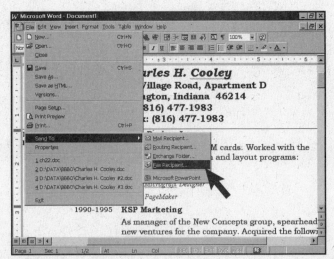

2 Open the **File** menu, point to **Send To**, and click **Fax Recipient**.

Do It Yourself   Fax Your Resume

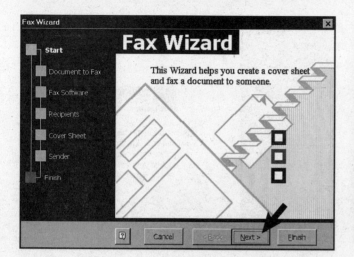

3 The Fax Wizard starts and displays an explanation of what it is about to do. Click the **Next** button to proceed.

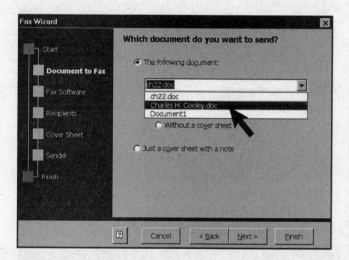

4 The next dialog box asks which document you want to send. You can send any document that is currently open in Word. Open **The Following Document** drop-down list, and click the document you want to fax. Click the **Next** button.

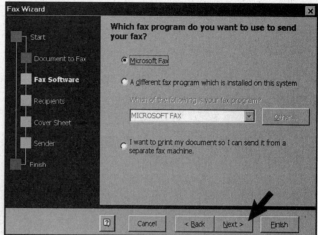

5 You are now asked which fax program you want to use. If you have another fax program installed on your computer, you can use it instead of Microsoft Fax to fax the document. Select the desired fax program, and click **Next**.

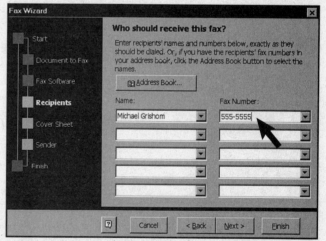

6 The next dialog box prompts you to enter the name and fax number of the recipient. Type the person's name in the first **Name** box, and then click the **Fax Number** text box, and type the fax number. You can send the fax to additional recipients, if desired. Click the **Next** button.

(continues)

Do It Yourself   Fax Your Resume

(continued)

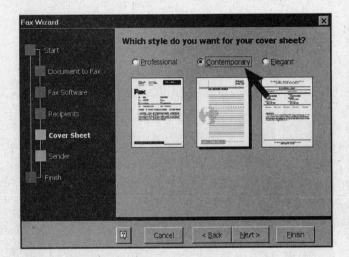

7 The next dialog box prompts you to pick a cover page design. Select the desired cover page, and click **Next**.

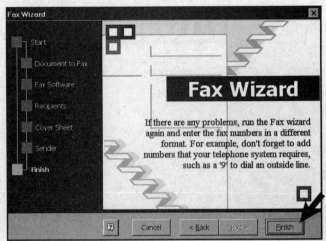

9 The Fax Wizard explains some common problems you may encounter when sending a fax. Click **Finish**.

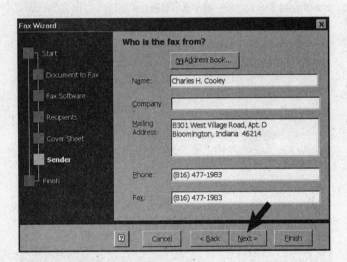

8 You are asked to enter information that the recipient will need to contact you. Type your name, mailing address, phone number, and fax number in the text boxes, and click **Next**.

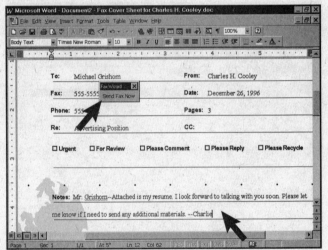

10 The Fax Wizard creates the cover sheet and displays it in Word, so you can add to it. Type any additional entries, and add a message, explaining that you have attached your resume. Click the **Send Fax Now** button in the Fax Wizard toolbar.

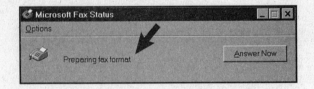

11 Microsoft Fax, or whatever fax program you use, transforms the cover sheet and resume into a faxable form, and uses your fax modem to dial the recipient's fax number and transmit the fax.

Create an Electronic Resume in PowerPoint

You've probably seen them on the news—electronic dating services that offer CD-ROM previews of potential mates. You can search for a person by hobbies, interests, education, and annual income, and then pull up a video clip of the person to see what he or she looks like on a good day.

What you rarely see on the news is that this same technology is being used in job searches. You can place your picture, work samples, music clips, video clips, a portion of your resume, letters of recommendation, and any other material on a disk and then send it off to companies in which you're interested, or place your resume on the Web. These electronic resumes are especially effective if you're looking for a job in the computer industry, advertising, marketing, graphics, or writing. An electronic resume shows not only that you have the basic qualifications for a particular position, but that you can use a computer to effectively present material.

The following project provides step-by-step instructions that can help you put together a basic PowerPoint resume.

Begin Do It Yourself   Fax Your Resume

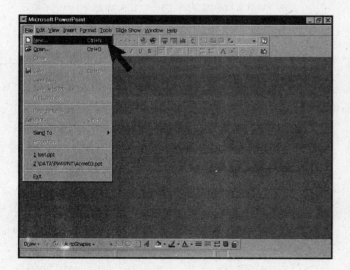

1 To create the electronic resume, we'll open PowerPoint's **File** menu and select **New**.

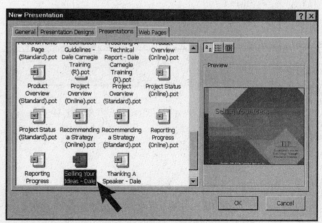

2 The New Presentation dialog box lets you select a design or sample presentation. Click the **Presentations** tab, and then click **Selling Your Ideas**.

(continues)

Begin Do It Yourself   Make a Multimedia Resume

(continued)

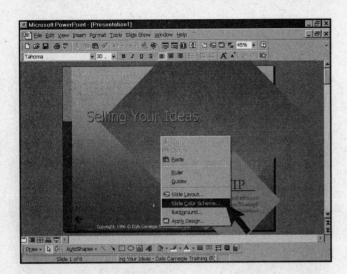

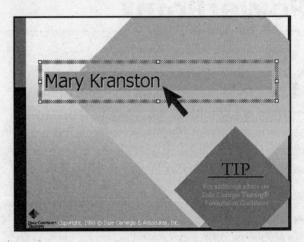

3 PowerPoint creates an eight-slide slide show. You can keep the slides dark, but I'm going to change the background, so it shows up better in this book. To change the background color, right-click the slide, and click **Slide Color Scheme**.

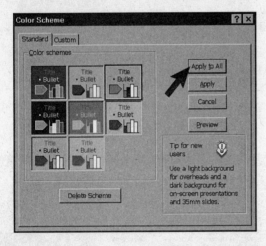

4 Click a color scheme, and then click the **Apply to All** button.

5 On slide 1, drag over **Selling Your Ideas**, and type your name.

6 Drag over **TIP**, and all the text below it, and type the name of the desired position. If the name is long, press **Enter** after the first line to place part of the name on a new line.

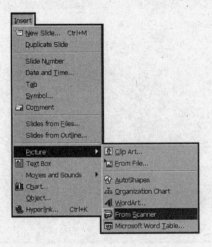

7 If you have a TWAIN compatible scanner, you can scan an image to place on your opening slide. Open the Insert menu, point to Picture, and click From Scanner. Follow the onscreen instructions to complete the operation.

Do It Yourself   Make a Multimedia Resume

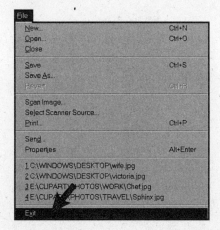

8 The image is scanned into Microsoft Photo Editor. Open Photo Editor's **File** menu, and choose **Exit**.

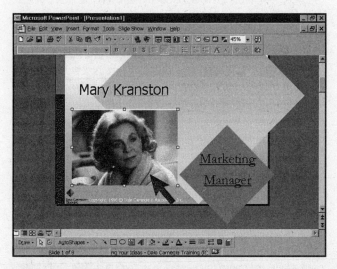

9 PowerPoint places the image on the slide. You can drag the image to move it, and drag any of the handles around the image to change its size.

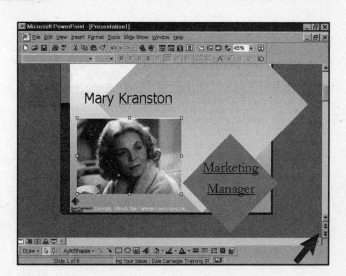

10 Once you've placed the image, there's probably not much room for anything else, so move on to slide 2. Click the **Next Slide** button.

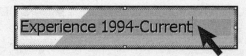

11 Remember, you started with a sales presentation, so you have to change the content. Drag over **Opening: Give Evidence**, and type **Experience** followed by the years you have held your current position (for example, **Experience 1994-Current**).

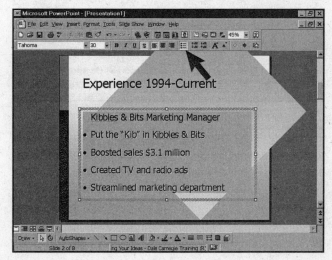

12 Delete all the text in the big text box below **Experience.** Click the **Bullets** button, and type a list of your job responsibilities and accomplishments at your current position. Press **Enter** after each item.

(continues)

Do It Yourself   Make a Multimedia Resume   *(continued)*

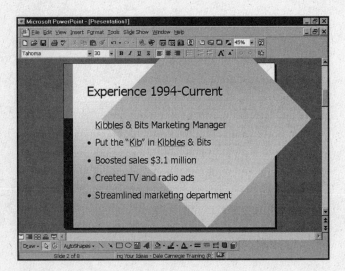

13 When you're done typing a list of accomplishments for your current position, click the **Next Slide** button to create a slide for your previous position.

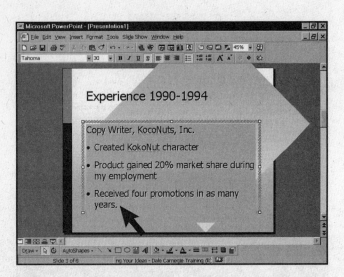

14 Continue creating slides to present all the information you would place on a paper resume, including education, training, awards, and professional organizations. (Don't worry about the order of the slides; you can rearrange slides later.)

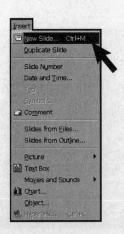

15 If you run out of slides, you can add slides anywhere inside the presentation. Use the **Next Slide** or **Previous Slide** button to display the slide after which you want the new slide inserted. Then, press **Ctrl+M** (or open the **Insert** menu and select **New Slide**).

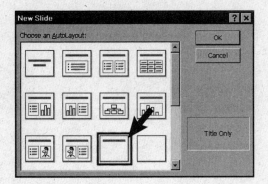

16 The New Slide dialog box appears, prompting you to pick an overall layout for the new slide. In this project, we will insert a video clip onto the new slide, so pick the **Title Only** slide layout to give the video clip plenty of room on the slide. Click **OK**.

17 The new slide appears, and displays text telling you to insert a slide title. Click the sample text, and type a title for this slide.

Do It Yourself   Make a Multimedia Resume

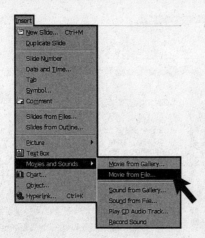

18 To insert the video clip (assuming you have a video clip on your hard drive or on CD-ROM), open the **Insert** menu, point to **Movies and Sounds,** and click **Movie from File**.

20 PowerPoint inserts the video clip, but it's too small to see. Drag one of the handles to make the video clip frame larger. You should make it as large as possible on the slide.

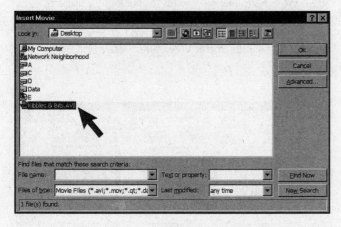

19 In the Insert Movie dialog box, change to the drive and folder that contains a video clip file. Then, click the name of the video clip file you want to insert. Click **OK**.

21 To make the video play automatically when this slide is displayed, right-click the video clip, and select **Custom Animation**.

(continues)

Do It Yourself Make a Multimedia Resume *(continued)*

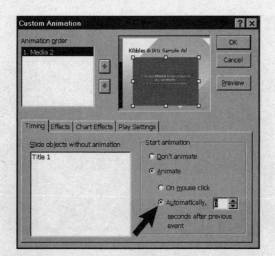

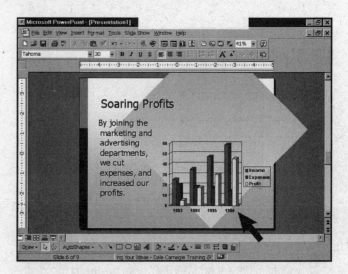

22 The Custom Animation dialog box lets you set several options for the clip. Click the **Timing** tab, click **Animate**, and click **Automatically** to have PowerPoint play the video clip automatically when this slide appears.

24 You can use the **Insert** menu to add sound clips, pictures, Excel charts, and other items to your slides. For example, here I pasted an Excel chart on a slide to illustrate how Mary Kranston helped boost profits at Kibbles & Bits. Now, let's sort the slides. Click the **Slide Sorter View** button located on the horizontal scroll bar.

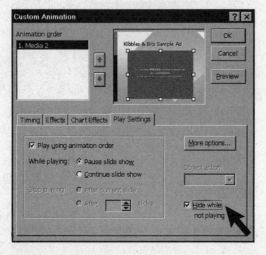

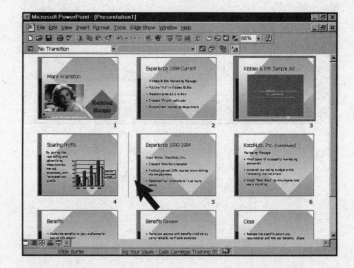

23 To hide the video clip while it isn't playing, click the **Play Settings** tab, and click **Hide while not playing** option. Click **OK**.

25 In Slide Sorter View, drag the slides around to place them in the desired sequence. As you drag a slide, a line appears to show where the slide will appear.

Do It Yourself Make a Multimedia Resume

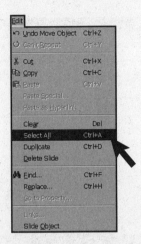

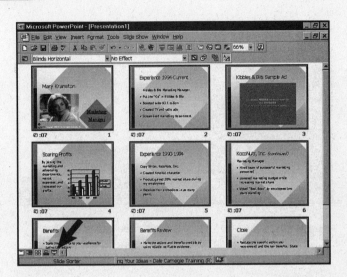

26 Once the slides are in order, add an animated build, so the slides will advance automatically. First, select all the slides. Open the **Edit** menu and choose **Select All**.

29 To preview your slide show, click the **Slide Show** button below the slide sorter area, and then sit back and watch. Make sure you have enough time to read all the text on each slide. If you don't have enough time, you may have to increase the transition time for that slide.

27 Right-click one of the slides, and click **Slide Transition**.

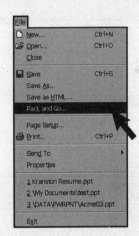

28 Use the Slide Transition dialog box to control the slide show. Here, I set the effect to Blinds Horizontal, at medium speed, using an automatic transition that changes the slides every seven seconds. I also added a camera sound that plays as the next slide comes up. Click **OK**.

30 Once your resume is perfect, you can place it on a floppy disk, so you can send it off. PowerPoint can package your resume with a viewer, so someone who doesn't have PowerPoint can still view it. Make sure you have three or four blank formatted floppy disks on hand. Then, open the **File** menu and select **Pack and Go**.

(continues)

Do It Yourself Make a Multimedia Resume *(continued)*

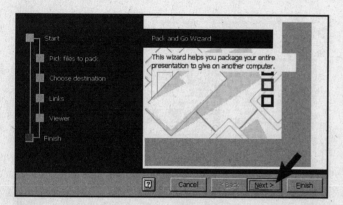

 31 The Pack and Go Wizard appears. Follow the on-screen instructions to complete the operation. (It may take more than one disk to store your resume.)

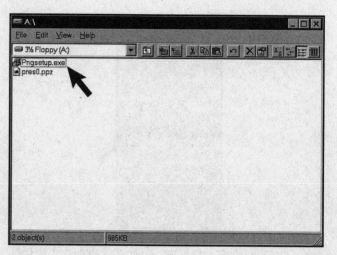

32 Once you store your resume on floppy disk(s), test it. Insert the first floppy disk into your floppy drive, use My Computer to activate the drive that contains the disk, and then double-click the **Setup** icon. Follow the on-screen instructions to play your resume.

Find a Job on the World Wide Web

After you have constructed the perfect resume, whether on paper or in an electronic form, you usually face a new challenge—finding someone to send it to. You can try the standard job search techniques: networking through friends and relatives, searching the want ads in the Sunday newspaper, and looking for businesses in the Yellow Pages.

All these approaches are useful, but if you have an Internet connection, you can use it to uncover additional positions that are not advertised through the standard channels. Many companies have Web sites on which they publish current job openings and contact information. You can find several job banks on the Web that are devoted to helping employers find qualified personnel for their businesses. You can even find places where you can post your own electronic resume.

The following Guided Tour helps you locate job banks and other employment services on the Web, and then use them to find some job leads, post your resume,

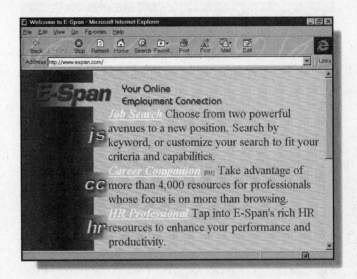

and gather contact information. The Guided Tour assumes that you have installed Internet Explorer and that you know how to navigate the World Wide Web. For details on installing and using Internet Explorer, see "Install Internet Explorer 3.0," on page 386.

Begin Do It Yourself   Find Employment Services and Job Banks

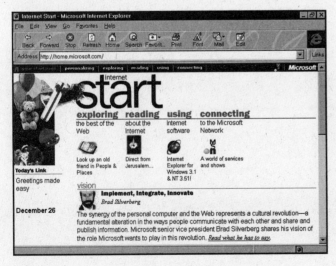

(1) Connect to the Internet, and run Internet Explorer.

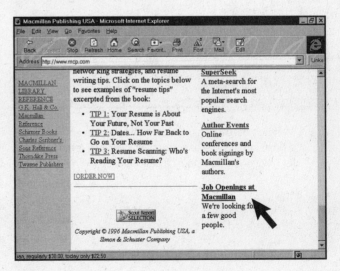

(2) If you know of a company where you would like to work, connect to its Web page, and look for a link that points to jobs. Here, we visit Macmillan Publishing's home page, which has a **Job Openings at Macmillan** link at the bottom of the page.

(continues)

Do It Yourself   Find Employment Services and Job Banks   (continued)

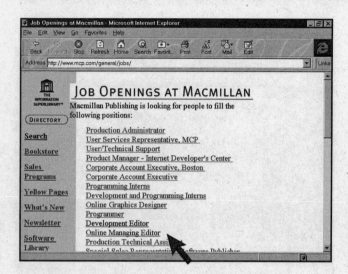

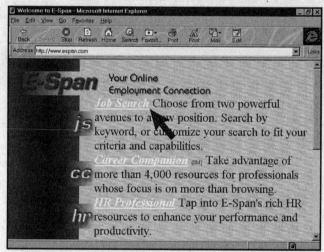

5 If you have no specific company in mind, check out E-Span's Online Employment Connection page. Type **http://www.espan.com** in the Address text box, and press **Enter**.

3 Clicking the **Job Openings** link displays a list of current job openings. You can click a link for information about a specific job.

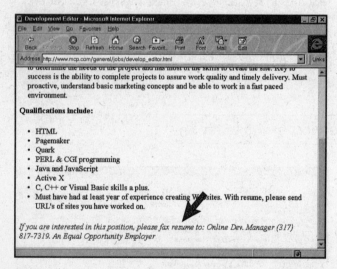

6 Click the **Job Search** link to search for a specific position, for jobs in a particular city, or for the job listings of a specific company.

4 Many job descriptions include information on how to submit your resume or contact the individual responsible for hiring the person to fill that position.

Do It Yourself Find Employment Services and Job Banks

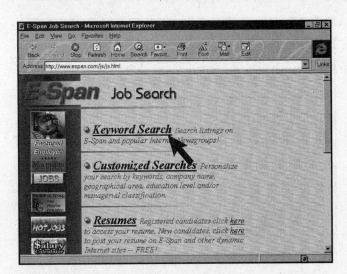

7 E-Span allows you to do a simple, keyword search or a more complex, custom search. Click the **Keyword Search** link.

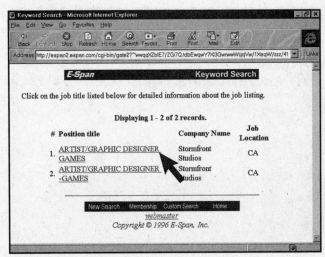

9 E-Span displays a list of all job postings that match your search instructions. Click a link for details about the job opening.

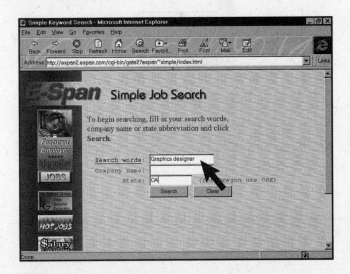

8 A simple online form appears. Click inside the **Search words** text box, and type the name of the position you want to search for. You can type a company name and the name of a state to narrow the search, but these entries are optional. Click the **Search** button.

10 Use the **Back** button to go back to E-Span's Job Search page, and then click the **Resumes** link.

(continues)

> **Do It Yourself** Find Employment Services and Job Banks *(continued)*

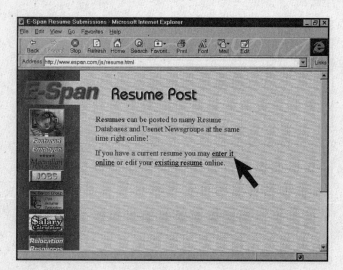

11 The Resume Post page explains that you can post your resume electronically. Click the **enter it online** link.

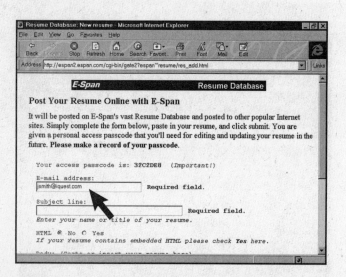

12 A simple form appears, prompting you to submit your resume. Be sure to write down the access passcode that's displayed so you can edit your resume later. Type your e-mail address in the **E-mail address** text box.

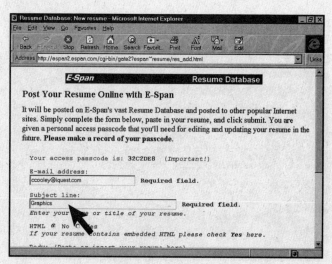

13 Click inside the **Subject line** text box, and type your name and the position you are seeking.

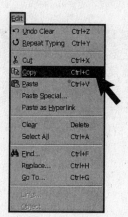

14 Open your resume in Word, highlight the entire resume, and then open the **Edit** menu and select **Copy**.

Do It Yourself   Find Employment Services and Job Banks

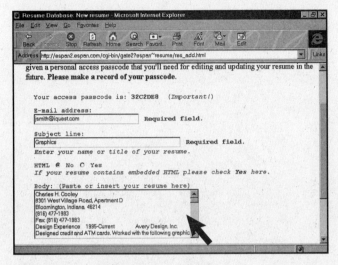

15 Switch back to Internet Explorer, click inside the **Body** text box, and press **Ctrl+V**. This inserts the copied resume into the text box as plain text.

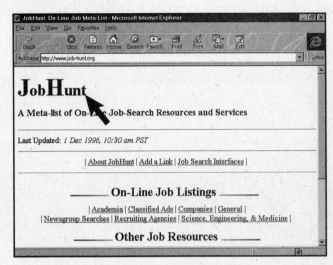

17 Job Hunt has lists of links to job banks, resume sites, and commercial employment agencies. You can find JobHunt at **http://www.job-hunt.org/**.

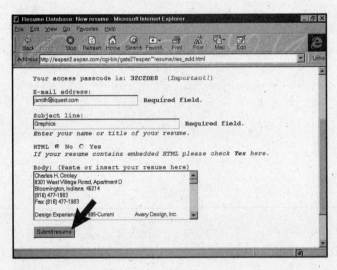

16 Click the **Submit resume** button. Your resume is now posted on E-Span's database.

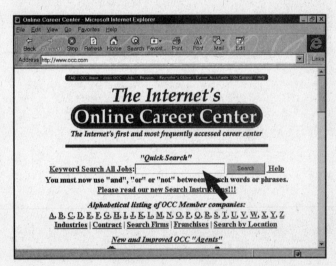

18 Visit the Online Career Center at **http://www.occ.com**. Here, you can search for jobs and find links to various other career help centers on the Internet.

When you're done exploring the sites in this Guided Tour, you can look for other job sites using any of several Web search tools. Go to Yahoo! at **http://www.yahoo.com** and search for jobs or career. You'll find more sites than you can visit in a single day!

DO IT YOURSELF

On the Job with Microsoft Office

Although Microsoft Office is handy around the house, it is designed especially for the high-powered environment of a corporation or business. With the Office applications and a little ingenuity, you can create the documents you need to correspond with customers and colleagues, publish your own news releases, write reports, manage and analyze data, and perform all of your other business-related tasks.

This section shows you how to use the various Office 97 applications and templates in a business setting. Here, you will find ideas for promoting your business with brochures, corresponding with colleagues by sending memos, keeping your customers informed with newsletters, and much more.

What You Will Find in This Section

Compose a Newsletter

Newsletters are great tools for keeping customers and employees informed and providing them with a sense that you care about their needs. If you own a small business, you can send newsletters to customers and prospective customers to let them know about new products (or new uses for old products), to notify them of upcoming sales, and to provide general information about your company.

Many corporations also create internal newsletters to inform their employees of benefit issues, company parties and picnics, promotions, and newly hired employees. These newsletters help generate a sense of camaraderie and show the employees that the company is sensitive to the needs of the employees.

You have probably received newsletters in the mail. They commonly have a headline (sort of like on a newspaper), and the text is arranged in columns. Some newsletters contain graphics. In this project, you will learn how to use the Columns feature in Word to create your own newsletter. In addition, you'll gain a little practice with fonts and type sizes.

The steps in this project show how to create a custom newsletter from scratch. Another way to create a newsletter is to use Word's Newsletter Wizard. Open the **File** menu and select **New**. In the New dialog box, click the **Publications** tab, and then double-click the **Newsletter Wizard** to start it.

Although the columns feature seems ideal for setting up newsletter columns, if you are working on a newsletter consisting of several pages, you might want to use text boxes instead. With text boxes, you can flow text from a text box on one page to a text box several pages later by linking the two text boxes.

Add a Graphic to Your Newsletter

You can really jazz up your newsletter by adding graphics or pictures to make it appear more professional. You can insert clip art included with Microsoft Office (these steps explain how) or insert your own graphics by using the **Insert, Picture, From File** command and then selecting the file. Here are the steps on how to insert a graphic from the Microsoft Clip Gallery:

1. To insert a graphic or clip art into your newsletter, open the **Insert** menu, point to **Picture**, and click **Clip Art**. The Microsoft Clip Gallery appears.

2. Click the Clip Art category from which you want to choose an image. The Microsoft Clip Gallery displays all the graphics in the selected category.

You can add bullets and numbered lists and change indents, fonts, font sizes, styles, and more. Basically, add or change any formatting as you normally would in any Word document.

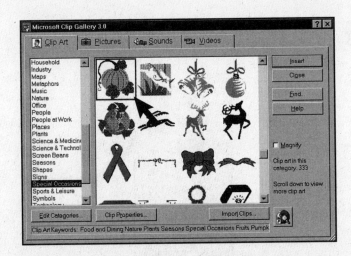

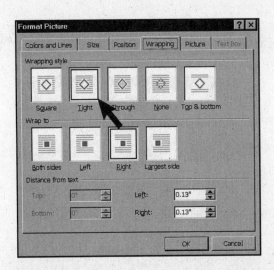

3. Scroll down the list of images, and click the desired image. Click the **Insert** button.

4. The image appears on the page, but usually not where you want it. Drag the image to the desired location.

5. If the graphic is not the size you want in the document, click the graphic (selection handles appear around the graphic). Drag one or all of the selection handles until the graphic is the size you want.

6. You can change the way the text wraps around the image, and change other properties of the image. Right-click the image, and select **Format Picture**. Enter any adjustments, and click **OK**.

Begin Do It Yourself   Put Together a Newsletter

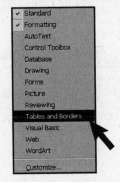

1 In Word, start with a blank document by clicking the **New** button. Right-click any toolbar, and click **Tables and Borders** to turn on the Tables and Borders toolbar.

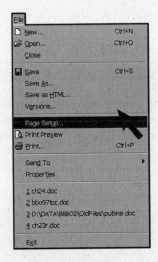

2 Set the page margins by opening the **File** menu and selecting the **Page Setup** command.

(continues)

Do It Yourself Put Together a Newsletter

(continued)

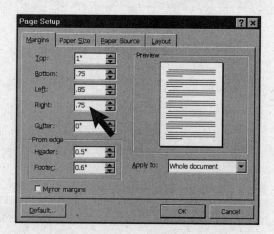

3 In the Page Setup Dialog box, click the **Margins** tab. Change the margin setting to Top: **1"**, Bottom: **.75"**, Left: **.85"**, and Right: **.75"**. Click **OK**.

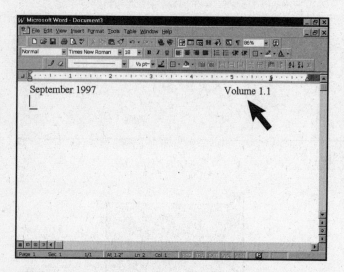

4 Set the Font to **Times New Roman** and the font size to **18** using the buttons on the Formatting toolbar. Then, type the date and volume number of the newsletter. Press **Enter** to move to the next line.

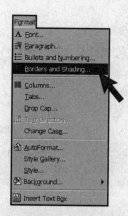

5 Select or highlight the line you just typed; open the **Format** menu and select **Borders and Shading**.

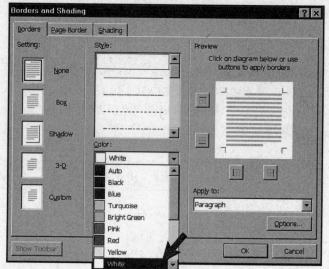

6 In the Paragraph Borders and Shading dialog box, click the **Borders** tab; click the **Color** drop-down list and click **White**.

Do It Yourself   Put Together a Newsletter

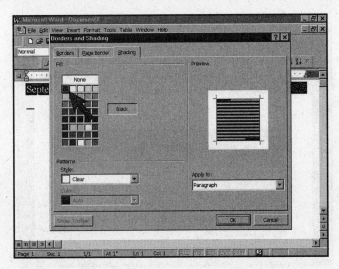

7 Click the **Shading** tab and click the black swatch under **Fill**. Click **OK**.

8 Move to the blank line after the date and volume and change the Font Size to **48**; type the title to your newsletter (in this case, **Legends Ledger**). Click the **Center** button on the toolbar to center the title and press **Enter** to move to the next line.

9 Select the title you just typed in and click the **Shading Color** drop-down list on the Tables and Borders toolbar. Click **Gray-15%**.

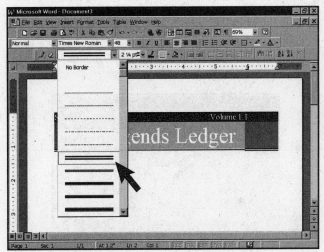

10 Let's add a double line below the title, using the Tables and Borders toolbar. Open the **Line Style** drop-down list, and select the double underline. Open the **Line Weight** drop-down list, and select **2 1/4 pt**. Open the **Border** drop-down list, and select **Bottom Border**.

11 Move to the blank line below the title, and press the **Enter** key two or three times to insert some space below the title. (If you do not insert this extra space, you'll have trouble setting up your columns in the next couple steps.)

(continues)

Do It Yourself   Put Together a Newsletter

(continued)

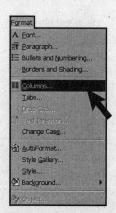

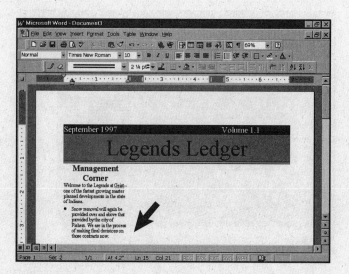

12 Press the up arrow key twice to move to the blank line below the title and click the **Font Size** button; set the font size to **10**. Then click the **Align Left** button on the toolbar. Now put your newsletter into three columns. Select the empty line you inserted, open the **Format** menu, and select **Columns**.

15 To enter the body text, click the **Font Size** button and select **10**; then click the **Align Left** button; then click the **Bold** button. Type your body text.

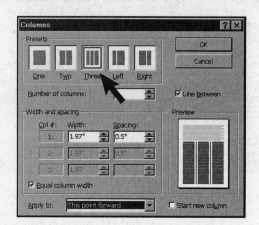

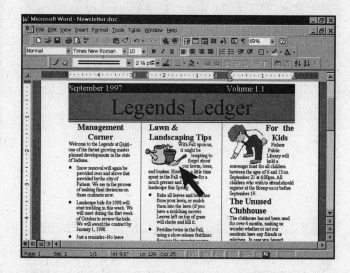

13 In the Columns dialog box, click **Three** under **Presets** and click the **Line Between** check box. Open the **Apply To** drop-down list, and click **This Point Forward**. Click **OK**.

14 The insertion point rests in the first column of the newsletter. To enter a heading, click the **Font Size** button on the toolbar and select **18**. Click the **Bold** button and then click the **Center** button. Type your first column heading, and press **Enter**.

16 To add a graphic to the newsletter, see the steps in the "Add a Graphic to Your Newsletter" task, page 482.

17 When you finish typing and formatting your text in the newsletter, you should save and print it. If you want to preview the newsletter before you print it, click the **Print Preview** button on the toolbar.

Create an Invoice

If you have your own business, you probably have to bill your customers before they'll pay you. Although handwriting an invoice is legal, it makes your company look like some fly-by-night operation. And pre-printed invoice forms may not be the perfect solution, either. The answer? Create your own, custom invoices in Excel!

The people at Microsoft were kind enough to provide an invoice template. All you have to do is adjust the invoice so it fits your needs, and then fill in the blanks. The steps in this task will walk you through creating a custom invoice for your own personal needs.

If you are not happy with the invoice template, you can create your own invoice from scratch and save it as a template. Use the **File, Save As** command, click the **Save as type** drop-down list and then **Template**. Then click **Save**.

If you are basically happy with the invoice template but want a few additions such as new text, a different term agreement, and so on, don't hesitate to add and delete elements from the existing template. Once you have made the changes, select the **File, Save As** command, click the **Save as type** drop-down list and

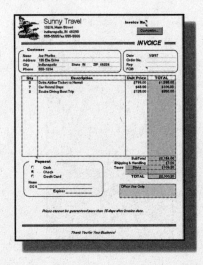

then **Template**. If you want to give a new name to your template, type the name in the File name text box and click **Save**. If you want to write over the existing template, simply click **Save**.

Once you have an invoice, you can print it and send it by standard mail, e-mail, or fax (if you have a fax modem). To fax or e-mail the invoice, open the **File** menu, point to **Send To**, and choose the appropriate command: **Mail Recipient** or **Fax Recipient**.

Begin Do It Yourself Create an Invoice

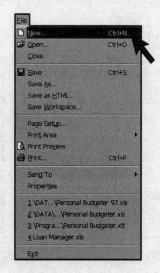

1 Open the **File** menu and select the **New** command. The New dialog box appears.

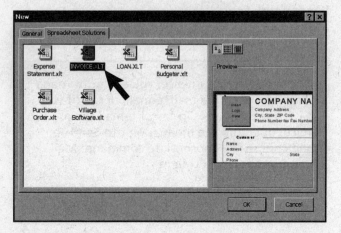

2 Click the **Spreadsheet Solutions** tab and then click the **Invoice** icon. Click **OK**.

Whenever you open a template which contains macros, such as the Invoice template, Office 97 displays a warning. If you think that your system may have been infected by a macro virus (if you share files with other people), you can click **Disable Macros** to prevent the macros from running. However, if you disable the macros, the template won't do everything it is designed to do. To load the macros, click **Enable Macros**. If you commonly share Office 97 documents, purchase a good anti-virus program, such as McAfee AntiVirus, and use it.

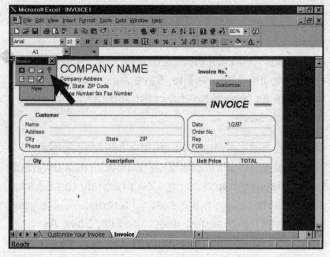

3 The Invoice template appears on-screen. You will also notice a new floating toolbar called **Invoice**. If the invoice is perfect for your needs, skip ahead to the steps titled "Fill in the Invoice."

To move the floating toolbar out of the way so you can see more of the screen in the steps, drag its title bar up over one of the other toolbars. When you release the mouse button, the toolbar will appear at the top of the window with the other toolbars.

Begin Do It Yourself   Customize the Invoice Template

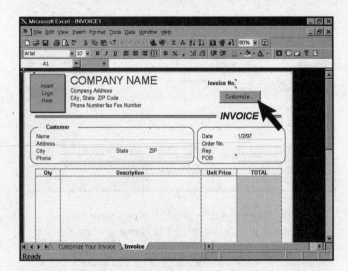

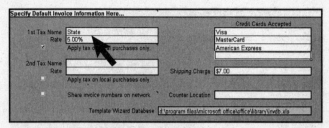

3 In the **Specify Default Invoice Information Here** area, enter pertinent information such as your state's tax rate, what credit cards you accept, and shipping charges. Select the check boxes that apply to your situation.

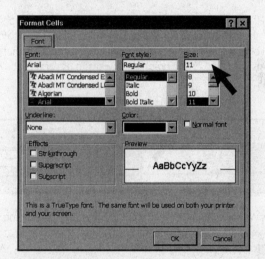

4 In the **Formatted Information** area, you will notice the company name shows the information you entered in step 2. If you want to change the font or font size, click the **Change Plate Font** button at the bottom of the invoice. The Format Cells dialog box appears. Make any changes in the dialog box you want and click **OK**.

(continues)

1 Before you begin typing information on the template, you need to make some custom changes, such as adding your company name. Click the **Customize** button in the top-right corner of the Invoice template.

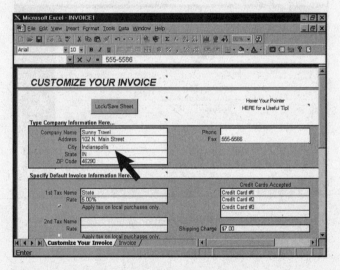

2 You'll see a screen that says **Customize Your Invoice**. In the **Type Company Information Here** area, type your company name and address in the text boxes.

Do It Yourself Customize the Invoice Template *(continued)*

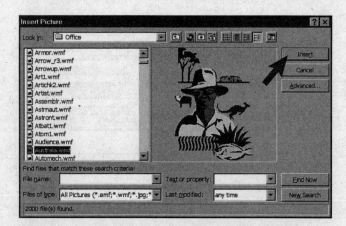

5 If you would like to add your company logo or a graphic to the invoice, click the **Select Logo** button at the bottom of the invoice. In the Insert Picture dialog box, select the file that contains your logo or the graphic you want to use and click **Insert**.

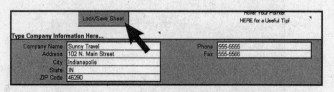

6 When you finish making the selections for customizing the invoice template, click the **Lock/Save Sheet** button at the top of the invoice.

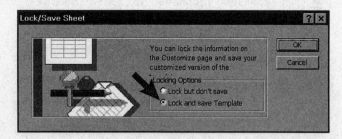

7 In the Lock/Save Sheet dialog box, click the **Lock and Save Template** option button and click **OK**.

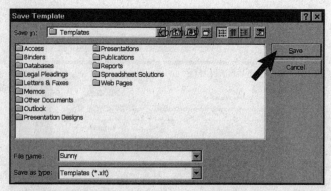

8 In the Save template dialog box, type a name for your customized template in the **File Name** text box and click **Save**. This doesn't overwrite the original invoice template. It creates another version of the template for you to use in the future.

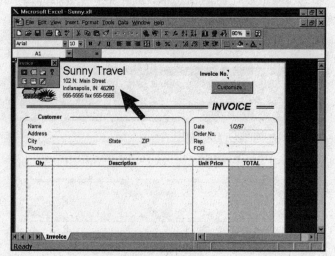

9 You'll notice that the information you entered when you customized the form, such as your company name and address, appears on the invoice.

Begin Do It Yourself Use the Customized Template to Create Your Invoice

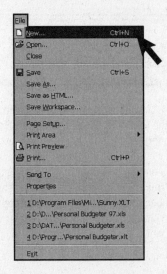

1 Open the **File** menu and click the **New** command.

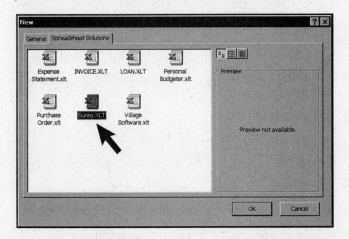

2 Click the template you saved in the previous set of steps; then click **OK**.

Any time you see a little red dot next to a cell, the cell includes a *comment* with helpful information on filling in the information. To see the comment, point at the red dot.

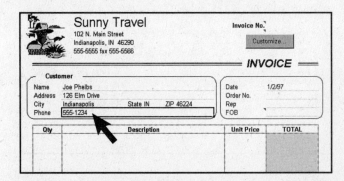

3 In the Customer area of the invoice, click the line you want to fill in and begin typing. Continue until you fill in all of the customer information.

4 To the right of the Customer area, Excel adds the current date (if you want to change it, click the field and type the new date). To fill in the remaining fields, click the field and begin typing.

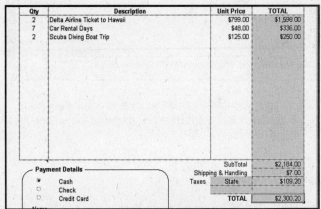

5 To fill in the body of the invoice, click the **Qty** field and enter your quantity per item. Enter a description of the item in the **Description** field and the individual price per unit in the **Unit** Price field. Excel automatically calculates the amount and places it in the **Total** field.

6 Continue entering your invoice information. Excel displays the grand total automatically at the bottom of the invoice after adding in the shipping charges and taxes.

(continues)

Do It Yourself Use the Customized Template to Create Your Invoice

(continued)

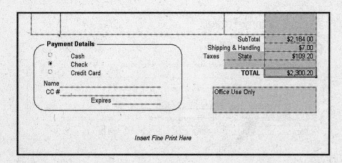

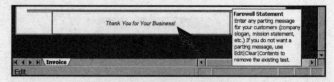

7 Fill in the **Payment Details** information areas as needed.

8 (Optional) In the **Office Use Only** area, fill in any information as necessary.

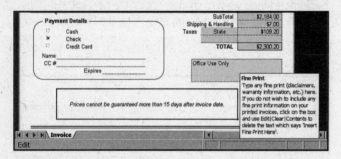

9 If you want special text on the invoice, double-click inside the **Insert Fine Print Here** box, drag over the existing text, and type your new text.

10 To add a closing statement to your invoice, double-click inside the **Insert Farewell Statement Here** box, drag over the existing text, and type the desired text.

11 To see a preview of your invoice as you create it, click the **Print Preview** button on the toolbar. When you finish your invoice remember to save the invoice as an Excel workbook with the **File Save** command as you normally would save a workbook. You can also print it or send it via fax or e-mail.

Put Together a Custom Purchase Order

If you do a lot of purchasing for your business, a purchase order is a necessity for staying organized. Using a purchase order is a clear and concise way to purchase items from a vendor. You give the vendor visual proof of what you are ordering, preventing the mistakes and misunderstandings which result from verbal orders.

Using a purchase order every time you purchase an item also allows you to assign a number to each purchase order. This provides an efficient way of tracking orders.

Microsoft Excel comes with a template for creating a professional looking purchase order. You are not limited to the existing template; you can customize it to meet your business needs, as explained in this project.

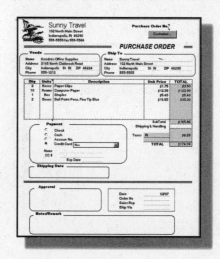

Begin Do It Yourself Create a Purchase Order Form

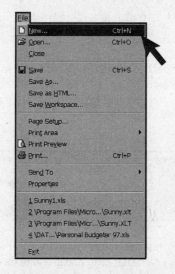

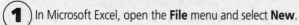

① In Microsoft Excel, open the **File** menu and select **New**.

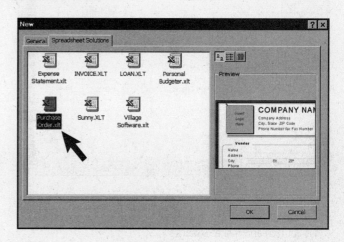

② Click the **Spreadsheet Solutions** tab, click the **Purchase Order** icon, and then click **OK**.

(continues)

Do It Yourself   Create a Purchase Order Form

(continued)

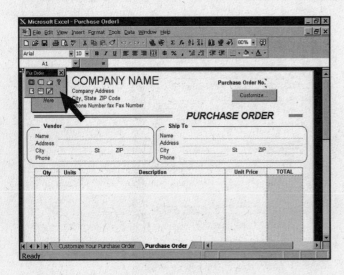

3 The Purchase Order template appears on-screen. You will also notice a new floating toolbar called **Pur Order**. You can use the purchase order as is, by filling in the necessary information. However, I suggest you customize the template first.

> Any time you see a little red dot next to a cell, the cell includes a *comment* with helpful information on filling in the information. To see the comment, rest the mouse pointer on the red dot.

Begin Do It Yourself   Customize the Purchase Order Template

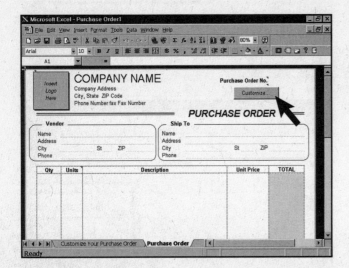

1 Before you begin filling in the information on the template, such as adding your company name, click the **Customize** button and makes changes.

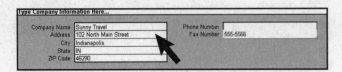

2 You'll see a screen that says **Customize Your Purchase Order**. In the **Type Company Information Here** area, type your company name and address in the text boxes.

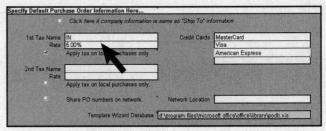

3 In the **Specify Default Purchase Order Information Here** area, enter the pertinent information such as your state's tax rate and your credit card number(s). Select the check boxes that apply to your situation.

4 In the **Formatted Information** area, you will notice the company name has been updated with the information you entered in step 2. If you want to change the font or font size, click the **Change Plate Font** button, at the bottom of the purchase order. The Format Cells dialog box appears. Make any changes in the dialog box you want and click **OK**.

Do It Yourself   Customize the Purchase Order Template

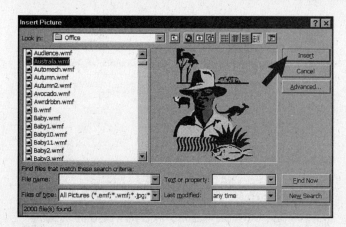

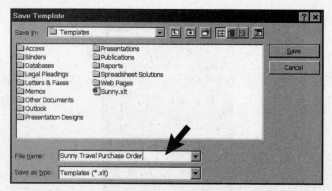

8 In the Save template dialog box, type a name for your customized template in the **File Name** text box and then click **Save**.

5 If you would like to add your company logo or a graphic to the purchase order, click the **Select Logo** button to the left of the Change Plate Font button. In the Insert Picture dialog box, select the file that contains your logo or the graphic you want to use and click **Insert**.

6 When you finish making the selections for customizing the purchase order template, click the **Lock/Save Sheet** button located at the top of the purchase order template.

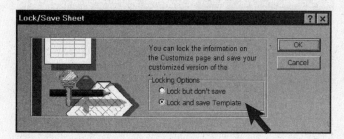

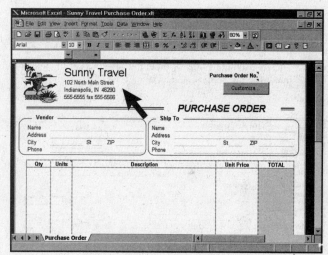

7 In the Lock/Save Sheet dialog box, click the **Lock and Save Template** option button and click **OK**.

9 You see the information on the purchase order that you entered when you customized the form. At this point, the Purchase Order dialog box is displayed, where the template has been saved. It instructs you to "Click **Close** from the **File** menu and then click **New**" to open the template so you can begin using it.

Begin Do It Yourself Use the Customized Template to Create Your Purchase Order

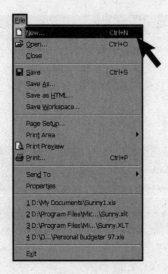

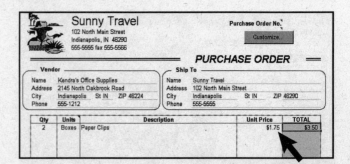

5 Click the **Qty** field and enter your quantity per item. In the **Units** field, enter the unit size as it applies to the unit price, such as a case, box, dozen, and so on. Enter a description of the item in the **Description** field, and the individual price per unit in the **Unit Price** field. Excel automatically calculates the amount and places it in the **Total** field.

1 Open the **File** menu and click the **New** command.

2 Click the template you saved in the previous set of steps; then click **OK**.

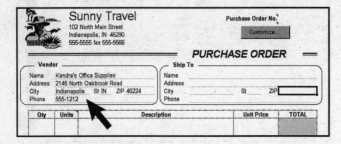

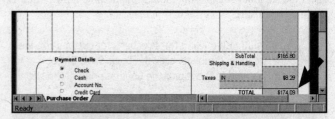

6 Continue entering your purchase order information. Excel displays the grand Total automatically at the bottom of the invoice after adding in the Shipping & Handling charges and Taxes.

3 In the **Vendor** area of the invoice, click the line you want to fill in and begin typing. Continue until you fill in all of the vendor information.

4 In the **Ship To** area, click the line you want to fill in and begin typing. Continue until you type in all of the Ship To information.

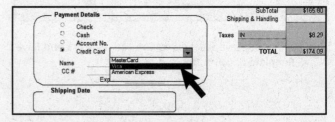

7 In the **Payment Details** information area, click the method of payment. If you select **Credit Card**, a drop-down list appears with the credit cards you entered when you customized the purchase order. Click a credit card and Excel adds the information about that card in the appropriate fields. Fill in all of the remaining fields as needed.

8 To see a preview of your purchase order as you create it, click the **Print Preview** button on the toolbar. When you finish your purchase order, remember to save it as an Excel workbook with the **File, Save** command as you normally would.

DO IT YOURSELF

Create Your Own Web Page

As we evolve into a paperless society, printing documents on paper is becoming passé. Companies, organizations, and even individuals are beginning to publish their documents electronically on the Web. In addition to making these documents available to a new market or audience, electronic publishing also allows people to create multimedia documents complete with text, pictures, sounds, animations, and interactive areas.

To join this revolution, you should consider publishing your own documents on the Web. Many Internet service providers offer a set amount of storage space for their members to use for publishing their Web pages. As long as you stay within the limits, your monthly connect fee will cover the cost of housing your publication.

The Office 97 applications all offer tools that enable you to create Web pages from scratch and quickly transform your existing documents into Web pages suitable for publication on the Web. This section shows you how to use these tools to create your own Web pages and place them on the Web.

What You Will Find in This Section

Make a Web Page in Word

The easiest way to make the transition from paper to electronic publishing is to use Word. With Word, you can create a Web page from scratch using the Web Page Wizard, or you can transform your existing Word documents into Web pages. The following *Project* shows you both techniques.

If you use the Web Page Wizard to create your document, the resulting document contains instructions on how to modify it and enter additional text. The Wizard formats the text specially for the Web and attaches a template containing the styles you need to format titles, headings, lists, and the other items that make up your Web page.

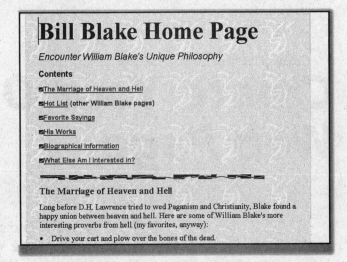

> The projects in this section assume that you have some knowledge of and experience with the World Wide Web. If you haven't yet dipped your toe in the Web, see "Use Office 97 on the Web," starting on page 385.

The Codes Behind a Web Page

All the pretty pages you encounter on the Web consist of nothing more than text and HTML (HyperText Markup Language) codes. The HTML codes provide basic instructions on how to display the text and insert pictures and other objects on a page. When your Web browser opens the page, it reads and interprets the codes, and then displays the page. For example, text coded like this `<b>This text appears bold</b>` appears like this: **This text appears bold.**

You can create your own Web page by typing a text document and typing the codes yourself, but the process is tedious and would require you to memorize many codes. By using Word's Web template, you can code your document using Word's formatting tools. When you make text bold, mark a heading, create a bulleted list, or insert a picture, Word inserts the correct HTML codes for you behind-the-scenes.

Although Word's Web page support helps you create HTML coded documents, you really should know the basics of HTML and how to edit the codes behind the page. These skills come in handy if you want to add advanced features to your Web page. For example, many Web search pages invite you to include their search tools on your Web page. They even provide you with the codes you need to do this. But you need to know how to edit HTML codes. An excellent HTML how-to document is available for free at **http:// www.ncsa.uiuc.edu/General/Internet/www/ HTML Primer.html**.

> If you want to learn how to use HTML codes, the best way is to view them in action. You can view a coded version of any Web page in Internet Explorer. First, open the page. Then, open Internet Explorer's **View** menu and select **Source**. Internet Explorer displays the coded text file in a separate window. If you are working on the document in Word, open the **View** menu and select **HTML Source**.

Work with Links

No Web page is complete without links to other Web pages. The page you create using the Web Page Wizard will have links to other sections in the same document, but these links do not point to other pages on the Web.

After you create your Web page, look for text that is blue and underlined to identify the links. To insert additional links, enter the **Insert, Links** command after creating the Web page. For detailed instructions on how to insert links, see "Insert Links to Other Documents and Web Sites," on page 503.

Begin Do It Yourself   Make a Web Page from Scratch

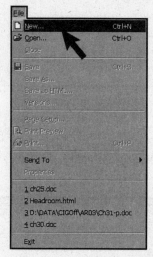

1 Use the Web page Wizard to create a Web page from scratch. To run the Web Page Wizard, open Word's **File** menu and select **New**.

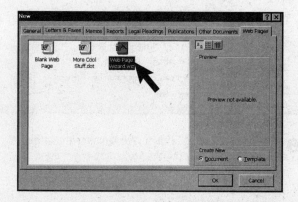

2 In the New dialog box, click the **Web Pages** tab and double-click **Web Page Wizard**.

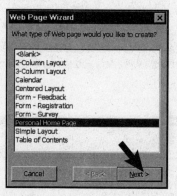

3 The Wizard creates a simple Web page and opens it in a new document window. In front of the page, the first Wizard dialog box pops up, asking you to specify the type of page you want to create: Survey, Calendar, Personal Home Page, Table of Contents, etc. Make your selection and click the **Next** button.

4 The second dialog box (there are only two) asks you to pick an overall design: Contemporary, Professional, Elegant, and so on. Pick the design you want.

(continues)

Do It Yourself Make a Web Page from Scratch *(continued)*

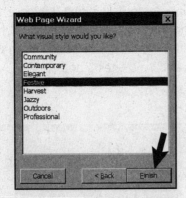

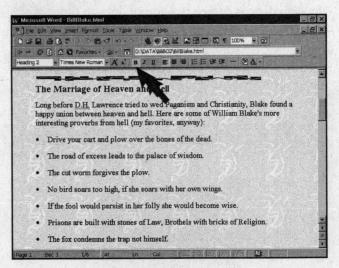

5 The Wizard applies the selected design immediately so you can see how it will affect your page. Click the **Finish** button.

7 Use the Word formatting tools that you have already mastered to format your text. You can make text bold, italic, or underlined; change fonts; create bulleted or numbered lists; change the text color; and even insert tables.

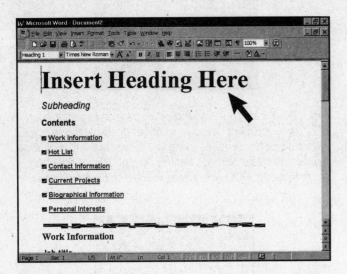

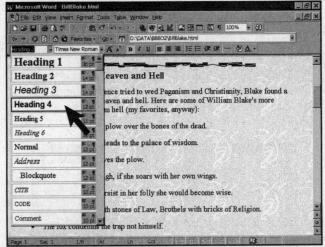

6 The Wizard disappears, leaving you with a fill-in-the-blanks Web page. To modify the page, follow the instructions on the page itself. For example, to add a title to the page, drag over **Insert Heading Here** and type the title.

8 The Web Wizard attaches a Web template that offers many styles. Check out the **Style** drop-down list in the formatting toolbar for heading styles.

Do It Yourself Make a Web Page from Scratch

9 Use the **Insert** menu to insert pictures, charts, video clips, audio clips, and horizontal lines.

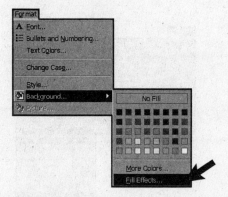

10 Use the **Format, Background** submenu to pick a background color for your Web page, if desired. (Be careful not to choose a color that is going to make the text difficult to read.)

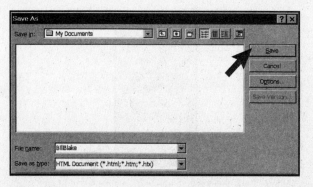

11 As always, you should save your work. Open the **File** menu, select **Save**, and use the Save As dialog box to name the file. By default, Word saves the file using the HTML extension, marking the file as a Web document.

> The Web page you created very likely contains graphics that the Web template inserted. In order to display the page properly, these graphic files must be placed on the Web along with the HTML coded file. It's a good idea to save the Web page into its own folder, so you will have all the files you need to copy to the Web in a single location.

Begin Do It Yourself Save a Word Document as a Web Page

1 If you have already created a document that you want to place on the Web, you can save it in HTML format. First open the document. Then, open the **File** menu and select **Save as HTML**.

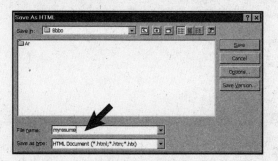

2 The Save As HTML dialog box appears. Type a new name for the file, using all lowercase characters and no spaces. Make sure **HTML Document (*.html;*.htm;*.htx)** is selected in the Save as Type drop-down list, and click **Save**. Word automatically adds the file name extension .html.

(continues)

Do It Yourself Save a Word Document as a Web Page *(continued)*

3 To see the codes that Word has added to your file, open the **View** menu and select **HTML Source**.

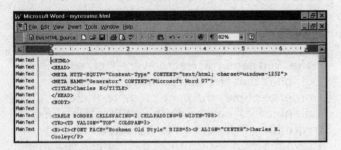

4 The coded document appears. Click **Exit HTML Source**. Word attempts to add the correct codes to the document, but you should check the formatting. Use any of Word's formatting tools to recode the document.

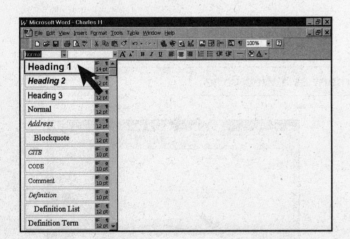

5 When you save a Word document as an HTML file, Word attaches the Web page template to it, making Web page styles available. Select the text you want to reformat, open the **Style** list (in the Formatting toolbar), and click the desired style.

6 You will probably want to add pictures and other objects to your page. Check out the options on the **Insert** menu to see what you can add.

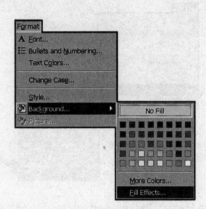

7 To change backgrounds, open the **Format** menu, point to **Background**, and select a desired background color. The **Fill Effects** option calls up a dialog box that lets you add a textured background to a page. When you are done fine-tuning your page, be sure to save it. Open the **File** menu, and select **Save**.

Insert Links to Other Documents and Web Sites

Assuming you used a template to create your Web page, your page probably already contains a few links to other sections of the Web page (or to other slides, if you're working with a PowerPoint presentation). However, you will probably want to insert additional links pointing to other pages on the Web or other documents at your Web site.

The Standard toolbar in all of the Office 97 applications has an Insert Hyperlink button that allows you to quickly insert links into your documents. The links might point to other Web pages, to other Office 97 documents, or to any files on your hard drive or network. You can use links to stitch your documents together even if you're not on the Internet! Whenever you click a link to a file, Windows opens the file in the associated application.

The procedure for inserting a link varies depending on whether you are linking to a different section of the same document or to a different file (on your hard drive, the network, or the Internet). When creating a link to an external file, you simply mark the link text and then specify the address or path of the file you are linking to. Creating an internal link is a two-step process; you must mark the link text, and then insert a *bookmark* where the link points to.The following *Project* shows you how to create both types of links.

Hera's Home Page

Your links to the hottest pages on the Web!

- Hollywood Online
- Kraynak's InKredible Links
- The Character Shop
- Kiplinger Online
- Time Magazine
- InfoSeek
- Games, Games, and More Games
- Wacky World of Finger Painting
- NBC
- FOX Network

You can have your Office application automatically transform Web page and e-mail addresses into links. Open the **Tools** menu and select **AutoCorrect**. Click the **AutoFormat As You Type** tab, and make sure there is a check mark next to **Internet and Network Paths with Hyperlinks**. Click **OK**. With this option on, whenever you type a page address, network path, or e-mail address (and press the spacebar), the Office application converts the text into a link.

Begin Do It Yourself Create a Link to an External File

1 Drag over the text or select the object that you want to use as the link. (This is the text or object a person will click.)

2 Click the **Insert Hyperlink** button in the Standard toolbar.

(continues)

Do It Yourself Create a Link to an External File *(continued)*

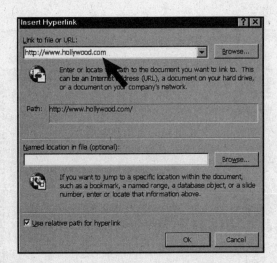

3 The Hyperlink dialog box appears, prompting you to specify the address of the page you want the link to point to. In the **Link to File or URL** text box, type the page's address. (If you are linking to a file on your hard drive or on the network, you can click the Browse button and select the file from a list.)

5 This dialog box prompts you to select the bookmark to which you want the link to point. Select the bookmark, and click **OK**. If the document contains no bookmarks, the list is empty. (See the next task to learn how to create bookmarks.)

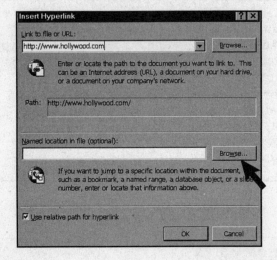

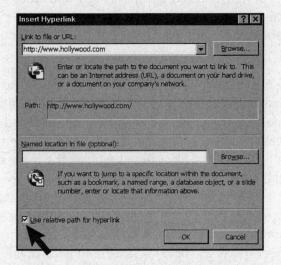

4 If you want to point to a specific location in the selected document or file (and you inserted a bookmark to mark it), click the **Browse** button next to **Named Location in File**.

6 Leave the **Use Relative Path for Hyperlink** option on, if you plan on keeping all the connected files in the same folder. If you are creating a link to a file in a specific folder, and you don't plan on moving that file, turn this option off. If you turn the option off, the entire path and name of the file are used as the link. Click **OK**.

Do It Yourself Create a Link to an External File

If you decide to remove the link from your page, highlight the link, click the **Insert Hyperlink** button, and click **Remove Link**.

7 The selected text is transformed into a link and appears blue (or whatever color you choose for displaying links) and underlined. (Because most users expect unvisited links to appear blue and visited links to appear red, think twice about changing the link colors.)

Begin Do It Yourself Use Bookmarks to Link Within the Same Document

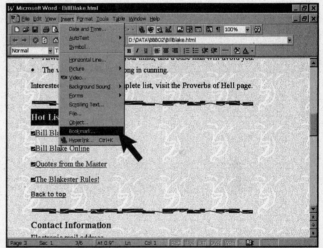

1 If you have a long document that uses several subheadings, you may want to include a table of contents at the beginning of the document that contains links to the various sections of the document.

2 Mark each section you want to link to using a bookmark. To do this, drag over the destination text, open the **Insert** menu, and select **Bookmark**.

(continues)

Do It Yourself Use Bookmarks to Link Within the Same Document   *(continued)*

3 The Bookmark dialog box appears. Type a name for the bookmark and click the **Add** button. The name is added to the list of bookmarks in this document.

4 You can now create a link that points to the bookmark. Drag over the text you want to use as the link and click the **Insert Hyperlink** button.

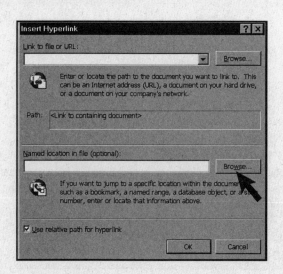

5 The Hyperlink dialog box appears. Click the **Browse** button next to **Named Location in File**.

6 The Bookmark dialog box appears, listing all the bookmarks in this document. Select the bookmark to which you want this link to point, and click **OK**. Click **OK** to create the link.

Place Your Web Document on the Web

You have created your own Web page, but it's not going to do you any good sitting on *your* computer. You need to place it on a Web server, where fellow Web surfers from all over the world can open it and experience your vision.

If you work for a company that has its own Web server, you can save your Web pages to the server. If you are not so fortunate, you can usually post a relatively small Web document on your Internet service provider's Web server. Most service providers and many of the major online services (America Online, CompuServe, and The Microsoft Network) allow members to post their personal pages in a special area on the service.

To post your page on your Internet service provider's Web server, call your service provider for details. The service provider will tell you what to name your file and in which directory you must save it. You will have to *upload* the file to the service provider's computer via FTP. To do this, you will need an FTP program (you can find one at **www.stroud.com**). The following *Project* shows you how to obtain and install a popular FTP program called WS-FTP and use it to upload your Web files.

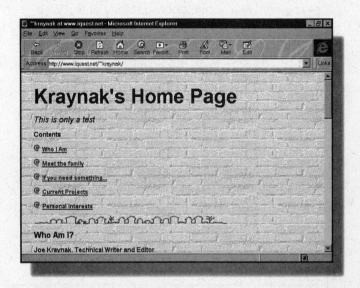

Test Your Page

Before you place your finished page on the Web, run a spell check, and read the page again, just as if you were creating a paper document. In addition, open your page in Internet Explorer, to make sure it looks okay. Click the links to see if they work; you might have to edit them. Make sure all the graphics are being inserted properly. Sometimes, the page might look fine in Word, but have problems in real life (on the Web).

Check the page again after placing it on the Web, especially if your page contains links to files and graphics on your hard drive. Sometimes, the links may work properly locally (on your hard drive), but when you transfer the files to a remote server, the links point to the wrong directories. Check your graphics and links again.

> FTP stands for *file transfer protocol*, a set of rules that govern the transfer of files on the Internet. Currently, Internet Explorer allows you to download files (copy them to your computer) using FTP, but does not allow you *upload* files (copy them from your computer to another computer on the Internet).

FTP with the File, Save As Command

If you create a simple Web page, containing no graphics, you can use the **File, Save As** command to upload your document to the Web. However, if the page contains any graphics, File, Save As does not copy them along with the page, and the page will appear incomplete when opened. Many of the Web page templates insert graphical bullets and separator lines and background textures, which are graphic files. If you want to keep the graphics on your page (you probably do), follow the steps in the *Project*.

If your page does not contain graphics, open the page in the Office application you used to create it. Open the **File** menu and select **Save As**. In the Save As dialog box, open the **Save In** drop-down list, and click **Add/Modify FTP Locations**. This opens a dialog box prompting you to enter the address of the FTP site, your username, and your password. Enter the requested information and click **OK**.

This returns you to the Save As dialog box, which now contains the address of the FTP site. Click the address and click **Open**. If you are not connected to the Internet, the Connect To dialog box appears; click **Connect**. Once you are connected, the Save As dialog box lists the directories (folders) on the remote computer. Change to the folder in which your service provider told you to save the Web page file, and then click the **Save** button.

If your Web page contains graphics, a warning dialog box appears, telling you that the graphics are not being sent to the remote computer but are being stored in the Windows\Temp folder.

Begin Do It Yourself Obtain and Use an FTP Program to Place Your Page on the Web

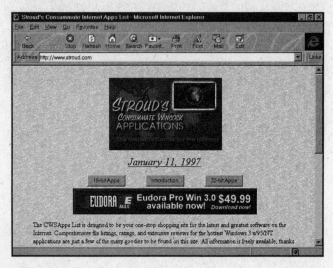

1 You can find a link to FTP programs at Stroud's. Connect to the Internet, run Internet Explorer, and go to Stroud's at **www.stroud.com**.

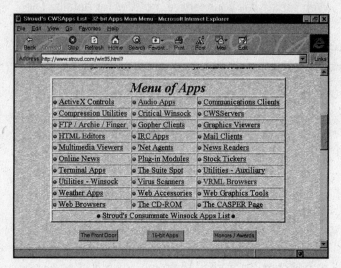

2 Click the **32-bit Apps** button, scroll down the page to the **Menu of Apps**, and click the **FTP** link, as shown here.

Do It Yourself Obtain and Use an FTP Program to Place Your Page on the Web

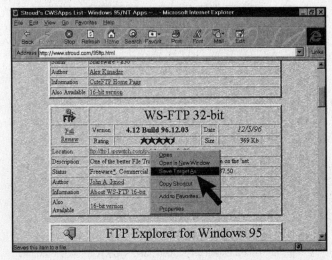

3 Scroll down to WS-FTP 32-bit. Right-click the **Location** link, and click **Save Target As**.

4 In a few seconds, the Save As dialog box appears. Use this dialog box to select the folder in which you want the WS-FTP installation file saved. You can simply save it to the Windows desktop, as shown here. Click **Save**.

5 Internet Explorer starts downloading the file, and displays a dialog box showing the progress. Wait until the operation is complete.

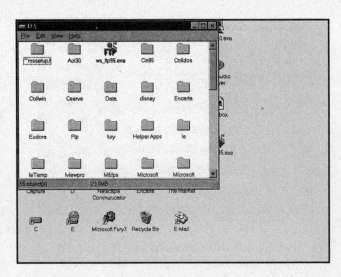

6 After you've copied the file, double-click its icon to run it. Read the license agreement, and then click **Accept**.

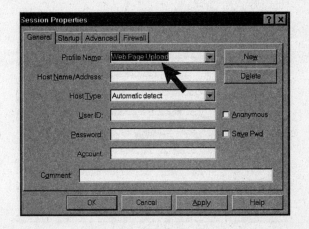

7 The Session Properties dialog box appears. You can type anything in the **Profile Name** text box. This just identifies a particular connection you are trying to establish.

(continues)

Do It Yourself Obtain and Use an FTP Program to Place Your Page on the Web *(continued)*

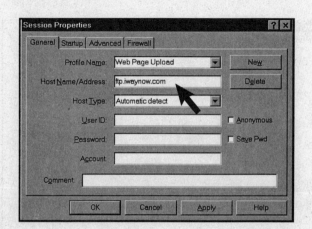

8 Click inside the **Host Name/Address** text box, and type the address of the FTP site to which you want to copy the files. Get this address from your Internet service provider. The address usually starts with ftp; for example, `ftp.serviceprovider.com`.

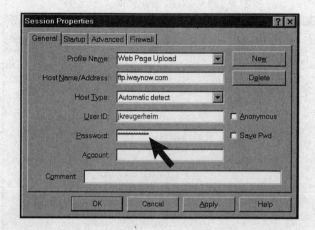

10 Most FTP sites require a password to upload files. Click inside the **Password** text box, and type your password. As you type, the password appears as a series of asterisks. You can click **Save Password**, if you want WS-FTP to remember the password for the next time. Click **OK**.

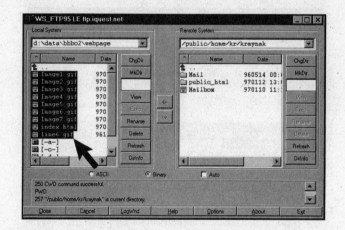

9 Leave **Host Type** set to **Automatic Detect**. Click inside the **User ID** text box, and type your username. (This is usually the same name you use in the Connect To dialog box to establish your Internet connection.)

11 WS-FTP connects you to the FTP site and displays the window shown above. Use the left pane to change to the folder in which your Web page and associated files are saved. Click a file to select it; Ctrl+click additional files to select them. (Make sure you select all the files that your Web page needs, including graphics.)

Do It Yourself   Obtain and Use an FTP Program to Place Your Page on the Web

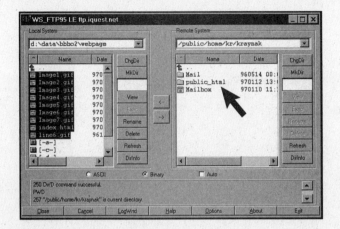

12 The right pane shows directories on the remote computer. Change to the directory in which your service provider told you to copy your Web files.

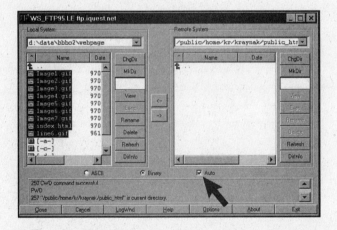

13 Click **Auto** to place a check mark next to the Auto option. This tells WS-FTP to automatically transfer text files as ASCII (plain) text, and transfer other files (such as graphics) as binary files.

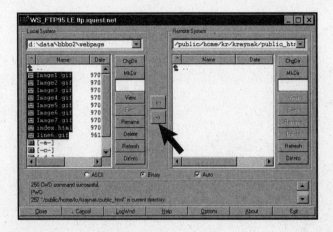

14 Click the arrow button that points toward the right pane to begin uploading files from your computer to the remote computer.

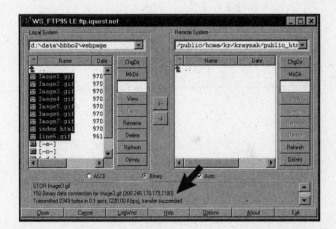

15 The bottom of the window shows the progress of the operation. When the files have been copied, click the **Close** button.

16 Your Web page is now on the Web. Your service provider should have given you some indication of the page address. Use Internet Explorer to visit the page, and make sure it looks and behaves as you intended it to.

Always check a Web page after placing it on the Web. Make sure all the links work, recheck your spelling, and make sure the background and text colors don't clash. Tell a friend to check the page for you and give you honest feedback. You can use WS-FTP to delete the files or replace them with new, updated versions.

PART 3

Quick Fixes

This is the section of the book that no one really wants to read. If you have turned here, it means you are having a problem. But don't despair. Here are some of the most common problems, along with their solutions. You won't have to fumble through the whole book saying, "I know I've seen the solution in here somewhere." The problems and solutions are here for easy reference.

To use this section, look for your problem in the Quick-Finder tables at the beginning of each problem type. If you can't find your particular problem, try looking in the Integration Problems, which covers problems that affect all of the Office programs. Once you find your problem in the table, turn to the Quick Fix to find the solution.

What You Will Find in This Part

Questions and Answers

Installation Problems

Halfway through installation, a message was displayed that said, "Installation did not complete successfully." What do I do now?

Any other application that is running can interfere with the installation. Make sure you close all other applications (especially virus checking software) and run the installation program again.

I got partway through installation and Office told me that I didn't have enough disk space.

Office can take up a lot of disk space. Typical installation needs 121 MB of disk space, and the Run From CD-ROM installation needs 60 MB.

One way to solve the problem is to create more disk space. Click the **Exit Setup** button and try to free up some disk space. Copy files that you no longer need to a floppy, and delete the files from your hard drive. You might even want to run the Drivespace program (Start/Programs/Accessories/System Tools/Drivespace) to increase the total amount of space on your disk. Then run Setup again.

If you were unable to free up enough space, you can install only some of the Office components by doing a Custom installation. Follow these steps to change the Setup options:

1. In the Setup program, at the screen where you choose between Typical, Custom, and Run From CD-ROM, choose **Custom**.

2. Deselect all the check boxes except for those for the Office programs you need the most. Remember, you can always add or remove options after you have installed Office. You can also highlight an option and click the Change Option button to uncheck individual components of an option.

3. Continue to uncheck options until the required disk space is less than the available disk space (you can see the totals at the bottom of the dialog box). Click the **Continue** button to finish the installation.

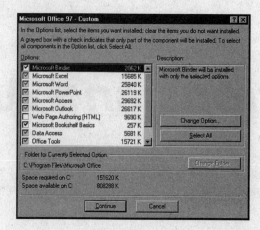

Setup told me I had enough disk space, but when it was almost finished, it told me it couldn't finish because there wasn't enough disk space.

You are probably using a disk compression program such as DriveSpace. When you use a disk compression program, the amount of hard drive space that Setup thinks you have is only an estimate of how much free disk space you actually have. Since DriveSpace doesn't know what kind of files you will be adding or how much they will be able to be compressed, the free space reported is only an educated guess. Even though Setup thought you had enough space, you really didn't.

During installation, Setup asked me to insert disk 2. I inserted disk 2 and it asked me again to insert disk 2.

This problem can be caused by two different things. Either you have bad disks or there is a problem with your floppy drive. We'll address the bad disk theory first. Exit the setup program by clicking the **Exit Setup** button and do the following:

> The following commands assume that your drive A: is the drive you are installing from. If you are using drive B:, substitute B for A in the commands.

1. From the **Start** menu in Windows, point to **Programs**, and click **MS-DOS Prompt**.

2. All of the disks except for disk 1 are in the DMF format. This format allows Microsoft to store more information on a floppy disk, but it keeps you from using standard copy commands on the disk. Therefore, you will have to use the EX-TRACT program to test the other disks. Create a temporary folder on your hard

drive to test the disks. You can call it OFFTEMP. Type the following to create the folder:

MD C:\OFFTEMP

3. Copy all files from the Setup disk to the temporary folder by typing:

Copy A:*.* C:\OFFTEMP

4. You now need to extract the Cabinet files from disk 2 to your temporary folder. Insert disk 2 in your A: drive and type the following:

A:FOR %1 IN (*.*) DO C:\OFFTEMP\EXTRACT /C A:\%1 C:\OFFTEMP\%1

If you cannot extract these files successfully, disk 2 is bad. Contact Microsoft for replacement disks.

> If disk 2 checked out okay and you would like to check the rest of your disks, you can check them using the same command as in step 4. Insert each disk in your A: drive and repeat step 4.
>
> If you don't have any problems extracting all of the disks, your disks are okay. You can delete the files from the OFFTEMP folder to free up disk space, and you can delete the OFFTEMP folder itself too.

If all of the disks checked out, there could be a problem with how your floppy drive is communicating with your computer. To alleviate the problem, you may be able to do the following:

1. From the **Start** menu, point to **Programs**, point to **Accessories**, and click **Notepad**. Use the **Open** command on the **File** menu to open **C:\CONFIG.SYS**. Scroll down to a blank line and add the following command:

   If your 1.44 MB floppy drive is drive A:

   DRIVPARM=/d:0 /f:7

   If your 1.44 MB floppy drive is drive B:

   DRIVPARM=/d:1 /f:7

2. Now, check your CONFIG.SYS file to make sure you do not have the following line:

   DEVICE=DRIVER.SYS

   If you do have this line in CONFIG.SYS, type **REM** in front of the line to disable it.

3. Restart your computer and run Setup again.

If setup still does not work properly, remove the statement you added in step 1 from the CONFIG.SYS file. If you typed **REM** in front of any lines in step 2, delete the **REM** that you added. Contact your computer manufacturer and tell it that change-line support is not functioning properly.

Windows 95 itself does not come with the DRIVPARM command but if you upgraded from Windows 3.1 and DOS, you still have the command on your system. If your PC came new with Windows 95, however, the preceding procedure may not work because you may not have DRIVPARM available.

Partway through installation I got the error message: Setup could not open FINDFAST.CPL: it is in use by another application.

You probably ran Setup from **Add/Remove Programs** in the Control Panel, or you had Control Panel open for another reason. Whatever the reason, having the Control Panel open is your problem. Click **Control Panel** on the taskbar to switch to Control Panel. Close Control Panel and switch back to Setup. Click the **Retry** button in the message box and Setup will continue.

I want to make backup copies of the installation disks but I keep getting an error.

Microsoft invented a way to store 1.7 megabytes of data on a 1.44 megabyte floppy drive. This saves Microsoft money because they don't have to distribute as many disks. Unfortunately, it also means that you cannot make backup copies of the disks. If it's any consolation, Microsoft will replace defective disks at no charge.

I have uninstalled Office, but the Microsoft Office folder is still on my hard disk.

When Office uninstalls, it removes only the files that it put there itself during installation. Office leaves any folders that contain files that it doesn't recognize. For example, if you created your own templates, the Templates folder will remain within the Microsoft Office folder, along with the templates you created. And of course, the Microsoft Office folder can't be removed if it still contains anything.

If you leave these folders on the hard disk, Office will use any custom settings that you changed in your application if you reinstall it. If you're sure that you won't be installing the program again, or if you don't care about any changes you've made to the setup, you can delete these folders.

Word Problems

I displayed a different paragraph on-screen by scrolling with the scroll bar, but when I started typing, the typed text showed up where I was before.

Simply moving the display to a different place does not move the insertion point (the flashing bold vertical line). You must scroll the screen to show where you want it and then click the left mouse button to move the insertion point. Now when you type, the text will go where you want it.

When I try to add text in the middle of a document, it types over the text that is already there.

Someone has set up your copy of Word to be in Overtype mode. You can tell because there's an OVR in the status bar. Some people prefer that editing mode. If you want to go back to Insert mode (the default), in which characters move over to make room for the new ones, follow these steps:

1. Select **Tools**, **Options**.

2. Click the **Edit** tab in the Options dialog box and uncheck the check box next to **Overtype Mode**.

3. Click **OK** to close the dialog box.

All the toolbars and menus are gone. The only thing on my screen is the document. How can I get them back?

You are in Full Screen mode. In this mode, all that is visible is your document, which can be handy if you just want to type or read what you have written. You can still use the menus if you remember the shortcut keys to bring them up. There is a floating toolbar near the bottom of the screen with only one button in it: Close Full Screen. Click that button to return to normal editing. By the way, if you ever want to try full screen mode again, select **View**, **Full Screen**.

I've set up Word to have two columns, but there is only one column on the page.

You are in Normal view. Normal view is the view you will use most of the time. You can see more of what you are typing and Word runs faster in Normal view. Unfortunately, you cannot see graphics characters, headers and footers, or columns in Normal view. Your columns will print correctly even though they do not appear on-screen. To view your columns, choose **View**, **Page Layout**, or click the Page Layout button in the lower-left corner of the screen.

When I type things, Word keeps changing them. What's going on?

Word is actually helping you out. This is the AutoCorrect feature. It automatically corrects common typing errors as you enter them. For example, if you type "teh," Word changes it to "the." Follow these steps to edit which mistakes Word automatically corrects:

1. Select **Tools**, **AutoCorrect**. The AutoCorrect dialog box appears.

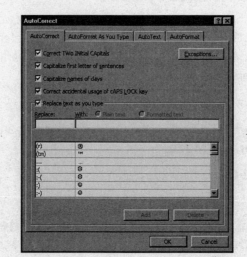

2. In the AutoCorrect dialog box, you can check the check boxes next to the following options to turn them on:

   - **Correct TWo INitial CApitals** Automatically changes the second letter to lowercase if you accidentally capitalize the first two letters of a word.

   - **Capitalize First Letter of Sentences** Automatically capitalizes the first letter of the first word when you begin a new sentence.

   - **Capitalize Names of Days** Automatically capitalizes the first letter of the names of the days.

   - **Correct Accidental Usage of cAPS LOCK Key** Automatically deactivates Caps Lock when you use it incorrectly. For example, if you have **Caps Lock** activated and you hold down the Shift key to capitalize the first letter of a word, Word knows that you really didn't mean to have Caps Lock activated, so it deactivates it for you and corrects the word you were typing.

   - **Replace Text as You Type** Turns on/off the main AutoCorrect feature—the list of words to correct.

3. If you have a word that you misspell frequently, enter the misspelled word in the **Replace** box.

4. In the **With** box, type the correct spelling of the word.

5. Click the **Add** button.

6. Repeat steps 3 through 5 to add more words if necessary. When you finish making changes, click **OK** to close the dialog box.

If you don't like the AutoCorrect feature at all, you can turn it off by clearing the **Replace Text as You Type** check box in the AutoCorrect dialog box. If there are certain AutoCorrect words that you don't want replaced, just select them from the list and click **Delete**.

I want to open a document I created in another program, but when I open it, there are a lot of funny characters on the screen.

Word did not convert your file correctly because it didn't have the right converter at its disposal. Not all of the converters are installed by default. Sometimes Word will tell you it can't open the document, but other times it will try to do so with imperfect results, causing the funny characters you see.

You can install the converter you need, along with a bunch of others by following these steps:

1. Close all open applications, including Word.

2. Locate your Microsoft Office CD or disks. You will need them for this procedure.

3. From the Control Panel, double-click the **Add/Remove Programs** icon.

4. Click the **Install/Uninstall** tab.

5. Click **Microsoft Office** from the list of programs and click the **Add/Remove** button.

If you are running the Microsoft Office Shortcut Bar, you can do the following instead of steps 3 through 5. Right-click the colored cube at the end and select **Add/ Remove Office Programs**. Then from the Office Setup and Uninstall dialog box that appears, click **Microsoft Office 97** and click **OK**.

6. Windows will prompt you to insert your Office 97 disk 1 or Office 97 CD (depending on how you installed it). Insert it into the appropriate drive and click **OK**.

7. When the Microsoft Office 97 dialog box opens, click the **Add/Remove** button.

8. Click **Converters and Filters**, and then click the **Change Option** button.

9. Click **Select All** to select all converters to install.

10. Click **OK** to return to the main screen, and then click **OK** again to install the converters.

11. A message box will pop up telling you when Office setup is complete. Click **OK** to close the message box.

The next time you try to open your document, it will be converted correctly.

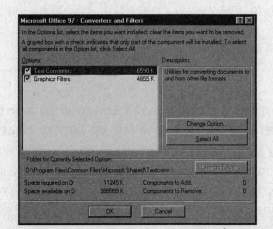

I am editing a document my coworker gave me, but every time I try to change something, Word puts a line through it and adds the new text in a different color.

Your coworker has turned on revision marks. This marks the changes that reviewers make in a special color so that the original author can see what changes have been made. The changes can later be accepted and merged into the document. When you delete text, instead of deleting it, it formats it as strikethrough (with a line drawn through it).

If you want to turn off the revision marks, follow these steps:

1. Select **Tools**, **Track Changes**, **Highlight Changes**. The Highlight Changes dialog box appears.

2. Deselect the **Track Changes While Editing** checkbox.

3. Click **OK** to close the dialog box. Future revisions you make to the document will not be marked.

To get rid of the revision marks already in the file, select **Tools**, **Track Changes**, **Accept or Reject Changes**. In the Accept or Reject Changes dialog box, click **Accept All**. Then click **Close**.

> If you turn revision marks on/off frequently, consider creating a toolbar button for the action. To do so, right-click any toolbar and select **Customize**. Click the **Commands** tab, and select **Tools** from the list. Then find the **Track Changes** entry on the Commands list and drag it up to a toolbar. When you close the dialog box, you will have a button on the toolbar that toggles revision mark tracking on and off.

I accidentally deleted a whole paragraph. Is there any way to get it back?

 Fortunately, Word has a wonderful command called Undo. You can select **Edit**, **Undo**, or click the **Undo** button on the toolbar, or press Ctrl+Z. If you did something else after you deleted the paragraph, you can keep selecting Undo until it brings the paragraph back.

I've added a bulleted list to my document. Now every time I press Enter it adds a new bullet.

 To turn off the Bullet attribute for the new line, just click the **Bullet** button in the Formatting toolbar to turn it off. When you want to create another bullet item, click the **Bullet** button again to turn that attribute back on.

If you just want more space between items on your bulleted list, select the paragraphs, then select **Format**, **Paragraph** and enter some spacing in the **After** text box. (For example, if you are using a 12-point font, you could enter **12** to create a blank line after each bullet item.)

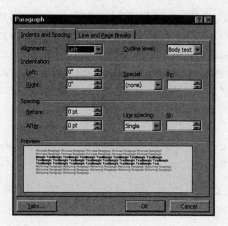

Word isn't using the right numbers for the numbered list.

There are two kinds of problems typical here. Either you want to start a new numbered list but Word insists on picking up at the number where the last list left off, or you want to pick up where the other one left off but Word insists on starting a new one.

Either way, you need to right-click the numbered list item and select Bullets and Numbering from the shortcut menu. The Bullets and Numbering dialog box appears. From there:

- If you want to restart numbering at 1, click the **Restart Numbering** button.
- If you want to continue the previous list's numbering, click the **Continue Previous List** button.

I'm entering text in a table, but it won't all fit. Can't the table automatically adjust to fit my text?

You need to change the row height of your table to Auto. This will allow the height of the row to grow large enough to fit the contents. Follow these steps to change the row height:

1. Highlight the row(s) of your table that you want to change. If you want to select the entire table, click the table and, with Num Lock off, press **ALT+5** on the numeric keypad.

2. Select **Table**, **Cell Height and Width**.

3. Click the **Row** tab, and select **Auto** from the drop-down list in the **Height of Row** box.

4. Click **OK** to close the dialog box.

I changed the paragraph alignment to justified. Now there are big gaps between the words.

When you use justified alignment, Word makes the left and right edges of your paragraph even with the left and right margins. The only way Word can do this is by adding space between words to spread them out. To avoid large gaps, you must use hyphenation. The easiest way to hyphenate is to let Word do it for you automatically. Follow these steps to turn on automatic hyphenation:

1. Select **Tools**, **Language**, **Hyphenation**.

2. In the Hyphenation dialog box, check the **Automatically Hyphenate Document** check box.

3. Click **OK** to close the dialog box. Word will go through your document and hyphenate words at the appropriate places.

While using the spelling checker I accidentally added a word to the custom dictionary that was spelled incorrectly. How can I change it?

You need to edit your custom dictionary to delete the incorrectly spelled word. The dictionary can be edited as a Word document. Follow these steps to open your custom dictionary:

1. Choose **Tools**, **Options**.

2. Click the **Spelling and Grammar** tab in the Options dialog box.

3. Click the **Dictionaries** button.

4. In the Custom Dictionaries dialog box, make sure there is a check mark next to the name of your custom dictionary (it is usually called CUSTOM.DIC) to check it. Then click the **Edit** button.

5. A message box will open telling you that Word will disable automatic spell checking when you edit the dictionary. Click **OK** to continue.

6. Your custom dictionary will open in Word. You will see a single column of words. Scroll through the dictionary until you find the word that you incorrectly added to the list. Highlight the word and press the Delete key to erase it. If there are other words that you do not want in the dictionary, go ahead and delete them too.

7. When you are finished editing the dictionary, choose **File**, **Close**. Word will ask you if you want to save the changes. Click **OK** to save the dictionary.

> You might get a message that the document contains formatting that cannot be saved in text format. If this happens, click the **Yes** button. Word will then tell you that your dictionary is a Text Only document. Click the **Text Only** button to save the dictionary in Text Only format.

8. Since automatic spell checking was disabled in step 4, you will need to manually turn it back on. Choose **Options** from the **Tools** menu. Click the **Spelling and Grammar** tab and check the check box next to **Check Spelling As You Type**. Click **OK** to close the Options dialog box.

I've looked up several meanings in the Thesaurus, and I can't remember what the original word was.

Click the drop-down box in the Looked Up section of the Thesaurus dialog box. The word you started with is always at the top of the list.

The last two lines of my paragraph are on the second page. How can I keep them all on the first page?

 If you have just a line or two on the last page of the document, there is an easy way to move those lines to the previous page. Select **File**, **Print Preview** and click the **Shrink to Fit** button in the toolbar. This will compress the lines on the previous page to allow all the lines to fit. It won't look right from full-page zoom, so click the Zoom feature to zoom in and make sure you are happy with the appearance of the shrunken lines. If you're not, select **Edit**, **Undo Shrink To Fit** to return your document to regular size.

There is a blank line below each paragraph, but Word won't let me delete them.

Word allows you to automatically add spacing before or after a paragraph. With this option you can separate your paragraphs without having to manually add a line each time you start a new paragraph. To set the spacing, follow these steps:

1. Highlight the paragraph(s) you want to set the spacing for.

2. Click the **Format**, **Paragraph**.

3. In the Paragraph dialog box, click the **Indents and Spacing** tab. In the Spacing section, you can either add space before or after the paragraph using the **Before** or **After** options. The spacing is given in point size. If you're using a 12-point font,

6 points would be half a line; 12 points would be a whole line. To eliminate the spacing, set these values to zero.

4. When you finish, click **OK** to close the dialog box.

> If you find this problem occurring in all your paragraphs, you may want to change the style definition. Click in the paragraph that you need to change the Style and choose **Format, Style**. Click the **Modify** button in the Style dialog box. In the Modify Style dialog box, click the **Format** button and click **Paragraph**. Adjust the spacing as described in step 3 above and click **OK**. Click **OK** again and click **Apply**. This will change the Style for all paragraphs that are based on the style.

I see dots between all my words and paragraph marks at the end my paragraphs. How can I get rid of them?

 You have inadvertently clicked the Show/Hide button on the toolbar. With this button activated, you see paragraph marks at the end of each paragraph and dots to indicate spaces, but these characters will not print with your document. If you don't want to look at them, simply click the **Show/Hide** button again.

I have changed to a larger font and can only see a part of the width of a page at a time. How can I see more of the page?

You can see more of the document by adjusting the Zoom control on the toolbar. If you want to see the entire width of the page, open the **Zoom** drop-down list on the toolbar and select **Page Width**. Or you can experiment with different percentages to get the size you like the most. Even though your type looks smaller on-screen, it will print full size.

After I move a table, I can't see enough of my document.

Sometimes, when you move a table, it shifts the viewpoint of the document past the left or right margins. This shows a column of blank space to the left or right of your text. To display the document correctly, click to the right of the horizontal scroll box; then move the scroll box all the way to the left.

When I tried to move one item in a numbered list, the text moved but the number didn't. How can I get them to move together?

 To move the number along with the text, you have to include the paragraph mark with the selection. To be sure that you have selected the paragraph mark, click the **Show/ Hide** button on the toolbar to make the paragraph marks visible. Select the paragraph mark along with your text, and the number or bullet will move with the text.

I changed the font at the beginning of the document, but it keeps changing back to the original font.

Word will revert to the default font for the template you used to create your document. One way to change the font throughout your document is to wait until you have typed the whole document and then select the entire document by pressing **Ctrl+A**. Then change the font. If you always want to use this font for the template your document is based on, follow these steps to change the default font:

1. Choose **Format**, **Font**.

2. Choose the desired font from the dialog box and click the **Default** button. A message box opens asking if you are sure you want to change the default font. Remember, this will change the default font in all new documents you create using this template. If you are sure you want to change the default font, click **Yes**.

I selected a block of text and my cursor changed to an arrow with a box around the tail. What's happening?

This is the *drag-and-drop* pointer. Drag-and-drop enables you to save time by not having to click the Cut and Paste buttons to move a block of text. To use drag-and-drop, follow these steps:

1. Select the block of text you want to move.

2. Click the text again and hold down the mouse button to bring up the drag-and-drop pointer.

3. Move the cursor to the point in the document where you want the beginning of the selected text to be moved to. Release the mouse button, and the block of text moves to the new location.

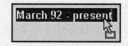

If you accidentally got the drag-and-drop cursor, immediately move the cursor into the selected text and click the mouse again. This will cancel your selection. If you don't use drag-and-drop, and this feature annoys you, you can turn it off. Choose **Tools**, **Options** and click the **Edit** tab. Uncheck the Drag-and-Drop Text Editing check box and click **OK**.

I want to add page numbers, but Page Numbers is gray in the Insert menu.

You are in Outline, Online Layout, or Master Document view. You cannot add page numbers in these views, so choose **Normal** or **Page Layout** view by clicking its button in the lower-left corner of the window or selecting a view from the View menu.

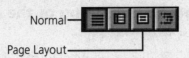

Normal
Page Layout

When I print a Word document, it numbers all the pages including page 1. How can I turn off the page numbering on page 1?

By default, when you add page numbers to a document, Word numbers all of the pages. In some documents, however, you may not want to number the first page. Fortunately, there is an easy way to suppress the page number on the first page. Follow these steps:

1. Choose **Insert**, **Page Numbers**.

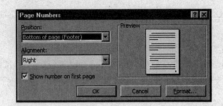

2. In the Page Numbers dialog box uncheck the **Show Number on First Page** check box.

3. Click **OK** to close the dialog box.

When I type in (c) or (r), Word changes it to © or ®.

AutoCorrect is changing the text for you. With this feature, you can easily insert the © or ® symbol. Unfortunately, it is very difficult to type a C or R in parentheses. If you need to use a C or R in parentheses in your document, follow these steps to tell AutoCorrect that you don't want to change those:

1. From the **Tools** menu, choose **AutoCorrect**.

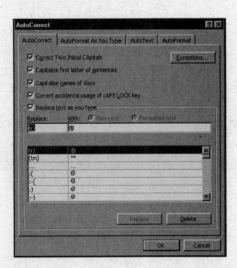

2. At the bottom of the AutoCorrect dialog box, select the (c) entry.

3. You now have two choices. You can completely delete the © shortcut, or you can define a different key sequence to type to make the © symbol appear.

   - To delete the © shortcut, click the **Delete** button.

   - To define a new sequence, type the new sequence (for example, **{C}**) in the **Replace** box and click the **Add** button. Now highlight the original **(c)** entry and click the **Delete** button.

4. Repeat for ® if you want to change that one too.

5. Click **OK** to close the dialog box.

I want to use a wizard, but when I try to open a new document, the wizard I want is not available.

Not all of the Wizards appear on the default tab in the New dialog box. If you don't see the one you want, try clicking the other tabs in the New dialog box to see if it's on one of those.

If you still can't find the wizard you are looking for, it may not have been installed when you installed Office. In a typical installation, not all of the wizards install. Follow these steps to install more wizards:

1. Close all of your open applications.

2. From the Control Panel, double-click the **Add/Remove Programs** icon. Then click the **Install/Uninstall** tab.

3. In the Add/Remove Programs Properties dialog box, click **Microsoft Office 97** and click the **Add/Remove** button.

4. Setup will prompt you to insert your Office for Windows 95 CD (or disk 1 if you installed from floppy). Insert the disk and click **OK**.

5. In the Setup dialog box, click the **Add/Remove** button.

6. Click **Microsoft Word** in the Options list and click the **Change Option** button.

7. Click **Wizards and Templates** and click the **Change Option** button again.

8. Scroll through the Options list and click the wizards you want to install, or click Select All to choose them all. Click **OK**.

9. Click **OK** to close the dialog box, and click the **Continue** button.

10. A message box will open telling you that Microsoft Office Setup was completed successfully. Click **OK** to close the message box.

Excel Problems

If I type a long name in Excel, the end of it cuts off when I type something in the next column.

The name is still there; you just can't see it all because the column is not wide enough to show the full name. The easiest way to change the column width is with your mouse. Follow these steps:

1. Move your cursor to the right side of the column heading (the gray-lettered area at the top of the column) until it turns into a vertical bar with arrows on each side.

2. Click-and-drag the edge of the column until it is the width you want. If you double-click the right side, the column width will change to fit the largest value you have in that column.

I set up a calculation to add the numbers in a column, but Excel displays #######.

The result of your calculation is too wide to fit in the cell. Change the column width using the technique in Quick Fix until it is wide enough to display the result.

If I type in 100000000 Excel displays 1E+08. How can I get it back to 100000000?

You need to format the cells to display the number in the way you prefer. Follow these steps to change the number format:

1. Highlight the range of cells you want to format.

2. From the **Format** menu, choose **Cells** and click the **Number** tab.

3. In the Format Cells dialog box, choose **Number** in the **Category** box. There is a sample at the top of the dialog box that shows you how your numbers will look with the selected format.

4. If you like, you can also use the 1000 separator to make your number look like 100,000,000. Just select the check box next to **Use 1000 Separator (,)**. You can also change the number of decimal places that are in the **Decimal Places** box.

5. Once you have the number looking like you want it, click **OK** to close the dialog box.

> After you finish, if the number looks like ########, your column width is too small. Use the technique in Quick Fix to change the column width.

I entered a function in a cell, but Excel displays #NAME?.

There are two things that could be causing this problem. First, make sure that you have spelled the function correctly. If it isn't misspelled, you may have used a range name that doesn't exist. To check, click the arrow toward the left edge of the formula bar to drop down a list of valid range names. If there are no names on the list, or the one you specified isn't there, you need to define the range you wanted to calculate. Follow these steps to define a range:

1. Highlight the range of cells you want to name.

2. Select **Insert**, **Name**, **Define**.

3. In the Define Name dialog box, type in a name for your range in the **Names in Workbook** box (make sure it's the same name that's in your function) and click **OK**. Your function will now work correctly.

The answer is not correct when I calculate a range of cells.

Some of the entries in the range may not have been entered correctly. Check each cell to ensure that the numbers are not stored as text. To do this, click the cell and look it up in the formula bar. If there is an apostrophe before your number, it is formatted as text. Excel won't use text in your calculations, so you need to remove the apostrophe to let Excel know you have a number in the cell.

The other possibility is that Calculation is set to manual. Try pressing F9 to recalculate.

I entered a calculation in a cell, but it displays the text of the calculation instead of the answer.

You have forgotten to put an equal sign before your formula. Excel needs this to let it know there is a formula in the cell. Edit the cell, insert the equal sign, and your calculation will work correctly.

When I entered a date in a cell, Excel changed it to a number.

Most of the time, when you enter a date in a cell, Excel is smart enough to know that it is a date. However, if you already have the cell formatted in something other than date format, Excel will change it to the format you have specified. Follow these steps to fix the problem:

1. Highlight the range of cells that contain the dates.

2. Select **Format**, **Cells** and click the **Number** tab.

3. In the Format Cells dialog box, select **Date** from the **Category** box and select the desired date format from the **Type** box.

4. Click **OK** to close the dialog box.

I am trying to enter 01214 (a ZIP Code) into my worksheet, but the first zero doesn't display, or it puts a comma in the number.

By default, Excel drops all leading zeros in your numbers. To display the leading zeros, you need to use the ZIP Code format for the range of cells that contains your ZIP Codes. Follow these steps to change the format:

1. Highlight the range of cells that contain the ZIP Codes.

2. Choose **Format**, **Cells** and click the **Number** tab.

3. In the Format Cells dialog box, select **Special** in the **Category** box.

4. In the **Type** box, select **Zip Code** or **Zip Code + 4** (depending on which one you are using).

5. Click **OK** to close the dialog box.

I changed some numbers in a column, but the total didn't change.

You probably have automatic calculation turned off; this is a useful way of speeding up your work if you have a very large worksheet because Excel can take a while to recalculate. To see the correct total press **F9**. Excel will recalculate the worksheet. If you want Excel to calculate automatically, follow these steps:

1. Choose **Tools**, **Options** and click the **Calculation** tab.

2. Choose **Automatic** from the Calculation section of the Options dialog box.

3. Click **OK** to close the dialog box.

There is a flashing vertical bar in one of the cells. What does it mean?

If you double-click a cell you can edit its contents right in the cell. This is a convenient way to edit because you don't have to keep moving to the formula bar when you are editing cells. The flashing bar is an insertion point, like in your word processor. It simply indicates you are in Edit mode and shows you where text you type will appear.

I want to sort my data, but Excel sorts the column headings too.

 There are two ways to fix this problem. The easiest way is to select the range of cells you want to sort (don't include the headings) and click the **Sort Ascending** or **Sort Descending** button.

Another way is to do the following:

1. Select the data to be sorted, including the headings.

2. Select **Data**, **Sort**.

3. In the **My List Has** section of the Sort dialog box, click **Header Row**.

4. Open the **Sort By** drop-down list and choose a column to sort by.

5. Click **OK** to close the dialog box and sort the data.

I inserted a page break, but I don't want it there anymore. How can I remove it?

This can be a little tricky because the Remove Page Break option doesn't even appear in the Insert menu until you select the correct cell. To select a horizontal page break, select a cell directly below the page break. To select a vertical page break, select a cell directly to the right of the page break. To remove the page break, choose **Remove Page Break** from the **Insert** menu.

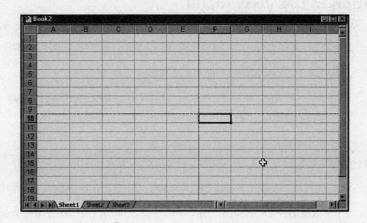

If you can't see page breaks on-screen, switch to Page Break Preview view (**View, Page Break Preview**). Or, if you prefer to see the page breaks in Normal view, select **Tools, Options,** and click the **View** tab. Then select the **Page Breaks** check box and click **OK.**

I entered a formula, and Excel displays the message: Error in formula.

Excel will try to help you by moving the cursor to the part of the formula that has the error. If you're not sure what the problem is, click the **Help** button in the error message dialog box. Excel will give you a list of common mistakes to look for, like having the wrong number of arguments in a function, invalid characters, missing operand (such as =2+3+), or an external reference without a workbook name (such as =!B2). These types of mistakes can be frustrating to find because they usually involve a simple typing error or a missing sign. If you get tired of looking at the formula, remove the equal sign at the beginning of the formula and press **Enter.** This will allow you to continue working and come back to the formula later. When you are ready to tackle the formula again, make sure you reenter the equal sign.

When I enter a formula, Excel displays the error message: Parentheses do not match.

Remember, when you use parentheses in a formula, they must equal out. That is, for every open parenthesis there must be a closed parenthesis. Carefully check your formula to be sure you have used the parentheses correctly. To have Excel help you find the missing parenthesis, click the left edge of the formula in the formula bar. Move the insertion point through the formula with the right arrow key. As you move through the formula, matching parentheses will bold. This may tip you off to where you need to add the missing parenthesis.

I want to create a report, but I can't find the Report Manager option in the View menu.

If the **Report Manager** option is not in the **View** menu, it means the Report Manager is not loaded with the Add-Ins. To load it, follow these steps:

1. Choose **Add-Ins** from the **Tools** menu.

2. In the Add-Ins dialog box, check the **Report Manager** check box in the **Add-Ins Available** box.

3. Click **OK** to close the dialog box.

The next time you select the **View** menu, the **Report Manager** option will be available.

If the **Report Manager** was not available in the **Add-Ins Available** box, it was not installed during your Office installation. Follow these steps to install the Report Manager:

1. Close all your open applications.

2. Select **Start**, **Settings**, **Control Panel**.

3. Double-click the **Add/Remove Programs** icon.

4. In the Add/Remove Programs Properties dialog box, click **Microsoft Office 97** and click the **Add/Remove** button.

5. Setup will prompt you to insert your Office for Windows 95 CD (or disk 1 if you installed from floppy). Insert the disk and click **OK**.

6. In the Setup dialog box, click the **Add/Remove** button.

7. Click **Microsoft Excel** in the **Options** box and click the **Change Option** button.

8. Click **Add-ins** in the **Options** box and click the **Change Option** button again.

9. Check the **Report Manager** check box and click **OK**.

10. Click **OK** to close the dialog box, and click the **Continue** button.

11. A message box opens telling you that Microsoft Office Setup was completed successfully. Click **OK** to close the message box.

I tried to center text across several columns, but the Merge and Center command did not work.

 The Merge and Center command will not work properly if the cells you are centering across (except for the cell with the data in it) are not empty. To be sure there is no data in the cells, select the seemingly empty cells and press the **Delete** key. The easiest way to merge cells and center across them is to highlight the range of cells you want to center across (including the cell with the data in it) and click the **Merge and Center** button in the toolbar.

PowerPoint Problems

I accidentally selected the wrong template in the wizard I used to create my presentation. How can I change it?

It's easy to change the design template in a presentation. Just follow these steps:

1. Choose **Format**, **Apply Design**.

2. In the Apply Design dialog box, choose the desired template from the list in the **Name** box. If you're not sure which one you want, click a template and you will see a preview of what it will look like.

3. Once you have chosen the correct template, click the **Apply** button.

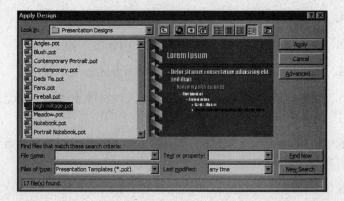

I accidentally deleted a slide from my presentation. How can I get it back?

Choose **Edit**, **Undo** to bring back the slide. If you've done a few things since you deleted the slide, keep selecting **Undo** until the slide comes back. Unfortunately, you will lose anything you have done after you deleted the slide.

When I add a long line of text to my slide, it goes off the edge of the slide.

You have entered your text as a label instead of in a text box. You did this by selecting the **Text** tool from the Drawing toolbar and clicking and releasing the mouse button somewhere on your slide. When you entered the text as a label, the text box expanded to fit whatever you were typing and did not wrap to the next line. If you would rather have the text wrap automatically, you need to create a text box. To do this, click the **Text** tool and click the mouse button at the upper-left corner of where you want the box to start. While holding the mouse button down, drag the box to the desired size. Now, the text you type will wrap when it gets to the edge of your text box.

I want to remove the bullets from my slide, but PowerPoint won't let me.

 To remove the bullets, select the lines beside the bullets you want to remove and click the **Bullet** button in the toolbar.

I added transitions in my slide presentation, but they are too fast to see.

The transition speed is set to Fast by default. You can change the speed to Slow or Medium if Fast is not effective. Follow these steps to change the transition speed:

1. Switch to Slide Sorter View by clicking the **Slide Sorter View** button in the lower-left corner of the window.

2. Select all the slides that have a fast transition.

3. Select **Slide Show**, **Slide Transition**.

4. In the Slide Transition dialog box select **Slow** or **Medium** in the **Speed** section.

5. Click **Apply** to Apply the changes to the selected slides, or click **Apply to All** to apply the changes to the entire presentation.

I have some hidden slides in my presentation. How can I show them?

Hidden slides can be very useful tools for presentations when you may need to show a little more data than you expected. When your presentation gets to the slide just before the hidden slide, click the right mouse button to bring up the menu. Point to **Go** and click **Hidden Slide**. If you'd rather use the keyboard just press the **H** key.

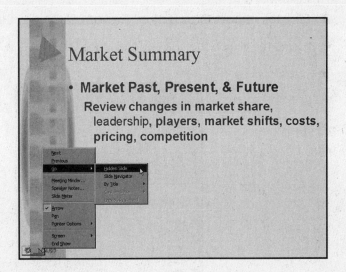

How can I bypass PowerPoint's starting dialog box when I start the program?

The PowerPoint dialog box that appears each time you start the program can be disabled by selecting **Tools**, **Options**. Click the **View** tab, and then deselect the **Startup Dialog** check box.

I installed some new clip art on my computer, but I can't find it in the Clip Gallery.

Whenever you install new clip art, you have to add it to the Clip Gallery. Follow these steps to add your new pictures:

1. Choose **Insert**, **Picture**, **Clip Art**.

2. If you see a message about additional clip art being available, click **OK**. The Clip Gallery appears.

3. Click the **Import Clips** button. The Add Clip Art to Clip Gallery dialog box appears.

4. Locate the clip on the disk and then click **OK**. The Clip Properties dialog box appears.

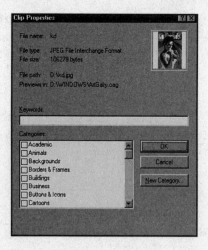

5. Fill in the Clip Properties by specifying keywords and to what category the clip belongs. Then click **OK**. The clip art is added.

You can also download clip art from Microsoft's Web site by clicking the globe button at the bottom corner of the Clip Gallery. When you add clip art in this way, it is automatically added to the Clip Gallery, in a category called Downloaded Clips.

I don't like the categories used to organize clip art.

You can create your own clip art categories in the Clip Gallery, and move clips freely between categories.

To create a new category, follow these steps:

1. In the Clip Gallery, click **Edit Categories**.

2. Click **New Category** to create a new category.

3. Type the name for the category.

4. Press **Enter** or click **OK**.

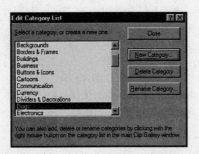

While you are editing categories, you can also rename existing categories or delete them. Click the **Rename Category** or **Delete Category** button to do so.

To change what category a clip appears in, follow these steps. Clips can appear in more than one category.

1. Select the piece of clip art that you want to recategorize.

2. Click **Clip Properties**.

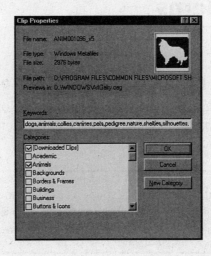

3. Click to place or remove check marks in the check boxes for the categories.

4. Change the keywords if you want. Separate each keyword with a comma.

5. Click **OK**.

I added ClipArt to my presentation, but it fills up the whole slide.

When you insert ClipArt on your slide, it is always the same size. It's pretty easy to change the size after you insert it. Just follow these steps:

1. Click the picture to bring up the sizing handles (sizing handles are the little squares that surround the picture).

2. Using the mouse, point to one of the sizing handles until the mouse pointer turns into a double-headed arrow. Click the left mouse button and drag the picture to the desired size. Use the corner sizing handles if you want the picture to change proportionally.

3. When you get the picture to the correct size, you may need to move it to a different location on the slide. Just click in the middle of the picture and drag the entire picture to the desired location.

I can't select some of the objects on my slide.

The objects you can't select are probably on the slide master. To select these objects, select **View**, **Master**, **Slide Master**, or hold the **Shift** key and click the **Slide View** button to the left of the horizontal scroll bar. You will now be able to change the objects in the slide master. To get back to your slides, choose **Slides** from the **View** menu or click the **Slide View** button. Remember, any changes you make to the slide master will affect all of the slides in your presentation.

Outlook Problems

How do I set up Outlook to check my e-mail?

When you first install Outlook, it gives you the option of choosing what online services it can manage the mail for. It sets them up automatically then, but if you want to add another service later, you must do it manually.

> Not all online services are supported by Outlook. In fact, most of the big-name ones, like America Online and Prodigy, aren't. However, you can use Outlook to check your e-mail from most dial-up Internet Service Providers (ISPs).

1. Select **Tools**, **Services** to open the Services dialog box.

2. Click the **Add** button to see a list of services you can set up.

3. If you do see the service you want (for example, Internet Mail), click it and then click **OK**. A dialog box appears asking for information about your connection to that service.

4. Fill in the information. If you don't know what to put in a field, contact your ISP for advice.

5. Click the **Connection** tab, and select **Connect Using the Network** or **Connect Using the Modem**, depending on which type of connection you have to your service. If you choose modem, choose which modem you want to use from the drop-down list.

6. Click **OK.** You see a message saying that the service will not be available until you log off and exit Outlook. Click **OK** to acknowledge this, and then **OK** again to close the Services dialog box.

7. Select **File**, **Exit and Log Off**. The next time you start Outlook, that service will be available.

Whenever I start Outlook, it automatically logs onto my online service to check my mail; I don't want this.

Outlook checks for new mail on all services by default. You can prevent it from checking a certain service automatically by following these steps:

1. Select **Tools**, **Options**, and click the **Email** tab.

2. In the **Check For New Mail On** list, remove the check mark beside the services you don't want Outlook to automatically check.

3. Click **OK**.

To check your mail manually, select **Tools**, **Check For New Mail On**. Select the services you want to check, and click **OK**.

I can't find an important address because I forgot the last name.

Outlook allows you to search for items (contacts, tasks, appointments, and so on) by any field, not just last name. To search for an item:

1. Select **Tools**, **Find Items**.

2. Select where you want to look from the **Look For** drop-down list (for example, Contacts).

3. Type any word you remember from the record in the **Search For the Word(s)** text box.

4. If you know what type of field that text is in, select it from the In drop-down list (for example, **Name Fields Only**). If you aren't sure, select **Frequently Used Text Fields**.

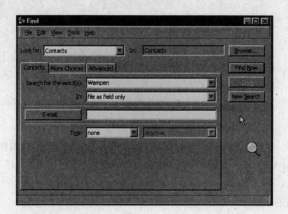

5. Click **Find Now** to see a list of records that match.

I don't want my calendar available to other users.

By default, Outlook publishes three months of your calendar on the server so that others can schedule meetings with you. If you don't let your calendar be shown, you limit Outlook's usefulness. However, if your calendar contains very sensitive information, the inability to schedule through Outlook may be of less importance than your information security.

To set Outlook so that your calendar is not published on the server, select **Tools**, **Options**. Click the **Calendar** tab, and click the **Advanced Scheduling** button. In the Publish text box, enter **0**. Then click **OK** twice to return to Outlook.

Miscellaneous Problems

I closed the Office Assistant window when I first started the program, and now I need help. How do I get the Office Assistant back and ask it a question?

The Office Assistant is a great feature. It starts automatically the first time you start an Office product, but after that you must ask for its help. To do so, click the **Office Assistant** button on the Standard toolbar, or press **F1**.

To ask the Office Assistant a question, just type your question and press **Enter**. The Office Assistant presents you with a list of topics to help narrow down the search; click one of them to view the information.

The toolbar is in a box in the middle of the screen. How can I get it back under the menu bar?

If you double-click the toolbar's title bar or drag it from its place at the top or bottom of the screen, it will turn into a toolbox (MenuBar). You can move the toolbox anywhere on the screen. Double-click the title bar of the toolbox to change it back into a toolbar. If you can't find the toolbar at all, right-click any toolbar and select the one you want from the list that appears.

My toolbar no longer has the buttons I need. How can I get it back to the original configuration?

If you or someone else has changed the configuration of your toolbar, it's easy to reset the default configuration. You can set it back to the default for individual document templates or for the Normal document template (which governs all new documents unless you specify otherwise). Follow these steps:

1. Right-click any toolbar and select **Customize**.

2. Click the **Toolbars** tab.

3. Select the toolbar you want to reset.

4. Click the **Reset** button. A dialog box appears with a drop-down list of document templates. Normal is the default one. Select a different template if needed, and click **OK**.

5. Click **Close**.

Someone customized my menu. How can I get it back to the way it used to be?

Believe it or not, the menu bar is just another toolbar. To reset it, follow the preceding steps in "My toolbar no longer has the buttons I need. How can I get it back to the original configuration?" but choose Menu Bar (or Worksheet Menu Bar in Excel) as the toolbar to reset.

Integration Problems

When I try to open a Word outline in PowerPoint it tells me that it cannot modify the file because it is in use.

You probably forgot to close the file in Word. PowerPoint cannot open a file that is open in another program. Click over to Word using your taskbar or **Alt+Tab** and close the file. Now you should have no problem using the outline in PowerPoint.

When I copy an Excel worksheet into Word, it doesn't update automatically when I edit it in Excel.

You need to create a link between Excel and Word. When you link an object, Excel will automatically update your worksheet. To link your Excel worksheet to Word, follow these steps:

1. Open the document in Word and move the insertion point where you want the Excel worksheet to be inserted.

2. If you want to insert an entire worksheet that you already have made up, choose **Insert**, **Object** and click the **Create from File** tab.

3. Enter the name and folder of your Excel file in the **File Name** box (if you don't remember where it is, click the **Browse** button). Be sure to check the **Link to File** check box.

4. Click **OK**. This will establish the link between the two files. Any changes that you make to your worksheet in Excel will be reflected in the Word document.

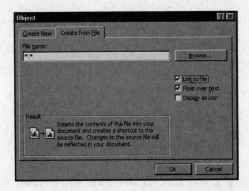

If you would rather link only part of the worksheet, follow these steps:

1. Select the desired range in Excel and click the **Copy** button on the toolbar.

2. Open Word and bring up the document that you want to link the Excel worksheet to. Move the insertion bar to the desired location in your document and choose **Edit**, **Paste Special**.

3. When the Paste Special dialog box appears, choose **Microsoft Excel Worksheet Object** from the **As** box and click **Paste Link**.

4. Click **OK**, and the selected range in your worksheet will be linked to your Word document.

Now that I have my worksheet linked to Word, it still won't update when I edit it in Excel.

Somehow, the link between the files has been broken. This may have happened if you renamed the Excel file or moved it to a different folder. You can try to relink the files by doing the following:

1. Choose **Edit**, **Links**.

2. In the Links dialog box, click the link you are having trouble with in the **Source File** box.

3. Click the **Change Source** button and choose the name and folder where your worksheet is located.

4. Click the **Open** button.

5. Click the **Update Now** button to update the link.

When I tried to copy an Excel worksheet into PowerPoint, the data was not lined up.

When you pasted the Excel data into PowerPoint, you probably used the **Edit**, **Paste** command. This will not work correctly because the Paste command tells PowerPoint that you are pasting plain old text. You need to let PowerPoint know that you are pasting Excel data. To do this, follow these steps:

1. Highlight the range of data in Excel and click the **Copy** button in the toolbar.

2. Switch to PowerPoint, click where you want to insert your Excel data, and choose **Edit**, **Paste Special** to bring up the Paste Special dialog box.

3. Click **Microsoft Excel Worksheet Object** in the **As** box (it should already be highlighted) and click **OK**. Your worksheet will be inserted as an object. If you need to edit the data, double-click in the middle of the Excel object.

I want to copy an Excel worksheet into PowerPoint, but it won't fit on the slide.

Edit your worksheet to remove any unnecessary data before you copy it to PowerPoint. If you need all the data, you can reduce the size after you have inserted it into PowerPoint. First, be sure to copy your worksheet as an Excel Object (see Quick Fix "When I copy an Excel worksheet into Word, it doesn't update automatically when I edit it in Excel"). To change the size, single-click in the middle of the Excel worksheet in PowerPoint. You will notice little squares surrounding the picture. These are called sizing handles. To change the size, click one of the sizing handles and drag the edge/corner until the data is the desired size. Be careful shrinking your data too much, though; it may make it so small that it is unreadable to your audience.

I used Find to search for a document, but it didn't find it.

You may not be searching enough places. Try choosing a drive in the **Look in** box and check the Include subfolders check box. It may take longer to search all the subfolders, but if the file is on the drive, it should find it. Also, click the **Date Modified** tab and select **All files**. Click the **Advanced** tab. Check that the **Of type** box is **All Files and Folders** and the **Containing text** and **Size** boxes are blank. This will give you the widest possible search.

I want to edit a linked object, but nothing happens when I double-click it.

Whenever you double-click a linked object, the source application should open to edit the object (the source application is the one that created the object). If the source application doesn't open when you double-click the object, choose **Edit**, **Links**. Click the **Open Source** button to bring up the source application.

When I double-click an Excel worksheet I have embedded in Word, it looks more like a worksheet, but Excel never opened.

This is one of those cases where Word and Excel work so well together that you can't even tell they are two different programs. When you double-click your embedded worksheet, look up at the toolbar. You'll notice that it is the Excel toolbar even though it looks like you are still in Word. Also, your embedded worksheet will change to show your column and row headings. You can edit the worksheet as though you were in Excel. When you are done, click somewhere else in your document and the Word toolbar will once again appear.

The Shortcut bar takes up too much space.

You can make the shortcut bar share space with maximized windows' title bars with a simple change. Just right-click the multicolored square at the end of the shortcut bar and select **Customize**. Click the **View** tab and select the **AutoFit Into Title Bar Area** check box. Then click **OK**.

Printing Problems

I can't print because the print option is grayed out.

You probably do not have a printer installed. To install your printer do the following:

1. From the Windows **Start** menu, select **Settings** and **Printers**.

2. Double-click the **Add Printer** icon.

3. The Add Printer Wizard will open to help you add your printer. Choose your printer from the list of **Manufacturers** and **Printers**. If you have a disk from your printer manufacturer, click the **Have Disk** button. After you have chosen your printer, click **Next**.

4. Choose the port that you want to use with this printer. Most printers are connected to the parallel port (LPT1). Click **Next**.

5. Type a name for the printer, and click Yes if you want to use this printer as the default printer. If this is your only printer, it is the logical choice. Click **Next**.

6. Click **Yes** to print a test page and click **Finish**. It is a good idea to print the test page to see if your printer will work correctly.

7. A dialog box will appear asking if your test page printed correctly. If it did, click **Yes** and your printer is set up. If it didn't print correctly, click **No**. Windows will bring up the Help menu to aid in troubleshooting the problem. Check to make sure that you attached the cable to the computer and the printer. Also, make sure that the printer is turned on, online, and loaded with paper.

My printer prints a blank page after my document is printed.

You probably have some blank lines at the bottom of your document. To check, click the **Show/Hide** button in the toolbar. If you see one or more paragraph marks on blank lines at the end of your document, highlight and delete them. You can see if this fixed your problem by choosing **Print Preview** from the **File** menu and scrolling to the last page to see if it is blank.

My pages print in reverse order when I print my Word document.

Your printer controls the order that your pages print. It can be annoying to have to re-order all your pages every time you print a document, so Word has given us a way to fix the problem. Follow these steps to change the print order:

1. Select **Tools**, **Options**, and click the **Print** tab.

2. Click the **Reverse Print Order** check box to change it (uncheck it if it's checked; check it if it's not).

3. Click **OK** to close the Options dialog box.

When I create a table in Word, the gridlines show up on the screen, but they don't print.

Gridlines do not normally print. They are there to show the position of your table on the screen. To print the gridlines, follow these steps:

1. Select the table (click somewhere in the table, and then press **Alt+5** on the numeric keypad with Num Lock off).

2. Choose **Format**, **Borders and Shading**.

3. In the Borders and Shading dialog box, click the **Borders** tab and click the **Grid** button. If you want, you can change the thickness and style of the lines in the **Style** box.

4. Click **OK** and you'll have lines around your table suitable for printing.

When I print my document, it doesn't look as good as it does on the screen.

Your printer probably doesn't support the font you have chosen. Check the printer documentation to see what fonts your printer supports and use one of those. Another alternative is to use a *TrueType* font (the ones with **TT** beside them in the font list). These fonts will print well on virtually all printers. If you want to check which TrueType fonts are available for use, do the following:

1. From the Windows **Start** menu, select **Settings** and **Control Panel**.

2. Double-click the **Fonts** icon. A folder opens showing all of the installed fonts. The TrueType fonts have **TT** in the icon. Standard fonts have an **A** in the icon.

3. If you double-click one of the font icons, you see some information about the font and a sample of what the font looks like.

4. Click the **Print** button to print a sample.

5. When you finish, click the **Done** button.

When I print graphics, the lines are all jagged.

You may have the print resolution set too low. The resolution is how many dots per inch the printer will use to print your graphics. The higher the resolution, the better it looks, but it will also take longer to print. To change the resolution, do the following:

1. From the Windows **Start** menu, select **Settings** and **Printers**.

2. Right-click the printer icon you are using to print your graphics and choose **Properties** from the menu.

3. Click the **Graphics** tab and click the drop-down list in the Resolution box. The list will show all of the resolutions supported by your printer. Click the highest one.

4. Click **OK** to close the dialog box.

> Jagged edges on an individual graphic (rather than on the entire page's printing) might be the result of resizing it. When you resize raster-based images (that is, images composed of little dots rather than images generated mathematically), they sometimes lose their smooth edges. There is not much you can do about this other than try to create or acquire images in approximately the same size as you will be using them.

When I try to print a PowerPoint slide on my laser printer, it only prints half the slide.

Your laser printer doesn't have enough memory to print the entire slide. Unlike dot-matrix or inkjet printers, laser printers have to load the entire page into their memory before they can print. The best way to fix the problem is to add more memory to your printer. Consult your printer documentation for information on what type of memory to buy. If you can't afford an upgrade right now, try printing with a lower resolution. Follow these steps to change the printer resolution:

1. From the Windows **Start** menu, select **Settings** and **Printers**.

2. Right-click the printer icon you are using to print your graphics and choose **Properties** from the menu.

3. Click the **Graphics** tab and click the drop-down list in the **Resolution** box. Choose a lower resolution from the list.

4. Click **OK** to close the dialog box.

More of your slide should print. If the full slide still doesn't print, you may have to choose a lower resolution than you did in step 3, or shrink the size of the slide so it doesn't take up the whole page.

> If you are using a lot of different fonts on your printout, you might try experimenting with the Fonts settings on your printer's Properties sheet. To display it, right-click your printer's icon in the Printers window (Start/Settings/Printers) and select Properties, and then click the Fonts tab. Click the Send Fonts As button at the bottom of that tab and experiment with the Send TrueType Fonts As setting to see if any of the settings will enable your entire page to print.

I loaded 8 1/2 x 14-inch paper in my printer, but it only prints on the top 11 inches.

You have to tell Office when to change paper sizes. Follow these steps to let your Office application know there is different paper in your printer:

1. From the Office application, choose **File**, **Print**.

2. Choose the desired printer from the drop-down list in the **Name** box and click the **Properties** button.

3. Click the Paper tab and click the appropriate paper size in the **Paper size** box. In this case, select **Legal**.

4. Click **OK** to close the dialog box. Remember to change the paper size back to 8½×11 inches when you finish. You may also have to set up your printer to accept the larger paper. Consult your printer manual for information on how to do that.

The edges of my document do not print.

You are probably trying to print on too much of the paper. Most printers require you to have at least a 1/2-inch margin on all edges of the paper. Consult your printer manual for specifics. To fix this problem, the first thing you need to do is find out if your print driver has the correct settings for the unprintable area. Follow these steps to check:

1. From the Windows **Start** menu, select **Settings** and **Printers**.

2. Right-click the printer icon you are using to print your document and choose **Properties** from the menu.

3. Click the **Paper** tab and click the **Unprintable Area** button.

4. In the Unprintable Area dialog box, check your printer documentation and ensure that the values in **Left**, **Right**, **Top**, and **Bottom** are correct. The units are in .001 inch, so a value of 250 will be .25 inch (1/4 inch). You can also select the units in .01 millimeter by selecting it in the **Units** box.

5. Click **OK**; then click **OK** again to close the dialog boxes.

Once you are satisfied that you have the unprintable area configured correctly, you must change the margins in your document to match these settings.

I want to print only my embedded Excel chart, but it prints the whole worksheet.

To print a chart embedded in your worksheet, click the chart and choose **File**, **Print**. Check that the selected chart is highlighted in the Print What section of the Print dialog box. Click **OK** and only your chart will print.

When I print my Excel report, all the pages are numbered page 1.

Even though it seems obvious, you have to let Excel know that you want to number the pages continuously. To do this, follow these steps:

1. Choose **Report Manager** from the **View** menu.

2. In the Report Manager dialog box, choose the desired report from the **Reports** box and click the **Edit** button.

3. At the bottom of the Edit Report dialog box, check the **Use Continuous Page Numbers** check box and click **OK**.

4. Click the **Print** button in the Print Report dialog box to print out your report using continuous page numbers.

I have a date field in my document, but the correct date does not print.

The field has not been properly updated. The date that is printing is the date that was current when you inserted the field in your document. To update the field to today's date, highlight the field and press **F9**. If you would like your fields to be updated automatically when you print, choose **Tools**, **Options** and click the **Print** tab. Under **Printing Options** check the **Update Fields** check box and click **OK**.

File Creating and Saving Problems

I want to save my document, but my application tells me I haven't chosen a valid file name.

You may have tried to save your file using a name that contains a control character. With Windows 95, you can use long, descriptive file names to name your files. You can even use spaces in the names. There are still a few characters that you cannot use, however. You can pretty much use any character except a control character (for example, CTRL+A, CTRL+B, and so on) or the following: ? \ < > | / * " : ;

I want to open a file, but it doesn't show up on the list of files in the dialog box even though I'm in the right folder.

You have probably saved your file with an extension other than the default for the program you are using (for example, XLS for Excel files). In the File Open dialog box, the program only shows files with the default extension for that program. To see all the files, select the drop-down list in the **Files of Type** box to display a list of choices. Choose **All Files** from the list and all the files in the folder will appear. In the future, you should let the application assign the extension for you when you save your files. This makes it less confusing when you are trying to open the file again.

I can't find the file I'm trying to open. What should I do?

You probably saved the file in a different folder than the one the program uses as the default. The easiest way to find it is to point to **Documents** on the **Start** menu in Windows. Windows will display the 15 most recently used files. If the file you are looking for is in the list, click the name of the file to open it. If the file is not on the list, use the **Find** option. Follow these steps to find your file:

1. From the Windows **Start** menu, select **Find** and **Files or Folders**.

2. If you remember the name (or part of the name) of the file, click the **Name & Location** tab and type the name in the **Named** box. You can use wild cards if you like.

3. If you can't remember the name, but you remember when you worked on it last, click the **Date Modified** tab.

   Click the radio button next to **Find all files created or modified**, and click one of the following options:

   between If you know that you last modified your file between two dates, select this option and type in the dates.

   during the previous month(s) Select this option if you want to find files that you modified within a certain number of months. Type in the number of months you want to look back.

   during the previous day(s) Select this option if you want to find files that you modified within a certain number of days. Type in the number of days you want to look back.

4. If you don't remember when you last worked on the file, click the **Advanced** tab. Choose one or a combination of the following options:

   - If you know what type of file it was (such as a Word document), choose it from the drop-down list in the **Of type** box.

   - If you know that the file contains certain text, type the text in the **Containing text** box; this search will take a while because Windows has to search the contents of each file on the drive.

If you know that the file is greater than (or less than) a certain size, choose the appropriate entries in the **Size is** box. First, choose **At least** or **At most** from the drop-down list. Next, type in the size in KB (kilobytes).

You can also choose combinations of steps 2 through 5, for example, if you know the date the file was modified, and you know that it contains a certain text phrase.

5. Click the **Find Now** button to begin your search. A window will appear below the Find dialog box with a list of files that it finds. The window will show which folder the file is in. If you want to edit the file now, double-click it. The application that created it will open to edit the file.

I saved my file using a password. Now I've forgotten the password. Is there any way to open this file?

Unfortunately, you're out of luck. There is no way to open this file short of typing in every combination of characters and numbers until you come up with the correct password (this could take years). Next time, write down your password and put it in a place where you won't lose it.

My files always end up in different folders. How can I get the folder I want as the default?

By default, the Office applications save the files you are working on in the same folder that they store their program files. This can make it very hard to find your files later because these directories contain so many files. Therefore, it is a good idea to store your files in a different location. You can set the default location for your files, but each application does it a little differently.

For Word, follow these steps:

1. Choose **Tools**, **Options**.

2. Click the **File Locations** tab. Click the folder you want to change under **File Types** and click **Modify**.

3. Choose the desired folder from the Modify Location dialog box (you can also create a new folder with the Create New Folder button in the toolbar). A good example would be a folder called Documents for Word files.

4. Click **OK** to close the dialog box; then click **Close**.

In Excel, follow these steps:

1. Choose **Tools**, **Options**, and click the **General** tab.

2. Type in the desired drive and folder in the **Default File Location** box.

3. Click **OK** to close the Options dialog box.

In PowerPoint, follow these steps:

1. Choose **Options** from the **Tools** menu, and click the **Advanced** tab.

2. Type in the desired drive and folder in the **Default File Location** box.

3. Click **OK** to close the Options dialog box.

I can't get Word to open my Word for Macintosh document. It tells me that the disk drive is not valid.

The disk that contains your file is probably formatted for Macintosh. Windows-based computers cannot read Macintosh disks. Take a Windows formatted disk over to your Macintosh and tell it to save the file in MS-DOS format. If you have already done this, but you still get the error, you probably have a defective diskette. Get another one and try again.

I tried to copy a file to a floppy disk, but got an error message telling me that the disk is write-protected.

All floppy disks can be write-protected. When a disk is write-protected, it keeps you or someone else from accidentally deleting or changing files on that disk. It is a good idea to write-protect floppies when you have important data on them. If the data on the disk is not that important, or you just want to add a file to the disk, you can unprotect it. You do this differently depending on the type of floppy disk.

- For a 3 1/2-inch floppy disk, turn the disk to the back side. There is a square piece of plastic in the upper-left corner of the disk that you can move to cover or un-cover a square hole. If the square hole is visible, the disk is write-protected. If the hole is covered by the plastic piece, the disk is not write-protected. Use your fingernail or the end of a pen to move the piece of plastic to the desired location.

- For a 5 1/4-inch floppy disk, there is a notch on the right edge of the disk about an inch from the top. To write-protect these disks, get a piece of tape and cover the notch (packages of disks come with pieces of tape for this purpose). To unprotect the disk, simply remove the tape.

System Problems

The screen redraws very slowly in Word. How can I speed it up?

When you have a lot of fancy fonts and graphics on the screen in Word, the screen can update rather slowly. To speed up the redraw, click the **Normal View** button in the lower-left corner next to the horizontal scroll bar. Your fonts and graphics will not display correctly, but if you are just adding text, it won't matter. When you want to see how things actually look, or change the layout, switch back to **Page Layout View** by clicking the **Page Layout View** button.

The toolbar buttons are too small for me to see very well.

The toolbar icons are small enough that they all fit comfortably on the screen at once. But if you use a higher-resolution than 640x480, you have some room to make them bigger and more visible without sacrificing any of them. Just right-click a toolbar and select **Customize**. Then click the **Options** tab and select the **Large Icons** checkbox. Click OK.

When I double-click a document in My Computer or the Explorer, a dialog box pops up asking me what I want to open the file with. I know I created the document in Word. What's the problem?

You have probably saved your document with an extension other than DOC. The extension is the three characters to the right of the period in your file name. If your file has a DOC extension, Word knows that it needs to open when you double-click that file. If you choose another extension for your file, Word won't know to open. When a certain extension is associated with the program that created it, such as DOC for Word documents, it is known as file association. So, when you save your files in Office, don't put any extension on the file name. Then, the Office program will automatically put the correct extension on them and know to open when you double-click the file in My Computer or the Explorer. If you want to associate another file extension with one of the Office programs, follow these steps when you get the Open With dialog box:

1. From the list of programs, click the one you want to use to open this file. If the program is not on the list, click the **Other** button and navigate through the folders until you find your program.

2. If you check **Always use this program to open this file** check box, Windows will remember to use this program the next time you double-click the file.

3. Click **OK** to open the file using the program you chose in step 1.

When I try to select something using the left mouse button, a menu pops up next to the mouse pointer. Whatever I'm trying to select doesn't get selected.

When we refer to the left mouse button, we really mean the primary button. If you normally use the mouse with your left hand, and have your mouse set up that way, the right button will be the primary button. Therefore, whenever we tell you to click the left button, click the right button. If you don't want your mouse set up left-handed, do the following:

1. From the Windows **Start** menu, select **Settings** and **Control Panel**.

2. Double-click the **Mouse** icon.

3. Click the **Buttons** tab and click the radio button next to **Right-handed**.

4. Click **OK** and your mouse will be set up Right-handed.

When I was in a dialog box, I clicked Help in the menu bar, but nothing happened. Why can't I get help in a dialog box?

The **Help** commands on the menu bar and toolbar will not work when there is a dialog box on the screen. To get help, click the ? button in the top-right corner of the dialog box. Your mouse pointer changes to a pointer with a question mark. Now click the dialog box element that you need help with.

Mouse pointer —

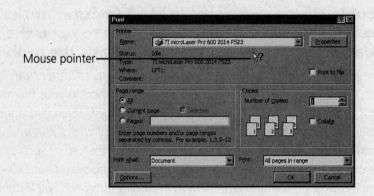

PART 4

Handy References

Use this handy references section to help you with common shortcut keys, toolbars, and Excel functions. This reference section helps you find the more common shortcut keys for the tasks you perform in Word, Excel, and PowerPoint.

Also included in this section is a listing of all buttons on the major toolbars for Microsoft Word, Excel, PowerPoint, and Outlook. The buttons are in the order they appear on each toolbar with a short description for each button. Don't forget that you can always use the ToolTip feature; just move your mouse pointer over the toolbar button and pause. The button's name appears on-screen.

For those of you who want to become more fluent in the language of Excel functions, there is a listing of common functions. Categorized by subject, this list is handy when designing complicated worksheets. The major arguments for each function have been included where appropriate.

Also, when using Outlook, you'll notice that an icon appears in front of each item. A listing of these icons and their meaning is included here.

What You Will Find in This Part

HANDY REFERENCES

Handy Reference

Use this handy reference section to help you with common shortcut keys, toolbars, and Excel functions. This reference section helps you find the more common shortcut keys for the tasks you perform in Word, Excel, and PowerPoint.

Also included in this section is a listing of all buttons on the major toolbars for Microsoft Word, Excel, PowerPoint, and Outlook. The buttons are in the order they appear on each toolbar with a short description for each button. Don't forget that you can always use the ToolTip feature; just move your mouse pointer over the toolbar button and pause. The button's name appears on-screen.

For those of you who want to become more fluent in the language of Excel functions, there is a listing of common functions. Categorized by subject, this list is handy when designing complicated worksheets. The major arguments for each function have been included where appropriate.

Also, when using Outlook, you'll notice that an icon appears in front of each item. A listing of these icons and their meaning is included here.

What You Will Find in This Section

Microsoft Office 97 Shortcut Keys

General Shortcut Keys for All Windows Programs

Shortcut Key	Desired Command
Ctrl+Esc	Displays Task Bar and Start menu
Alt+Tab	Switches to next window
Ctrl+X	Cuts selection
Ctrl+C	Copies selection
Ctrl+V	Pastes selection
Ctrl+W	Closes the active document window
Ctrl+F6	Switches to the next document window
Shift+F10	Displays the shortcut menu
Alt+underlined letter	Opens a menu
Underlined letter	Selects a command from an open menu
Esc	Closes a menu
Ctrl+Tab	Moves to next tab in a dialog box
Tab	Moves to next option in dialog box
Alt+down arrow	Opens a drop-down list box
Spacebar	Turns an option on or off
Esc	Closes dialog box and cancel command
Enter	Closes dialog box and perform command
F1	Gets help from Office Assistant

General Formatting Commands

Shortcut Key	Desired Command
Ctrl+B	Bold text
Ctrl+I	Italic text
Ctrl+U (or Ctrl+Shift+U)	Underlines
Ctrl+5	Applies or removes strikethrough, not a general command; works in Excel, but not Word
Shift+F3	Toggles case
Ctrl+Shift+F	Changes fonts; works with Office 95, but not 97

Shortcut Key	Desired Command
Ctrl+Shift+P	Changes point size
Ctrl+Shift+>	Increases font size
Ctrl+Shift+<	Decreases font size
Ctrl+E	Centers paragraph
Ctrl+J	Justifies paragraph
Ctrl+L	Left-aligns paragraph
Ctrl+R	Right-aligns paragraph

Word Shortcut Keys

Formatting Text	
Shortcut Key	Desired Command
Ctrl+Shift+A	All uppercase letters
Ctrl+Shift+K	All small capitals
Ctrl+Shift+H	Makes text hidden
Ctrl+Shift+W	Underlines words but not spaces
Ctrl+Shift+D	Double underlines
Ctrl+=	Subscript
Ctrl+Shift++	Superscript
Ctrl+Spacebar	Removes character formatting
Ctrl+1	Single-spacing
Ctrl+2	Double-spacing
Ctrl+5	One and one-half line spacing
Ctrl+0	Adds or removes the line preceding a paragraph
Ctrl+M	Indents a paragraph
Ctrl+Shift+M	Removes an indent; this shortcut works in Office 95 but not in 97
Ctrl+T	Creates a hanging indent
Ctrl+Shift+T	Removes a hanging indent
Ctrl+Q	Removes paragraph formatting
Ctrl+Shift+S	Applies a style

(continues)

Formatting Text   *Continued*

Shortcut Key	Desired Command
Alt+Ctrl+K	Use AutoFormat
Ctrl+Shift+N	Applies Normal style
Alt+Ctrl+1, 2, or 3	Applies Heading 1, 2, or 3 style

Working with Documents

Shortcut Key	Desired Command
Ctrl+N	Creates a new document
Ctrl+O	Opens a document
Ctrl+W	Closes a document
Ctrl+F	Closes current window
Alt+Ctrl+S	Splits a document
Ctrl+S	Saves a document
F12	Saves a document with a new file name
Ctrl+P	Prints
Ctrl+F2	Prints Preview

Deleting, Copying, and Inserting

Shortcut Key	Desired Command
Backspace	Deletes a character to left
Delete	Deletes a character to right
Ctrl+Backspace	Deletes previous word
Ctrl+Delete	Deletes current word
Ctrl+Shift+Enter	Inserts column break
Alt+Shift+D	Inserts date field
Ctrl+Enter	Inserts page break
Shift+Enter	Inserts line break
Alt+Shift+T	Inserts time

Working with Text

Shortcut Key	Desired Command
F3 (or Ctrl+Alt+V)	Creates AutoText; Alt+F3 displays the Create AutoText dialog box used to name your AutoText entry
F8 or Shift key	Begins selection
F8 twice	Selects a word
F8 three times	Selects a sentence
F9 four times	Selects a paragraph
Shift+left arrow	Selects character to left
Ctrl+Shift+right arrow	Selects to end of word
Shift+End	Selects to end of line
Ctrl+Shift+down arrow	Selects to end of paragraph
Ctrl+A	Selects entire document
Ctrl+Shift+F8	Selects a vertical block of text F8 works in Office 97
F7	Spell Check
Ctrl+Z (or Alt+Backspace)	Undo
Ctrl+Y	Redo
Ctrl+F	Finds text
Alt+Ctrl+F	Repeats last find
Ctrl+Alt+N	View normal
Ctrl+Alt+O	View outline
Ctrl+Alt+P	View page layout

Moving in a Document

Shortcut Key	Desired Command
Alt+Page Up	Go to start of column
Alt+Page Down	Go to end of column
Ctrl+Home	Go to start of document
Ctrl+End	Go to end of document
Home	Go to beginning of line

(continues)

Moving in a Document *Continued*

Shortcut Key	Desired Command
End	Go to end of line
Ctrl+down arrow	Go to next paragraph
Ctrl+up arrow	Go to previous paragraph
Tab	Go to next cell in a table
Shift+Tab	Go to previous cell
Ctrl+Page Down	Go to next page
Ctrl+Page Up	Go to previous page
Alt+Ctrl+Page Up	Go to top of window
Alt+Ctrl+Page Down	Go to end of window
Page Up	Up one screen
Page Down	Down one screen
Ctrl+G	Go to a particular page
Shift+F5	Go to last location when document was closed

Excel Shortcut Keys

Entering and Manipulating Data

Shortcut Key	Desired Command
F2	Edits the current cell
Enter	Completes the cell entry
Tab	Completes cell entry and moves to the next cell
Shift+Tab	Completes cell entry and moves to the previous cell
Esc	Cancels an entry
Alt+Enter	Inserts a carriage return
Backspace	Erases character to left
Delete	Erases character to right
F4	Repeats the last action
Shift+F2	Edits a cell comment
Ctrl+D	Fills down

Shortcut Key	Desired Command
Ctrl+R	Fills right
Ctrl+Enter	Fills selected range
=	Starts a formula
Ctrl+A	Displays the Formula Palette
Alt+=	Inserts the AutoSum formula
F3	Pastes a name into a formula
Ctrl+F3	Creates a name
Ctrl+;	Enters the date
Ctrl+Shift+:	Enters the time
Ctrl+K	Inserts a hyperlink
F9	Calculates all worksheets
Shift+F9	Calculates current worksheet only
Ctrl+'	Displays formulas

Selecting Cells

Shortcut Key	Desired Command
Ctrl+Shift+*	Selects region bordered by blank cells
Shift+arrow key	Selects cell to left, right, up, or down
Ctrl+Shift+arrow key	Selects all cells to the last non-blank cell in the same column or row
Ctrl+Shift+Home	Selects from current cell to beginning of worksheet
Ctrl+Shift+End	Selects from current cell to end of worksheet
Ctrl+Spacebar	Selects current column
Shift+Spacebar	Selects current row
Ctrl+A	Selects entire worksheet

Moving and Scrolling Inside Worksheets

Shortcut Key	Desired Command
Arrow key	Moves to the next cell
Ctrl+arrow key	Moves to edge of data region
Ctrl+Backspace	Scrolls to display the active cell

(continues)

Moving and Scrolling Inside Worksheets *Continued*

Shortcut Key	Desired Command
Alt+Page Down	Moves right one screen
Alt+Page Up	Moves left one screen
Ctrl+Page Up	Moves to the previous sheet in the workbook
Ctrl+Page Down	Moves to the next sheet in the workbook
Ctrl+F6	Moves to next workbook
Ctrl+Shift+F6	Moves to previous workbook
Home	Moves to the beginning of the row
Ctrl+Home	Moves to the beginning of the worksheet
Ctrl+End	Moves to the last cell in your worksheet
Ctrl+Spacebar	Selects the entire column
Shift+Spacebar	Selects the entire row
Ctrl+A	Selects the entire worksheet

PowerPoint Shortcut Keys

Deleting and Copying Text and Objects

Shortcut Key	Desired Command
Backspace	Deletes character left
Ctrl+Backspace	Deletes word left
Delete	Deletes character right
Ctrl+Delete	Deletes word right
Ctrl+Z	Undoes previous changes

Selecting Text and Objects

Shortcut Key	Desired Command
Shift+right arrow	Selects right character
Shift+left arrow	Selects left character
Ctrl+Shift+right arrow	Selects to end of word
Ctrl+Shift+left arrow	Selects to beginning of word

Shortcut Key	Desired Command
Tab	Selects an object
Ctrl+A	Selects all objects (Slide view)
Ctrl+A	Selects all slides (Slide Sorter view)
Ctrl+A	Selects all text (Outline view)

Running a Slide Show

Shortcut Key	Desired Command
<Number>+Enter	Goes to slide <number>
F1	Displays shortcut menu
B	Displays a black screen
W	Displays a white screen
Ctrl+P	Changes the pointer to a pen
Ctrl+A	Changes the pen to a pointer
Ctrl+H	Hides the pointer
S	Stops/restarts automatic show
E	Removes on-screen notations
Esc	Ends show
H	Displays hidden slide
N	Displays next slide
P	Returns to previous slide

Outlook Shortcut Keys

Working with Items

Shortcut Key	Desired Command
F2	Edits a field
Esc	Cancels Edit
+ (On the numeric keypad)	Expands a group

(continues)

Working with Items   *Continued*

Shortcut Key	Desired Command
- (On the numeric keypad)	Collapses a group
Arrow key	Moves from item to item
Ctrl+Shift+>	Opens next item
Ctrl+Shift+<	Opens previous item
F6	Displays Folder List

Formatting Items

Shortcut Key	Desired Command
Ctrl+Shift+L	Creates bulleted list
Ctrl+T	Adds indent
Ctrl+Shift+T	Removes indent

Working with the Inbox

Shortcut Key	Desired Command
Ctrl+N	Creates e-mail message
Ctrl+Q	Marks as read
Ctrl+R	Replies to message
Ctrl+Shift+R	Replies to All
Ctrl+K	Inserts hyperlink

Working with Calendar

Shortcut Key	Desired Command
Ctrl+Shift+A	Creates appointment
Ctrl+Shift+Q	Creates meeting request
Alt+1	Views one day
Alt+number	Views x days
Alt+-	Views a week
Alt+=	Views a month
Ctrl+Tab	Moves between Calendar, TaskPad, and Folder List
Tab	Moves to next appointment
Shift+Tab	Moves to previous appointment

Shortcut Key	Desired Command
left arrow	Displays previous day
right arrow	Displays next day
Alt+up arrow	Displays same day, previous week
Alt+down arrow	Displays same day, next week
Alt+Home	Goes to first day of week
Alt+End	Goes to last day of week
Alt+Page Up	Goes to first day of month
Alt+Page Down	Goes to last day of month

Working with Contacts

Shortcut Key	Desired Command
Ctrl+N	Creates contact
Ctrl+Shift+B	Displays Address Book
Ctrl+Shift+D	Dials a contact

Working with Other Outlook Programs

Shortcut Key	Desired Command
Ctrl+Shift+J	Creates Journal entry
Ctrl+Shift+N	Creates a note
Ctrl+Shift+K	Creates a task
Ctrl+Shift+U	Creates a task request

Toolbar Buttons

Microsoft Office Default Shortcut Bar

Icon	Program
W	Starts Microsoft Word
X	Starts Excel

(continues)

Microsoft Office Default Shortcut Bar *Continued*

Icon	Program
	Starts PowerPoint
	Starts Binder
	Opens the Getting Results book
	Creates a new Office document
	Opens an existing document
	Starts Internet Explorer
	Starts Access
	Opens Bookshelf Basics
	Creates a new note in Outlook
	Sends an e-mail message with Outlook
	Creates a Journal entry in Outlook
	Starts Microsoft Outlook
	Creates a new appointment in Outlook
	Creates a new task in Outlook

Excel Functions

Financial Functions

Function	Arguments	Purpose
ACCRINT	(issue, first_interest, settlement, rate, frequency)	Calculates the accrued interest for any security that pays periodic interest
ACCRINTM	(issue, maturity, rate)	Calculates the accrued interest for any security that pays interest at maturity
CUMIPMT	(rate, nper, pv, start_period, end_period, type)	Calculates the cumulative interest paid between two periods
CUMPRINC	(rate, nper, pv, start_period, end_period, type)	Calculates the cumulative principal paid on a loan between two periods

Function	Arguments	Purpose
DB	(cost, salvage, life, period)	Calculates the depreciation of an asset for a specified period using the fixed-declining balance method
DDB	(cost, salvage, life)	Calculates the depreciation of an asset for a specified period using the double-declining balance method or some other method you specify
EFFECT	(nominal_rate, npery)	Calculates the effective annual interest rate
FV	(rate, nper)	Calculates the future value of an investment
FVSCHEDULE	(principal, schedule)	Calculates the future value of an initial principal after applying a series of compound interest rates
IPMT	(rate, per, nper, pv)	Calculates the interest payment for an investment for a given period
IRR	(values)	Calculates the internal rate of return for a series of cash flows
NOMINAL	(effect_rate, npery)	Calculates the annual nominal interest rate
NPER	(rate, pv)	Calculates the number of periods for an investment
PMT	(rate, nper, pv)	Calculates the periodic payment for a loan
PPMT	(prate, per, nper, pv)	Calculates the payment on the principal for an investment for a given period
PV	(rate, nper)	Calculates the present value of an investment
RATE	(nper, pv)	Calculates the interest rate per period of an annuity
RECEIVED	(settlement, maturity, investment, discount)	Calculates the amount received at maturity for a fully invested security
YIELD	(settlement, maturity, rate, pr, redemption, frequency)	Calculates the yield on a security that pays periodic interest
YIELDMAT	(settlement, maturity, issue, rate, pr)	Calculates the annual yield of a security that pays interest at maturity

Date and Time Functions

Function	Arguments	Purpose
DATE	(year, month, day)	Calculates the serial number of a particular date
DATEVALUE	(date_text)	Converts a date in the form of text to a serial number
DAY	(serial_number)	Converts a serial number to a day of the month
DAYS360	(start_date, end_date)	Calculates the number of days between two dates based on a 360-day year
HOUR	(serial_number)	Converts a serial number to an hour
MONTH	(serial_number)	Converts a serial number to a month
NETWORKDAYS	(start_date, end_date)	Calculates the number of whole workdays between two dates
TODAY	( )	Calculates the serial number of today's date
WEEKDAY	(serial_number, return_type)	Converts a serial number to a day of the week
WORKDAY	(start_date, days, holidays)	Calculates the serial number of the date before or after a specified number of workdays
YEAR	(serial_number)	Converts a serial number to a year

Math and Trigonometry Functions

Function	Arguments	Purpose
ABS	(number)	Calculates the absolute value of a number
ROUND	(number, num_digits)	Rounds a number to a specified number of digits
ROUNDDOWN	(number)	Rounds a number down, toward zero
ROUNDUP	(number num_digits)	Rounds a number up, away from zero
SUM	(number1)	Adds numbers in cells

Statistical Functions

Function	Arguments	Purpose
AVERAGE	(number1, number2, ...)	Calculates the average of its arguments
COUNT	(value1, value2, ...)	Counts how many numbers are in the list of arguments
COUNTA	(value1, value2, ...)	Counts how many values are in the list of arguments
MAX	(number1, number2, ...)	Calculates the maximum value in a list of arguments
MEDIAN	(number1, number2, ...)	Calculates the median of the given numbers
MIN	(number1, number2, ...)	Calculates the minimum value in a list of arguments

Text

Function	Purpose
CONCATENATE	Joins several text items into one text item
DOLLAR	Converts a number to text, using currency format
FIXED	Rounds a number as text with a fixed number of decimals
LOWER	Converts text to lowercase
TEXT	Formats a number and converts it to text
UPPER	Converts text to uppercase
VALUE	Converts a text string that represents a number to a number

Logical

Function	Purpose
AND	Returns TRUE if all its arguments are TRUE
FALSE	Returns the logical value FALSE
IF	Specifies a logical test to perform
NOT	Reverses the logic of its argument
OR	Returns TRUE if any argument is TRUE
TRUE	Returns the logical value TRUE

Index

F

X-Y-Z